TORAH FROM THE INTERNET

Intriguing Insights into Jewish Holidays and the Weekly Torah Reading

by Rabbi Mordecai Kornfeld

THE JUDAICA PRESS, INC.
New York, 1998

ISBN 1-880582-23-6

THE JUDAICA PRESS, INC.
123 Ditmas Avenue
Brooklyn, New York 11218
718-972-6200 800-972-6201
JudaicaPr@aol.com

Manufactured in the United States of America

Rabbi Nachman Bulman
Yeshivat Ohr Somayach
Ohr Lagolah

הרב נחמן בולמן
ישיבת אור שמח
אור לגולה

סיון תשנ"ו פה עיה"ק ת"ו
June 11, 1996

Our times are blessed with ever growing interest in Torah studies in English. And even many of limited background seek greater depth rather than easy, superficial treatment. On the other hand, time constraints require condensed, abbreviated approaches to highly complex themes in Torah thought.

The *Weekly Parasha* by a gifted young scholar—Rabbi Mordecai Kornfeld—addresses that need in a clear, learned, and richly varied manner. With striking scholarly and popular orientation, R. Kornfeld assembles the teachings of our Sages to illuminate our *Parashoth* in Halacha and Agaddah, in recounting *Chumash* lives and *Chumash* themes.

The undersigned does not feel qualified to endorse Torah studies of this kind. It is however a pleasure to extend greetings and appreciation to Rabbi Kornfeld, as well as hope that his *Weekly Parasha* may be widely welcomed.

הכותב לכ' התורה ולומדי'
נחמן בולמן

137/21 Ma'alot Daphna, Jerusalem 97762 Israel • Tel: 02-824321 :מעלות דפנה 137\21 ירושלים 97762 • טל

Dedicated to memory of the members of my father's family and the six million Jews who perished in the Holocaust.

מים רבים לא יוכלו לכבות את האהבה ונהרות לא ישטפוה...
(Shir Hashirim 8:7)

"...Hashem said to his people, 'Even if all the leaders of the world were to join forces, they would not be able to annihilate you.'"
(Targum, ibid.)

TABLE OF CONTENTS

Preface vii
Introduction ix
Acknowledgements xv
Glossary 295

Sefer Bereishis

Chapter 1: Bereishis 1
Chapter 2: Noach 7
Chapter 3: Lech Lecha 10
Chapter 4: Vayera 15
Chapter 5: Chayei Sarah 19
Chapter 6: Toldos 24
Chapter 7: Vayetze 28
Chapter 8: Vayishlach 32
Chapter 9: Vayeshev 37
Chapter 10: Miketz/Chanukah 41
Chapter 11: Vayigash 46
Chapter 12: Vayechi 52

Sefer Shemos

Chapter 13: Shemos 59
Chapter 14: Vaera 64
Chapter 15: Bo 71
Chapter 16: Beshalach 75
Chapter 17: Yisro 80
Chapter 18: Mishpatim 83
Chapter 19: Terumah 88
Chapter 20: Tetzaveh 92
Chapter 21: Ki Sisa 97

Chapter 22: Vayakhel 102
Chapter 23: Pekudei 106

Sefer Vayikra

Chapter 24: Vayikra 111
Chapter 25: Tzav 116
Chapter 26: Shemini 122
Chapter 27: Tazria/Hachodesh 128
Chapter 28: Metzorah 133
Chapter 29: Acharei Mos 136
Chapter 30: Kedoshim 140
Chapter 31: Emor/Holidays 146
Chapter 32: Behar 152
Chapter 33: Bechukosai 156

Sefer Bamidbar

Chapter 35: Bamidbar/Shavuos 161
Chapter 36: Naso 167
Chapter 37: Bahaaloscha 172
Chapter 38: Shelach 177
Chapter 39: Korach 183
Chapter 40: Chukkas 187
Chapter 41: Balak 194
Chapter 42: Pinchas 198
Chapter 43: Mattos 205
Chapter 44: Masei 212

Sefer Devarim

Chapter 45: Devaraim/Tisha b'Av 217
Chapter 46: Vaeschanan 223
Chapter 47: Eikev 235
Chapter 48: Re'eh 240
Chapter 49: Shoftim 245
Chapter 50: Ki Setzei 251
Chapter 51: Ki Savo 256
Chapter 52: Nitzavim-Vayelech/Rosh Hashanah 259
Chapter 53: Ha'azinu/Yom Kippur 263
Chapter 54: Ha'azinu/Sukkos 267
Chapter 55: Vezos Habrachah/Simchas Torah 273

Jewish Holidays

Chapter 56: Jewish Holidays 277
Chapter 57: Parshas Zachor 285
Chapter 58: Purim 289

PREFACE

By HaGaon HaRav Aharon Feldman

The Talmud (Avoda Zara 5a), relates that Adam the First was shown the scholars and the teachers of Torah of all future generations. If we presume that Adam saw them in action, he certainly must have found many scholars in our times hunched over a computer console preparing lectures to be delivered to a worldwide audience by means of the Internet.

The Internet has become one of the prime means of communication—particularly international communication—of our times. The learning potential of this medium is enormous, if only because of the vast millions throughout the world who subscribe to it. Its development is a modern equivalent of the invention of the printing press five centuries ago. The years to come might well indicate that the Internet has influenced the quality and quantity of the teaching of Torah as much as the printing press did in its time.

Fortunately, a few individuals have recognized the potential of Internet as a Torah vehicle and have begun designing lectures and courses appropriate for this medium. One of the pioneers in this field is Rabbi Mordechai Kornfeld, an expert Torah scholar who has spent two decades studying and teaching Torah. He has designed a fascinating, popular series on the weekly Torah portion which is estimated to have tens of thousands of readers throughout the world. The present book is a compilation of this series adapted for book form.

Like a precious jewel which has a beauty from whichever perspective it is viewed, Torah conveys wisdom at whatever level it is studied. On its simple level, Torah describes the roots of the Jewish people and informs them of G-d's demands from them. At its deepest level it reveals the secrets of Creation, the workings of Providence, and the forces driving history. At points in between, a serious student can gain anything from wondrous insights into human psychology to learning how man can conquer the evil in his nature.

Just as science never ceases to discover new insights into the infinite wisdom of G-d's nature, so it is with G-d's Torah. The Torah has been propounded for three and a half thousand years, and until this day, Torah scholars have never ceased to discover in it new insights.

This series gives the reader a glimpse into this infinitude. With a remarkable mastery of his subject matter, Rabbi Kornfeld permits us to indulge in brilliant commentaries by Torah masters of previous generations, often startling in the manner in which they unmask the hidden meanings of the Torah or of its Aggadic interpretations.

The very strength of this book is its unassuming posture. The author does not seek to impress readers with his own prodigious scholarship, but rather to offer readers a taste of the variegated richness of the Torah as expressed in the wisdom of the sages.

Everyone can benefit from this book. The learned will discover commentaries they had never known existed. Beginners will be exposed to a new level of meaning in Torah. Everyone will be rewarded with intriguing, thought provoking and inspiring ideas.

INTRODUCTION

All For The Sake Of The Torah

"In the beginning (*beReishis*) of Creation..." The entire world was created for the sake of the Torah, which is called "*Reishis*," and for the sake of the Jewish people, who are also called "*Reishis*" (Rashi, Bereishis 1:1).

What makes the Jewish people unique among the rest of Creation?

"The Holy One, blessed be He, created the world solely in order that His creations should fear Him (i.e., perform His commandments)" (Shabbos 31b).

The Gemara in Berachos 6b says that the world in which we live was created for one purpose—to allow mankind the opportunity to become eternal through the service of the Creator. Since the Jews chose to receive the Torah—Hashem's manual of Divine service—and teach the rest of the world Hashem's ways, it is for them and those who follow their lead that the world was created. The remainder of the world's inhabitants serve but a secondary purpose—to provide company for those who fear their Creator.

It is for the purpose of studying the Torah that the world was created and it is for this purpose that it remains in existence until today. In Berachos 8a it says that "since the Beis Hamikdash was destroyed, all that Hashem values in His world are the few square feet where halacha is learned." Similarly, *all* creative acts that take place on earth are meant to further the study of Torah and the performance of mitzvos. In Koheles 2:26 we read that Hashem puts in the mind of a sinner the drive to amass great wealth, so that it may eventually be passed on to one who does good before Him. In the Rambam's (Maimonides) Introduction to the Mishnah, he writes that if a sinner succeeds in erecting an enormous palace, it was actually not constructed for the sinner's benefit, but in order to save the life of the righteous person who, in some future generation, will find shelter from the blazing sun in the shade of one of its walls.

The Brisker Rav (Parshas Bereishis) develops this theme further, while offering a brilliant insight into an Aggadah in Avoda Zara:

"On the Day of Final Judgment, the Roman Empire will be brought before the Creator to be judged. When Hashem asks them, 'What have you accomplished?' They will reply, 'We established many markets; we built many bathhouses; we amassed great wealth...all in order that the Jews may learn Torah!' 'Fools!' Hashem will retort, 'You did so only to serve your own selfish desires!' " (Avoda Zara 2b).

What could have prompted Rome to make such a bizarre statement? The persecutions that Israel suffered at the hands of Rome are no secret. Was Rome trying to fool the Creator?!

To the contrary, answers the Brisker Rav, Rome replied in earnest. On the Day of Final Judgment the full truth will be revealed: Rome will realize that the purpose of all that they accomplished—and all that was ever constructed or invented in this world—was to benefit the righteous. For the sake of Torah...for the sake of the Jewish People. Nevertheless, since Rome established their markets and built their bathhouses for entirely selfish reasons, they can claim no reward for their inventiveness.

II

The new medium for communication

This past century has seen an unparalleled explosion of growth in science and technology, particularly in the field of communication. Like the Roman markets and bathhouses, this new technological advance was certainly granted to the world in order to enhance the study of Hashem's Torah. As different media of communication were developed, each was put to its proper use. Torah was taught through the medium of telephone wires, HAM radio, and eventually public radio and television broadcasts. As the Internet ushers in a new age in communication, Torah Judaism is preparing itself to teach Torah in a manner more global than has ever been possible in the past. When the Torah was given on Mt. Sinai, "the voice of Hashem was heard from one end of the earth to the other" (Zevachim 116a). This expression takes on new meaning now, as the Torah travels regularly from one end of the world to the other in minutes or even seconds. The thousands of regular subscribers to my weekly Internet Parasha-Page include residents of the U.S., Canada, Australia, South Africa, Central and South America, Great Britain and most of the European countries, including such Eastern European countries as Poland. From Alaska to Tasmania, thanks to the Internet, the Parsha is being seen in a new light.

Torah over the Internet has humble enough beginnings. In 1993, numerous publishers of weekly Torah publications began to prepare electronic copies of their publications and make them available to the world Jewish community through the Internet. Perhaps the first weekly Torah publication prepared *exclusively* for the Internet is the still active "Byte of Torah" parsha mailing-list (bytetorah@shamash.org) by Rabbi Zev Itzkowitz, a former student of mine. I myself began to take advantage of the Internet to deliver my thoughts on the weekly Torah portion to my parents and students overseas in late '93 (5754). Since then, dozens of parsha and Torah-oriented mailing-lists have benefitted hundreds of thousands of subscribers the world over.

People can now use the Internet to forward questions to Rabbinical authorities, access databases listing rabbis and kosher eateries around the globe, attend virtual *shiurim* [Torah lectures] and halacha-oriented discussion groups, and much more. Most Yeshivos that cater to English-speaking students, both in Israel and in the Diaspora, can now be contacted through an e-mail address. A very exciting new development is my recent establishment of Kollel Iyun Hadaf, a small group of Torah scholars who together prepare study material to distribute via e-mail to learners of the *Daf yomi*—a Talmud study program popular among Jews from all walks of life. At our Website (http://www.shemayisrael.co.il/dafyomi2/) visitors can join free mailing-lists which cater to learners of all levels, from the most basic to the most advanced.

III

The Internet vs. the WWW

Where does one find this wealth of Torah knowledge on the Internet? And how can one take advantage of the wondrous technology of the Internet for the purpose of Torah study without falling into the bottomless abyss of pornography, racism, gaudy advertising and (arguably worst of all) empty hours wasted at the computer console, for which the Internet has become notorious? These are always the first questions I am asked by friends without Internet access. In order to address these questions, I would like to first dispel a popular misconception shared by nearly all non-users of the Internet.

Contrary to what most people think, the Internet and the World Wide Web (WWW) are *not* synonymous. They are two distinct concepts, which are meant to be exploited in different ways. The Internet itself is simply a means of rapidly communicating information between computers separated by vast distances. The technology behind it dates back some 30 years, when it was first developed by the U.S. Department of Defense. The WWW, on the other hand, is a four to five year old set of software rules that *uses* the Internet to allow the rapid transfer of information in a graphical environment. It also makes it possible to link information from very disparate sources in a manner that seamlessly leads a user from one computer or country to another as the user pursues subjects of interest with the click of a mouse. And herein lies the danger: who knows just what the next click will bring? And when one is presented with an endless world of links, when does someone's curiosity stop driving him or her further away from home-base?

The good news is that there is plenty of Internet or Net territory, including some (if not all) of the most useful information available on the Net. All of which can be gleaned without once using the World Wide Web. As I mentioned, the WWW is a relatively recent development. When I began to distribute the Parsha-Page through the Internet, 99 out of 100 Internet users were unfamiliar with the World Wide Web. In those days, the Internet was used mainly for the transfer of e-mail, which on most networks can be accomplished through the use of entirely independent (and free) e-mail software which cannot be used to view the WWW. Such viewing requires Web-browsing software. Although such software is included free in most Internet packages (or operating systems), it can be easily deleted (or hidden). The computer will then remain Web-free, yet it will be able to receive all the various Torah publications available through the Internet just as easily as any other computer! (Exceptions to this include the large online networks such as Compuserve and America Online, which use the same program for receiving e-mail and for viewing their other services. However, software is available which can limit access of these networks to e-mail only. There are also numerous networks which are often free—such as juno.com in New York which offer e-mail-only accounts for those willing to forego the option of using the WWW.)

In addition, even if you choose to allow your computer to access the WWW, many readily available software packages can limit Web access exclusively to Torah-true networks. The major Jewish networks can usually be trusted to monitor their Web sites for offensive postings (it is in their best interests to keep their sites holy!). If you limit your Web browsing to networks such as shemayisrael.co.il, shamash.org, ou.org, aishdas.org, torah.org, torahnet.co.il, jewishnet.net, 613.org, yated.com, chabad.org etc., you will be playing it pretty safe.

Having made that clear, let us have a brief look at the cornucopia of Torah now lying at our feet and how it can be accessed.

IV

What's out there?

Those familiar with the Web will be quick to advise that the first place to look for Jewish Web material is Matthew Album's listing of Jewish resources on the Internet, now merged with Virtual in the Maven index (http://www.maven.co.il). Be aware, however, that if you are looking for Torah postings, nearly everyone posting Torah on the

Web on a regular basis is distributing it simultaneously through a free, automatic Internet mailing-list. Since these lists are generally run by the major Jewish networks listed above (especially virtual.co.il, shemayisrael.co.il and shamash.org), you should get a current list of the mailing-lists available on these networks. To obtain such a list, either (if you use the WWW) visit www.aishdas.org's Web site, browse, and then join the list of your choice. The List mailing-list index also has an extensive listing of Torah mailing lists at http://www.liszt.com/select/Religion/Jewish/Torah/. Another useful URL is http://www.neosoft.com/internet/paml/, an official list of all the internet mailing lists. Search for Torah or Judaism. You can probably get an e-mail version of the list by writing to its compiler, arielle@taronga.com.

If you do not wish to use the WWW, address an e-mail message to listproc@name.of.the.network (or, if that doesn't work, to majordomo@name.of.the.network) and put in the message area one word only: lists. (The name of the network is generally the same as their URL—that is their WWW address—but without the prefix "http://www.".) In reply, the automatic mailing-list processor will send you a full listing of that network's mailing-lists along with one-line descriptions of each list. To the best of my knowledge, all of the Torah mailing-lists available through these networks are distributed free of charge.

When you have chosen the mailing-list you would like to join, address a message in the same manner as mentioned above and type as your message body the words: "subscribe listname [your name]" (without the quotes). (To remove yourself from a list to which you have subscribed, send a message to the same address you used to subscribe to the list, and type as your message body the words: unsubscribe listname—it is not necessary to include your name when you unsubscribe.) Remember, your mail will be sent to an automatic list processor and will not normally be seen by human eyes. Do not add any other words to your message or the list processor will not process the entire message.

Since this book comprises a collection of insights into the weekly Parsha, I will include here a very brief sampling of Internet publications that offer insights into the weekly Parsha for readers with a broad range of backgrounds in Torah study:

Name of list
network
description

parasha-page virtual.co.il My own publication, from which this book was compiled weekly. **virtual.co.il** Ohr Someach's review of the parsha (for beginners). **parashaqa virtual.co.il** Ohr Someach's quiz on the parsha (with Rashi). **yhe-parsha virtual.co.il** R. Leibtag's mailing (Yeshivat Har Etzion). **lifeline shamash.org** Project Genesis' parsha mailing (R. Yakov Menken). **byte-torah shamash.org** R. Zev Itzkowitz delves into a verse from the parsha. **shabbatshalom shamash.org** R. Packouz of Aish Hatorah (for beginners).

drasha shamash.org R. Mordecai Kaminetzky's weekly Drasha. **ravfrand shamash.org** taken from R. Yissachar Frand's weekly lecture. **ohr-torah sitt.com** published by Toronto's Ner Israel Kollel (advanced)...and there's much, much more! Many list authors will be glad to respond to questions as well. All of the above-mentioned lists provide English language literature only. (Unfortunately, due to problems of compatibility, to my knowledge Torah insights are not yet being distributed in Hebrew through Internet mailing lists).

Parasha-Page archives on the web are presently not up to date, the best archives at the moment appear to be the computerized ones at reference. com, http://www.reference.com/cgi-bin/pn/go.py?choice=authorprofile& email=kornfeld@netmedia.net.il, click on any months mailings to find the archives. If you would like a specific issue, just write me an e-mail message and I'll be glad to pass it along to you.

May Hashem grant me the strength and wisdom to continue to dwell in the "tent of Torah" in Jerusalem and bring the sweet words of the Torah to Jewish homes around the world. "For Torah goes forth from Zion; the word of Hashem, from Jerusalem!" (Yeshayah 2:3).

Mordecai Kornfeld (kornfeld@netmedia.co.il)
Rosh Chodesh Iyar, 5757

ACKNOWLEDGEMENTS

It is finally time to give credit where credit is due. I would certainly never have been able to achieve what I have without the boundless patience and constant support of my dear wife, Ayeleth—even when it meant giving up her husband for long hours to a computer. All that is mine, and all that I have given you, is hers! (Kesuvos 63a). May Hashem grant her the strength and wisdom to raise our children to serve Him with love. I also thank my wife's parents. Rabbi and Rebbetzin G. Rabinowitz, for their constant encouragement and support.

In all that I learn, I am constantly inspired by the image of my great mentor, Hagaon Rav Yisroel Zev Gustman of blessed memory. His quest for the truth, his passion for the study of Torah, the joy and exhilaration of his classes will always remain before my eyes. A teacher, a father, a counselor all combined, he embodied the spirit of the Torah scholar of old.

The Parasha-Page benefited greatly from the Talmudic, scholarly and linguistic talents of my good friend and editor, Rabbi Yakov Blinder, presently of Yeshivat Reishit Yerushalayim, Jerusalem. I would like to thank as well the various other editors who, at one point or another, left their mark on the Weekly Parasha-Page—among them, Rabbi Gavriel Rubin, Rabbi Chananya Greenwald, Aaron Feuer and, more recently, Dovid Himelson. I am indebted to Rabbi Yonasan Rosenblum for the hours he put into editing the "Seven Liquids" essay (page 277) and for his invaluable stylistic advice. I would also like to acknowledge the glimpses that I have been given into less obvious aspects of the Torah by the many Torah scholars with whom I have become associated. The insights of my father-in-law Hagaon

Rav Gedaliah Rabinowitz, My Rebbi Hagaon Rav Moshe Shapiro, Hagaon Rav Shlomo Fisher, Harav Chagai Preschel, Harav Avraham Miller, and numerous others have frequented the Parasha-Pages.

With regard to my Internet mailing-list, I would like to acknowledge the tremendous help that the staff members of Jerusalem One and, later, Virtual Jerusalem have given me in arranging and maintaining the Parasha-Page mailing-list. Special thanks to Zvi Lando, Danny Schilo, Avi Moscowitz and Mike Greenberg. To all of you subscribers who have dedicated issues of the Parasha-Page—*chazak ve'ematz*! I couldn't have done it without you! May the words of the Torah always be on your lips and provide you and your families with all of your material and spiritual needs.

I thank Aryeh Mezei, Bonnie Goldman and Zisi Berkowitz of Judaica Press for lending this manuscript the benefit of their publishing expertise and experience. They took a different sort of manuscript and managed to mold for it the perfect home. I am truly thankful for all the dedicated efforts they put into its production, from start to finish, while electronic communication shortened the distance between us.

The unceasing stream of love and encouragement that my parents poured upon me is what gave me the boldness to undertake this task. I cannot begin to describe their enormous help in every realm of my life (not to mention editing this book for publication). Their living example of love for a fellow man stands before my eyes in all that I do. May Hashem grant them long life and the *yiddishe nachas* of seeing all their children and grandchildren grow up in the ways that they have taught us.

May Hashem grant me the strength and wisdom to continue to dwell in the "tent of Torah" in Jerusalem and bring the sweet words of the Torah to the houses of Jews around the world. "For Torah goes forth from Zion; the word of Hashem, from Jerusalem!" (Yeshayah 2:3).

Mordecai Kornfeld
Rosh Chodesh Iyar, 5757

TORAH FROM THE INTERNET

Intriguing Insights into Jewish Holidays and the Weekly Torah Reading

by Rabbi Mordecai Kornfeld

PARSHAS BEREISHIS

In The Beginning
6,000 Years Ago Or 15 Billion Years Ago?

In this week's Parsha we find a description of the events that took place at the time of the creation of the universe. Hashem created the universe and all that is in it in six days and "rested" from creating on the seventh day—events which we commemorate weekly with our observance of the Shabbos day. From the chronology given in this Parsha and in the following one, it is clear that this creation took place approximately 6,000 years ago.

How old is the universe?

Modern scientists, however, would tell us quite a different story of the beginning. During recent years, a mounting body of evidence drawn from such varied disciplines as astronomy, cosmology, geochronology, paleontology, radiocarbon dating techniques and dendrochronology (tree-ring analysis), seems to indicate that the universe is much older than this. Although all experts essentially agree that civilization as we know it (i.e., the written word and the appearance of commercial societies) is about 5500-6500 years old, scientists' picture of prehistory is not at all similar to the biblical one. Scientists estimate that the universe has been around for 10-20 "billion" years; the earth, for 4 billion years; and multicellular life on earth, for 650 million years.

How can the account of the Torah be reconciled with these scientifically established conclusions? Let us take a look at some of the approaches that have been suggested to deal with this problem.

II

The first, and most obvious approach is to invoke the opinion of the Rambam (Maimonides) in his introduction to *Moreh Nevuchim* (*Guide to the Perplexed*).

The Rambam asserts that some of the events described in the Torah—including those involved in the story of creation—should not be understood literally. Rather, they are to be taken in an allegorical sense, as allusions to profound or esoteric concepts. If we understand the six days of creation as an allegorical, rather than a chronological, description of the events of creation, the contradiction between the Torah's account and scientists' account is obviously resolved.

Two allegorical approaches to creation

What allegorical meaning can be attached to the story of creation? What can the six days of creation be said to represent? The Ramban (Nachmanides) in a number of places in his commentary on the Torah, points out some of the underlying themes of the six days of creation.

The Ramban points out (Bereishis 1:3) that according to the Kabbalists, the word "days" can be taken to mean "emanations of Divine power" (or *sefiros*). The seven days of the story of creation can thus be understood as referring to seven of the *sefiros* involved in the creation of the world.

In other places (Bereishis 2:1, Vayikra 25:2) the Ramban suggests another theme to which the six days of creation may be alluding. In Tehillim 90:4 we read "A thousand years in Your eyes is like a single day that passes by." Hashem's "days" can be seen as the equivalent of one thousand years. Each of the six days of creation may thus represent one thousand years of the six thousand years we are told (Sanhedrin 97a), will pass between the time of Adam and the end of time.

(Rabbeinu Bachye ben Asher, in his commentary to the Torah, follows in the Ramban's footsteps and even adds a few points to the Ramban's words. Similar approaches were developed by Rav Avraham ben Rebbi Chiyya HaNassi in his *Megillas Hamegillah,* and by Abravanel in his commentary to Bereishis 2:1. According to Abravanel, this theme is actually hinted at in a Midrash Hazohar ad loc. See the following essay for a synopsis of their suggestions.)

III

As we have described above, the six days of creation may be understood allegorically. It should be noted, however, that the Ramban (Bereishis 1:3), and even the Rambam (*Moreh Nevuchim*, part II, chap. 30), seem to take the six-day account of creation literally (Ramban only presents the above allegories as an "added" aspect to the literal interpretation of the verse). If the six days are taken literally, how is it possible to reconcile the Torah's account with present-day scientific knowledge? Two basic approaches have been offered to answer this question.

Four literalist approaches to creation

(1)

Some have noted that the Midrash (Bereishis Rabbah 3:7) states that before the creation of the world as we know it, Hashem created and destroyed several other "proto-worlds." This would fit in neatly with our current understanding of the pattern of mass extinctions found in the annals of world history. (See Tiferes Yisrael, in his essay *Drush Ohr Hachayim*, section 3, printed among the commentaries at the end of Mishnayos Yachin U'Voaz, Nezikin II.)

The pre-Genesis worlds

We may point out, however, that according to the Kabbalists, the durations of these "proto-worlds" may not be able to account for the billions of years that the scientists speak of. In Kabbalistic literature, the length of this period of "the creation and destruction of worlds" is sharply limited. According to *Sefer HaTemunah* (preface to Temunah #3), this period of time was 7,000 years; according to Rabbeinu Bachye (to Bereishis, end of 1:1) it was 2,000 years; and according to the renowned medieval Kabbalist of Safed, Rav Yitzchak Luria (Sha'ar Ma'amarei Rashbi, commentary to the Idra Rabbah in Zohar 3:135a) it was only seven *days* long.

(2)

All in the first six days

There are those who suggest that when the Torah speaks of "days" in the account of creation, it simultaneously means the 24-hour period we are accustomed to call "day," and billions of years. This can be explained in several different ways.

(2a)

According to Einstein's theory of general relativity, time is not an absolute measurement. The experience of time changes relative to the speed at which an object is traveling and the gravitational forces acting upon it. What seems to be one day to someone in one situation, may actually be perceived as many days to another observer subject to a lower force of gravity or is traveling at a slower velocity. If we measure "six days" from the standpoint of someone outside the universe—from God's perspective, as it were—it could correspond to billions of years as measured from a human, earthly point of view. Perhaps during the first six days, when there was no human yet to measure time from an earthly standpoint, Hashem counted His days from a different perspective. (Dr. Gerald Schroeder in his book *Genesis and the Big Bang*, ch. 2. See also Aaron Vecht in *Challenge*, p. 186.)

(2b)

Rav Shimon Schwab (*Challenge*, p.165-174) suggests a different way the six days of creation correspond to billions of years. It is possible, he asserts, that during these six days Hashem "sped up" time, compressing billions of years into what we now sense as a 24-hour period. Consider, for example, a movie played at very high speed—a three-hour film can be seen in its entirety in a few short minutes.

It may be asked, however, that if all of the events of the unfolding of the universe were uniformly speeded up, in what way could their speed be measured? Relative to what absolute frame of reference was the process of creation "speeded up"?

The answer, Rav Schwab says, is that the Torah's frame of reference is the *ohr haganuz*—the primordial light created on the first day of creation. It was this spiritual light that, by its waning and reappearance every 24 hours (according to present day clocks), formed the basis for the first few evenings and mornings (the sun was not even in the skies until the fourth day!). It is by comparison with the cycle of this light, that has remained constant ever since its creation, that the billions of years of creation can be seen as compressed into six 24-hour days. It was only on the seventh day that Hashem slowed down the pace of the universe so that the cycle of the primordial light corresponded to our 24-hour day.

(2c)

A common approach is suggested by the Lubavitcher Rebbe (in a letter cited in *Challenge*, pg. 147, suggestion "B." See also Sanford Aranoff, *Challenge* pgs. 151-162.) The Torah tells us that when the first man and woman were created they were fully grown and developed, physically and mentally, although such a state of growth usually takes many years to materialize. Similarly, the animals of the world and the plants and trees were created at an advanced stage of development (Chullin 60a).

Since all the creatures in the world were created in a state that seemed to attest to many years of previous growth, perhaps the earth—and the entire cosmos—was also "born" bearing signs of many, many years of development. For instance, there are stars whose light seems to come to us only after traveling in space for many billions of years. The stars and the traveling rays of light were all created on the fourth day. This is all part of the scheme of creation, by which objects were created bearing all the physical signs of a long period of development.

If so, when Hashem created the earth and its inhabitants, perhaps He also created artifacts to attest to their ancestry. Thus, on the day that the animals were created, their prehistoric remains were created along with them.

IV

Why the conflicting evidence?

There is, however, a disturbing question that may be asked concerning Rav Schwab's approach (the "high-speed" theory) and the Lubavitcher Rebbe's approach (the "built-in history" theory)—as their authors themselves point out. Since Hashem did in fact create the universe in six days, why would He have altered it in a way that it gives the impression of being much older than it really is? He could have performed a six-day creation without leaving behind such misleading evidence.

Rav Schwab suggests that Hashem created the world this way in order to allow humans the possibility of denying creation. If Divine creation of the world would be obvious to all, there would be no challenge in accepting this doctrine, and there would thus be no reward for those who accepted Hashem's mastery upon them.

The suggestion that the creation was intentionally made to mislead us seems less than satisfying, however. Besides, didn't Adam, Eve and their son Kayin manage to sin, as obvious as creation was to them? And didn't the Jews and gentiles sin for thousands of years until Darwinism and paleontology made their impressions? Apparently enough challenge exists even without this added confusion. (More moderate suggestions, such as those of Rav Kanievsky in *Chaye Olam* 1:19 and 2:7, may also be applied here.)

V

A new approach

The world around us was intended to encourage us to analyze the works of Hashem, and to convey to us many moral lessons. The Gemara (Eruvin 100b) tells us for instance that we can learn moral conduct from various animals; see also Rambam Yesodei HaTorah 2:2. If so, nature itself may be seen as a Torah in its own right, teaching us the will of Hashem. Thus, there are two guidebooks to the ways of Hashem: the Torah, and the natural world.

The "book" of nature has a unique quality, though. Nobody, no matter how ardent an atheist, can ever claim that it nature is a "forgery." Even if someone refuses to see the hand of Hashem in nature, the lessons that it teaches us about life and human nature are still there to appreciate. Perhaps it is for this reason, then, that this "book" was modeled to present quite a different story of creation than the Bible. The two "books" present different pictures of the world because they were written for different audiences, as we shall explain.

The Gemara (Sanhedrin 38a) asks why it was that humans, the crowns of creation, were the very last thing that God created. One of the answers the Gemara gives is that this was done to ensure that humans would not let their elevated status in the world go to their head. In the words of the Gemara, "If a person becomes overly arrogant, he is reminded of the fact that even the fleas were created before him." Humans were created last to remind them of their puniness.

The Gemara there poses another answer, however, that seems to present precisely the opposite theme. When a person invites guests home, the Gemara explains, the food is prepared and the table and chairs set before the guests arrive. Similarly, Hashem first finished the preparations of all the ingredients of the universe before His "guests" were brought to partake of

His "feast" in the Garden of Eden. The very fact that humans were created last thus attests to the human being's centrality in the scheme of creation.

It may be said that these two answers complement each other. We find in the Midrash (Bereishis Rabbah 8:1) that when someone follows the will of Hashem he is told, "Your spirit was created even before the angels of the Heavens"; but if he does not follow the will of Hashem, he is scolded with the reminder that "even the bodies of the fleas were created before your body was!" The Midrash means to say that when one does Hashem's will, one should realize that one ranks even higher than the angels of Heaven. If, however, one is arrogant and defies the will of his Creator, one must be humbled by the knowledge that he is only a tiny part of the cosmos.

The message that a believer learns from the Torah's account of creation 6,000 years ago is the pivotal role that humans play in this world. If human beings follow the ways of Hashem and the words of His Torah, they will raise themselves spiritually and raise all of nature along with them.

However, Hashem knew that there would always be people who would not accept the veracity of the Torah. For them He created a universe full of indications of the vastness of the forces of nature and the humbleness of human's origins. How humbling it is to ponder the scientific version of where humans came from—"Even fleas preceded you!" Furthermore, by considering the long history of extinctions caused by rather sudden changes in the earth's makeup over the ages, humans come to realize that the universe is not ours to abuse. Humans live in a world which hangs in a very delicate ecological balance. If we do not respect the rights of other people and creatures to exist, we are liable to face natural disasters such as those visited upon the earth in the past. Today's ecological awareness can be directly related to the recent scientific discoveries about the past history of this planet.

Thus the creation of the world was carried out on two distinct planes—according to a six-day creation, to teach people who accept the Torah the centrality of the human being's role in carrying out Hashem's will in the world, and according to a 20-billion year apparent creation, to teach those who do not accept the Torah these humbling lessons in a different manner.

Further reading

For further reading on this subject, I recommend the following books: *Challenge* edited by C. Domb (Feldheim Publishing, 1976), pp. 124-186; *Genesis and the Big Bang* by G. Schroeder (Bantam Books, 1990); *In the Beginning* by N. Aviezer (Ktav Publishing House, 1990); *Immortality, Resurrection, & the Age of the Universe* by Rav Aryeh Kaplan (Ktav Publishing House, 1993).

PARSHAS NOACH

The Seventeenth Of The Second

"In the 600th year of Noach's life, in the second month on the 17th day of the month all the fountains of the deep burst forth and the windows of the heavens were opened to let forth rain upon the earth for forty days and forty nights" (Bereishis 7:11-12).

The day of the year which marked the start of the great flood seems to be entirely random. What made the 17th day of the second month such a fateful day? A friend, haRav Chaggai Preschel offered the following explanation.

II

The timing of the great flood

Rebbi Eliezer (Rosh Hashanah 11b) informs us that the "second month" quoted in the above verse is Cheshvan, the second month counting from Tishrei, the month during which Hashem created the world. On the previous first of Tishrei (Rosh Hashanah, the Day of Judgment) Hashem deemed the world to be unworthy and decreed upon it the great flood (Rosh Hashanah 12a).

When the city of Ninveh was to be punished Hashem granted them a 40 day reprieve, giving them a last chance to repent and change their evil ways (Yonah 3:4). This is Hashem's way; even after He decides to eradicate a city or nation as punishment for its sinful ways, He still allows them an extra 40-day opportunity to repent. When the Jewish People sinned by serving the golden calf (Shemos 32), Hashem did *not* wipe them out immediately, as had been decreed. Rather, He gave them 40 days to repent, during which Moshe prayed from the Jews and Hashem accepted his prayers (Rashi, Devarim 9:10). Before bringing the great flood as well,

Hashem gave the world 40 last days to repent.

But 40 days after the first of Tishrei only brings us to 10 Cheshvan—why did the flood begin only seven days later, on 17 Cheshvan? Rashi provides us with the last piece of this puzzle:

"'In another *seven days* I will bring rain upon the earth...' (Bereishis 7:4) —the seven days mentioned here were the days of mourning that followed the passing of the righteous Mesushelach (Methuselah). In order to allow people to pay their respects to Mesushelach, Hashem delayed the flood for seven days" (Rashi Bereishis 7:4, from Sanhedrin 108a).

III

Exactly seven days after 10 Cheshvan, the great flood began!

The beginning of the flood: Cheshvan or Iyar

Unfortunately, Rebbi Eliezer's opinion that the great flood began in Cheshvan is not agreed upon by all. According to Rebbi Yehoshua, the "second month" of the verse, during which the flood started, was *Iyar*! As the Gemara tells us:

Rebbi Eliezer said: The world was created in the month of Tishrei...Rebbi Yehoshua said: The world was created in the month of Nissan....

Consequently the two differed as to when the great flood took place. Rebbi Yehoshua maintained that the rain started on the 17th of Iyar...while Rebbi Eliezer said that it began on the 17th of Cheshvan (Rosh Hashanah 11a, 11b).

Even in regards to halachic matters there remains a controversy among the early commentators whether to accept the opinion of Rebbi Eliezer or Rebbi Yehoshua (See Rashi, Tosafos and Ritva to Rosh Hashanah 8b, 12a, 27a) there any way to explain why, according to Rebbi Yehoshua, the flood began specifically on the 17th of Iyar?

IV

In a Midrash (Vayikra Rabbah 29:1), Rebbi Eliezer tells us why the first of Tishrei is the yearly Day of Judgment. The first man was created on the first day of Tishrei. He sinned, was judged and was granted life despite his sin on that same day. Hashem chose to judge mankind on the first of Tishrei every year as an omen that they too will merit atonement and be granted life on that day.

Why Tishrei is the Day of Judgment

As the Ran (14th cent. Spain) points out (Rosh Hashanah 16a), this only accounts for the opinion of Rebbi Eliezer. Why should the Day of Judgment be on the first day of Tishrei according to Rebbi Yehoshua, who believed that man was created in the beginning of Nissan? (See Rosh Hashanah essay p.259). We may suggest a novel approach to this question.

The Torah tells us that although Rosh Hashanah marks the beginning of the New Year, when it comes to numbering the months, Nissan is month #1 (that is, the New Year begins with month #7!). We count our months from Nissan to commemorate our Exodus from Egypt which took place in the month of Nissan (Shemos 12:2 and Rashi). Radak (13th cent. Spain) to I Kings 8:2, Ritva (14th cent. Spain) to Rosh Hashanah 11b and others point out that it seems to be clear from the verse in Shemos that *until* the Exodus, Tishrei not only marked the beginning of the *year*, but it was also labeled "month #1" when numbering the months. Nissan was granted special status only after the Exodus, in order to commemorate that event.

This is all fine, however, only according to Rebbi Eliezer. Since he held that the world was created in Tishrei, there was no reason for Nissan to be the first of months before the Exodus occured. According to Rebbi Yehoshua, however, the world was created in Nissan. Shouldn't Nissan have been considered the first of months, then, from the beginning of time?

The answer to this question may be that before the Exodus, Nissan was indeed both the first of all the months and the beginning of the year according to Rebbi Yehoshua. What changed at the Exodus was that the beginning of the *year*—not the beginning of the month-count—was shifted. In order to make Nissan a unique month for the Jewish People (who commemorated in it the Exodus) and for them alone, Hashem started to treat Tishrei (the month of the autumnal equinox rather than the vernal equinox) as the beginning of the year for all of mankind! This curious situation, whereby we celebrate the New Year and its accompanying Day of Judgment in Tishrei while counting our months from Nissan, makes it clear that Nissan does not derive its elevated status simply through chronological precedence.

Before the Exodus, in Rebbi Yehoshua's opinion, Nissan was the beginning of the year, the time for judgment and the beginning of the month-count. Only *after* the Exodus did the first of Tishrei become the beginning of the new year and the Day of Judgment. This explains why the first of Tishrei—rather than the first of Nissan, the day of Creation—is celebrated today as the day that mankind is judged, according to Rebbi Yehoshua.

We can now apply Rabbi Preschel's formula to Rebbi Yehoshua's opinion just as simply as we applied it to Rebbi Eliezer's opinion (in section II). The great flood started exactly 47 days after the first of Nissan, according to Rebbi Yehoshua, because that was the Day of Judgment throughout the era preceding the Egyptian Exodus!

PARSHAS LECH LECHA

The Prophetic Experiences Of The Avos

"Avraham passed through the land (of Israel) until he reached the area of Shechem; until the plains of Moreh" (Bereishis 12:1).

Ramban explains this as follows: "Let me tell you a rule worth keeping in mind when reading this parsha and the parshiyos that follow—all of which discuss the adventures of our forefathers. Our Sages hinted to this rule in brief by stating, 'Anything that occurred to the *Avos* (our forefathers, Avraham, Yitzchak, and Yaakov) is a sign of what will happen to their children' (Tanchuma Lech Lecha # 9). It is for this reason that the Torah discusses at length the travels of Avraham, the wells that Yitzchak dug, and other such stories. The innocent reader may think these stories are superfluous. In truth they all presage future events in the lives of our people. When something happened to any of the three prophets referred to as 'the *Avos*,' the prophet was able to deduce from his experiences what was destined to happen to his descendants" (—i.e., the experiences themselves were prophecies—MK).

It is clear from the Torah that our forefathers were prophets, and received prophetic visions. The Ramban, however, adds a new dimension to their prophecy.

Experiences that are prophecies

He states that prophecy does *not* come in verbal form only—even a physical experience can be a prophecy. The *Avos* were subject to many such "prophetic experiences" throughout their lives, which were analogous to verbal prophecies. These experiences revealed to them the destiny of their descendants, the Bnai Yisrael.

II

The Ramban refers to this theme quite often in the book of Bereishis. For example, when Avraham comes to Eretz Yisrael, his first stop is "the area of Shechem; until the plains of Moreh" (Bereishis 12:6). This hints to the fact that the very first territory his descendants would conquer would be Shechem, the city which two of the children of Yaakov captured and plundered (Bereishis 34:25). Similarly, Elon Moreh was the Jewish nation's first stop upon crossing into Eretz Yisrael with Joshua (see Rashi Bereishis 12:6, Tosafos Sotah 33b s.v. *Mul*).

Examples of prophetic experiences

Immediately after the stop in Shechem, Avraham Avinu camped between Beth El and Ay, which Ramban points out (Bereishis 12:6) marked the exact location of the first war the Jews would have to fight upon entering the Holy Land.

Later, driven by famine, Avraham Avinu travels to Egypt. He and his wife, Sarah, fear abuse and death. It is Pharaoh, however, who ends up suffering. By the end of Avraham and Sarah's trip, Pharaoh sends Avraham and Sarah off accompanied by some of his own people and laden with Pharaoh's gift to them of immense wealth (Bereishis 12:10-20). This episode, Ramban explains (12:10), clearly hints to the experiences of Bnai Yisrael during their bondage in Egypt and their eventual exodus. Yaakov and the tribes were forced by famine to move to Egypt; the Jewish nation suffered greatly there, but were later released from bondage and sent out of Egypt by a beleaguered Pharaoh; they were joined in their exodus by Egyptian converts and were given great wealth by their former captors (Shemos 12:38). Both Rashi and Ramban explain that when Avraham returned to Eretz Yisrael, he was told to, "Get up and walk about the entire land" (13:17), symbolizing that Avraham's progeny would be the future heirs of that land, and would easily conquer it.

Avraham goes to war against four powerful kings and their armies and defeats them. Ramban points out (14:1) that this symbolizes the Four Exiles that the Jewish nation was to experience. Each exiling nation would in turn succumb, while the Jewish nation would survive them all.

Similarly, during the famed *bris ben habesarim* or covenant between the parts vision, Avraham experiences four types of fears. This, says Rashi and Ramban (15:11, 12) symbolizes the periods of terror that the Jews would face during their four exiles.

Ramban also applies this theme to the experiences of Yitzchak and Yaakov (see, for example, Ramban to Bereishis 25:23, 26:1, 27:20, 29:2, 33:26, 34:18). In many instances, the Ramban brings further Midrashic support for his interpretations.

III

Upon a closer examination of the sources, a pattern emerges in the prophetic experiences of the *Avos*. As the Gemara tells us, there are only three men we refer to as the *Avos*, or founding fathers, of our nation: Avraham, Yitzchak and Yaakov. It is their experiences that provide us with insight into what will befall the Jewish nation throughout the ages, as the Ramban established.

Three Avos; three eras in Jewish history

Perhaps we may add, then, that the experiences of the three *Avos* reflect the events of three distinct periods in Jewish history. Each one of the *Avos* corresponds, chronologically, to a different period in the future history of the Jewish nation.

It would seem that the experiences of Avraham Avinu correspond to those that affected the Jewish nation during its period of incubation, birth and maturation. We find hints in the experiences of Avraham to events that occurred from the time of Yitzchak's birth, through the lives of Yaakov and the twelve tribes, the Egyptian exile, the Exodus, the years of wandering, and finally the conquest and settlement of Eretz Yisrael—a total of 880 years.

The life of Yitzchak, on the other hand, corresponds to the golden period of Jewish history. This period begins with the construction of the First Temple and its 410 year history, and includes the 70 years of Babylonian exile that followed the destruction of the First Temple and the 420 years that the Second Temple stood—900 years in all.

Yaakov's life corresponds to the third period of Jewish history, during which we suffered greatly and found ourselves homeless and powerless, at the mercy of our enemies. This third period began with the destruction of the Second Temple and continues until today. The end of this period will herald our final redemption, our return to the Holy Land, and the coming of the Messiah.

In fact, we find a chronological theme in the order of the *Avos* elsewhere. We are told in Berachos 26b that our forefathers were the ones who instituted the daily prayers. Avraham Avinu instituted the morning prayer, Yitzchak, the afternoon prayer, and Yaakov, the night prayer. According to what we have proposed above, the same can be said of their prophetic experiences: Avraham foresaw the morning, or birth, of the nation. Yitzchak foresaw the afternoon—when the sun is fully risen and shines brightly. Yaakov prophesied the Jewish nation's long dark night, i.e., exile and suffering, often compared to the dark of night (see Tosafos, Taanis end of 3a). Just as the evening prayer is recited between sunset and daybreak, so too, the "night" of exile stretches on until the appearance of the rays of the morning light, an allegory for redemption.

With these insights, let us now take a fresh look at the lives of the *Avos*.

IV

According to the Midrash, Avraham Avinu's first prophecy was the *bris ben habesarim*, (Bereishis 15:7-21 see Rashi's comments on Shemos 12:40, Tosafos Shabbos 10b). During this vision Avraham is told that his children (i.e., Yitzchak and his descendants) would be in a land that was not theirs for 400 years. It is appropriate that Avraham's first vision would describe the very first events in Jewish history. This vision began to materialize only thirty years afterwards, with Yitzchak's birth.

Avraham

The *bris ben habesarim* took place in Eretz Yisrael. Avraham afterwards returns to his family in Ur Kasdim, where he is commanded to return to Israel. He returns, and then leaves Israel again, this time for Egypt. After his experiences in Egypt, he returns for the third time to Israel.

Similarly, Yitzchak, the first "born Jew," lived in Eretz Yisrael all his life. His son, Yaakov, traveled out of Israel to father the twelve tribes. Yaakov returned to Israel, and from there went to Egypt. After suffering through years of Egyptian persecution, the Jewish nation eventually returns to Eretz Yisrael for the third time, thereby completing the pattern described by Avraham's experiences.

As we have outlined above, Avraham's travels in Eretz Yisrael foreshadowed the Jewish conquest of Canaan which followed their exodus from Egypt.

Avraham twice experienced a taste of the Four Exiles that the Jews would have to endure (see section II). Although this does not seem to fit the pattern we are trying to establish, further examination reveals that it very well may belong to the same category as the rest of Avraham's prophecies.

Various commentaries tell us that although the Jews were supposed to remain in Egypt for 400 years, Hashem saw that they weren't able to handle such an extended oppression. Instead of having them stay in Egypt the entire 400 years, Hashem redeemed Bnai Yisrael after only 210 years. However, it was necessary for the Jews to "make up" time in exile, and to experience four future expulsions. Indeed, Rashi on Shemos 3:14 states that when Moshe is originally told to take the Jews out from Egypt, Hashem hints to Moshe that there would be future periods of exile.

The Egyptian exile was the source from which all other exiles evolved. The part that exile plays in Jewish history is the completion of a process that began in Egypt. It is as part of a revelation of the Egyptian oppression, that Avraham was shown the Four Exiles that the Jews experienced at a later time in history.

Yitzchak is described by Rashi on Bereishis 26:2 as "an unblemished burnt offering" due to his part in the Akeida (see Bereishis 22:9). A living sacrifice, Yitzchak's life symbolizes the golden period of Jewish history, during which the Temples stood and the sacrificial service dominated daily Jewish life.

As the Ramban (26:1) points out, Yitzchak's short stay in the land of the Philistines is premonitious of the Jewish exile in Babylon, between the First and Second Temple periods. Yitzchak's subsequent excavation of three wells is a prophetic allegory hinting to the three Temples (the two that were, and the third that will soon be rebuilt, speedily in our days)—Ramban 27:2. Yitzchak never left Eretz Yisrael, except for a short visit in the "pseudo-Israel" land of the Philistines (see Rashi 26:12). Similarly, the Jews during the Temple periods comfortably inhabited Eretz Yisrael. Even during the 70-year exile in Babylon, the Torah centers of Israel were transferred along with them, intact, to Babylon (Gemara Gittin 88a).

Yitzchak

Yaakov wrestled with his twin brother, Esav while in his mother's womb. This clearly hints to the suffering our nation was to experience at the hands of Esav's descendants—the Roman nation—which destroyed the Second Temple and exiled us from our land (Rashi 25:22; Ramban 25:23, 33:26). It is this Roman exile, the fourth of the Four Exiles, whose burden we still bear today.

Yaakov

Yaakov is forced to flee Eretz Yisrael to escape the grasp of his murderous brother, Esav (Bereishis 27:42). Throughout his life he is forced to deal with the evil plotting of Esav and other oppressors. Even upon his return to Eretz Yisrael, Yaakov's torment does not end. For twenty-two years Yaakov lives in anguish, believing that his beloved son Yosef had been killed (Rashi 28:9, 37:1). Eventually, Yaakov returned to the Diaspora where he passes away after a "short and miserable life" (Bereishis 47:9). Yaakov's experiences represent the suffering of the Jews in the Diaspora since the destruction of the second Temple.

The only moment that Yaakov lives peacefully with his evil brother, Esav, occurs on the day that Yaakov returns to Israel after an extended stay in the house of Lavan (Rashi 33:4). On this day Yaakov envisages the time, yet to come, when all the Jews would return from the diaspora and live in peace and tranquillity in their land (Rashi 33:14). Similarly, the return of Yaakov's body to Eretz Yisrael after his death in Egypt symbolizes the victorious return of a despondent Jewish nation to its homeland, in the End of Days (Taanis 5b).

It is perhaps significant to note that during the last moments of Yaakov's life he attempted to reveal to his children the day of the Final Redemption (Rashi 49:1). It was only after Yaakov had "lived" the history of the Jewish nation up until the End of Time, that he was able to say when the time of the final redemption would come—may we merit to see its arrival, speedily in our days!

PARSHAS VAYERA

A Mountain, A Field, A House: One Place; Three Names

"And Avraham prayed in that place saying, 'May future generations serve you in this place;' therefore people now say, 'This is the mountain upon which Avraham served Hashem' (Bereishis 22:14).

R. Elazar asked: What does the verse mean when it says (Yeshayah 2:3), "Many nations will go and say, 'Let us go up to the mountain of Hashem, to the house of the God of Yaakov"? Why is only Yaakov mentioned? Is He only the God of Yaakov and not the God of Avraham and Yitzchak?

The Gemara answers: At the time of the redemption [the Holy Temple] will not be as it was in the days of Avraham when it was called a *har* [mountain], as it says (Bereishis 22:14), "On the mountain Hashem will be seen". Nor will it be as it was in the days of Yitzchak when it [the place of the Temple] was referred to as a *sadeh* [field], as it says (Bereishis 24:63), "And Yitzchak went out to pray in the field". Rather it shall be as it was in Yaakov's days, who called it a *bayis* [house], as it says (Bereishis 28:19), "And he called the name of the place, 'The house of Hashem'" (Pesachim 88a).

In succession Avraham, Yitzchak and Yaakov came to the place where the Holy Temple was destined to be built. They each perceived this coveted place differently. To Avraham, it was a mountain; to Yitzchak, it was a field; and to Yaakov, it was a house. It is this last perception that will be shared by all upon the Final Redemption.

We know that in *every* statement of Chazal many deep concepts have been encapsulated. What are Chazal trying to teach us in the passage quoted above? What is the significance of the allusions to a "mountain", a "field" and a "house"? Let us see what insights we can glean from this passage with the help of the great scholars.

II

On a simple level the passage can be explained as follows: The Beis Hamikdash is where Hashem reveals His glory to us here on Earth in a way that all can appreciate His dominion [see Parsha page Tetzaveh 5755, section II]. This is referred to as the dwelling of the Divine Presence in this world [*Hashra'as haShechinah*].

The cumulative effect of our forefather's prayers

When each of the *Avos*, in turn, visited the site where the Beis Hamikdash was to be, they prayed there that Hashem would reveal His Presence to the world and let everyone see His glory. They asked Hashem to cause His *Shechinah* to dwell in this world, and to establish the Beis Hamikdash on this spot. The prayers of each of the *Avos* had a cumulative effect until eventually they succeeded in accomplishing their goal. Our Sages conveyed this thought to us through a series of metaphors, referring to the place of the future Beis Hamikdash first as a mountain, then as a field, then as a house.

When Avraham Avinu first approached the site, he saw a mountain. The place on which the Beis Hamikdash was to be built resembled a raw mountain, because one could not see any sign of its owner, or Creator, by looking at it. By Yitzchak's time, however, Avraham's prayers had already had an effect. Yitzchak saw a field. A field shows signs of an owner since crops are growing in it in an organized manner. However, one does not see the owner since the owner usually does not live on his field.

When Yaakov Avinu came and experienced a vision there he called the Temple Mount "the 'House' of Hashem". He saw that the Bnai Yisrael would eventually merit that this place would resemble a house where the owner can constantly be seen. A Beis Hamikdash would be built and Hashem would reveal His glory there on a permanent basis. It is in this manner that the Temple will again be perceived upon our redemption.

III

We can add yet a deeper dimension to our understanding of this passage with the help of some ideas primarily culled from the commentary of the Maharsha (Pesachim 88a).

Maharsha: three names, three Temples

Although Avraham, Yitzchak and Yaakov each had a vision of the Beis Hamikdash, each of them saw a *different* one of the three Temples which were to be built in the course of Jewish history. Avraham Avinu saw the First Temple, Yitzchak saw the Second Temple, and Yaakov saw the Third Temple, which is to be built in the time of the future redemption. The first one—the one which Avraham Avinu saw—lasted 400 years before it was destroyed. After it was destroyed, it was referred to as, "The 'mountain' of Zion which is desolate" (Eichah 5:18).

Avraham Avinu referred to this spot as a mountain, because he saw that after the destruction of the First Temple it was to become a bare mountain.

Yitzchak saw the second Beis Hamikdash, also destined to be destroyed. Of its destruction it is said "Zion will be plowed as a 'field' " (Micha 3:12—see Rashi, Taanis 29a, s. v. *Nechresha Ha'ir*). This Beis Hamikdash, Yitzchak saw, would end up an open field. (I.e., although it was destroyed, it still bore signs of having once been settled.)

Yaakov Avinu, though, saw the Third Beis Hamikdash, which will never be destroyed. This Beis Hamikdash could be referred to as a house since it was destined to endure and to remain a house for all eternity. This is the "house" that those who return at the end of days will see in Yerushalayim.

IV

The Belzer Rebbe: encampments of heavenly hosts

An ingenious suggestion for an entirely different approach to our passage was offered by the Belzer Rebbe, haGaon Rav Sarshalom of Belz (*Chidushei Maharash*, Parshas Vaeschanan—see also *Sefer Ben Yehoyada*, Pesachim 88a). Embellished with some additional insights of our own, it will round out our understanding of this teaching of the Sages.

In Nedarim 39b are told that the creation of the Beis Hamikdash preceded the creation of the entire world (see Ran ad loc.). Now, we know that there was no Beis Hamikdash on *earth* until 480 years after the exodus from Egypt. However, we find (Rashi Bereishis 28:17) that besides the earthly Beis Hamikdash, standing on the Temple Mount in Jerusalem, there is a "heavenly" Beis Hamikdash situated opposite the earthly one. This "heavenly" Beis Hamikdash existed even before the Beis Hamikdash was built on earth.

If so, perhaps we can suggest that the Beis Hamikdash which preceded the creation of the earth was the "heavenly" Beis Hamikdash. Our Beis Hamikdash was built from stone and wood, but the heavenly Beis Hamikdash certainly could not be built from such materials. In the desert, the Bnai Yisrael surrounded the Mishkan on four sides with four different camps. Our Sages tell us that so too, in Heaven, Hashem surrounds Himself with four different camps of angels (see Midrash Shemos Rabbah 2:9, quoted by Ramban, Bamidbar, end of 2:2). Perhaps it is these camps of angels that are referred to as the "heavenly Beis Hamikdash." The heavenly Temple, then, is made up of the four *machanos* [camps] of angels encamped around the Divine Presence. (See Bereishis 32:3, where a group of angels is referred to as a *machaneh*. The encampments of the Jews which surrounded the Mishkan are also referred to as *machaneh*—Bamidbar 2:3).

However, as long as Hashem had not yet fully revealed His presence on earth, and there was no earthly Beis Hamikdash, the heavenly Beis Hamikdash was also incomplete. Before Avraham Avinu came along, four *machanos* of angels did not surround the *Shechinah*. There was a heavenly Temple (the one that preceded the creation of the world) but it consisted of only one wall surrounding the *Shechinah*, made up of one camp of angels—one *machaneh* Elokim. As the *Avos* began to reveal the presence of Hashem on earth to its inhabitants, so too, the heavenly Beis Hamikdash became more and more complete.

According to the numerical system known as *gematria*, each letter of the Hebrew alphabet is assigned a numerical value. *Alef* = 1, *beis* = 2, *yud* = 10, etc. Our Sages have taught us that the numerical value of the Hebrew letters comprising each word can yield insights into the deeper meaning of a word. *Machaneh*, for instance, has a *gematria* value of 103 (*mem* = 40, *ches* = 8, *nun* = 50, *heh* = 5).

Avraham Avinu came and prayed on the place where the Temple was to be, opposite the heavenly Temple. With his prayers Avraham added an additional wall to the heavenly Temple—a second *machaneh* of angels. *Machaneh* (103) plus *machaneh* (another 103) equals 206. That is why Avraham called this place a *har*, the *gematria* of which is 205 (*heh* = 5, *reish* = 200. One of the rules of *gematria* is that one may, at times, add one number to the combined numerical value of a word's letters. This extra number corresponds to the word as a whole. Adding an extra one in such a manner is referred to as *im hakollel* [with the total]. In such a manner, *har* equals exactly 206, or 2 x 103.)

When Yitzchak prayed there he added another *machaneh* of angels to the heavenly Beis Hamikdash, giving it a third "wall." Now that there were three *machanos*, Yitzchak referred to this place as a *sadeh* which has the *gematria* of 309 (*sin* = 300, *daled* = 4, *heh* = 5), or three times *machaneh* (103). When Yaakov prayed there he added a fourth wall, making it a *bayis*. *Bayis* has the *gematria* of four times *machaneh* (103), or 412 (*beis* = 2, *yud* = 10, *saf* = 400).

The Belzer Rebbe adds that the heavenly Beis Hamikdash did not yet have a ceiling—similar to the tabernacle in the desert which had four walls but no ceiling, only a covering of cloth. Later on, before Moshe Rabbeinu was taken away from the Bnai Yisrael, he was shown all of Eretz Yisrael, including the place of the Beis Hamikdash (Rashi, Devarim 3:25). At that time Moshe Rabbeinu prayed for the completion of the heavenly Beis Hamikdash. He prayed using the word, "*vaeschanan* [and I pleaded]" (Devarim 3:23). Moshe used this word because his prayer was to add a ceiling—a fifth *machaneh* of angels—to the heavenly Beis Hamikdash. Five times *machaneh* is 515, exactly the *gematria* of *vaeschanan* (*vav* = 6, *alef* = 1, *saf* = 400, *ches* = 8, *nun* = 50, *nun* = 50)!

PARSHAS CHAYEI SARAH

Themes In The Hebrew Alphabet

Upon Sarah's death, Avraham approached Ephron the Hittite and offered to buy from him the cave of Machpelah. Ephron answered Avraham saying, "My lord, listen to me! What is a four hundred silver shekel piece of land, between you and me? Just take it and bury your dead!"

So Avraham weighed out the amount of money Ephron had mentioned..."four hundred silver shekels of tradable currency" (Bereishis 23:14-16).

Ephron had said, "Between me and you"—which implied, "Between two good friends such as us, why should this be important?"

"Avraham weighed out to Ephron"—we see in this verse that the *vav* is left out of Ephron's name. According to Rashi this was done because, although Ephron said a lot (i.e., he offered to give the land for free), he did nothing (i.e., he ended up being paid for the full value of the land). Not only that, but Ephron took four hundred large shekalim—"centenaria"—as it says, "tradable currency." The shekels were of such high quality that they were acceptable as shekels anywhere in the world (Rashi to vs. 15,16).

Why the missing letters?

The beginning of this week's Parsha discusses Avraham's purchase of the Cave of Machpelah in Hebron from Ephron the Hittite. Our Sages point out that the unusual spelling of Ephron's name in the verse that discusses the sale, indicates a lack of sincerity and generosity on Ephron's part. While Ephron had originally claimed that he was not interested in receiving any money for the Cave of Machpelah, he subsequently gladly accepted even more money than the field was worth.

How does Rashi infer this from the missing *vav*? The most obvious explanation is that if Ephron's name is written "lacking" something it demonstrates that Ephron himself was "lacking" something. Thus it is implied that he was not sincere when he made his magnanimous offer.

We find a similar theme in Rashi's comments (Bereishis 25:24 and 38:27) on the strange spelling of the word *te'omim* [twins] in parshas Toldos. In this parsha, when the Torah speaks of the birth of Yaakov and Esav, *te'omim* is spelled without the letter *alef* (*tomim*). In describing the birth of Yehudah's twins (Bereishis 38:27), Zerach and Peretz, the word *te'omim* is spelled with an *alef*.

Rashi explains that in the case of Yehudah's twins, both these twins became righteous men. This is why their birth is described with the "full" word, *te'omim*. In the case of Yitzchak and Rivkah's twins, however, one of them was the wicked Esav. Since one of the twins was evil and "lacked" completion, the word describing their birth has a letter lacking—it is spelled *tomim*. We can derive from this the following principle—in a situation where there is something lacking, the word describing it may be spelled without one of its letters. According to this understanding, the particular letter that is dropped is of no consequence.

II

HaRav Yaakov Blinder suggested to me that Rashi's comment in this case might be understood in a deeper sense. The letter *vav*, he points out, is the letter prefixed to Hebrew words to indicate that they are connected to the words that precede them. (*Vav* is usually translated in English as "and," but it often has other conjunctive connotations as well.) Rashi, for example, comments on Shemos 21:1 that, whenever the Torah says *eleh* ("these are") it indicates that what follows is not related to what preceded. When the Torah says *v'eleh* (with a *vav*, meaning "*and* these are"), a connection to the previous passage is implied." In fact, the very name of the letter—*vav*—actually signifies in Hebrew "a hook (or peg) which is used for attaching" (Shemos 26:32 ff.). The elongated line that represents the letter *vav*, actually resembles a hook.

Why specifically those letters?

Perhaps, then, there is a reason that this particular letter was left out of Ephron's name. Perhaps Ephron's *vav* was omitted in order to show the lack of "connection," or endearment, between himself and Avraham. Ephron had just boasted how he and Avraham were such good friends that money need not pass between them. But by taking the full price of the field—and then some—Ephron showed that he, in fact, felt no friendship at all for Avraham. "He said a lot but did nothing" (Rashi 23:16). In reality, as the lack of *vav* shows, there was no connection between the two men at all.

Following Rav Blinder's line of reasoning, we may explain Rashi's other example of a word that is "lacking." The word for twins *te'omim* is spelled *tomim*, with the letter *alef* lacking when referring to Yaakov and Esav. This shows that one of the twins would be wicked and would not serve his Creator. Rav Blinder suggests that perhaps the *alef* was dropped because this letter represents Hashem, the Creator, as we find in many Midrashim (Yerushalmi Chagigah 2:1 quoted by Beis Yosef to Orach Chayim 36, letter *beis*; Midrash Osios d'Rabbi Akiva, letter *alef*. See also Chagigah 16a, "*Aluph* [chief] always means Hashem, as it says in Yirmiyahu 3:4 'You are the *Aluph* of my youth'"; Bereishis Rabbah 20:2 and Rashi Mishlei 16:28 where Hashem is referred to as "*Alupho shel Olam*").

III

Rav Blinder used this idea to explain another episode in our Parsha where there are missing *vavs*.

Other missing* vavs *explainable in this manner

Avraham sent his faithful servant, Eliezer out of Israel to find a bride for his beloved son, Yitzchak. Eliezer goes, and succeeds in his mission. While at the bride's house, Eliezer tells Rivka and her family the entire story of how he accepted his mission and accomplished it. In passing, Eliezer mentions that when he was originally presented with the mission he had asked Avraham, "Perhaps I will find a suitable bride, but she will not be willing to follow me back to Israel. What should I do then?" The word for "perhaps" in Eliezer's query (*ulai*) is spelled without its usual *vav*. Rashi, quoting the Midrash, explains this ommission in the following way:

"The word *ulai* is written here without a *vav* so that it may also be read as *elai* [to me]. Eliezer had a daughter, and he had hoped that, if all else failed, Avraham would allow Eliezer to marry off his daughter to Yitzchak. But Avraham said to him, 'My son is blessed, and your daughter is cursed' (see Bereishis 9:25). A cursed person cannot be joined together with a blessed person" (Rashi Bereishis 24:39).

It is interesting to note that when the Torah first recounts Avraham's appointment of Eliezer to his mission, it also records Eliezer's query. Over there, however, the word *ulai* is spelled normally, with the *vav* (Bereishis 24:5). It is only when Eliezer repeats his conversation with Avraham to the parents of the bride that *ulai* is spelled with a *vav* missing. This may be understood in light of Rabbi Blinder's suggestion. The missing *vav* in the bride's house is hinting that Eliezer, after having heard and accepted Avraham's answer to his query, understood that he was trying to connect two people who were inherently apart from each other—the cursed and the blessed could never be joined together. It is to stress this lack of possible connection between the two parties that *ulai* is written here without the *vav*. This is how Chazal infer that Eliezer had attempted to "connect" himself to Avraham, and Avraham had refused the connection.

We may add that Rav Blinder's idea can help us gain a better understanding of some other statements of Chazal as well.

***Another example of a missing* vav**

For instance, in Vayikra 26:42 ("I will remember My covenant with Yaakov") the name Yaakov is spelled with an "extra" *vav.* Rashi explains this as follows:

"Yaakov has a *vav* added to his name in five places, because Yaakov took a *vav* from the name of Eliyahu (which is spelled in five places with a missing *vav*) as 'security' to guarantee that he (Eliyahu) would come to announce the dawn of the Messianic era to his (Yaakov's) descendants."

Why did Yaakov specifically take this letter from Eliyahu and append it to his own name? And how did he take it? How do we know the missing *vav* from Eliyahu is added to Yaakov?

We know from Yeshayahu that Eliyahu is supposed to be the one who will usher in the era of "peace" when the Messiah will rule—"the herald ascending the mountains announcing peace" (Yeshayahu 52:7).

In the words of the Mishnah, "Eliyahu's mission will only be to bring peace to the world" (Mishnah, end of Eduyos). Since we have shown that a *vav* represents a connection between people, we suggest here that the *vav* that Yaakov took from Eliyahu denotes that he wanted to ensure that Eliyahu would indeed come to instill brotherhood and mutual friendship (a connection between people) among mankind.

We see that in Megillah 16b that "One should read the names of the evil Haman's ten sons in one breath, to indicate that they were all hanged at one time. One should lengthen the *vav* written in the name of Vaizasa (one of Haman's sons), to indicate that all the ten sons were hanged on the same pole."

A third example of a missing vav

Once again we see that the *vav* represents a connection. The long *vav* in Vaizasa's name hints that Haman's sons were hanged at once, and on the same pole.

IV

As we mentioned earlier (section II), the letter *vav* is an appropriate choice to be used as a prefix denoting connectivity, since in Hebrew the word "*vav*" means hook. Similar themes have been pointed out regarding the use of some of the other letters of the Hebrew alphabet as prefixes. The Gemara tells us:

The symbolic significance of prefixes in Hebrew

"This (physical) world was created by Hashem with the letter *heh*; the (spiritual) World-to-Come was created with the letter *yud*" (Menachos 29b).

The letter *yud* is used in Hebrew as a prefix to indicate the future tense of a verb. The reason that of all the letters in the Hebrew alphabet specifically the *yud* is used, may be connected to the fact that it was the letter *yud* that was used to create the world of the future, i.e., the World-to-Come.

The Maharal suggests a related idea to explain another prefix used in Hebrew. The letter *heh* is attached to a word to show that the word refers to a specific item, an object that is already known to the reader. (*Heh* corresponds to the definite article—the word "the" in English.) Why is this particular letter used for this purpose? The Maharal explains that since *heh* was the letter used to bring all physical, tangible things into existence in the world at the time of creation, it is appropriate that it also is the letter that describes a known, concrete item—an item that has already been recognized and identified in the past!

PARSHAS TOLDOS

What Did You Call Esav?

"The youths grew up. Esav was an expert hunter (*yodea tzayid*), a man of the field. Yaakov was a studious person, and he dwelled in the tents of Torah study" (Bereishis 25:27).

The Torah describes Esav as *yodea tzayid* translated by Onkelos in Aramaic as *nachshirchan.* However, the word *nachshirchan* does not appear anywhere else in Talmudic literature—which presents a major problem for those trying to understand the teachings of the Targum.

Onkelos, was the nephew of a Roman Emperor. He converted and became one of the Torah Sages in the times of the Mishnah. His verse by verse rendering of the Torah into Aramaic, known as Targum Onkelos or simply Targum, is a fundamental tool for understanding the nuances of the Bible. The Targum uses a most unusual word to translate the phrase *yodea tzayid,* used in the Torah to describe Esav's character.

Aside from the lack of cross references, there is a problem establishing the correct pronunciation of this strange Targum. One version replaces the *reish* with a *daled* (two close look-alikes), rendering *nachshid chan.* Even if we maintain the spelling as it appears in our copies of the Targum, it is unclear whether the word is spelled with a *shin* or a *sin* (the two are identical in written form). Perhaps it should be read *nachs irchan.* Thus we already have three possibilities: *nachshirchan*, *nachshidchan*, and *nachsirchan.*

Aside from the spelling of the world, there is another problem. It is unclear whether this Targum is meant to be read as a single word—perhaps it is actually two distinct words. And if it is two words, it isn't clear where the first word ends and the second one begins: Are the first two letters a separate word, or do the first three letters go together? All of these variations may result in differing interpretations regarding the meaning of the word.

One of the simplest readings is that of the *Aruch* (a Talmudic dictionary written by R. Nasan b. Yechiel, eleventh century Italy). Under his second entry for *shin*, *daled*, *chaf*, he asserts that the proper reading is *nach shadchan*, two words of similar meaning. *Nach* means at rest, and *shadchan* means (in Aramaic) quiet or unaccomplished. Thus, the Targum is describing a *yodea tzayid*—a hunter—as a person who does not accomplish anything with his life; an idler. He hunts for pleasure and is not involved in any creative pursuits. Tosafos (Bava Kama 92b) points out that even if one spells the word with a *reish* (as our texts do) and with a *sin*, it can still be understood in the same way—as two words meaning a person who is at rest and idle: *nach sirchan.*

It is worthy of mention that the *Aruch haShalem* (B. Kahut, Germany, nineteenth century) writes that *Nachsharchan* is a single word that in Persian means hunter. If so, this would be an even simpler way to read the Targum, using a Persian word to translate the literal meaning of the Hebrew word *tzayid* [hunter]. However, this raises the question of why the Targum chose to use a rare Persian word which occurs nowhere else in rabbinic literature, instead of the usual Aramaic word. Perhaps this is an indication that even if the *Aruch haShalem* is correct, Chazal chose this unusual word in order to hint at a deeper meaning.

II

The sefer *Pane'ach Raza* (Rav Yitzchak Yehudah haLevi, twelfth century France) tells us that the Targum is supposed to be read as two words—*nachash yarchan. Nachash* means sorcery (see Bamidbar 24:1). *Yarchan* means thigh or hip. In other words, when the verse says that Esav was *yodea tzayid*—that he *knew* how to hunt—it means that he knew a special *nichush* [magic spell] which enabled him to run extraordinarily swiftly in pursuit of his prey. (Rashi comments on Shoftim 15:8 that the word thigh is interchangeable with the word runner.)

Another explanation: it's two words

In giving this explanation, Pane'ach Raza may have had in mind the passage in *Pirkei d'Rabbi Eliezer*, chapter 24, which tells how Esav acquired special clothes which caused every beast or fowl to fall before him whenever he wore them. Perhaps this is the same *nichush* to which the Targum refers. (See also Rav Yehudah heChassid's commentary on the Torah, who quotes a similar reading of the Targum but explains it somewhat differently).

The Tzioni (sixteenth century) also reads the Targum as *nachash yarchan.* However, he suggests that *nachash* here does not mean a spell, but rather a snake. Esav had tattooed a snake on his thigh. This translation may be seen to conform generally to the approach of the Pane'ach Raza. This tattoo may have been a form of sorcery. Esav cast his spells through the medium of a snake which was tattooed on his thigh, the snake symbolizing the swift dispatchment of one's prey.

III

Let us follow through on the suggestion that the word *nachash* in this Targum refers to a snake. Perhaps we can discover a deeper significance to this snake.

Further insight into the Nachash

We know that every nation has a guardian angel. This angel signifies the essential character of the nation, and the nation is the representative of that angel (or the angel's traits) on earth. The angel of Esav is the angel Samael (Rashi, Sukkah 29a and Sotah 10b, from Tanchuma, Vayishlach 8). This means that Esav is Samael's agent on earth. Samael is described as the chief Satan [prosecuting angel], as well as the Angel of Death at the end of Midrash Rabbah on the Torah.

There is another famous persona described in terms similar to those used in describing Samael. In the Zohar (1:35b), we find that the *Nachash haKadmoni*—the primordial snake of the Garden of Eden—is identified with the *yetzer hara* [the evil inclination] and the Angel of Death. It is, in fact, no coincidence that he is referred to by the same titles as Samael. As is made explicit in Pirkei d'Rabbi Eliezer chapter 13, everything which the snake said and did, he did at Samael's behest. It, too, is viewed as Samael's agent on earth. Both Esav and the *Nachash* are earthly representatives of Samael, the Satan—the force which Hashem created to challenge human beings. They deny Hashem's kingship in this world. They urge people to sin, to refuse to become disciples of Yaakov, and to rebel against God rather than submitting to Him.

This may be the implication of the verse we quoted at the beginning of this essay: "And Esav was a man who was *yodea tzayid*—a hunter—but Yaakov was a straight person." The verse contrasts Esav's *yodea tzayid* with Yaakov's straightforwardness. Yaakov was straight whereas Esav, in his crooked ways, set out to ensnare others in the web of the wicked. The Bereishis Rabbah (63:10) in fact teaches us that *yodea tzayid* means that Esav "ensnared people with his words"—just as the snake did. This is the job of the Satan, and both Esav and the snake are his agents.

Perhaps this is what the Targum meant by saying that Esav had a snake upon his thigh (*nachash yarchan*). The snake on the thigh of Esav was the primordial snake itself, to show that Esav was his heir; he was continuing the snake's assignment. (The Tzioni, too, hints at this interpretation.)

IV

We have not yet discussed the significance of the thighs. Why was Esav's *nachash* tattooed specifically on his thigh? The words of Maharal (16th century Poland), in explanation of a Gemara in Bava Kama, can enlighten us here:

Further insight into the Yarchan

"A man's spine after seven years becomes a snake—but only if he did not bow down during the *Modim* prayer [the prayer of thanks and acknowledgment to Hashem]" (Bava Kama 16a).

"The snake originally walked with an upright posture, for he was originally the king of the beasts. But because he persuaded Man to become a complete heretic (Sanhedrin 29a), and to refuse to bow down to Hashem, the snake was cursed. His curse was that he must walk upon his belly; that he should lose his upright posture. Therefore anyone who does not bow down before Hashem, his spine will also become a snake; he will lose his upright posture" (Maharal of Prague, *Nesivos Olam, Nesiv haAvodah*, chapter 10).

The Maharal says that an upright posture shows pride and independence. The human being's upright stance—his unique thigh—distinguishes him from other creatures. When a person voluntarily bows down—at his thighs —he lowers himself and symbolically humbles himself. The snake refused to bow down and humble himself before Hashem, therefore his upright posture—his thigh that wouldn't bow down—was taken away.

In a similar vein, a human being owes Hashem a debt of gratitude for all that he has. The spine of a person who does not wish to bow down to Hashem in grateful acknowledgment will turn into a snake, in order to show that his crime is that of the snake. Just like the snake, he refused to humble his upright posture (see also Maharsha Kiddushin 29b, s.v. *Ketanina).*

We may add that Esav shared this characteristic of the primordial snake as well. He, too, refused to humble himself before Hashem. The ability to stand upright is dependent upon the hips and thighs, and it is with the hips that one bows down. Esav had the quality of the snake in his thighs, which expressed itself in his not wanting to bow down to Hashem. This is why he is called *nachash yarchan*—snake thighed! (See also Daniel 2:32.)

PARSHAS VAYETZE

"Hashem Has Ended My Disgrace"

"Hashem remembered Rachel and heard her prayers and caused her to conceive. She became pregnant and gave birth to a son, and said, 'Hashem has ended my disgrace' " (Bereishis 30:22-23).

"My disgrace"—I was disgraced since my barreness, they said would lead Yaakov to divorce me and I would marry Esav instead. [This is the simple understanding of the verse.]

According to the Midrash, however, the disgrace to which Rachel was referring was that a childless woman has no one else to blame for her misdeeds. Once she has a son she can blame him: "Who broke this vessel? It must have been your son! Who ate these figs? It must have been your son!" (Rashi, ad loc.).

Rachel's strange statement of thanks

As the verse quoted above tells us, Rachel called her son "Yosef" because "Hashem has ended (*asaf*) my disgrace." What disgrace was Rachel referring to? Having no children is not a disgrace. Only a misdeed can be a source of disgrace. Childlessness might be a source of depression, or a feeling of lack, but it is not a *disgrace*, i.e., a cause for others to disgrace her. This is the question that Rashi is addressing in the above selection (as pointed out by Yefe To'ar to Bereishis Rabbah 73:5, s.v. *Taluy*).

Rashi suggests two ways of understanding Rachel's disgrace: One possibility is that she was concerned lest she be sent away and left with no way to stay in Yaakov's family other than to marry Esav. Becoming a part of Esav's family would surely be a disgrace (see Bereishis Rabbah 80:8, "*Ki Cherpah Hi Lanu...*").

The second interpretation Rashi offers is that a childless woman is blamed for everything that goes wrong in the house—this is her disgrace. Now that Rachel bore Yaakov a child, if anything breaks in the house it would be blamed on her son.

This second explanation is very difficult to understand. After waiting all these years for a child, and after all that she has been through, is this what Rachel thanks Hashem for when her prayers are finally answered? That if she breaks a pot now she can blame it on her son? Is this a proper show of gratitude to Hashem for bestowing upon her such a tremendous blessing?

The commentaries to whom we generally turn are silent concerning this Midrash. (See *Sichos Mussar* by Rav Chaim Shmulevitz, 5732, ch. 6, for the *mussar* [personality development] school's interpretation of this Midrash.) However, Rav Asher Sternbuch of Har Nof, Jerusalem (son of Rav Moshe Sternbuch, author of *Moadim Uzmanim*), recently shared with me a beautiful thought that sheds much light on this cryptic Midrash. Let us first study the background of Yoseph's birth, in order to appreciate Rav Sternbuch's explanation.

II

The first point we must clarify is, in what merit was Rachel granted a son? The Midrash answers this question.

The deed that earned Rachel a child

When Rachel was due to marry Yaakov, Yaakov suspected that her father might try to cheat him by giving him Leah instead. To this end, Yaakov gave Rachel a secret password by which he would be able to identify her under a veil or in the dark. Should Lavan indeed try to make the switch, Yaakov would be able to catch Lavan immediately.

Things did not work out as planned, however. Lavan did, in fact, make the switch. But Yaakov didn't manage to catch him in time. As Rashi writes:

"And in the morning, behold it was Leah"—but in the night Yaakov did not realize that it was Leah. Why? Because although Yaakov gave a password to Rachel, when Rachel saw that her father was substituting Leah for her, she said, "What a tremendous embarrassment this will be for my sister!" (Yaakov would discover that it was Leah and send her out right in middle of the wedding.) Rachel decided to give the secret password to Leah (Rashi, Bereishis 29:25).

Rachel selflessly gave her sister Leah her secret password so that Leah should not be publicly disgraced. Yaakov unwittingly married Leah. By morning, after ostensibly agreeing to take this woman as his wife, Yaakov already kept Leah. Our Sages tell us that the cure for Rachel's infertility came as a reward for this altruistic act. As Rashi tells us:

"Hashem remembered Rachel and heard her prayers"—Hashem remembered that Rachel gave the secret password to her sister when she got married (Rashi, Bereishis 30:22).

The Sages have taught us in numerous places that all of the rewards and punishments that Hashem gives are always "measure for measure" (Sanhedrin 90a; see Tishah b'Av essay section I, p. 217, Re'eh essay section V, p. 244). This being the case, we may ask what "measure for measure" was involved in this instance? Why was it that because she gave the secret password Rachel deserved to receive a child? After all, she did not give Leah a child, but rather a husband!

III

According to Rashi's first explanation of Rachel's "disgrace," that by bearing a son Rachel was saved the disgrace of falling into the hands of Esav, the measure for measure is not hard to find. Rashi (Bereishis 29:17) tells us that Leah's eyes were weak from crying because she thought that she would end up having to marry Esav. People had been saying that since Yitzchak had two sons and Lavan had two daughters, the elder son should marry the elder daughter and the younger son, the younger daughter.

Measure for measure #1

Indeed, had Yaakov married Rachel (the younger daughter) as planned, Leah would have been left with no choice. In order to marry into the family of Avraham, she would have had to marry Esav. By giving Leah the password, Rachel enabled Leah to marry Yaakov, since once she had been with him for the night he would accept her as a wife and not send her away. In this manner Rachel saved her sister from marriage to Esav.

Now that Rachel was barren she was afraid that Yaakov would divorce her and *she* would fall to Esav. At this point Hashem remembered that she had saved her sister from this fate. He now saved Rachel from the same fate by granting her a child and thereby securing her husband, measure for measure. (See Maharal's *Gur Aryeh*, ad loc.)

IV

One might ask, however, why Yaakov would divorce Rachel for being childless? After all, he already had children with Leah, so he did not have to divorce her in order to have children with someone else. In numerous places we see that Yaakov loved Rachel even after Leah bore him children. Why, then, would she think that he might divorce her, leaving her to fall into Esav's hands? Perhaps it was this difficulty that prompted Rashi to seek another explanation of the "measure for measure".

Measure for measure #2; answer to our original question

What other "measure for measure" might there be? In what way is having a child a proper reward for giving her sister the secret password? The answer lies in Rachel's words upon Yoseph's birth: "Hashem has ended my disgrace." We noted that Rachel had saved her sister from disgrace ("What a tremendous embarrassment this will be for my sister!"). Now, at Yosef's birth, Rachel expressed her gratitude that she, too, had been saved from disgrace, measure for measure.

But what disgrace was Rachel saved from? As we pointed out earlier, childlessness may be a cause for sadness and depression, but it is not a cause for disgrace!

The Midrash that Rashi cites enlightens us in this matter. There is indeed an aspect of disgrace involved in the state of childlessness; it leaves the mother subject to hypercriticism. She can be blamed for everything. This, suggests Rav Sternbuch, is the key to understanding what Rachel meant. Rachel realized that it was this aspect of disgrace that comes with childlessness which allowed the principle of "measure for measure" to come into play in granting her a son.

This is why Rachel thanked Hashem upon Yosef's birth for sparing her from being embarrassed by her misdeeds. It was not that she did not have a greater reason for giving thanks than the fact that she would no longer be blamed for breaking things. Her major cause for thanks was of course the fact that she would be the mother of a tribe of Israel. However, Rachel meant to acknowledge the determining factor that gave her the merit of having a child in the first place. She saw that sparing her sister from disgrace had earned her this child, who would, to some degree, spare *her* from disgrace. She thanked Hashem for the child by thanking Him for dealing her "measure for measure!"

PARSHAS VAYISHLACH

The Rise Of The Sun

"When Yaakov was all alone, a man came and struggled with him until the breaking of dawn.... Then the man said 'Let me leave, for the sun has risen!' " (Bereishis 32:25-27).

Throughout the generations, the Torah commentaries have been intrigued by the story of Yaakov's struggle with a mysterious man. Who was this anonymous stranger who came to struggle with Yaakov just before his historic reunion with his brother, Esav? What is the significance of this incident and what can we learn from it?

Rashi reveals some of the secrets of this passage. According to the Midrash, Rashi tells us, this "person" was none other than Esav's guardian angel. (Each nation has a representative in Hashem's heavenly court—(Shemos Rabbah 21:5), see also Rashi Devarim 2:31. Esav, as forebear of the Roman nation, had his own "guardian angel.") His struggle with Yaakov was intended to foreshadow Esav's eventual domination over Yaakov. Instead, however, it was the angel that succumbed to Yaakov. Yaakov's symbolic victory was a sign that he was destined to overpower Esav and to survive Esav's attempts to crush him.

Yaakov's struggle with the angel

The commentaries agree that this encounter did not merely foreshadow the interaction between the two brothers at their impending meeting. Rather, it served as a prophetic synopsis of the relationship between their descendants throughout the generations.

The Kli Yakar offers his interpretation of the struggle, encapsulating many of the suggestions of his predecessors. He maintains that the struggle between Yaakov and the guardian angel of Esav represented the struggle between the descendants of Yaakov and the forces of evil who try to obscure Hashem's presence in this world. The struggle is constant. The descendants of Yaakov are continually trying to show the world that there is a Creator. They must both bolster their own faith and spread the fear of Hashem throughout the world—while simultaneously facing the harsh opposition of Esav and his emissaries. This is the struggle between Yaakov and the angel of Esav (who is actually none other than the Satan himself—see Toldos essay, section III, p. 26)

II

According to all of these explanations we may ask, why did Esav's angel stop fighting with Yaakov just because the sun was rising? What is the significance of the sun rising?

The rising of the sun (First analysis)

The Kli Yakar explains that the sun is the great witness to Hashem's power in this world (as will be explained at length in the Sukkos essay, section II, p. 268). When one contemplates the sun—with its tremendous display of energy and its life giving functions—it makes one aware of the power that Hashem exerts on this world. Armed with this reminder, one is able to overcome all the seductions the material world presents to draw one away from our Creator.

This is the reason the angel fought only until dawn. With the rising of the sun, the angel said, "I have no more power over Yaakov." And this is the manner in which we must fight against the forces of Esav throughout the generations. We must encourage ourselves to fear none but Hashem Himself, by taking note of the signs of Hashem's power that we constantly see in this world.

III

We may present a deeper analysis of the allegorical meaning of the sun's rise, with the help of some additional passages from the Midrash.

"The sun has arrived!" (Further analysis)

In the beginning of Parshas Vayetze, we are told that Yaakov, during his travels, was forced to stop "because the sun had arrived" (this is the literal translation, although idiomatically it is usually rendered, "the sun set"). The Midrash explains:

"What does it mean that Yaakov stopped 'Because the sun had arrived?' Yaakov, upon his arrival at that place, heard the ministering angels saying, 'The sun has arrived, the sun has arrived!' "

Years later, when his son Yosef said (Bereishis 37:9) "I dreamed, and behold the sun and the moon (which, as Rashi tells us, represent Yosef's father and mother)...were bowing down to me," Yaakov exclaimed, "Who revealed to my child this secret, that I am called the sun?!" (Bereishis Rabbah 68:10).

Yaakov himself is referred to as "the sun." This interesting nickname, which was originally coined by the ministering angels, was reinforced in Yosef's vision.

We find a similar theme in another Midrash:

"And Hashem called the light (which he created on the first day of Creation) 'day' " (Bereishis 1:5)—this refers to Yaakov.

"And the darkness he called 'night'" (ibid.)—this refers to Esav.

"And there was evening" (ibid.)—this is the dominion of Esav.

"And there was morning" (ibid.)—this is the dominion of Yaakov (Bereishis Rabbah 2:3).

Again, Yaakov is likened to light.

The name "Yaakov" is often used to refer not only to the patriarch himself, but to the entire Jewish people (see, for example, Bamidbar 24:5). Yaakov, or the Jewish nation as a whole, is compared to light. The mission of the Jewish people is to bring the light of Hashem's teachings—i.e., the Torah of Hashem—to the world at large. In this way, the Bnai Yisrael are the "light" of the world. The forces trying to stop them are the "darkness" of the world. This is the meaning of the Midrash which states that Esav is darkness. Esav represents the forces which are trying to keep the world in the dark and to prevent Yaakov from spreading his light.

This is also the message of the first Midrash quoted above. The angels informed Yaakov—as he left his father's house and began to make his way into the open world—that his mission was to be like the sun—to be a beacon of spiritual light to nations of the world. When Yosef saw in his dream that his father was represented by the sun, it was a sign that Yaakov would continue to fulfill this mission upon his descent to Egypt, after Yosef was appointed to a position of influence in that country.

With this in mind, perhaps we can suggest a deeper meaning behind the wrestling angel's statement about the sun. The angel gave up the fight when he saw that "the sun was rising." The angel realized that Yaakov would never succumb to the material enticements presented to him by the surrounding nations. *Yaakov's* sun was rising, and would repulse the forces of evil and not be subdued. Yaakov himself would forever be a beacon of light to the nations of the world. That is what the angel meant by saying, "Let me leave, for the sun has risen"—"You have succeeded in your mission, Yaakov; I have no more power over you." And just as Esav's forces lost in their struggle with Yaakov, so too, whenever Yaakov's children fulfill their mission, by revealing Hashem's presence in the world, Esav will have no power over them.

IV

We can use our new understanding of the metaphor of the sun to shed light on many other statements of our Sages involving the sun. Let us take one particularly enigmatic example:

The sun's din and the sun's sawdust

"Rav Levi said: Why is a person's voice not heard as well by day as it is by night? Because of the sound produced by the sun's disc as it saws its way through the Heavens like a sawyer cutting down cedars.

The dust which can be discerned hanging in the air where the sun shines is the sawdust that is produced by the sun's progress. It is referred to in Hebrew as *lo*—'nothingness.' This is what Nevuchadnetzar (the Babylonian king who destroyed the First Temple) meant when he said (Daniel 4:32): 'All of the inhabitants of the earth are as *lo* [to Hashem].'" (Gemara Yoma 20b)

What a strange presentation this Aggadah [words of Chazal that consist of homiletics or narratives, rather than discussions of legal issues] makes of the daily solar cycle! The Gemara seems to treat the Heavens as some sort of solid body through which the sun must drill its way, producing visible sawdust! (See *Be'er haGolah*, ch. 6, for the Maharal's approach to this Aggadah.) Perhaps we can gain insight into this passage based on what we have prefaced above.

As we learned above, the night—when the great beacon of Hashem is not shining on the land—is Esav's dominion. It is a time when we do not see Hashem's hand clearly in the world. Under the cover of night a person is particularly susceptible to the persuasions of the forces of evil. This is what the Midrash means when it says, " 'And there was evening'—this is the dominion of Esav." The darkness of night allows one to forget one's Creator.

When Rav Levi asked, "Why is the voice of person heard better at night," he meant, "Why is a *person* dominated by his physical, worldly impulses at night more than by day?" His answer was that by day, the sun can be heard boring through the heavens like a man sawing through cedars. The daytime is dominated by the "voice" of the sun, that great harbinger of Hashem's mighty presence. This bolsters a person's faith, and makes him less susceptible to the persuasions of the evil inclination.

The manner in which the sun cuts through the firmament is compared to "a man cutting through cedars." The tall, erect cedar tree is used by the Torah as a symbol of haughtiness (Rashi, Vayikra 14:4). As the sun cuts its way through the heavens, Hashem cuts the haughty down to size. The sun humbles the arrogant by openly demonstrating Hashem's power.

"The dust which can be discerned hanging in the air where the sun shines is the sawdust that is produced by the sun's progress." —The dust that reflects light in the sun's rays, reminds us of the lesson in humility that we derive from the sun. Wherever the sun shines, we are reminded that "You are dust, and you will return to dust" (Bereishis 3:19). We are made aware of Hashem's overwhelming power, compared to our own impotence. This is precisely the context in which *lo* is quoted in Daniel—"All of the inhabitants of the world are like nothingness [to Hashem]."

This, then, is the lesson of the sun's "sawing," a lesson of which we are reminded every time we see dust suspended in a beam of sunlight. The passage in Yoma, rather than being an outdated lesson in astronomy, is actually a deep philosophical lesson of faith in Hashem.

PARSHAS VAYESHEV

...But The Will Of Hashem Will Prevail

Yosef's brothers went to graze their father's sheep in Shechem. [Yaakov] said to Yosef, "Aren't your brothers grazing the sheep in Shechem? Come, let me send you to them." Yosef replied, "Here I am, ready to do your will!" (Bereishis 37:12-13).

The Torah tells us that Yaakov sent his son Yosef to bring tidings of his brothers' welfare. Yosef's brothers were, by that time, extremely jealous of him (see Bereishis 37:11). When the brothers saw Yosef approaching, they knew that this was their opportunity. Now they had him all alone, with no one to protect him or to report to their father what became of him. They conspired at first to kill him, but moderated their plans and sold him as a slave instead. For twenty-two years, Yaakov believed that his beloved son, Yosef, was dead. Meanwhile, Yosef slowly rose in rank from slave to custodian, to a member of the king's court. Eventually, he was appointed vizier over all of Egypt...and the rest is history.

The dangers of Yosef's mission

When considering the circumstances of Yosef's sale, many people are bothered by a nagging question. Yaakov was aware of the tremendous jealousy which Yosef's brothers harbored towards him for reporting their actions to their father in the past (see Rashi, Bereishis 37:10, s.v. "*Vayigar Bo*"). Why did Yaakov not foresee that the brothers might take advantage of this opportunity to give vent to their jealousy? Should his ten strong brothers try to harm him, Yosef would be defenseless! Didn't Yaakov realize the perils of sending Yosef alone on this mission?

In fact, there is a principle in Torah law (Mishnah Berurah 603:4), which states that if one sends a friend on a mission and the friend is killed (in a manner unrelated to the mission) during the course of performing the task, then it is appropriate for the sender to repent for his friend's death. The sender is considered culpable to some extent even though he merely sent him on an unrelated mission. Certainly in the case at hand, where Yaakov sent his son into a situation that he *knew* to be perilous, Yaakov should be held responsible for what befell Yosef! How could Yaakov have committed such a grave mistake in judgment?

It is noteworthy that when the news of Yosef's supposed death reached Yaakov, Yaakov responded by saying, "Now I will certainly go to Gehinnom [purgatory] in my mourning" (Bereishis 37:35). Yaakov should have simply said, "I will mourn eternally for my son"—why did he mention Gehinnom? (See Rashi ad loc., s.v. "*Avel She'olah.*") Perhaps we may suggest that Yaakov was concerned about the very principle mentioned above. He had sent someone on a dangerous mission, and his emissary was (he believed) killed by a wild animal. According to the above principle, Yaakov—the sender—still bears guilt for the death. (Pane'ach Raza and Chizkuni, loc. cit.)

In any event, it remains to be answered how could Yaakov have sent Yosef alone to his brothers when he knew how much they hated him? A closer analysis of the verses may lead us to an answer to this puzzle.

II

Shechem: A safe haven?

As we have seen, the verse tells us that Yosef's brothers were grazing the sheep in Shechem. On the other hand, Yaakov was living at that time in Hebron, not in Shechem (as we find in Bereishis 37:14). Shechem is quite a distance from Hebron—why would the brothers be grazing the sheep in Shechem, rather than in the area of Hebron where they lived?

The answer to this may lie in the fact that the Patriarchs, as we are told in many places, were very conscientious about not taking anything that did not belong to them. They were careful to graze their flocks only on property which belonged to them, or in the wilderness (see Rashi to Bereishis 13:7 and 24:10). It is true that Yaakov was living in Hebron at the time, but his own grazing land and the wilderness in the area of Hebron may have become depleted. It may be that Yaakov was forced to seek other pastures for his flocks. We know that while Yaakov was living in Shechem, he bought the property on which he was encamped (Bereishis 33:19). If so, perhaps that is the reason he sent his sons to graze the flocks in Shechem; there he owned private property. He could allow the animals to graze without any fear of committing theft, and his children would have a home nearby (Yaakov's Shechem homestead).

If Yaakov owned land in Shechem, he would certainly not have left it unattended when he moved to Hebron. That would have been an invitation to squatters as well as a waste of productive land. Clearly, he must have left some of his many servants in Shechem. If this was indeed the case, then when the brothers went to graze in Shechem they would have been grazing in the company of Yaakov's servants, who would remain with them to help with the flocks. Furthermore, the brothers would have necessarily been accompanied by some of the servants wherever they were grazing the sheep. Only the servants who lived there full-time would have been certain which fields either belonged to Yaakov or were ownerless, and which fields belonged to someone else.

Now we can understand why Yaakov felt safe sending Yosef to Shechem even though the brothers were filled with animosity towards Yosef. Yaakov knew that the brothers would be constantly in the presence of Yaakov's servants, who would be able to keep an eye on Yosef. The brothers would be afraid to harm Yosef in the presence of their father's servants lest they report the matter back to Yaakov.

This may be what Yaakov was hinting at when he "*Aren't* your brothers grazing in Shechem?" He did not simply state, "Your brothers are grazing in Shechem," but rather he asked rhetorically, "*Aren't* they grazing in Shechem." In other words, "If they were in the open pastures near Hebron, I would be afraid to send you. Were you to find them there, you would be alone with them, and vulnerable. But since they are grazing in Shechem, they are certain to be accompanied by my servants. My servants will be there to watch over you, and your brothers will be afraid to harm you. Therefore I can send you with confidence to Shechem!"

III

What, then, was Yaakov's miscalculation? How were the brothers able to catch Yosef all alone?

Grazing themselves Rashi tells us (Bereishis 37:12) that the brothers did not go to Shechem only to graze their sheep. They went to "graze themselves" as well—to eat and drink and enjoy themselves. Thus they did not actually remain with the sheep in Shechem the entire time. In fact, they do not seem to have been with the sheep when Yosef met them. The sheep are not mentioned at all at the time of their meeting. The sheep were presumably left with the servants in Shechem.

When Yaakov first sent Yosef on his mission, he told Yosef to check up on "the welfare of his brothers and of the sheep." When Yosef first arrived in Shechem he saw the sheep, but did not find his brothers. Thus, he felt it necessary to go and look for them.

(Although his father had made the introductory remark, "Aren't your brothers grazing in Shechem?" Yosef felt compelled to seek them out even though they had moved from Shechem. A source for this reaction can be found in Gittin 65a, where we are told that if a man tells his friend, "Give this document of divorce to my wife, she can be found in such-and-such a place," the carrier of the document may present the wife with the document *anywhere* that he finds her. The husband only mentioned the location as a pointer—"you'll probably find her here, but you may give her the divorce document elsewhere as well." He did not mean to limit the location of the divorce to any particular place. So too, Yosef felt that his father had mentioned Shechem only as a pointer. Yaakov did not mean to limit the search to Shechem alone.)

IV

The man in the field

Yaakov may have foreseen such an eventuality, but he did not see it as a cause for concern. If the brothers were not found together with the sheep, how would Yosef find them? The brothers were not obligated to report their movements to anyone, and they might have gone anywhere at all! It would be impossible for Yosef to locate them, and there would therefore be no cause for concern. Yosef would simply have to wait in Shechem for their return. Therefore Yaakov felt safe sending Yosef to Shechem.

However, as Rashi tells us (Bereishis 37:14), everything which befell Yosef here was predestined. Hashem had already decreed that Yosef would be sold to Egypt, in order to pave the way for the Egyptian Exile (Bereishis 15:13).

Yaakov had calculated correctly that in the natural course of events the brothers would have been unable to harm Yosef—either because of the presence of the servants, or because Yosef would be unable to find them. However, when Yosef went looking for his brothers, he *happened* to meet a man in the field. The man told him that he *happened* to overhear the brothers saying that they were going to Dosan (Bereishis 37:15,17).

There was no reason for them to have told this stranger where they were going; he just *happened* to overhear it. As a result of this seemingly chance encounter, Yosef was able to locate his brothers in Dosan. (Rashi, in fact, tells us that the stranger Yosef met was none other than the angel Gavriel. This can either be taken literally, or it can be taken to imply that the man was a tool of Hashem's Providence for bringing about an otherwise unlikely course of events.) Yosef went to Dosan to find his brothers. When he found them, he was all alone—and that is how he ended up as a slave on a caravan headed towards Egypt.

"A man makes for himself many calculations, but the will of Hashem shall prevail!" (Mishlei 19:21).

PARSHAS MIKETZ

Chanukah—Yosef And The Hazards of Beauty

On Chanukah we celebrate the victory of the meager, ill-equipped Jewish militia against the vast and mighty Greek legions. The Jewish victory was more than physical. It was a victory of the God-fearing Kohanim [priestly tribe] over the Hellenized secularists—of the Torah's eternal teachings over materialism. The Jewish victory was climaxed by the restoration of the Temple service, and the rekindling of the golden menorah [seven branched candelabra] in the Holy Temple.

Every year during the festival of Chanukah, in the regular cycle of weekly Parsha readings, we read the story of Yosef and his brothers. This could be taken as mere

Yosef and Chanukah

happenstance, since, after all, the fixed yearly Torah-reading cycle happens to reach the story of Yosef and his brothers around this time of year. However, great Kabbalists throughout the ages have pointed out that there is more to it than that. According to Rav Nasan Shapiro (16th century Poland) in *Megaleh Amukos* (Parshas Vayeshev), the Greek domination over Israel came about as Divine retribution for the sale of Yosef. Rav Zvi Elimelech of Dinov (*Bnai Yisaschar*, Kislev, 4:119) points out further that the name of the Greek king at the time of the Chanukah story, "Antiochus," has the same numerical *gematria* value as "Yosef" (=156). It is as if the Greek king Antiochus somehow derived his power through what transpired with Yosef! (See also *Bnai Yisaschar*, Kislev, #13).

How are we to understand this? What is the connection between the Greek conquest and the Chanukah story on the one hand, and the story of Yosef on the other?

II

"Yosef was beautiful of form and beautiful in appearance" (Bereishis 39:6). "When Yosef saw that he was successful in Potifar's house, he began to eat, drink and curl his hair. Hashem said to him, 'Your father is mourning for you and you are busy curling your hair? I am going to set the bear upon you!' " (Rashi, ad loc.)

The ugly side of beauty

Yosef was extremely handsome. Rashi (Bereishis 49:22) tells us that Yosef was so attractive, the Egyptian women would climb on top of a wall in order to catch a glimpse of him as he passed by. Yosef sometimes acted in a conceited manner, due to his good looks. Rashi (37:1) tells us that while he was still in his father's home, Yosef used to act childishly, fixing his hair and touching up his eyes to look more beautiful. He continued this behavior in the house of Potifar, after being sold into slavery. Hashem punished Yosef for his conceit with the advances and seductive pleas of Potifar's wife, and with her subsequent false accusations.

Being overly conscious of one's personal beauty can lead to more than simple arrogance. One who becomes obsessed with himself will want to become more and more beautiful—to amass all the beauty that money can buy. He will want to ornament himself with gold and jewelry, and with the riches of royalty. The obsession will gradually turn into self-idolization, and to more than that—into idol-worship itself!

The idol worshiper believes that he will obtain whatever he wants by procuring it through his idols. He aims to satisfy his physical desires with nothing in mind but his own personal gain. There is no responsibility, no accountability, no sense of fairness, in idol-worship. He serves the sun god so that the sun should bestow its bounty upon him, the god of the sea so that the sea should bestow its blessings upon him, and the god of gold to acquire more gold. He plays a game with the gods in order to get what he needs.

This is the culmination of an obsession with one's self. "I have given [Israel] much wealth, and they made their gold into an idol" (Hoshea 2:10). The more gold, or beauty, that a person has, the more at risk he is of falling into idolatry (see Berachos 32a).

III

This is the pitfall that Yosef's brothers saw in Yosef's actions. "The brothers [of Yosef] said one to the other, 'Behold, the *baal hachalomos* [dreamer] is coming' " (Bereishis 37:19). The brothers said, "This is the one who will lead them all to the Baal [a form of idolatry]" (Bereishis Rabbah 84:14).

Golden calves

When the brothers saw Yosef coming they remarked, "This is the one who will bring idol worship to Israel!" Yosef's descendant, Yeravam ben Nevat broke away from the Davidic kingdom to form the kingdom of the ten northern tribes, and set up in his kingdom two golden calves. He forbade his subjects from going to the Temple in Jerusalem, forcing them to serve his golden calves instead. This, the brothers foresaw, would be the result of Yosef's preoccupation with his own beauty. This is the reason they felt it necessary to stop Yosef at all costs. They felt that they could not allow him to be a part of the holy nation that was to descend from them. Thus they agreed to sell him as a slave, where his erroneous ways would not be able to affect others.

It was this same abuse of beauty that Yosef demonstrated, which brought about the worship of the golden calf that the Jews served after receiving the Ten Commandments (Shemos, ch. 32). Rashi (Shemos 32:4) explains that after Aharon had cast the gold that was brought to him into the furnace, one of the Jews threw into the fire a slate engraved with an incantation. This gave the golden calf the appearance of life. The background of this slate and its incantation is as follows:

Before Yosef died, he left instructions that his body be transported out of Egypt when the time for the exodus arrived (Bereishis 50:25). In the meantime, however, his body was placed in a leaden coffin and sunk to the bottom of the Nile River. When the time came for the Jews to leave Egypt, Moshe took a slate and wrote on it the phrase, "*aleh shor, aleh shor*"—"Arise bull, arise bull!" (See Bereishis 49:6, where Yosef is compared to a bull.) Moshe threw this slate into the Nile, and Yosef's coffin miraculously rose to the surface (see Sotah 13a). It was this slate, with its reference to Yosef, which the worshipers of the golden calf cast into the furnace, causing the calf to mystically take on the appearance of life.

The Midrash is telling us that the Jews came to worship the golden calf through an expression of the same lust for beauty—and riches—that Yosef had shown. Indeed, the Gemara tells us, "Moshe protested to Hashem, 'It was the tremendous amount of gold and silver that you granted the Jews [upon their exodus from Egypt] that caused them to build the golden calf!' " (Berachos 3:2a).

And it was this very attribute which brought about Yeravam's worship of golden calves, and, eventually, the Greek exile. "The very day that Yeravam brought his golden calves to Beis El and Dan, a shanty was built, which grew through the centuries into the city Italy of the empire of Yavan [Greece]" (Shabbos 56b, and Rashi).

Greece, the nation of self-worship—the nation which epitomized the idolization of beauty and the worship of pagan gods—overpowered Israel when the Jews themselves showed a weakness in this regard. And the root of this weakness lay in Yosef's actions as a youth—those same actions upon which Yosef's brothers based their decision to sell him. "The brothers said, 'This is the one who will lead them all to the Baal!"

IV

There is, however, another side to beauty. "Beauty and favor are false, but a woman who fears God should genuinely be praised" (Mishlei 31:30).

Beauty coupled with the fear of heaven

If a woman uses her beauty to invoke the fear of God, then even her beauty can be praised. It is not "false" beauty, but "true" beauty. If beauty is used to inspire awe and admiration for the Almighty, then it is a praiseworthy trait. That is the purpose of gold and silver, and that is when beauty should be expressed.

The Midrash describes the Mishkan which the Jews built to worship Hashem in the desert, as the "beauty of Israel" (Tanchuma Ki Sisa, #13). This may be what Chazal meant when they said, "Let the gold of the Mishkan come and atone for the gold of the calf" (Tanchuma Terumah, #8). By properly using gold, wealth and beauty to increase the awe of Heaven, the Jews were able to rectify the wrongdoing of making the golden calf.

The Temple in Jerusalem is also referred to as "the beauty of the world" (Zevachim 54b). Similarly, "This is my Lord, I shall beautify Him" (Shemos 15:2) "This is my Lord, I shall build Him a Holy Temple" (Targum Onkelos, loc. cit.).

"One who never saw Jerusalem during the days of the Temple, never saw a coveted city in his life! One who never saw the Holy Temple while it was erect, never saw a beautiful building in his life!" (Gemara Sukkah, 51b).

"Zion [Jerusalem, while it was crowned with the glory of the Holy Temple], the all-beautiful" (Tehillim 50:2). "From Zion sprouted forth all of the beauty of the world!" (Gemara Yoma 54b).

The victory over Greece represented the victory of God-fearing beauty over pagan beauty. The rededication of the Holy Temple symbolized the use of beauty to serve Hashem, rather than to serve one's self. By channeling their appreciation for beauty in the proper direction the Jews were able to free themselves of the pagan Greek rule. They were able to rebuild Zion and the Holy Temple—the "beauty of the world."

Yosef set the pattern for the rectification as well as for the sin. Ultimately, he conquered his impulse to be led astray by his beauty. He refused to give in to Potifar's wife, even though it meant his long imprisonment and near death (see Sotah 36b). So too, the Chashmonaim [Hasmoneans] were able to withstand the Hellenistic pressures of the assimilated Jews.

V

The very name "Zion" actually contains within it the name "Yavan". Yavan is spelled: *yud, vav, nun*. Zion also ends with *yud, vav, nun*—but these letters are preceded by the letter *tzadi*. The letter *tzadi* alludes to the fear of G-d, the trait of the tzaddik [G-d fearing person]—"A tzaddik rules himself through the fear of Hashem" (Shmuel II 23:3). By using the quality of the tzaddik—i.e., the fear of Hashem—the beauty of Yavan is transformed into the beauty of Zion.

The fall of Yavan in the hands of Zion

An interesting Midrash draws a close parallel between the life of Yosef and the history of Zion. "Take note of the fact that all of the adversity that Yosef faced, Zion faced.... About Yosef we are told, 'They hated him' (Bereishis 37:4); Of Zion we are told, 'Therefore I hated her' (Yirmiyah 12:8). About Yosef, 'They plotted against him' (37:18); Of Zion, 'They schemed secretly against your nation' (Psalms 83:4). About Yosef, 'The Midianites sold him to Egypt' (37:36); Of Zion, 'You have sold the children of Yehudah and of Jerusalem to the children of *Yavan*.'

'...And all of Yosef's good fortune also befell Zion:'

About Yosef we are told, 'Yosef was beautiful of form and beautiful in appearance.' (Bereishis 39:6); Of Zion we are told, 'Beautiful land, joy of all the world!' (Psalms 48:3). About Yosef, 'There is no one greater than I *in this house*' (39:9); Of Zion, 'The glory of this latter *Temple* shall be even greater than that of the former' (Chaggai 2:9)."—(Tanchuma Vayigash, #10)

The Midrash continues at great length, bringing many other parallels between the history of Zion and Yosef's life. As the commentary Etz Yosef points out, even the numerical values of Zion and Yosef are identical. They both equal 156!

The fate of Zion, the city of beauty, is patterned after Yosef's life. As Yosef misused his beauty, so too, Zion lost its "tzaddik." This brought about Zion's eventual subjugation, or "sale," to Yavan, just as it had caused Yosef himself to be sold. When Yosef conquered his temptations and refused the advances of Potifar's wife, it caused him to be called by a new title: Yosef the tzaddik (Zohar 1:194). Through this accomplishment, Yosef was able to add the "tzaddik" to "Yavan" (*yud, vav, nun*), making it "Zion" (*tzadi, yud, vav, nun*). Fortified with this spiritual armor, he eventually became freed of his bondage, and rose to rule over the entire land. It was in this manner, too, that the weak forces of the Chashmonaim were able to defeat the mighty Greek armies. Yosef set the pattern of history for the Chanukah miracle. He turned the "Yosef = Antiochus" into "Yosef = Zion." And Zion has what it takes to overcome the forces of Yavan—"I will awaken your children *Zion* against your children *Yavan*!" (Zecharyah 9:13).

May we merit to bring about the final return to Zion, soon and in our days!

This essay is based on the works of Rabbi Mattisyahu Weinberg, who resides in Jerusalem. *Patterns in Time*, Rabbi Weinberg's series on the Jewish festivals, weaves a beautiful tapestry from the words of our Sages revealing to us many of the striking and profound motifs of the Jewish calendar that hitherto went unnoticed. This essay is based on his volume on Chanukah, pp. 74-81; 224-227 (along with some embellishments of my own).

PARSHAS VAYIGASH

The Brothers' Mistake

Yosef told his brothers, "Come close to me," and they came close. He then said, "I am Yosef, whom you sold to Egypt!...Behold, you see with your own eyes...that it is my mouth that is speaking to you." (Bereishis 45:4,12)

"You see with your own eyes"—...that I am your brother, because you see that I am circumcised, just as you are, and also that "it is my mouth that is speaking to you," i.e., I am speaking the Holy Tongue (Hebrew). (Rashi ad loc.)

A matter of recognition

Rashi tells us that these two statements of Yosef were intended to convince his brothers he was indeed their brother Yosef. He told them to "come close" to show them that he was circumcised, and he pointed out to them that he was speaking the Holy Tongue a sure sign of the family of Yaakov Avinu. Apparently the brothers did not believe Yosef at first. It was necessary for him to prove to his brothers that he was indeed telling the truth.

A number of questions arise concerning this description of the events. Firstly, as the Ramban points out, why did the brothers not believe Yosef when he identified himself? Rashi tells us in several places (Bereishis 42:3,13,14) that the brothers were aware of the possibility that they might encounter Yosef in Egypt, and were in fact anxious to find him, buy him back and bring him home. Here they find a man who mentioned Yosef's name, as well as the fact that his brothers sold him as a slave to be taken to Egypt. Both of these facts were never divulged by the brothers in their conversations with him. Wouldn't they be the perfect proof of his identity? How could there possibly be any room for doubt in the brothers' minds after this?

It should also be recalled that in Bereishis 43:33 we are told that Yosef was able to seat his brothers at the table in precise age order, a feat at which they themselves marveled (ibid.). Even if the brothers did not guess Yosef's identity then and there, in retrospect, this production should at least have verified the truth of Yosef's statement when he eventually did reveal himself. (See also Rashi to Bereishis 43:7, who adds that Yosef displayed to his brothers a familiarity with even their private lives, based on his memories of them from his youth.)

Another difficulty presents itself. How could the brothers ignore Yosef's constant efforts to have Binyamin brought to him, his profuse show of favor to Binyamin when he did come (see Bereishis 43:34 and Rashi to 43:33), and finally Yosef's attempted abduction of him? Surely the peculiar attitude of the viceroy of Egypt toward Binyamin, coupled with the fact that he seemed to know so much personal information about them and their family, should have given them enough evidence to at least suspect that they had found the man for whom they were so anxiously looking!

Thirdly, even if we accept that the brothers needed further convincing for some reason, how would these two items prove Yosef's identity at all? Rashi tells us (in Bereishis 41:55) that all the Egyptians underwent circumcision during the first stage of the famine. Besides, all the various nations that descended from Avraham practiced circumcision, so how could this be considered an identifying characteristic of a son of Yaakov? (This problem is raised in the super commentaries on Rashi—Mizrachi, Gur Aryeh.)

Using his knowledge of Hebrew to prove his identity is no less perplexing. As the Ramban asks, wasn't Hebrew the language of the land of Canaan? Why, then, would it be so unusual for a high governmental official to be able to speak many foreign languages, especially that of a neighboring country? Surely many Egyptians spoke Hebrew well! Besides, what motive would anyone else have—especially a powerful governor of a powerful nation—in claiming to be Yosef?

II

In order to address these questions, let us first examine another comment of Rashi's in last week's Parsha:

The owner or the slave? "Yaakov saw that the sale (*shever*) of food was taking place in Egypt..."—Yaakov saw, through divine inspiration, that there was something for him to look forward to (*sever*) in Egypt. It was not a clear enough prophecy, however, for him to realize that this glimmer of hope was the discovery of Yosef (Rashi to 42:1).

Perhaps it was not simply a flash of divine inspiration that occurred to Yaakov that gave him the premonition that Yosef might be found in Egypt, but also an insight into the course of events happening there, as follows:

The Gemara tells us that Yaakov was the personification of the Talmudic statement that "With the arrival of the Torah scholar, there arrives blessing" (Berachos 42a). Indeed, in Bereishis 31:9-12 we see that Yaakov was blessed, through supernatural means, with an inordinate amount of economic success in his dealings with Lavan. Lavan himself noted the connection between Yaakov's presence and financial prosperity (Bereishis 30:27). Furthermore, after Yaakov had just lavished a fortune of gifts upon his brother, we read that Yaakov arrived in Shechem "complete," which Rashi (ibid. 33:18) explains to mean that he immediately regained all the money that he had spent on Esav. Even in the years of famine, when the rest of the residents of Canaan had long since depleted their supplies of grain, Rashi (ibid. 42:1) tells us that Yaakov and his family were blessed with sufficient food for themselves. In fact, when Yaakov arrived in Egypt, we are told that the famine, which was to have plagued the area for another five years, abruptly ended in his merit (Rashi ibid. 47:19). Wherever Yaakov went, and in whatever situation he was to be found, there was sure to be prosperity and blessing—both for him and for those in his vicinity.

In Bereishis 37:2 Rashi (quoting Bereishis Rabbah) points out the amazing similarities between the life's events of Yaakov and those of Yosef (both were hated, both were pursued by their brother(s), etc.). The Gemara in Berachos (ibid.) tells us that Yosef shared with his father the quality of bringing blessing to his surroundings, as well. This can indeed be seen explicitly in several places in the Torah: "Everything he did, Hashem made successful in his hands" (Bereisis 39:3); "Everything that he did Hashem made successful" (ibid. 39:23). (And of course, let us not forget that he became the viceroy over all of Egypt!) And, like his father, his ability to bring blessing wherever he went extended to those around him as well: "As soon as (Potifar) appointed him to be in charge of his house...Hashem blessed the household of the Egyptian because of Yosef" (ibid. 39:5).

Yaakov saw that whereas the famine was affecting the *entire* region, the seven years of plenty were mysteriously limited to Egypt alone (see Ramban to 41:2). If Egypt was benefiting from such an unusual degree of prosperity, it occurred to Yaakov, it might be that Yosef had something to do with it. The fact that this prosperity started as soon as the new leader took control in Egypt only heightened Yaakov's feeling that a single person was somehow involved in the turn of events. The brothers may have come to the same conclusion. This may be why they came to Egypt with full confidence that Yosef was to be found there (Rashi, Bereishis 42:3,13,14).

This analysis of their thinking, however, only seems to *add* to our wonder. Why did the brothers not suspect that the ruler himself was Yosef, especially after he told them his identity outright?

The answer is that the brothers did not consider even as a remote possibility that their brother could have ascended to such a senior position in

Egypt. He could not speak Egyptian; he was a foreigner; and he had—at least at one time—been a slave. Any one of these factors, as the *sar hamashkim* [chief butler] pointed out, would have disqualified Yosef for any senior appointment under normal circumstances (see Rashi to Bereishis 41:12). Furthermore, the brothers knew that this ruler was married and had children. They knew that Yosef was a holy man and would never have married an idolatrous Egyptian woman! (In fact, the Midrash [*Pirkei d'Rabbi Eliezer*, 38] says that the "daughter of Poti Phera" whom Yosef married was actually an adopted daughter, for Poti Phera had adopted a foundling from the land of Canaan—who turned out to be none other than the daughter of Dinah, and Yaakov's granddaughter!)

No, the possibility that this ruler of Egypt was Yosef was out of the question. If so, what was Yaakov's, and the brothers', premonition? Perhaps they suspected that this ruler had been Yosef's *master* in the past. It was this man's association with the righteous Yosef that brought such unusual prosperity to his land (the same kind of prosperity that Potifar, Yosef's first master, had indeed experienced)!

Now we can understand why the brothers did not become suspicious when they saw that the ruler had so much personal information about them and their missing brother. A master may certainly have questioned his slave about his past, and this would be especially true in the case of such a holy and extraordinarily successful servant. The brothers indeed knew that they were on to something when they heard all that Yosef told them, but they thought that "something" was not Yosef himself, but the man who *owned* Yosef!

III

The plan for Binyamin's capture

With this in mind, we can explain how the brothers viewed the curious behavior of Yosef towards Binyamin, and why they suspected the Egyptian ruler of falsely representing himself as their brother. The brothers knew that the famine was now affecting Egypt as well as all the other surrounding countries. Whatever mysterious merit had been working on its behalf during the seven years of plenty seemed to have dissipated. Since it was well known that the Egyptian culture was steeped in lewdness and immorality (see Rashi Bereishis 12:19), the brothers suspected that Yosef, as righteous as he was, may have succumbed to the licentious temptations of his surroundings and thereby lost his ability to be a source of blessing to himself and to his environment. Alternatively, they may have reasoned that Yosef did indeed remain steadfast in his righteous ways, and was persecuted for doing so (as did in fact happen to him in the house of Potifar—39:7-20). He would therefore be no longer in the service of this viceroy.

If this ruler was now deprived of the services of his righteous servant, as indicated by the fact that Egypt was now suffering along with the rest of the region, it would be quite understandable that this man would now want to find a substitute of equal qualifications. Surely he would have learned from Yosef that he had other brothers and that one of them was a full brother (and was more likely to share his characteristics) who was, moreover, not involved in the grievous sin of selling Yosef as a slave. This was Yosef's only brother who remained righteous, and would therefore be able to bring blessing himself. It was only natural, therefore, that the viceroy would want to use all means possible to entice Binyamin to Egypt and seize him as his slave.

Bearing all this in mind, we can now understand the manner in which Yehudah tried to persuade Yosef not to keep Binyamin. He told Yosef that keeping Binyamin would certainly lead to their father's death. This father, as the ruler certainly knew, was the source of all the blessings that Yosef merited. Bringing about his death would definitely frustrate any plans he might have of obtaining the blessing of prosperity through enslaving Binyamin. Furthermore, Yehudah argued, if Binyamin leaves his father he himself will die (see Ramban to Bereishis 44:22), and there will certainly be no benefit gained by keeping him away from his father!

We can now understand why the brothers refused to believe Yosef even after he revealed himself. They were suspicious that he was responding to Yehudah's argument. He had become convinced that keeping Binyamin would not accomplish anything, as the blessing that the ruler was seeking would not be able to function. "This ruler is now trying to get us to bring our father Yaakov himself to join him in Egypt, in order that he may herald the return of the rescinded blessing!" they thought. "To this purpose, he has taken up the tactic of masquerading as Yosef himself!"

Since this was the brothers' suspicion, it is obvious that hearing the viceroy mention Yosef's name and the fact that he was sold by his brothers would do nothing to alleviate their skepticism toward the ruler.

IV

But if so, how did Yosef's signs of circumcision and knowledge of Hebrew manage to convince the distrustful brothers after all else had failed? As we pointed out earlier, circumcision and knowledge of Hebrew were themselves far from "solid" proofs of Jewish identity in the land of Egypt!

Unmasking an impostor: The Vilna Gaon's strategy

There is an authoritative story about the Vilna Gaon, recorded at the end of the book *Divrei Eliyahu* as follows:

Once there was a man who fled to an unknown location shortly after his wedding, leaving his wife an agunah (i.e., unable to remarry, as her husband had never formally divorced her). About fifteen years later a man came to her town claiming to be the abandoned woman's long-lost husband. No one in town was familiar enough with the man to be able to positively identify him after so long a lapse of time. He tried to prove his identity by mentioning all sorts of personal details about himself and his wife, including very private matters that only a husband could know. Nevertheless, the woman didn't trust him. She insisted that she would not accept him until the matter was brought before the Torah scholars of the generation. The family decided to refer the question to the Vilna Gaon: How could they ascertain whether this man was indeed the long-absent husband, or not?

The Gaon suggested that the man be asked to show his alleged father-in-law the seat in the synagogue in which the father-in-law sat. A new husband normally accompanies his father-in-law to the synagogue on the first Shabbos after the wedding and sits next to him, so the man should have no trouble identifying the seat. His advice was taken. The man was unable to identify his supposed father-in-law's seat, and was exposed as an impostor. As it happened, this man had simply met the true husband, and had learned from him all the details about the husband, his wife and her family. Shortly thereafter, the true husband returned, and was immediately recognized by all.

When asked how this particular test of true identity occurred to him, the Gaon replied that if someone would stoop to such depths of deceit—and the sin of adultery—to steal someone's wife, he would never have the slightest interest in anything that has to do with sanctity or religion. He may have quizzed the husband about many personal matters, but the thoughts of the synagogue would certainly never enter his mind.

Perhaps we can apply the moral of this story to our Parsha. If Yosef was suspected of being an impostor, the only way to disprove this allegation would be to show that he was aware of matters of *holiness.* A charlatan might know every detail about the person he is trying to impersonate through extensive questioning, but he would not think of asking questions involving sacred issues! Yosef was not exhibiting the physical property of being circumcised or the intellectual ability of being able to master the Hebrew language; he was showing the brothers that he was aware that the circumcision was a sign of the *sanctity* of the House of Israel, and that the Hebrew language was the *Holy Tongue,* which embodies the sanctity of prophecy and of Divine creation (see Ramban, Shemos 30:13). When the brothers saw that this man was aware of these facts, they were convinced that they were not dealing with an Egyptian scoundrel, as they had originally suspected. This man was indeed their brother, Yosef!

PARSHAS VAYECHI

Tehillim: 147 Psalms Or 150 Psalms?

"The days of Yaakov, the years of his life, were one hundred and forty-seven years" (Bereishis 47:28). There are one hundred forty-seven Psalms in the book of Tehillim, corresponding to the 147 years of Yaakov's life, as suggested in the verse "You are Holy, enthroned upon the praises of Yisrael [another name for Yaakov]" (Masseches Sofrim 16:11).

What did Yaakov say (during the nights when he would stay up tending Lavan's sheep)? ...The entire book of Tehillim, as it says, "You are Holy, enthroned upon the praises of Yisrael (Yaakov)" (Bereishis Rabbah 74:11).

The discrepancy in the Psalm-count

It comes as quite a surprise to the modern reader to hear that there are 147 Psalms in the book of Tehillim. In all printed editions of Tehillim there are 150 Psalms! Apparently the arrangement of the Psalms in the days of the Talmud differed somewhat from that which appears in today's texts. It is inconceivable that three Psalms that were not in the ancient edition were added from some other source; the comments of the Sages of the Talmud cover every single one of the Psalms in our current editions. The answer to the mysterious addition of three Psalms over the centuries must lie rather with the rearrangement of the existing Psalms—i.e., the splitting of what was originally one Psalm into two separate units, in three places in Tehillim.

One such instance is in fact recorded in the Talmud itself. In Berachos 9b we are told that the first "two" Psalms in Tehillim should actually be counted as one long Psalm. Apparently the practice of splitting this Psalm into two parts was prevalent already in talmudic times, and the Gemara had to point out that this was not originally the case.

However, this is the only instance of such a phenomenon found in the Talmud. This accounts for only one of the three "missing" Psalms—i.e., the three Psalms that were "added" to the original 147 by breaking them off from their parent Psalm. How can we account for the other two missing Psalms? This question is discussed by the Yefe Mareh (to Yerushalmi Shabbos 16:1), and by Rav Elazar Flekles, in his responsa *Teshuvah Me'Ahavah* (part 1, res. 111), among others, but is left unresolved by them. (Rav David Cohen, in *Ohel David*, end of vol. II, offers some interesting insights on the subject, but leaves room for further research. See also Rav Wolfe of Heidenheim's essay on this subject—in the Tehillim he printed in Redelheim, Germany—based on the division found in the Salonika, 1521, print of the *Yalkut Shimoni*.) Very little has been written on this matter that is convincing, and keeps with the Talmudic and Midrashic sources. Let us attempt to reanalyze the situation.

II

There are several possibilities we may consider in our search for the extra Psalms.

According to one reading in Rashi on Megillah 17b (which is the reading found in all printed editions, and is the reading quoted by Tosafos ad loc.) it seems to be assumed that what we today call Psalms 9 and 10 are in fact counted as one Psalm. (The two Psalms indeed are related in theme. It is interesting to note also that Psalm 9 contains the beginning of a loose alphabetical acrostic—from *alef* to *kaf*—and Psalm 10 has the end of one—*lamed,* and later *kaf* through *taf*.—MK)

Two unacceptable solutions

It may also be understood from the *Toras Chaim* on Masseches Shavuos, that according to Rashi (Shavuos 15b), Psalms 90 and 91 should be considered as one. (It is interesting to note that the two are indeed combined in the prayers.—MK) We now have two candidates for the extra two Psalms.

Alternatively, the commentary attributed to Rashi on Divrei Hayyamim (I, 16:34) asserts that Psalms 105 and 106 are in reality one long Psalm, by showing that they are both reflected in the single prayer that King David offered in Divrei Hayyamim. Following through on that approach, it would have to be concluded that Psalm 96, is also part of the same long Psalm. Although it is not adjacent to #105, it is included in the same prayer of Divrei Hayyamim in its entirety. This may then offer us both of the extra Psalms; #96, #105, and #106 are all considered to be one Psalm!

We now have enough candidates to satisfy our quest for the extra Psalms. However, upon further analysis, it can be shown that none of these three possibilities are viable options. The Gemara (Berachos 9b) tells us that the Psalm beginning with the words *Barchi Nafshi* (now known as Psalm 104) is actually the 103rd Psalm, because, as mentioned earlier (section I), Psalms 1 and 2 should be considered as only one Psalm. Thus it is clear that the "added" Psalms cannot be found anywhere before #104, since the Talmud tells us that even in ancient times that Psalm was the 103rd chapter of Tehillim. All of our potential candidates are thus rejected, since they all involve Psalms before #103. (In fact, a more careful examination of the sources shows that in all these cases Rashi's words can indeed be interpreted in other ways. He does not necessarily mean to say that two of our Psalms are actually supposed to be one, large Psalm. The search for the two "added Psalms" must resume!

III

As was mentioned, the Psalms for which we are looking (that are today considered two Psalms but were originally one) must be located after what is today called Psalm 104. A number of other logical criteria may also be assumed:

Six rules: a process of elimination

1) It is known from Talmudic sources (Mishnayos Sukkah 5:4) that there are fifteen Psalms in the *Shir Hamaalos* series. None of these Psalms could ever have been joined to an adjacent one, as this would diminish the number of *Shir Hamaalos* Psalms (Psalms 120-134).

2) If a Psalm begins with an introductory epigraph, such as "A Psalm of David" or "A praise of David" it is clear that this Psalm cannot possibly be connected to the one before it. (Such as is the case in Psalms 108-110, 138-144).

3) Any Psalm written according to an alphabetical acrostic can be assumed to be in its original form; it is impossible that there was once another "piece" to such a Psalm that was subsequently broken off. An alphabetical acrostic must begin with *alef* and end with *taf*! (This rules out any connection between Psalms 111, 112, 145, 119 and an adjacent Psalm.)

4) If there are two adjacent Psalms, the first of which ends with the word *Hallelujah*, and the second of which begins with *Hallelujah,* it is clear that these two Psalms could never have constituted a single Psalm. (Rules out any connection between Psalms 105-106, and 145-150.)

5) Tosafos Kiddushin 33a (based on Midrash Socher Tov ch. 1) tells us that Tehillim is divided into five sections or "books." These books, as Tosafos points out, are clearly demarked in Tehillim. It is obvious that the last Psalm of one book could never be regarded as being attached to the following Psalm, which is the start of a new book. (Rules out Psalms 106-107.)

6) Psalm 136 has a constant refrain in every verse (*Ki Le'olam Chasdo),* and cannot be combined with the Psalms before it or after it, which do not have this refrain.

Even with all of this in mind, one still may surmise that Psalms 134-135 may be connected. The Gemara in Pesachim 117a, however, clearly negates this possibility, stating specifically that one of the two *Hallelujah*'s of Psalm 135 (verse 1 or 3) marks the beginning of a new Psalm.

If so, it becomes clear after processing all of the above criteria that we 'must' find the extra Psalms between Psalm 113 and Psalm 118. Our search for the extra two Psalms has been narrowed down to the six Psalms commonly known as *Hallel*!

(I later found that Rav Shlomo of Chelme, in his *Mirkeves haMishne*, [Salonika 1782, part II, Hilchos Chanukah 3:13] makes a similar calculation. However, because he did not mention rule six, his conclusion differs slightly from ours.)

IV

The added Psalms

The most obvious candidate for being combined with an adjacent Psalm is tiny 117, which, consisting of only two verses, is the shortest chapter in the entire Bible. Tosafos in Pesachim 117a asserts (apropos of a different question) that it is not possible that a Psalm should consist of only two verses. Obviously Tosafos is of the opinion that Psalm 117 is not an independent Psalm, but is rather the end of Psalm 116 or the beginning of Psalm 118 and was subsequently severed into a separate unit. In Sukkah 38b the verse "Give thanks to Hashem for He is good...," which is the first verse of Psalm 118 in contemporary editions, is referred to as "the beginning of the chapter," so it appears that the two-versed 117 should not be appended to the beginning of 118, but rather to the end of 116. (In fact Tosafos specifically groups Psalms 116 and 117 together, in Sukkah 54a.)

Thus we have accounted for two of the three "extra" Psalms: Psalms 1 and 2 were originally one, as were 116 and 117. But we must still find the third case where two of "our" Psalms were originally one unit.

Tosafos in Sukkah 54a seems to supply the missing information. Tosafos groups all of the Psalms from 113-115 together into one unit! This grouping would be "more" than enough, however, as it would remove "two" more Psalms from the total number, leaving us with only 146. However, this grouping together of Psalms 113-115 cannot be accepted in any case, when it comes to determining the number of Psalms. The Gemara in Pesachim (117a) specifically counts *Betzeis* (114:1) as the beginning of a Psalm. (Tosafos in Sukkah was dealing with the issue of the *tekios* that were blown in the Temple during the recitation of *Hallel*, and it was in *this* connection that he said that Psalms 113-115 are considered one unit, apparently, and not for purposes of calculating the number of Psalms in *Hallel*. See also Tosafos Sukkah 38b, *Mikahn*.) But if we accept Tosafos' partitioning of the Psalms of *Hallel except* for the one exclusion which is contradicted by Pesachim 117a, we will have removed our last extra Psalm. *Hallel* will now be divided into four sections:

(1) Psalm 113 (*Hallelujah Hallelu Avdei Hashem*);

(2) Psalms 114-115 (*Betzeis* and *Lo Lanu*);

(3) Psalms 116-117 (*Ahavti* and *Hallelu es Hashem Kol Goyim*);

(4) Psalm 118 (*Hodu Lashem Ki Tov*).

Perhaps we have thus found the third case of the compound Psalm: 114 and 115 were originally one long Psalm!

There are several indications that bear out our suggestion that 115 is not a separate Psalm. Firstly, according to this scheme it can be seen that every single Psalm of *Hallel* is separated from the next Psalm by the word *Hallelujah*, the word that exemplifies the praise of *Hallel*. (The first section begins *and* ends in *Hallelujah*, while the second and third section both end with the word.)

Another point of support for this theory is that the Aleppo Codex, the most ancient (and hence the most authoritative) complete manuscript of the Bible (Maimonides himself saw it and praised its accuracy!), has Psalms 114 and 115 written without any separation between them. In fact, Dr. Mordechai Breuer, a well-known expert in ancient biblical manuscripts, told me that *all* of the manuscript Tehillims that he has seen have these two Psalms as one, long one.

A third proof can be derived from Masseches Sofrim 20:9, which clearly enumerates the chapters in *Hallel*—and leaves out 115, apparently appending it to 114! Although the Vilna Gaon alters the text of M. Sofrim to agree to our numbering of Psalms, the Rambam (Hilchos Chanukah 3:13) seems to have had the text of M. Sofrim that we have. When he lists the chapters in *Hallel* (for a different halachic purpose) he also does not count 115 as an independent chapter! The Mirkeves haMishne ad loc. points out that the Rambam obviously had 114-115 together (see also Radak on Tehillim 115:1).

It should be noted, however, that the above Rambam and M. Sofrim just as clearly count Psalm 117 as an "independent" Psalm, which would seem to contradict our prior assumption. However, this need not force us to abandon that assumption. Psalm 117 is perhaps considered to be independent only in the context of the *Hallel prayer*. After all, Psalm 117 comes after the *Hallelujah* at the end of 116, and ends with its own *Hallelujah*, which perhaps grants it the Halachic status of a separate section of praise, in *Hallel*. However, as far as counting Psalms of *Tehillim* is concerned, it may have been joined with 116, due to its brevity.

Interestingly, Minhas Shai, an early commentary with superlative expertise in matters dealing with authenticity of manuscripts and various versions of the Biblical texts, also accounts for the 147 Psalms in Tehillim by joining Psalms 1-2, 114-115, and 116-117, just as we have, based on his findings in old manuscripts!

V

Why, then, do our editions of Tehillim have 150 Psalms? When and why did the three Psalms we have mentioned become split in two?

Anatomy of a typo The breakup of Psalms 1 and 2 into two Psalms was known even in Talmudic times, as can be seen from Berachos 9b, quoted above. The reason for the subdivision is suggested by the Maharsha to be as follows. The Gemara says that the reason the verse *Yihyu Leratzon*—"May the expression of my mouth...find favor..." (Psalm 19:15)—is appended to the end of the *Shemoneh Esrei* [Eighteen Benedictions] prayer is that David used this verse to conclude his eighteenth Psalm (according to the ancient division, where our Psalm 19 was really the eighteenth Psalm). It could be that when the eighteen-benediction prayer was expanded into nineteen during the late Tannaitic period, the need to keep the parallel between the number of Psalms preceding the verse of *Yihyu Leratzon* and the number of benedictions in the *Shemoneh Esrei* was addressed by changing those eighteen Psalms into nineteen—by subdividing one of them into two parts!

But when did the subdivision of Psalms 114 and 115 take place, and under what circumstances?

Perhaps we may suggest the following. A look in any Siddur will show that in *Hallel*, the first half of Psalm 115 is always printed as a separate paragraph from the second half. (In modern prayer books, this section often is printed in a different size or style of print, as well.) This is also the case with Psalm 116. The reason for this is that when the "short" version of *Hallel* is recited (on *Rosh Chodesh* [the first day of a lunar month] and the last six days of Pesach), the first half of these two Psalms is omitted. It is possible that the long Psalm which was originally comprised of *Betzeis*, *Lo Lanu* and *Hashem Zecharanu* came to be divided into two separate Psalms, due to this fact.

In order to let the reader know that he must, at times, skip *Lo Lanu*, the first half of the Psalm it had to be printed in the Siddur as the beginning of a new paragraph. (Before the paragraph would be printed a short note, informing the reader to skip until the words *Hashem Zecharanu* if today is *Rosh Chodesh* or the end of Pesach.) From the prayer books, the new paragraph division at *Lo Lanu* crept into our books of Tehillim, where it eventually was mistaken for a distinct Psalm!

My friend, haRav Yaakov Blinder, suggested that a similar theory may be presented to explain how Psalm 117 came to be split off from its parent Psalm, 116. The Rambam (Chanukah 3:8) tells us that the custom is, when reciting the "short version" *of Hallel*, to skip not only the first halves of Psalm 115 (*Lo Lanu*) and 116 (*Ahavti*), but also the entire Psalm 117 (*Hallelu es Hashem)* and the first four verses of Psalm 118. Maggid Mishneh attests to this being the prevalent custom in his days. (This custom is no longer followed in the standard Sephardi or Ashkenazi rites, but it is still practiced by the Yemenite Jews.) Thus, the early Siddurim, for the same reason described above, printed Psalm 117 as a new paragraph, in order to insert before it a note that one is to start skipping from that point until the words *Min Hametzar*, on *Rosh Chodesh* or the latter days of Pesach. This division in the Siddur eventually led to making Psalm 117 into a new Psalm altogether in the book of Tehillim! We can now understand how the 150 Psalms in our texts of Tehillim are actually the 147 Psalms of King David's ode to Yaakov Avinu.

In every generation, when confronted by any difficult situation, we offer Hashem our prayers in the form of the eternal chapters of Tehillim. We remember the difficult times our father Yaakov endured while in exile, slaving over the flocks of his devious uncle, and how he used the calming words of Tehillim to remind himself of Hashem's constant protection and the ultimate victory of good over all evil.

[Note: I presented a copy of this essay to Dr. Mordechai Breuer of Jerusalem, a modern expert in all matters relating to textual Masoret—and ancient biblical manuscripts. Dr. Breuer was kind enough to send me a lengthy reply, praising my work and the conclusions I reached. He also shared with me his personal approach to the discrepancy in the Psalm-count. He, too, judged the three Psalms we mentioned to be the extra ones. However, he did not propose, as we have, that some of the original 147 Psalms were later *split* in two. Rather, he suggested that perhaps the original *mesorah* [traditional rendering of the Scriptures] was 150 Psalms, and the *mesorah* of the Midrashim with which we started *combined* three Psalms with adjacent Psalms for various reasons—some of which we have touched upon here. (The arguments he bases his thesis on are primarily logical, not textual.) I shall not include a full English translation of his essay here, but I will be glad to send a copy of his essay (in Hebrew) to all who express interest in seeing it.—MK]

PARSHAS SHEMOS

The Sign Of The Serpent

When Moshe was first presented with the historic mission to lead the Jews out of Egypt, he hesitated. Moshe was concerned that neither the people nor Pharaoh would believe that he had been sent by Hashem. In order to bolster Moshe, Hashem supplied him with wonders to perform. These signs would prove that Moshe was indeed a Divine emissary. As the Torah tells us:

"Hashem said to Moshe, 'What is that in your hand?' Moshe replied, 'A staff.' Hashem told him, 'Throw it to the ground.' Moshe threw it to the ground and it became a snake, and Moshe fled from before it. Hashem said to Moshe, 'Put out your hand and grab it by the tail.' Moshe put out his hand and grabbed it, and it became a staff in his hand" (Shemos 4:2-4).

This feat was followed by two others (Shemos 4:6-9). When Moshe arrived in Egypt, he and his brother Aharon performed their repertoire of signs for the Jewish people (Shemos 4:30). Later, they repeated the wonder of the snake in Pharaoh's palace, with Aharon acting as Moshe's proxy:

The staff that became a snake

"Aharon threw down his staff before Pharaoh and before his servants, and it became a serpent! Pharaoh called upon his wise men and sorcerers, and the magicians of Egypt did likewise through their sorcery. Each one threw down his staff and they became serpents. Then, the staff of Aharon swallowed up their staffs!" (Shemos 7:10-12).

The ostensible purpose of this display was to prove to Pharaoh that Moshe indeed brought the word of God. Clearly, however, the choice of miracle was not random. If God chose this particular sign, it must bear a deeper, allegorical meaning somehow related to Moshe's mission. What could this hidden message be?

A number of suggestions have been made concerning the metaphorical significance of the transformation of the staff into a snake. Most commentaries see it as symbolic of the Jewish exile in Egypt, and of Pharaoh's ultimate downfall (Kli Yakar 4:9, 7:9; Ya'aros Devash 1:3; Chasam Sofer HaChadashos 4:3; Meshech Chochmah ibid.; Pardes Yosef 4:10). Others bring out the symbolism of Moshe's authority as an emissary of Hashem (Ha'amek Davar, Malbim, and R.S.R. Hirsch to 4:3). In general, however, these explanations fall short of explaining the rebuttal of the Egyptian magicians. What were they trying to say by turning their own staffs into snakes? What was their response to Moshe's proof of Divine agency?

Perhaps the most satisfying explanation of the allegory is from early commentators (Ibn Ezra 4:3; Chizkuni 7:9; Baal Haturim 7:9), who say that the staff's transformation into a serpent hinted to Pharaoh's behavior as king of Egypt; behavior which ultimately led to the ten plagues that Hashem brought upon the Egyptians. This interpretation actually has its basis in a Midrash. Let us take another look at Moshe's Divine sign in light of this explanation.

II

Staff = rod of retribution; Snake = self-willed murderer

"What message did the sign of the stick/snake carry for the Jews? Rabbi Elazar said: 'The stick that became a snake hinted to Pharaoh, who is called a 'snake'—'Pharaoh...the great serpent' (Yechezkel 29:3); 'The erect Leviathan snake' (Yeshayah 27:1). Pharaoh was compared to a snake because of the way he 'bit' the Jews. Hashem said to Moshe, 'Do you see how Pharaoh is like a snake? You will smite him with a staff, and he will end up as a piece of wood that cannot bite!' " (Shemos Rabbah 3:12).

"Why did Moshe perform for Pharaoh the miracle of the serpent? Because Pharaoh is compared to a serpent..... Whenever Moshe left Pharaoh's presence, Pharaoh would say, 'If I get hold of Moshe, I'll kill him! I'll hang him! I'll burn him!' But whenever Moshe entered the palace, Pharaoh would immediately become as a stick of wood" (Shemos Rabbah 9:4).

Moshe's miracle symbolized that a timid Pharaoh (a "staff") had become a venomous "serpent" (see Rashi 1:8). Hashem's message was that this serpent would be tamed and become harmless once again.

There may, however, be deeper significance to the staff than simple lifelessness. A staff, or stick, is used for striking and for punishing. When Hashem sent the nation of Aram to conquer the Jews, Hashem called them His "rod of retribution" (*shevet appi*—Yeshayah 10:5). So too, Pharaoh's position was one of a rod of retribution. As per the Divine decree (Bereishis 15:13), Pharaoh enslaved the Jews: "Your offspring will be strangers in a land not theirs, and they will serve the natives of that land, who will afflict them for four hundred years."

Such a "staff" is only a tool to be used by the person who holds it. The staff can accomplish nothing on its own. As Hashem chastened the nation of Aram, which prided itself in the destruction of Israel, "Can an ax in the hand of a wood-chopper take pride in its accomplishments? ...Does a staff [that strikes] pick itself up? No! Someone must raise it!" (Yeshayah 10:15). Pharaoh had nothing to gloat over. He was simply Hashem's tool.

But then, why should Pharaoh be punished with ten plagues? What did he do? The answer is that Pharaoh had turned himself into a snake!

Two reasons for the punishment of the Egyptians

The Ramban (Bereishis 15:4) gives two reasons for the punishment of the Egyptians. First of all, they did much more than was decreed. Hashem had only said that the Jews would be enslaved and oppressed. Pharaoh, however, gave them excruciatingly difficult labor, and even decreed the death of their babies. Ramban's second reason is that Pharaoh did not enslave the Jews *in order* to fulfill Hashem's will, but for his own selfish motives, because he hated the Jews, and desired to profit from their labor. Pharaoh's goal was not to fulfill the prophecy. This is why, according to the Ramban, Pharaoh was deserving of punishment for his deeds.

Ramban's suggestion that the Egyptians did much more than was decreed is clearly symbolized by the staff turning into a "serpent." When someone is hit with a staff, the place struck by the staff is bruised. But Pharaoh turned himself into a snake. The bite of a snake—unlike the bites of other animals —can cause poison to spread throughout the entire body of its victim (Yerushalmi Rosh Hashanah 3:9). Thus the effect of being bitten by a snake is much more severe than being struck by a stick.

The second reason Ramban gives for the punishment of the Egyptians— that Pharaoh did not enslave the Jews *in order* to fulfill Hashem's will, is also alluded to in the staff becoming a snake. The Gemara tells us (Sanhedrin 78a) that if a person scratches someone with the fangs of a snake, (according to the majority opinion) he cannot be sentenced as a murderer. The fangs of a snake are not comparable to knives dipped in poison because a snake's poison is contained in a duct, and the snake must exude the venom of its own volition. The snake is the killer; the man who holds the snake is merely a causative agent (*gerama*) in the murder and is not punishable as a murderer.

Similarly, Pharaoh tortured the Jews of his own free will. Instead of being Hashem's "staff," Pharaoh transformed himself into a "serpent." (See also Toldos essay, section IV, p. 27, for some more insights into the metaphor of a snake. I was later shown that much of the above thought can be found in Rav Yosef Salant of Jerusalem's *Be'er Yosef*, to Parshas Vaera.)

III

Pharaoh's magicians' response may now be viewed as a retort to Moshe's allegorical challenge. When Moshe threw down his staff so that it would turn into a snake, Pharaoh's magicians also threw down their staffs. Their message was, "We're right with you, Pharaoh! We, too, do not consider ourselves to be merely sticks in the hands of Hashem. We, too, wish to enslave Jews of our own free will! We will not accept the fact that it is only Hashem's will which has placed the Jews into our hands. Like Pharaoh, we too are serpents!"

The snakes of the magicians; becoming staffs once again

At this point, Moshe's staff swallowed up all of the other staffs. It is noteworthy that the Torah refers to them as "staffs" once more, and no longer as serpents. Moshe's serpent became a piece of wood once again, and then it "swallowed" the staff/serpents of the Egyptian sorcerers (Rashi). Perhaps this was a hint that, against his own will, Pharaoh would return to being a stick in Hashem's hands. He would end up doing things clearly against his own interests, simply because they fit into Hashem's plan. This is just what Hashem had already told Moshe (Shemos 4:21), "I will harden his heart so that he will not let the people go." Pharaoh would refuse to allow the Jews to leave, even after he had witnessed plague after plague, in order to reveal to the world through the plagues that Hashem was the Creator of the Heavens and Earth (Shemos 7:3). Pharaoh again became a staff in Hashem's hand—but this time, for punishing the Egyptians, not the Jews.

Perhaps this is why Moshe was told to pick up the snake by its "tail" when he turned it back into a staff. Moshe was to reverse the direction of this rod of retribution, making it smite the one who formerly wielded it!

Eventually, Pharaoh's own servants pleaded with him to let the Jews go, declaring, "Don't you realize that we're being destroyed?" (Shemos 10:7). Pharaoh refused to listen, and they became unwilling partners in his refusal to allow the Jews to go free. They, too, became sticks in Hashem's hands and were "devoured" by the "stick" called Pharaoh!

IV

The theme of a staff becoming a snake represents a humble pawn becoming haughty and proud. This theme can be used to explain numerous other appearances of the stick and the snake in the words of our Sages. For example, this is how we are told to bow to Hashem in the Amidah prayer:

Sticks & snakes in prayer

"One is to bow upon saying 'Blessed are you,' and stand erect upon reaching Hashem's name. Rav Sheshes would bow as a 'stick' (i.e., all at once, according to Rashi), and would return to an erect state as a 'snake' (i.e., Rashi says this is done slowly, first head, then neck, then trunk)" (Gemara Berachos 12a-b4).

"Bowing" to Hashem is to be done as a "stick". We demonstrate our humility and subjugate ourselves to Hashem's will, by showing that we are "sticks" in Hashem's hands. Without Hashem's help, we haven't the power to accomplish anything.

But when we reach the Holy Name in our prayers, we stand erect. This is the moment to display our pride in being Hashem's chosen nation, upon whom He rests His great name (see Ritva, loc. cit.). We return to holding our head "erect" the way a "snake" does. Even haughtiness has its place. "[Yehoshaphat's] heart was haughty when it came to following the ways of Hashem" (II Chronicles 17:6—see Shabbos 63a, Yoma 23a "*Talmid Chacham...Noter k'Nachash*"). We must be sure to recognize when we should be "snakes," and when we must be "sticks!"

PARSHAS VAERA

Rebbi Yehudah's Acronym

"These are the ten makkos [plagues] which the Holy One Blessed be He brought upon the Egyptians in Egypt. They are: blood, frogs, lice, mixed wild animals, pestilence, boils, hail, locusts, darkness, death of the firstborn. Rebbi Yehudah would make an acronym from the Hebrew words for the ten plagues: 'D'TZ'CH, A'D'SH, B'A'CH'V' " (Passover Haggadah; Sifri Parshas Ki Savo).

Rebbi Yehudah proposed an easily memorized acronym for the ten plagues: "D'TZ'CH, A'D'SH, B'ACH'V" (usually pronounced "DeTZaCH ADaSH B'ACHaV"). This simple mnemonic provides an easy way to recall the ten plagues.

We may, however, ask a very basic question concerning Rebbi Yehudah's mnemonic. Typically, a mnemonic is necessary to help us recall a matter which is *not* recorded in a readily accessible place—such as the opinion of a Sage in the Mishnah or Gemara, something which did not originally exist in written form. The ten plagues, however, are clearly written in the Torah, and every child can easily recite them by heart. Why then did Rebbi Yehudah need to create a mnemonic to help us recall the ten plagues?

Rebbi Yehudah and his acronyms

Commentators throughout the ages have discussed this issue—such as the authors of Tosafos in Da'as Zekenim and Hadar Zekenim, Shemos 7:25; Rosh, beginning of Vaera; Hagahos Maimonei, end of Chametz u'Matzah, #2; Avudraham and Kol Bo, in Haggadah shel Pesach; Pardes Yosef, Shemos 7:25. Let us examine some of their suggestions.

II

Suggestions from early commentators

(1)

The most obvious suggestion is that Rebbi Yehudah was not trying to help us remember the names of the plagues at all. Rather, he was emphasizing that the plagues are to be divided into three distinct groups. The first three plagues form one group, the second three form another group, and the last four form a third group.

The plagues are three distinct groups

There are a number of ways in which these three groups are distinct. (Please see Tosafos, Hagahos Maimonei and Avudraham.)

(2)

Da'as Zekenim suggests that perhaps Rebbi Yehudah's acronym is simply a mnemonic. However, it is not meant to remind us of the plagues. It is intended to record the correct "chronological order" of the plagues.

The order of the plagues

Two different chapters in Tehillim (78:44-51; 105:28-36) review the plagues which struck the Egyptians. These chapters, however, list them in a different order than the Torah. Since the Sages tell us that the Torah does not always relate events in chronological order (Gemara Pesachim 6b), one could assume that the order in Tehillim is the correct one. Rebbi Yehudah meant to assert, through his acronym, that the order in which they appear in the Torah is indeed correct.

(3)

Da'as Zekenim quotes a novel explanation for Rebbi Yehudah's acronym from RYBA [Rebbi Yitzchak ben Asher II], which is also cited in part by Hagahos Maimonei. RYBA makes two points. First, he remarks that if one writes the three sets of acronyms one on top of the other, the third letters of each grouping backwards spell "CHoSHeKH" which in Hebrew (*choshech*) means darkness:

Two acrostics

D-TZ-"KH"
A-D-"SH"
B-A-"CH"-V

RYBA derives from this that darkness accompanied all of the other plagues. What this means is that during the plagues of blood, frogs, lice, etc., there was darkness, as well. (Of course, the darkness of the actual plague of darkness, when its time came, was a much deeper darkness—see the text and Rashi of Shemos 10:21)

RYBA's second remark is that the plagues which occupy the third position in each set, always came together. That is to say, the plague of lice was accompanied not only by darkness, but by boils, as well. Similarly, the plague of boils was accompanied by lice and darkness, and the plague of darkness, was accompanied by boils and lice. (They are listed individually in the Torah because as the turn for each of them came, that particular plague was dominant. Thus lice was dominant when the time came for the third plague, boils at the sixth, and darkness at the ninth.)

RYBA contends that the inter-connectedness of these plagues is attested to through a diagram containing the three three-letter words "KiNiM" [lice], "SHeCHiN" [boils] and "CHoSHeKH" [darkness], arranged one on top of the other. Interestingly, the names of the three plagues are spelled out in such a diagram both horizontally and vertically:

CH—SH—KH
SH—CH—N
KH—N—M

The authors of the Tosafos are themselves perplexed by RYBA's explanation. Although these are intriguing observations regarding Rebbi Yehudah's acrostic, there would seem to be no source for RYBA's assertions in Talmudic literature. To make such assumptions solely on such vaporous "proofs" would seem to be taking too much for granted.

Perhaps we may suggest a new source for RYBA's claims. It may be that RYBA was alerted to his explanation by the differences between the Torah's version of the plagues and the versions presented in Tehillim.

In Tehillim 105, nearly all of the plagues are listed in their proper order. (The plagues of mixed animals and lice seem to be reversed in verse 31. However, upon further examination, that verse may be read, "Hashem plagued [the Egyptians] with mixed animals *while they were still recovering from* the lice that had filled their borders." A similar reading answers the apparent reversal of hail and boils in verse 32. According to this reading, the verse is connecting the last plague of each of Rebbi Yehudah's trios with the first of the next group. This is meant to emphasize that the Egyptians had no respite between the plagues.) Only the plague of darkness is out of place. It is listed first, instead of second to last.

This may be what prompted RYBA to suggest that darkness actually accompanied "all" of the plagues. In Tehillim, darkness is listed before the plague of blood, since from the beginning darkness was present. In fact, the entire year of the plagues may have been characterized by darkness.

Perhaps this is why Rebbi Yehudah's acrostic spelled CHoSHeKH "backwards", the way RYBA arranged it. Rebbi Yehudah was pointing out that the order in which *choshech* appears among the plagues must be "reversed"—as it indeed is, in Tehillim! RYBA's suggestion accounts for the order of the plagues in Tehillim 105, at the same time explaining Rebbi Yehudah's acronym.

The second half of RYBA's explanation may be connected to another verse in Tehillim. In Tehillim 78, when the plagues of the Egyptians in Egypt are specified, three of the plagues are omitted altogether. The three which are left out are none other than lice, boils and darkness. If we accept the RYBA's proposal that these three were *not* three distinct plagues, but rather they always came simultaneously, then it may be that they actually were not omitted. They are alluded to in verse 43, which tells us, "He performed 'signs' in Egypt, and 'wonders' in the field of Tzoan [the Egyptian capital]." This verse can be seen as alluding to an unspecified group of mixed signs and wonders that struck the Egyptians all at once. Since lice, boils and darkness are not mentioned elsewhere in the psalm, the RYBA may have concluded that they are the plagues to which the verse is referring!

(In Psalm 105 the plague of pestilence appears to be omitted. However, since verse 27 states, "[Moshe and Aharon] put on *them* [the Egyptians] the signs," the reason for this omission is quite evident. Unlike the other plagues, pestilence did *not* affect the Egyptians bodily. The rest of the plagues either harmed the Egyptians physically, or deprived them of their primary food source. Pestilence, however, only affected the Egyptian's livestock.)

Although we have found a possible source for RYBA's proposal, it remains to be explained *why* these three plagues function differently than the other plagues. Why did *these* three plagues specifically always come together?

The answer to this may lie in an observation made by Hadar Zekenim (on Shemos 7:25) in the name of Rebbi Yosef Bechor-Shor, in a different context. Rebbi Yosef notes that, as opposed to *all* the other plagues, lice, boils and darkness are phenomena which naturally occur from time to time. This statement may lend us insight into RYBA's assertion. The Egyptians might have been inclined to deny that these three plagues were signs from Hashem. Therefore, they always came together. This demonstrated to everyone that the plagues were *not* simply a natural occurrence. The plagues of lice, boils, and darkness were each accompanied by two "witnesses"—i.e., the other two plagues—to testify that they were indeed punishments sent by G-d!

III
Later commentaries offer other explanations for Rebbi Yehudah's acronym

(4)

A readable sentence

Tosafos Yom Tov (Avos 5:4) remarks that Rebbi Yehudah's acronym, "DeTZaCH ADaSH B'ACHaV," can be read as actual words. "ADaSH," or "ADuSH," means "I will trample" (exegetically exchanging the *alef* for an *ayin*); "B'ACHaV" means "with a slaughtering sword" (transposing the *ves* and the *ches*. In Yechezkel 21:20—"*ivchas cherev.*" The word "*ivchas*" *alef, ves, ches*, means to slaughter [or intimidate] with a sword.)

Tosafos Yom Tov does not explain how we are to understand "*Detzach*," but we may suggest that it be read "*Ditzach*," meaning "your joy"—i.e.,, referring to the firstborn, who are their parents' pride and joy. The entire acronym would now read, "Your joy, I will trample and slaughter with a sword!" Read in this manner, Rebbi Yehudah's acronym alludes to the killing of the firstborn. (The Haggadah—s.v. "*Bizroa Netuya*"—in fact uses "the sword" as a description for the killing of the firstborn.) Rebbi Yehudah's acronym hints at the fact that all of the plagues were simply stepping stones to the climactic plague that freed us from bondage—The death of the firstborn. Witness to the centrality of this plague in the story of the Exodus, is the fact that the very first statement Moshe is told to make to Pharaoh is, "If you refuse to let My children go, I shall kill your firstborn!" (Shemos 4:23).

Perhaps we may add a twist to Tosafos Yom Tov's suggestion, noting the point at which Rebbi Yehudah's acronym appears in the Haggadah.

The last of the ten plagues is not referred to as the plague of "*bechoros*" [the firstborn], but as the plague of *makkas bechoros* [the killing of the firstborn]. As various commentaries point out, this may be alluding to what the Midrash tells us about the last of the ten plagues. According to the Midrash, when Moshe warned Pharaoh that Hashem was going to kill the firstborn males, the firstborn Egyptians insisted that the Jews be allowed to leave. When Pharaoh refused, the firstborn took up their swords and waged a war against their countrymen, killing their own fathers. This is what the pasuk means in Tehillim 136, "He struck Egypt *with* their firstborn." (Pesikta Rabbasi 17:5; Rashi Tehillim 136:10; Tosafos Shabbos 87b.) This, then, is why the plague is referred to as "the killing of the firstborn"—in order that the phrase can be read in two ways. It can mean that the firstborn *were killed*, or that they *killed others.*

Perhaps Rebbi Yehudah, after hearing the words *makkas bechoros*, is proposing another way to hint at the Midrash's story through the mention of the ten plagues. His acronym is meant to be read, "Your joy, I will *cause to* trample and slaughter with a sword!"

(In fact, "B'ACHaV, instead of meaning "slaughter by sword," may be read as two words: *b'ach* [with a brother] and *av* [and father]. The acronym means that Hashem said He would cause the firstborn to "trample" their own "brothers and fathers"!)

(5)

The Gaon of Vilna (Shenos Eliyahu, end of Zera'im II), offers yet another approach to understanding Rebbi Yehudah's acronym.

The signs of the staff Shortly before the Haggadah cites Rebbi Yehudah, another statement of the Sages is cited asserting that the word *ossos* [signs] (in Devarim 26:8) is an allusion to Moshe's staff, with which he performed the miracles. Why is the staff alluded to in this manner? The staff "was used" to bring about the signs [the miraculous plagues]. Why should the staff itself be called a sign?

The Gaon of Vilna answers that in Shemos Rabbah 8:3, "Rebbi Yehudah" describes the staff that Moshe used. Moshe's staff was made of sapphire, and engraved with the acronym of the plagues—"DeTZaCH ADaSH B'ACHaV." This, then, may be why the staff is referred to as *ossos*. Inscribed in the staff were "signs" [letters, an acronym] alluding to the ten "signs" [plagues] that Hashem would bring upon Egypt!

If so, perhaps Rebbi Yehudah did not intend to "give" us a mnemonic by which to remember the plagues. Rather, he was informing us that this acronym had "already" been used as a way of packaging the plagues together. The acronym was used to symbolically invest Moshe's staff with the authority to act as the Divine agent for bringing the plagues upon the Egyptians. Rebbi Yehudah, following the opinion that he had presented in the Midrash, told us this in order to explain why the staff of Moshe is referred to as *ossos* in the preceding section of the Haggadah!

IV

Two gematrios:

Some of the commentators explain Rebbi Yehudah's acronym using gematria, where every letter of the Hebrew alphabet is accorded a numerical value, and any Hebrew word has the "value" of the sum of its letters.

(6)

"Asher"

Rav Shimshon of Ostropolier, a great Kabbalist of the 16th century, points out that the numerical gematria value of "DeTZaCH ADaSH B'ACHaV" is 501. This is the same value as the Hebrew word *asher* [that]. With this in mind, we may find many hints to the ten plagues in verses that use the word *asher*. Rav Shimshon quotes, for example, Shemos 4:17, "[Hashem said to Moshe,] Take this staff with you, that (*asher*) you may perform with it the signs." Take the staff and perform with it the *asher* [=501, or "DeTZaCH ADaSH B'ACHaV"] signs—the signs hinted at by the acronym equaling 501 that was engraved upon the staff! Similarly, "You shall tell your son and grandson the way that (*asher*) I punished the Egyptians" (Shemos 10:2, beginning of Parshas Bo). Tell them that I sent the Egyptians plagues with a numerical value totaling *asher* [=501].

Rav Shimshon was actually preceded in this gematria by Hagahos Maimonei, who fits it into another verse: "All the plagues that (*asher*) I have brought upon the Egyptians, I shall not bring upon you" (Shemos 15:26). All the plagues of Egypt, which total *asher* [=501], Hashem shall not bring upon us.

(7)

Finally, the Tosafists (in Hadar Zekenim) offer a unique gematria approach to Rebbi Yehudah's "DeTZaCH ADaSH B'ACHaV."

The portion of the Haggadah immediately following our acronym deals with a three-way argument as to how many plagues the Egyptians actually suffered. Although the Torah only openly mentions the ten plagues that affected the Egyptians in Egypt proper, the Torah hints that the Egyptians suffered "five times" as many plagues at the Reed Sea. This means that the Egyptians were plagued with "50" plagues at the sea, besides the ten plagues mentioned previously. Such is Rebbi Yossi haGlili's opinion.

The 600 makkos

Rebbi Eliezer disagrees. He contends that in Egypt, each plague was actually a "four-fold" plague. That brings up the mainland total to 40 *makkos*, and the sea-plague total to 5 x 40, or 200 plagues. Rebbi Akiva goes further, asserting that the plagues of Egypt were "five-fold" plagues. The mainland total is now 50 plagues, making the sea-plague total 250 plagues!

If we apply here the Talmudic dictum that, "These and those are both the words of Hashem" (i.e., all the opinions are correct to some measure), we can total all the suggested figures which makes a grand total of 100 plagues in Egypt itself, and 500 more by the sea. Rebbi Yehudah's acronym was meant as a mnemonic for the total number of plagues suggested by the Sages in the section following his "sign" in the recital of the Haggadah. "DeTZaCH ADaSH B'ACHaV" adds up to a gematria of 501, reminding us that the Egyptians suffered "500" plagues at the sea, plus another "1" hundred plagues in Egypt proper!

PARSHAS BO

Zrizus—The Quality of the Divine

BO

"Keep the matzos [of Pesach] from becoming chametz [fermented], for on this very day I took your multitudes out of the Land of Egypt" (Shemos 12:17).

R. Yoshiyah said, "Do not read the word as *matzos*, but rather read it as *mitzvos*—'Keep the mitzvos from becoming chametz'—since just as one should not allow matzos to ferment, so too one should not allow mitzvos to "ferment." Rather, if a mitzvah comes into your hand, do it immediately" (Rashi ibid., from Mechilta ad loc.).

The Mechilta tells us that in this verse the Torah is hinting at a much broader halachic concept than just baking matzos for Pesach. The Torah is teaching us that we must go to perform mitzvos [the commandments of Hashem] with *zerizus*—i.e., we must go swiftly.

The Maharal MiPrague raises two questions concerning the Mechilta's statement. Firstly, how can R. Yoshiyah change the reading of the word from the traditional vocalization in order to superimpose his homiletical interpretation on the Torah's words? Normally there must be some indication from the theme or context of a verse that supports such interpretations. The suggested "changes" in reading are only a tool to graphically demonstrate a point that can actually be learned from the traditional reading of the verse at hand.

Fermenting mitzvos

What, then, is the connection between the simple meaning of our verse and R. Yoshiyah's homily? Secondly, in what way does a mitzvah become "fermented", or spoiled, if it is not done immediately?

II

The Maharal addresses these two issues by assessing more carefully the nature of the mitzvah of matzah. In Devarim 16:3 we read "Do not eat leaven...; for seven days you should eat matzos...because you left Egypt with haste." The Torah clearly tells us that the mitzvah of eating matzah on Pesach is to remind us of the haste with which the Exodus took place. The matzah we eat brings to mind that when the Jews left Egypt they were so hurried that "they baked the dough which they had taken out Egypt into cakes of unleavened matzah, because they were expelled from Egypt and they were not able to delay" (Shemos 12:39).

The mitzvah of matzo

The Passover Haggadah makes this point even more clearly: "What does this matzah that we eat represent? It represents the fact that the dough of our forefathers had not had a chance to rise when Hashem suddenly appeared to them and redeemed them, as it says, 'They baked the dough which they had taken into matzos...'" (see also Sforno's comment on Shemos 12:17).

But this fact itself, the Maharal points out, requires explanation. Why is it important for us to remember that the Exodus from Egypt happened swiftly and suddenly? What is the underlying message in the great haste of the Jews leaving Egypt?

The Maharal explains that the lesson is that Hashem Himself—as opposed to any natural forces—took us out of Egypt. Any act done directly by Hashem takes place instantaneously because there is no element of mass or matter related to Hashem. A physical object has inertia to overcome in order to go into motion, but Hashem, Whose actions are purely spiritual, and are unimpeded by any physical qualities, can—and does—act with infinite speed. Besides, Hashem exists outside of the framework of space and time, and thus even when His actions take place on this physical world, they can take place without the passage of time.

(Although the Maharal does not openly make note of the fact, firm basis for his words can be found in the words of Chazal. In Chagigah 12b, the Gemara alludes to the fact that, in the words of Rashi (ad loc.), "all earthly acts are sluggish, while heavenly acts take place swiftly."—MK)

This, says the Maharal, is the key to the understanding of the mitzvah of matzah. The matzah that we eat reminds us of how rushed the events revolving around the exodus from Egypt were. This hurriedness is the mark of a divine act. It is the sure sign that the hand of Hashem was at work, shaping our destiny. " 'Hashem took us out of Egypt'—It was not an angel nor a seraph nor a messenger, but Hashem Himself Who took us out of Egypt"—(Passover Haggadah.) Therefore, it is necessary for us to remember the *swiftness* of the exodus. This is the Torah's way of insuring that future generations will always realize the extent of Hashem's love for the Bnai Yisrael.

Hashem took a "personal" involvement in the redemption—which is why it was carried out so suddenly.

III

Now we can explain Rav Yoshiyah's interpretation of our *pasuk*. The Maharal explains that the reason it is important to go to do a mitzvah swiftly is also related to what we have just explained. A mitzvah is the divine will on this world. When we perform a mitzvah, our intention is to demonstrate that it is not simply a mundane act. We would like to show that we are executing the will of our creator. Doing a mitzvah with *zerizus* accomplishes just that. By rushing to complete a mitzvah swiftly, we add to it the mark of our Creator, and show to everyone that what we are doing is His will!

A mitzvah is the Divine will on this world

This also explains what is meant by the "fermenting" of a mitzvah that is not done with the desired swiftness. Going to perform a mitzvah slowly, makes it appear to be a worldly act ("all earthly acts are sluggish"). In this sense, it is "fermented" or "spoiled." If we don't appreciate that the mitzvos we do are none other than the will of Hashem, even our mitzvos can become mundane acts! (Maharal, Gur Aryeh, Shemos 12:17; *Gevurot Hashem*, ch. 36)

IV

Perhaps the Maharal's insight into the concept of *zerizus* in performing mitzvos can be used to illuminate a seeming inconsistency in the words of Chazal regarding *zerizus*.

Two parts to zerizus

The Toras Kohanim (Tazria, Parsha I, quoted also in Gemara Pesachim 4a) teaches that although a circumcision may be performed at any time during a baby boy's eighth day, it is preferable to do it as early in the day as possible. This is derived from what the Torah writes about Avraham. The Torah tells us that "Avraham rose up early in the morning" to fulfill Hashem's commandment (Bereishis 22:3). Just as Avraham hurried to carry out Hashem's command first thing in the morning, so are we to take the first opportunity to perform a mitzvah. This concept is referred to as *zerizim makdimin lemitzvos* [the zealous do their mitzvos as soon as they are able].

Why is it necessary for Chazal to learn the importance of *zerizus* in performing mitzvos from two separate sources? If the Mechilta already learned the importance of swiftness from the matzos we bake for Pesach, why did the Toras Kohanim have to learn the same concept from Avraham's early rising?

Secondly, why do Chazal use two different expressions for describing the morals learned from these two *pesukim*? In one case, they tell us "*not* to ferment mitzvos," emphasizing the negative, while in the other case they tell us to "*do* mitzvos early", in the positive!

According to the Maharal's explanation, the above difficulties can be easily resolved. We may propose, based on the teachings of the Maharal, that there are two completely different ideas involved in doing a mitzvah swiftly.

Firstly, doing a mitzvah swiftly shows that one is anxious and eager to do mitzvos—*chibuv hamitzvah* [showing fondness for the mitzvah]. This is the more obvious reason for doing a mitzvah with *zerizus*. Secondly, as the Maharal pointed out, doing a mitzvah swiftly indicates that we consider it a heavenly act, and accordingly we would like to do it as heavenly acts are done, instantaneously. We may call this, *kiddush hamitzvah* [sanctifying the mitzvah].

It immediately becomes evident that the first concept only tells us *when* a mitzvah should be performed. It should be performed at the first opportunity. The speed at which the act is done, however, does not help to show *chibuv hamitzvah*. If anything, performing a mitzvah with undo haste would indicate a desire to get it over with, rather than eagerness. The second concept, though, does not relate to *when*, but to *how* the mitzvah should be done. It should be performed with haste and not sluggishly. Once the mitzvah is already under way it should be finished swiftly, in order to make it clear to all that it is a spiritual act; it is the will of Hashem. Doing the mitzvah at the first opportunity or leaving it to a later time, however, does not contribute any spiritual dimension to the act of the mitzvah.

We may now suggest that the Toras Kohanim is dealing with the first concept—*chibuv hamitzvah*. We learn from Avraham Avinu to rush to *start* the performance of a mitzvah at the first opportunity. The Mechilta, on the other hand, learns the other ideal—*kiddush hamitzvah*—from the matzos we bake before Pesach. If we want our mitzvah to be a spiritual act, then we must carry it out as swiftly as possible. This is what the Mechilta means by saying, "If a mitzvah *comes into your hand*, do it immediately", i.e., if you have already started to perform a mitzvah, then complete it *immediately* (—or, as the Midrash Lekach Tov puts it, "do it *swiftly*")!

This also explains the difference between the tone of the two expressions. The first expression is made in a positive manner, because it is only a recommended embellishment to the performance of the mitzvah that is added by doing it early. If we don't show our fondness for the mitzvah, however, the mitzvah that is eventually performed is in no way affected by this.

The second concept is stated in a negative tone. If the mitzvah is not done in accordance with this concept, it is not merely lacking embellishment. Rather, sluggishness in performing a mitzvah makes the mitzvah appear to be a mundane act, thus "spoiling" the mitzvah, as the Maharal so beautifully explained! Thus, the teachings of the Mechilta and of the Toras Kohanim do not contradict each other at all. Rather, they complement each other wonderfully!

PARSHAS BESHALACH

When Are We To Sing The Praises Of Hashem?

"On that day, Hashem saved Israel from the Egyptians, and the Bnai Yisrael saw the Egyptians dead on the shore of the sea.... At that time [*Az yashir*] Moshe and the Bnai Yisrael sang the following song to Hashem..." (Shemos 14:30, 15:1).

When the Israelites saw the downfall of their Egyptian oppressors they were moved to sing the "Song of the Sea" to praise Hashem for their miraculous exodus. Why, however, does the Torah emphasize that it was "at that time" that they sang [i.e., *Az yashir*]? It would seem more appropiate for the *pasuk* to simply state "*Then* Moshe and the Bnai Yisrael sang [*vayashir*]. The Torah seems to be bringing out a point involving the *timing* of the song. What is the message of the words *Az yashir*? (See Rashi ad loc.)

The Sh'lah (c. 1550) offers an interesting approach to explain why the Torah emphasizes that it was only "at that time" that the Bnai Yisrael sang their song of praise. In Divrei Hayyamim II 20:15-21 we read that a prophet named Yachziel promises the Jewish King Yehoshaphat victory in his battle against his enemies. Following this prophecy, the king appointed singers to go before the army's front lines and sing praises to Hashem for His salvation. From here, the Sh'lah points out, it is evident that when victory and salvation are assured through a prophet's prophecy, it is appropriate to praise Hashem for His salvation immediately, even *before* the predicted triumph actually takes place.

Singing before the salvation

(We may add an observation to that of the Sh'lah. Although a guarantee of victory is enough to elicit praises to Hashem even before a salvation actually occurs, the praises are *not* to be sung immediately upon hearing the prophecy. It is only when the salvation itself actually begins that we are to sing praises to Hashem for saving us. This can be concluded from the fact that even Yehoshaphat had the singers sing as they marched out to the battlefield. Or, based on D.H. II 20:19, perhaps it is appropriate to sing the praise of Hashem twice: the first time immediately, and the second time at the start of the salvation.—MK)

The Bnai Yisrael, the Sh'lah continues, were told on *Rosh Chodesh* Nissan of their impending liberation from the Egyptians, which was several weeks before the events at the Red Sea occurred (see Shemos 12:17-18). It would thus have been proper for them to break out in song before the drowning of the Egyptians. (As I noted above, it may not have been necessary to praise Hashem immediately upon hearing the prophecy on *Rosh Chodesh*. Nevertheless, on the fifteenth of Nissan—the night of the Exodus from Egypt—they should have already started to sing to Hashem, since at that point Hashem's promise actually began to come to fruition.—MK)

This, then, is the reason that the Torah stresses that the people did not sing to Hashem until after seeing the Egyptians dead on the shore. The Torah is admonishing the Bnai Yisrael for not having placed their full faith in Hashem's promise of salvation. They ought to have thanked Hashem immediately on the fifteenth of Nissan; instead it was only "at that time"—i.e., after the victory was complete—that the "people believed in Hashem and in Moshe" (14:31) and sang the song to Hashem.

Based on this insight the Sh'lah explains why the *Hallel* song is not recited in its entirety during the Pesach prayers except for the first day (or the first two days in the Diaspora). On Pesach we attempt to actually relive the Exodus from Egypt, as is mentioned several times in the Haggadah. Perhaps we are trying to counteract the weakness of faith shown by our forefathers, who waited to sing until the seventh day of Pesach, when the sea split. We therefore sing the praises of *Hallel* to Hashem for the *entire* salvation of Pesach on the first night (and day) of Pesach, which is the time of the *beginning* of Hashem's salvation. It is therefore no longer necessary for us to say *Hallel* throughout the remainder of Pesach!

II

Singing after the salvation

The Sh'lah teaches us that it is proper, as well as expected, to sing out to Hashem even before His salvation has been completed, as long as it has already begun. (See Rav Itzele of Volozhin, in *Peh Kadosh* to Shemos 15:19, who also seems to be of such an opinion. He contends that the Jews actually *did* sing to Hashem before the salvation was fully completed. Although the Jews didn't sing out on the fifteenth of Nissan, they did start to sing while they were still in the sea, even before the Egyptians were drowned.)

This would seem to stand in contradiction to the Vilna Gaon's words. In commenting on the blessing (in the *Shemoneh Esrei)* of *Re'eh Be'onyenu*, the son of the Vilna Gaon quotes his father's explanation of the verse in Tehillim 13:6: "I trust in Your kindness; my heart rejoices in Your salvation; I will sing out to Hashem when he deals kindly with me." The Gaon asserts that the three parts of this verse are discussing three different periods:

"I trust in Your kindness" means that Before the salvation, King David trusts that Hashem will save him.

"My heart rejoices in Your salvation"—means that As the salvation takes place, King David rejoices in it.

"I will sing out to Hashem when he deals kindly with me"—means that after the salvation has been completed, King David will then sing praise and thanks to Hashem (see Siddur haGra, *Birchas Re'eh Be'onyenu*).

From the Gaon's words it would seem that although one's heart may be filled with joy upon learning of Hashem's impending kindness, it is appropriate to sing thanks to Hashem only after the act of salvation is actually accomplished. (The Brisker Rav clearly states a similiar idea in the name of his father, Rav Chaim Soloveitchik [quoted in *Emek Borsch*, p. 124]. Basing his words on Tehillim 13:6 which is the *pasuk* that the Gaon explained, Rav Chaim contends that even if someone is assured by a prophet that salvation is guaranteed, it is improper to sing praise to Hashem for His kindness until it is actually experienced. The source for Rav Chaim's contention is undoubtedly the aforementioned comment of the Gaon. See also the Netziv's *Ha'amek Davar* to Shemos 15:1, who takes a similar position, bringing textual support to his stand from a Yerushalmi, Pesachim 10:6.)

Support can be found for the Gaon's words in the Midrash Shocher Tov. The verse in Tehillim 18:4 states: "I call out praise to Hashem, and I am saved from my enemies." Although on the surface this verse seems to imply that praises of Hashem are called for in *advance* of His salvation, the Midrash Shocher Tov (ad loc.) insists that this verse must be understood as if it were written in inverted order: "After I am saved from my enemies I call out praises to Hashem." (It is not infrequent for a *vav* which introduces a second clause of a sentence, to indicate a *cause* for the first clause, rather than an effect.—MK) This Midrash is clearly in agreement with the Gaon's understanding. Only after being saved does King David sing praise to Hashem. (See Emek Borsch, ibid., who did not see this Midrash and found in necessary to offer another interpretation of the verse instead.)

The Midrash continues, however, and quotes another opinion. According to Rav Huna the verse in Tehillim may be read as it stands, without inverting the order of the words: "I call out praise to Hashem, and (afterwards) I am saved from my enemies." It is a reference, says Rav Huna, to the episode that the Sh'lah had quoted, where Yehoshaphat had sung praises to Hashem *before* the salvation actually came about.

At first it would appear that there are two distinct opinions in the Midrash. According to one opinion, songs of praise are not to be sung until after victory is granted, in accordance with the view of the Gaon; according to the other opinion the songs may be, and should be, sung as soon as the act of salvation is begun. However, it does not seem likely that there are two disparate opinions in this matter. The story of Yehoshaphat in Divrei Hayyamim clearly seems to support Rav Huna's opinion. How, then, could there be disagreement on this matter? (See Emek Borsch, ibid., who offers a solution to the question by differentiating between *songs* and *thanks.* For lack of space, we will not discuss that theme here.)

III

It would appear that, in reality, both approaches to singing praise to Hashem are valid, but for different situations. There are times when song should precede salvation and times when it should follow, as follows:

Two types of salvations

When salvation is predicted by a prophet, a victory is so assured that there is no doubt whatsoever as to the outcome of the battle. Since success has been guaranteed by a prophet of Hashem, there is no reason to wait for the entire salvation process to come to its completion. However, when such salvation has *not* been promised by a prophet, and thus *not* guaranteed, then Hashem should be thanked only *after* the salvation is complete. Although one must always have faith that Hashem will do what is best for us, we cannot know that He will see fit to save us. Perhaps we are unworthy of His kindness! Therefore, only when full victory has been granted can a person sing out the praises of Hashem for His salvation.

King David, although his faith in Hashem was absolute ("I trust in Your kindness"), and he knew that Hashem would grant him only what was best for him, was nevertheless not *assured* that victory would be his. The Gemara (Berachos 4a) mentions that although David knew himself to be worthy and righteous, he was always concerned that he may sin at any moment. He was constantly concerned that he would disqualify himself from being deserving of unique Divine protection. Thus, although trusting in Hashem, David was never certain that victory would be his until he actually experienced it. That is why in his case, praises of Hashem were sung only "when He deals kindly with me"—after the salvation.

Yehoshaphat, on the other hand, was guaranteed victory through prophecy—and prophecies spoken through a prophet are never rescinded— and thus he was able to sing to Hashem even before the decisive victory occurred. The same applies to the Bnai Yisrael upon their liberation from Egypt. Since the prophet (Moshe Rabbeinu) had promised them salvation in

Hashem's name, they ought to have started singing praises to Hashem at the very start of the Exodus.

The Midrash is thus not recording two separate viewpoints about which should come first—salvation or song. If the verse in Tehillim 18:4 is taken to refer to David (which is the simple meaning of the verse) then it must be understood as an inverted sentence. If, however, it can be taken as a reference to the events of Yehoshaphat's battle, it may be interpreted without resorting to inversion!

(After writing this piece, I was proud to find that the conclusion I came to has been attributed to Rav Chaim Soloveitchik himself, according to the *Haggadah Mibeis Levi*, p. 186. See also Rav David Goldberg in *Shiras David* to Shemos 15:1, p. 260.—MK)

PARSHAS YISRO

A People United

"And all the people answered together and said, 'All that Hashem has spoken we will do [*na'aseh*]!'"(Shemos 19:8).

"Moshe came and told the people all the words of Hashem and all the laws, and all the people answered with one voice and said, 'All the things that Hashem spoke we will do [*na'aseh*]!' " (ibid. 24:3)

"[Moshe] took the Book of the Covenant and read it in the ears of the people, and they said, 'All that Hashem has spoken we will do and we will hear [*na'aseh v'nishma*]!' " (ibid. 24:7)

The three *pesukim* cited above describe the Bnai Yisrael's acceptance of the Torah at various stages in the drama of *Kabbalas haTorah* at Sinai. If we examine the wording closely, however, we will see that there are some interesting differences between these different stages. For one thing, in the first two verses the "togetherness" with which the people expressed their readiness to accept Hashem's words is stressed, a fact which is *not* mentioned in the account of the third stage. Also, the first two times the Bnai Yisrael only mention their eagerness to *do*, i.e., to act upon Hashem's commandments, while in the third verse they say that they will do "and hear" Hashem's commandments. What is the reason for these variations in the phrases the people used to demonstrate their willingness to accept the Torah?

United to "do," divided to "hear"

II

An interpretation of these verses is offered by my father-in-law, haGaon Rav

Gedalyah Aharon Rabinowitz, the Monastrishtcher Rebbe, who insightfully explains the discrepancies in the expressions used in the three verses in his work *Neveh Tzaddikim* on the Haggadah shel Pesach.

Unity and disunity may be complementary

Rabbi Rabinowitz explains that there are two parts to the acceptance of the Torah: (1) the acceptance to perform and obey the 613 mitzvos of the Torah in their entirety, and (2) the acceptance to study these mitzvos in order to better understand what exactly Hashem wants us to gain through their fulfillment. The first facet of Torah acceptance is what the Bnai Yisrael refer to as doing the commandments of Hashem, or *na'aseh*. The second facet is what they called *nishma*, or hearing the commandments of Hashem—with the connotation of *understanding* what is being heard. (The verb *shema*, which is usually translated as listen or hear can also signify to understand, as in the verse "They did not realize that Yosef 'understood them' [*shomea*]"—Bereishis 42:23.)

Regarding the first aspect of fulfilling the Torah's commandments, all Jews are equal. Every member of the community of Israel is obligated to perform the mitzvos that apply to them in the same fashion. (There may be varying opinions as to a *specific* detail in a particular mitzvah, but all agree on the *general* obligations entailed in keeping each of the mitzvos.

When it comes to the second aspect, however, this unity is not evident. Since Hashem created no two people with the same mind, there will always be differences between one individual and another regarding the understanding and meaning of the mitzvos. This, obviously, was all part of Hashem's will in the Giving of the Torah. These differences in understanding are expressed in the different attitudes that Torah scholars have towards the performance of the mitzvos. While some Torah scholars will demonstrate a boundless love for their Creator when performing the mitzvos, others show more of their awe of Hashem. Some Torah scholars approach Judaism with a more intellectual bent, while others may have a more emotional leaning. Some will choose to "specialize" in one particular mitzvah, giving it more emphasis than others in their daily lives, because they feel that this mitzvah in particular carries a special message for them, and can offer them guidance in life, ultimately bringing them closer to Hashem. No two human beings are exactly the same as far as the *nishma* of the Torah is concerned.

This, the Monastrishtcher Rebbe explains, is the difference between the expressions used in the above verses. When Moshe first went to the Bnai Yisrael, before the Giving of the Torah, he told them "the words of Hashem and all the laws" (Shemos 24:3), which, as Rashi explains, is a reference to the Seven Laws of Noach and the mitzvos given at Marah (Shemos 15:25). At that point the people answered "with one voice" that they would *do* these mitzvos. As far as the performance of the mitzvos are concerned, the Bnai

Yisrael accepted the Torah "with one voice"—in one unified fashion. Similarly, in Shemos 19:8, it was only in reference to the *observance* of the mitzvos that the people responded *together*.

But when Moshe "took the Book of the Covenant (Rashi explains this as referring to the entire Torah from Bereishis until the events of *Matan Torah*) and read it in the ears of the people," the people saw that the Torah was more than just a list of commandments and obligations, but an entire Sefer Torah, which had to be studied, analyzed and understood. To this, they exclaimed, "*na'aseh v'nishma*—we will do and we will understand!"

Now the people did not respond "together" or "with one voice". *Nishma* was to be a personal experience which would, of necessity, vary from one individual to the next. Every person would have his own unique approach in serving Hashem and understanding the meaning of the mitzvos. Therefore, when they accepted not only the "doing" but also the "understanding" of the Torah, they answered as individuals: "We will do and we will understand!" [Haggadah shel Pesach *Neveh Tzaddikim*, towards the end, on the verse "*legozer yam suf ligzarim*"]

III

A similar idea is expressed by haGaon Rabbi Akiva Eiger (c. 1800 C.E.). At the end of Masseches Taanis the Gemara says that in the future Hashem will have all the tzaddikim dance in a circle, and Hashem will sit in the center of the circle in Gan Eden. Each of the tzaddikim will then point to Hashem and say, "This is our G-d; this is Hashem, Whom we have so longed to behold!"

The circular dance of the righteous

What is the symbolism behind a dance that is specifically in a circle around Hashem? Rav Akiva Eiger explains the lesson of this dance of the tzaddikim as follows:

In this world every tzaddik has a unique, individual approach to serving Hashem. On the surface, each one of them appears to be heading in a completely different direction. The truth is, however, that this is not the case. All the different tzaddikim are united by a common goal—to draw closer to Hashem and fulfill His will in the best possible manner. In the World-to-Come this will become apparent to everyone. The tzaddikim will dance around Hashem *arranged in a circle*. In a circle, every individual faces a slightly different direction—yet they all revolve around the same central point. The tzaddikim, although each has a unique approach, are all trying to accomplish the same goal. Their lives revolve around the same central point, the point where "Hashem is sitting." In the World-to-Come, each tzaddik will point to Hashem and announce to everyone that this is their G-d to Whom they had strived to come close and serve throughout their lives! [Rabbi Akiva Eiger, quoted in *Chut Hameshulash* and *Toras Emes*].

PARSHAS MISHPATIM

Angel's Bread

"The man [who lived in Hebron] was the greatest of the giants" (Yehoshua 14:15). "This refers to our forefather Avraham, whose height was equal to that of seventy-four men. The amount of food and drink he consumed was enough for seventy-four men, and he had the strength of that many men as well" (Concluding Beraisa of Masseches Sofrim).

What message can we learn from this cryptic statement of the Sages? What is the significance of Avraham's gargantuan proportions? Was he literally seventy-four times as large as the average person? We find no hint in the Torah that Avraham was of such extraordinary dimensions! And what is the significance of the number seventy-four? The Vilna Gaon offers an enlightening interpretation of this Midrash based on an incident from this week's parsha.

Avraham's meal

II

Three guests visited Avraham after his historic circumcision (Bereishis 18:2). Avraham offered them a meal fit for kings (ibid. 5-8). Although we are told that these guests were actually angels (Rashi Bereishis 18:1), the Torah concludes that the guests ate what they were offered (18:8). Since when do the heavenly hosts eat food? The Gemara in Bava Metzia 86b asserts that the angels only appeared to be eating the food, but they didn't actually eat it. If so, however, why should the Torah itself refer to their action as "eating?" The Torah tells us in this week's parsha:

The 74 people

"Moshe, Aharon, Nadav, Avihu, and seventy of the elders of Israel climbed [Mount Sinai].... They gazed at Hashem and they ate and they drank. [They saw the

Divine Glory, and when He accepted the offerings they brought to Him, they were as happy as if they had been eating and drinking.]" (Shemos 24:9-11, according to Targum Onkelos).

"They were nourished from the Divine Presence, just as the angels" (Avos d'Rabbi Nasan, 1:8).

We are accustomed to thinking of eating as a singularly mundane act. The need to eat demonstrates our physical shortcomings. However, there is another, spiritual experience metaphorically referred to as "eating." When experiencing a "meal" of this sort, the soul itself is nourished in much the same way that our bodies obtain nourishment from the food that we eat. This spiritual nourishment is received from nothing other than the Glory of the Divine Presence of Hashem (*Ziv HaShechinah*). This non-physical culinary pleasure is an eternal one, that can take place without a physical world. It is this experience that is involved in the eternal bliss of the World-to-Come.

"In the World-to-Come there is no eating, and no drinking, no childbearing and no work, no jealousy, no hatred and no competition. Rather, the righteous sit with their crowns on their heads and enjoy the Glory of the Divine Presence, as it is stated, 'They gazed at Hashem and they ate and they drank' " (Berachos 17a).

This spiritual food can even provide, at times, physical sustenance. Moshe was in heaven for forty days. As he told the Jews, "Bread I did not eat; water I did not drink" (Devarim 9:9). What did his body subsist on, then? On the Glory of the Divine Presence! (Midrash Aggadah, ibid., see also Rabbenu Bachye loc. cit.)

Not only Moshe, but the entire Jewish nation once shared in such a Divine experience. For forty years, the Jews subsisted on heavenly Manna, which Hashem showered on the Jewish encampment in the desert (Shemos 16:35). What was this mysterious Manna, that had such amazing nutritional qualities? Rebbi Akiva tells us in the Gemara, "It was the bread upon which the angels subsist" (Yoma 75b). Rebbi Yishmael, though, found Rebbi Akiva's suggestion ridiculous. "Go and tell Rebbi Akiva that he is making a mistake. Do angels eat bread? Even when *Moshe*, a human being, was in heaven, he did not eat or drink!" What indeed did Rebbi Akiva mean? Rebbi Akiva must have been referring to the phenomenon we have mentioned above. The "bread" of the angels is the Glory of the Divine Presence, upon which they subsist. The Manna that the Jews ate had in it that quality. According to Rebbi Akiva, for forty years the Jews drew their physical sustenance from the Glory of the Divine Presence! (See *Keli Yekar*, Shemos 16:4.)

The meal on Mount Sinai that Moshe, Aharon and those who accompanied them experienced was not a physical cuisine. It was none other than the spiritual dining of the angels in heaven, and of the righteous in the World-to-Come. How many people partook of this "meal?" The seventy elders, Moshe and Aharon, Nadav and Avihu, or a total of *seventy-four* people. The meal that Avraham "fed" the angels, suggests the Vilna Gaon, consisted of the same Glory of the Divine Presence of which these seventy four men "partook." This is why his Divine visitors were able to "eat" with him. Although it looked as though they were eating the physical food, the angels were actually "eating" spiritual, other-worldly food. This is why the Torah refers to what the angels did as "eating." This is what Masseches Sofrim meant to say. The food and drink which Avraham served the angels was the same food and drink that is referred to in the story of the seventy-four people who climbed Mount Sinai! (Vilna Gaon, quoted in *Kol Eliyahu* #239, and in *Midrash Peliah*, Warsaw 1910, #17)

We may add, how did it come about that the angels found their spiritual food in Avraham's house?

Rashi (Bereishis 18:3) tells us that the Divine Presence did not depart from Avraham's tent while he was serving his three guests. If so, we can understand how the guests—who were actually angels—enjoyed the Glory of the Divine Presence while eating with Avraham. Hashem's Presence was right there with them, waiting for Avraham to finish entertaining his guests! In fact, this may be what the verse itself is describing when it tells us, "And he [Avraham] stood by them under the tree, and they ate." The Midrash tells us that Hashem appeared to Avraham in a *tree* (see Shemos 3:4). Perhaps, then, the verse can be read, "And He [Hashem] stood by them under the tree, and [because of that] they ate [the angels "dined" from the Glory of His Divine Presence]!"

III

What does the rest of the quote from Masseches Sofrim mean, then? How was Avraham's "height" and "strength" equal to that of seventy-four men?

The Divine meal

And why was it specifically at this point in Avraham's life, that his meal (and height and strength) is compared to that of seventy-four people? Let us first consider more thoroughly how "gazing at the Divine Presence" can be nourishing to the soul and to the body.

The Rambam describes the eternal bliss of the righteous in the World-to-Come:

"Our Sages said (in Gemara Berachos 17a, quoted above), 'In the World-to-Come there is no eating, and no drinking...rather, the righteous sit with their crowns on their heads and enjoy the Glory of the Divine Presence.'

'With their *crowns* on their *heads*'—Their knowledge and understanding of Hashem's ways, which brought them to merit a share in the World-to-Come, is with them. This is what the Gemara refers to as 'their crowns.' King Solomon refers to this as 'the crown with which his mother crowned him' (Shir HaShirim 3:11).

What knowledge and understanding [are we referring to]?

'They enjoy the Divine Presence'—they know and understand the truth of G-d, to an extent that would be impossible while they existed in a dusky and lowly physical body" (Rambam, Hilchos Teshuvah 8:2).

The "enjoyment of the Glory of the Divine Presence" involves the appreciation of Hashem's power, and the realization that He is the only true existence. Hashem "rested His Presence on Mount Sinai" (Shemos 19:18) in order to give us the Torah. In part, this means that Hashem appeared to us in a cloud of smoke, amidst the crack of thunder and the blast of the shofar, so that we would be able to grasp more fully His absolute majesty (see Tetzaveh essay, section II, p. 93). At that point, Moshe, Aharon, Nadav, Avihu and the seventy elders went up the mountain, each to a different height, while the rest of the nation remained at the foot of the mountain (according to Rashi to Shemos 19:24, 24:10). Hashem revealed His Presence to these seventy-four people to a greater degree than He did to the other Jews.

In fact, the very verse that the Rambam quotes about the crown of King Solomon, is taken by our Sages to refer to the time Hashem gave us the Torah. "Go out and see, daughters of Zion [nations of the world], King Shlomo [Hashem] adorned by the crown with which His mother [the Jewish nation] crowned Him on his wedding day [the day He gave the Torah to Israel, on Mount Sinai]..." (Mishna, Taanis 26b). Hashem was adorned by the Jews' newly achieved heights in the appreciation of His Divine Glory. In this manner, the seventy-four people partook of the "meal" of the righteous in the World-to-Come.

The same applies for those who ate the Manna. They saw with their own eyes that Hashem miraculously provided them with all their needs while they wandered helplessly in the desert. This brought them to a greater appreciation of Hashem's unlimited power. It was on this "Divine meal" that they subsisted.

IV

The enormous height and strength of Avraham

Avraham was "as tall as seventy-four people." This means he reached spiritual heights as great as the seventy-four people who climbed Mount Sinai. Hashem appeared to Avraham the same way He appeared to the Jews at the giving of the Torah. (In fact, the Midrash tells us that Hashem only gave the Torah to Moshe on Mount Sinai in Avraham's merit—Shemos Rabbah 28:1.)

Before Avraham had a Bris Milah, he was still a prophet. However, Avraham couldn't appreciate the full extent of Hashem's Presence until after he was circumcised (Rashi, Bereishis 17:3). The first time Hashem appeared to Avraham after his circumcision was when the angels came to visit him (Bereishis 18:1). It was specifically at this point in his life, that the Masseches

Sofrim reveals to us Avraham's greatness. Avraham now had achieved his greatest spiritual heights.

In what way was Avraham as "strong" as the seventy-four men? Rashi tells us that although the seventy-four men all "saw the Divine Glory," not all of them reacted to it properly. Moshe and Aharon acted with respect, but the others did not conduct themselves in a fitting manner. Their physical desires influenced their behavior (see Parasha-Page, Shemini 5754). Avraham, however, was as holy as the greatest of the seventy-four people. His spiritual base was strong enough to be able to experience such a Divine revelation, and come away unscathed!

PARSHAS TERUMAH

Just An Exaggeration...

"Make a *paroches* [a hanging curtain] of turquoise wool, purple wool, scarlet wool, and spun linen" (Shemos 26:31).

"There is a Mishnah that says: 'The pile of ash [from the burnt *korbanos*] in the middle of the altar sometimes had as much as three hundred *kors* of ashes in it.' Rava explained, 'This number is an exaggeration' " (Gemara Chullin 90b).

"There are three places where the Sages spoke with exaggeration: concerning the pile of ash on the altar, concerning the golden vine of the Beis Hamikdash and concerning the *paroches*. Concerning the *paroches*, the Mishnah (Shekalim 8:5) tells us: 'The *paroches* [of the Beis Hamikdash] was the thickness of a handbreadth ...and was forty by twenty *amos* (cubits)...and three hundred Kohanim would immerse it in a mikveh (to make it ritually pure for use in the Beis Hamikdash).' The exaggeration in the Mishnah is the claim that 300 Kohanim would immerse it" —(Rashi ibid.).

Our Sages seem to be telling us here that the Mishnah's text is not always meant to be taken literally. Even that great compilation is not free from exaggeration. This comes as a surprise, after reading tractate after tractate in which the Talmud meticulously infers halachic rulings not only from extra words in the Mishnah, but even from extra letters in a word of the Mishnah. How are we to relate to the statement that the Mishnah sometimes does not really mean what it says?

The Vilna Goan in *Kol Eliyahu*, Parshas Terumah, offers an ingenious explanation for the claim that three hundred Kohanim immersed the *paroches*. As the Mishnah mentioned, the *paroches*' dimensions were forty by twenty *amos*. The *amos* used in the Beis Hamikdash measurements consisted of five handbreadths each (Mishnah Kelim 17:10). Thus, the perimeter of the *paroches* was 2 x (40+20) = 120 *amos*, or 600 handbreadths. If the maximum number of Kohanim participated in the mitzvah of immersing the *paroches*, there would be room for exactly 300 people to grasp it, each one taking up two handbreadths of the perimeter with their two hands!

The paroches exaggeration

Why, then did the Gemara say that the number 300 was an exaggeration?

Because although it was *theoretically* possible for three hundred Kohanim to hold the *paroches*, it was never *actually* handled by this maximum number of people. It would be unlikely for the Kohanim's hands to be so closely spaced as to allow them to cover every inch of the perimeter.

Nonetheless, the Mishnah did not choose its "exaggerated" figure randomly. Rather, the number 300 was chosen because it represents the theoretical maximum number of Kohanim who could participate in this mitzvah. In this manner the Mishnah means to say that even the entire maximum of 300 Kohanim would have taken part in the immersion, had the circumstances to do so arisen.

II

An inconsistency in the Gaon's calculations?

The *Yefe Enayim* (beginning of Masseches Tamid), however, raises a serious objection to this calculation of the Gaon. According to the Mishnah (Kelim 17:10) and the Gemara (Menachos 97b), the special five-handbreadth *amah* measurement which was used in the Beis Hamikdash was only used for building the movable articles of the Beis Hamikdash, such as the holy ark, the table of the showbread, the golden altar, etc. When it came to the construction of the *buildings* of the Beis Hamikdash, however, the regular, sixhandbreadth *amah* measurement was employed. (This is the more liberal opinion of Rabbi Yehudah. Rabbi Meir maintained that the six handbreadth *amah* was used in an even more limited fashion.) The *paroches*, whose twenty-by-forty-*amah* dimensions were for the purpose of filling the entire breadth of the *Heichal* [Sanctuary building] in order to enclose the *Kodesh haKodoshim*, would then have to be measured with the same *amah* used for measuring the sanctuary itself, or a six handbreadth *amah*! The perimeter of the *paroches* would then measure 720—not 600—handbreadths!

In defense of the Gaon, it could be said that when grasping the *paroches* for the purpose of immersing it, the Kohanim would not hold it on all four sides. One side had to be left free, in order to lower the *paroches* into the mikveh. If the Kohanim held it on the three sides that measured 40, 40 and 20 *amos*, and left the other twenty-*amos*-side free, they would have covered 100 *amos*, or 600 handbreadths, of the perimeter. This is probably what the

Gaon said, and not as recorded in the *Kol Eliyahu.*

III

The Gaon's brilliant interpretation explains why the Mishnah used the figure of 300 Kohanim in its exaggerated statement. The Gemara, however, gives two other examples of exaggerated numbers mentioned in the Mishnah. Can a similar line of reasoning be used to account for the choice of the exaggerated numbers used in these Mishnayos as well?

The 300 kors of ash

I once heard an ingenious explanation for the exaggeration of the 300 *kors* of ash on the altar along these same lines, from Reb Dovid Yisrael Slutzkin, a retired banker who presently lives in Rechavya, Jerusalem.

The *kor* is a measure of volume corresponding to 30 *se'ah*-measures (between 900-1400 liters, or about 300 gallons). Mr. Slutzkin pointed out that according to the Gemara (Pesachim 109b), the minimum size of a mikveh—40 *se'ah*-measures of water—corresponds to three cubic *amos* of water. Accordingly, each cubic *amah* contains in it the volume of 40/3, or 13.33 *se'ahs.* Since a *kors* is equal to thirty *se'ahs*, the 300 *kors* mentioned by the Mishnah in connection with the ash on the altar would correspond to 9000 *se'ah* of ash. This is equal to 9000/13.33, or 675, cubic *amos* of ash.

In Mishnayos Middos 3:6 we learn that the base of the altar was 32 by 32 *amos.* We are told, however, that there were two places along the height of the altar where there were indentations that reduced the width and length of the altar. Since each indentation was one *amah* thick, there was a reduction of two *amos* in the dimensions of the altar on each of its sides—south, east, north and west. Thus, the top surface of the altar measured only 28 by 28 *amos.* On the four corners of the roof of the altar, there were four protrusions referred to as *keranos* [horns]. Each *keren* [horn] was one *amah* by one *amah* by one *amah*, a perfect cube. Because the *keranos* were an *amah* wide, the entire outer *amah* of the altar (even the part between the *keranos*) was referred to as the *keranos* area (Middos, ibid.), and was never used for burning *korbanos.* Therefore, the area on top of the altar that remained available for burning *korbanos* was 26 *amos* x 26 *amos*—an area of 676 square *amos.*

How high was the accumulation of ashes on the top of the altar allowed to reach? In Tehillim 118:27 it says, "Tie up the offerings, up to the *keranos* of the altar." The *keranos* of the altar, as we have already seen, jutted up one *amah* above the surface of the altar. The verse in Tehillim seems to imply that the sacrifices burned on the altar were never piled higher than the height of the *keranos*—a height of one *amah.* (Such a concept may be alluded to in Sukkah 45b, where we are told that the giant eleven-*amah*-tall willow branches that were propped up against the altar on Sukkos were bent over at their tops. Perhaps they had to be bent over, in order that they not be higher than the altar's *keranos*.)

Now that we have determined that the surface of the altar measured 676 square *amos* and that the ashes were never piled higher than one *amah*, we can see that the maximum volume of ash on the altar was 676 cubic *amos*. However, we know that there is a requirement to have a fire burning on the roof of the altar at all times (see Vayikra 6:6). If we allow for a space of one square *amah* to be left free of ash, to allow the fire to continue burning on the roof of the altar, we will have a maximum volume of 675 cubic *amos* of ash, which corresponds exactly to 300 *kors*, as shown above! Once again the Mishnah did not choose a random number in its exaggerated account of the ashes on the altar, but the exact number of *se'ahs* that could have accumulated in the theoretical maximum accumulation scenario!

Mr. Slutzkin added that the word Chazal use to describe an exaggeration, *guzmah*, might be understood as an abbreviation for the words *gam zo mah*—meaning, "this is also something." Even when the Sages exaggerated, they did so with an exact calculation in mind!

PARSHAS TETZAVEH

The "Misplaced" Incense Altar
Why Is The Incense Altar Mentioned In Tetzaveh?

"I will sanctify the Tent of Meeting and the altar, and I will sanctify Aharon and his sons to serve Me. I will dwell in the midst of the Bnai Yisrael, and I will be their G-d.... Make an altar for burning incense..." (Shemos 29:43-44; 30:1).

When Hashem commands Moshe to build the Mishkan and all its furnishings (Shemos 25-27), a very specific and logical order is followed. The commands begin with the innermost article of the Mishkan, the ark, situated in the Holy of Holies, and proceeds to the menorah and bread-table, situated in the anteroom of the Mishkan building.

The Torah continues with a description of the outer altar, to be located in the courtyard of the Mishkan. Following this the construction of the Mishkan itself is detailed, followed by instructions for enclosing the outer courtyard. Next the priestly clothes are described, and then the sacrifices of the inauguration ritual are stipulated.

There is one glaring exception to this otherwise perfect pattern—the command to make the incense altar. The incense altar is mentioned for the first time only after the description of the entire Mishkan edifice, and all its furnishings and the details of the Kohanim's vestments. Even the inauguration ritual for the Mishkan is described before any mention of the incense altar. It would have been logical for this altar—situated in the anteroom along with the menorah and bread-table—to have been described when these articles are first mentioned. What is the significance of the Torah's peculiar positioning of the description of this altar? Why is it presented as

A glaring exception to a perfect pattern

though an afterthought?

This question is addressed by early commentators, such as Ibn Ezra (Shemos 25:22) and Ramban (Shemos 30:1). Based on their words, Rav Ovadiah Sforno (c. 1300 C.E.) in his commentary to Shemos 25:23 and 30:1 presents the following answer to our question:

II

Actually, explains the Sforno, the entire concept of building a Mishkan to "house" Hashem, as it were, needs to be examined. As Shlomo noted in his inaugural prayer at the dedication of his Temple, "Behold, the heavens and the highest heavens cannot contain You, and certainly not this house!" What, then, is the idea of building a "house" for Hashem (for that is what the Temple is called throughout Tanach—*Bayis Lashem* (I Kings 5:19); *Beis Hashem* (I Kings 6:37)?

Sforno: How can the Divine Presence rest in a physical house?

Sforno explains this concept in the following manner. As human beings living in a physical world, we find it difficult to internalize completely ethereal and abstract concepts. We are able to relate to abstract concepts much more seriously if we see some physical representation. Through a tangible representation, we can visualize the concept as something more concrete, and more easily relate to it both emotionally and intellectually.

Seeing a skull and crossbones, for instance, has a much stronger effect than seeing the word "poison." Reading about a bomb-blast in the newspaper cannot be compared to actually hearing one, or seeing its debris.

The building of a splendid Temple, which resembles, in its external details, a house prepared for a great earthly king, is intended to impart to us the idea that Hashem's presence resides here on earth among humans. This idea would otherwise be quite difficult for us to fully appreciate emotionally and perceptually. The Mishkan "concretizes" our perception of the presence of Hashem. This stronger realization of the presence of our Creator, which comes from seeing the glory of the Holy Temple, referred to as *Veshachanti Besocham* (Shemos 29:44), or *Hashra'as haShechinah.* (See also Chinuch, mitzvah #95.)

The Mishkan "concretizes" our perception of the presence of Hashem

The Sforno uses this idea to explain the particular furnishings placed in the Mishkan, and later in the Beis Hamikdash. We read in II Melachim (4:9) that the woman who often hosted the prophet Elisha said to her husband, "Behold...the holy prophet passes by us regularly. Let us make him a...room... and place there a bed, a table, a chair and a candelabra."

When preparing a room for an important holy person, then, we see that the expected furnishings are a bed, table, chair and lamp. When the Bnai Yisrael built the Mishkan, which, as was explained earlier, was intended to be patterned after a palace built for royalty, they were to include the same basic items. The ark, the Sforno says, resembled a chair, and to this were added a table and a candelabra, all to prepare a room for a royal guest! (Making a bed would be inappropriate, however, since a bed is not prepared *in honor* of a royal guest, but for his *use*—for sleeping. A bed is not a decorative piece of furniture which lends dignity to a room. There is no place for such an article in Hashem's "house," even on a totally symbolic level, because "the Guardian of Israel neither sleeps nor slumbers."—MK)

The inclusion of these articles in the Mishkan was thus intended to produce a realization of Hashem's presence, by preparing a "room" for the most exalted King. The animal sacrifices of the inauguration of the Temple were also intended to bring about a greater appreciation of Hashem's presence, i.e., a "dwelling of the *Shechinah,*" in a manner witnessed publicly. (An understanding of animal sacrifice based on the words of our Sages, is a discussion for a different occasion.)

Sforno says that the incense altar, however, is not one of the objects normally used when setting up a room for a king, and is thus not a part of the preparations made to bring about a "dwelling of the *Shechinah*." What then was the purpose of the altar? When the king comes to visit, it is important for the host to have a suitable frame of mind for the presence of such an exalted guest. The host dares not act or think in his ordinary manner, but must feel the importance and magnitude of this special situation. The aromatic incense was used during the inauguration to bring out a special feeling of love and dedication for the Divine "Guest." In short, the other articles of the Mishkan were intended to *bring about* the dwelling of the Divine Presence on earth, while the intent of the altar was to *act upon* this Divine Presence once it was already there, to ensure that we are actually affected and moved by this Presence.

Thus, it is only after the construction of the Mishkan was described and the sacrifices of the inauguration outlined, after we are told that Hashem will dwell in our midst, that the command comes for the building of the incense altar. It is only after the *Shechinah* is brought to dwell in its "house," the Sforno explains, that it is appropriate to proceed to the next step—how we should react to this Presence!

Support for Sforno's comparison between the furnishings of the Mishkan and the furnishings used in the preparation of Elisha's room may be found in the Gemara. In Berachos 10b the Gemara describes the thrust of the prayers of the deathly ill King Chizkiyahu (II Melachim 20:2). "You revived the son of the woman of Shunem because his mother prepared a furnished room for Elisha," said Chizkiyahu. "How much more so should You heal me, because my ancestor Shlomo built an entire Temple with furnishings for You!"

III

Another answer altogether to our original question—why the Torah seemingly "misplaces" the description of the altar—is suggested by the Chidah in his *Nachal Kedumim*, in the name of Rav Moshe Galanti.

Rav M. Galanti: Only an "extra"

In Zevachim 59a we learn that the daily incense service of the Temple may be performed even without the incense altar. The incense would simply be burned on the floor of the Temple Sanctuary, on the spot where the altar was supposed to be located. This, however, could not be done with the large external altar situated in the courtyard of the Temple. If this altar had even a small chip, no sacrifices were allowed to be offered on it. Similarly, if there is no bread-table it was not permissible to bring the breads that were normally placed on the table and lay them on the floor in the place where the table should stand. The candles, too, could not be lit on the floor in the absence of a menorah, and it is absurd to think that the Tablets of the Ten Commandments could be left on the floor if the ark is not present. Every article of the Mishkan had a function, and this function could not be carried out in the absence of that article. The only exception to this was the incense altar, which, as noted above, was not absolutely necessary for the burning of the incense.

This, proposes R. Moshe Galanti, is why the description of the incense altar is presented almost as an afterthought. The incense altar was only an "extra," in the sense that its functional purpose was not imperative. It does not belong together with the other articles of the Mishkan, which were necessary for the functioning of the Mishkan. (See also Aderes Eliyahu, Meshech Chochmah, Maharil Diskin and others, who answer our question similarly.)

It should be noted that this explanation is not necessarily in opposition to the Sforno's interpretation. The two may in fact be said to complement each other. *Why* is it that the incense altar was not imperative to the function of the Mishkan? Because, as the Sforno explained, its goal was different from other articles of the Mishkan. It wasn't placed in the Mishkan to honor the One who dwells there, but rather was meant to facilitate the offering of incense.

Its functional purpose was not imperative

(For other explanations for the strange placement of the commandment to build the incense altar, see Ohr Hachayim [end of Shemos 25:9], Kedushas Levi, Kli Chemdah to Parshas Korach #1.)

IV

I once heard another intriguing answer to this question from haGaon Rav Leib Heiman, rabbi of the Bayit Vegan section of Jerusalem. (The same thought can be found in Rav Mordechai Miller's 1979 volume of *Shabbos Shiurim*.]

Moshe's Parsha vs. Aharon's

It is well-known trivia that the Parsha of Tetzaveh is the only one in the Torah (after Moshe's birth) that does not mention Moshe's name at least once. (See Baal Haturim at the beginning of the Parsha, and Pane'ach Raza.) Rashi (Shemos 6:26) tells us that Moshe and Aharon were both considered to be on an equal level. It may be suggested that the merits of both brothers were responsible for bringing the *Shechinah* to dwell in the Mishkan. Perhaps, in order to illustrate this joint merit, we split up the description of the Mishkan and its functions into two reading portions. The first is Terumah, which discusses the Mishkan building and its associated furnishings. This was Moshe's share in the Mishkan, for Moshe too administered the sacrifices and served in the Mishkan until Aharon's initiation ceremony was complete (Rashi Vayikra 8:28). The second portion is Tetzaveh, which is devoted to a description of the priestly vestments. These were never worn by anyone but Aharon and his descendants (Moshe wore a simple white linen robe when he performed the sacrifices mentioned above, Rashi ibid.). Thus, in order to stress the contribution of Aharon to the bringing of the Divine Presence to the Mishkan, Tetzaveh is dedicated exclusively to Aharon, and there is no mention of his more renowned brother!

In Avos 4:13 we learn that there are three "crowns" (i.e., three sources of honor and praise) in the world—the crown of Torah, the crown of Kingship and the crown of Priesthood (*Kehunnah*). Rashi (in Shemos 25:21,24 and 30:3) points out that these three crowns are represented in the Mishkan by the three articles which had a raised golden border-decoration on them.

The raised border around the top of the holy ark represents the crown of Torah, the raised border on the bread-table represents the crown of Kingship, and that on the incense altar represents the crown of Priesthood.

Moshe was considered to be a "king" over the Bnai Yisrael (Zevachim 102a; see also Devarim 33:5—"There was a king in Yeshurun" and Ibn Ezra ad loc., and Bereishis 36:31 and Rashbam ad loc.). The crown of Kingship was his, as was, obviously, the crown of Torah. The two objects that symbolize these crowns—the table and the ark—are thus mentioned in "Moshe's Parsha"—Parshas Terumah. The crown of Priesthood, however, belonged to Aharon alone (it too was originally supposed to be taken by Moshe, but he lost the right to it).

Therefore, the incense altar, which represents the crown of Priesthood, was not discussed until "his Parsha"—namely, Tetzaveh! This is why the Torah did not describe the incense altar in Parshas Terumah, which would seem to be its proper place.

PARSHAS KI SISA

Moshe's Radiance

"The two Tablets of Testimony were in Moshe's hands when he came down from the mountain, and although Moshe did not realize it, the skin of his face shone after Hashem had spoken to him. Aharon and all Bnai Yisrael looked at Moshe and saw that the skin of his face shone, and they were afraid to approach him...and [Moshe] put a mask on his face" (Shemos 34:29-30,33).

After Moshe finished writing the Torah, there was a small amount of ink left over in the pen. Hashem dabbed the ink onto Moshe's head, and it was from this ink that Moshe's radiance stemmed (Yalkut Shimoni #407).

The ink that shone

The Midrash in the Yalkut associates a drop of ink leftover from the writing of the Torah, with Moshe Rabbeinu's radiance. The Midrash obviously requires some added explanation. What is the meaning of identifying this ink as being the cause of Moshe's radiance? Also, why was there any extra ink—couldn't Hashem have apportioned the exact amount of ink necessary?

The Beis Halevi (Rav Yosef Dov Soloveitchik the first, c. 1900, in Drush #18, printed after section 2 of his responsa) offers a striking and compelling suggestion for the deeper meaning of this Midrash.

II

To introduce his explanation, the Beis Halevi quotes another Midrash. "When Hashem gave the Torah, He revealed to Moshe the Biblical text (i.e., the written law), the Mishnah (the oral law), the Aggadah and the Talmud (explanations for the laws given in the Mishnah)—as it says (Shemos 20:1), 'G-d spoke *all* these words, saying....' This includes even questions that would one day be brought up for discussion by students before their teachers.

To write or not to write? "Hashem then told Moshe, 'Now, go and teach it to Bnai Yisrael!' Moshe said to Him, 'Why don't You write it down for them?' Hashem answered, 'I would have liked to have the oral law committed to writing as well, but I know that the Bnai Yisrael will eventually be subjugated by the nations of the world and that their enemies will take away the written Torah from them and appropriate it for themselves (as in the times of Ptolemy—see Megillah 9a). If everything were to be written down, the nations of the world would take the entire Torah from the Bnai Yisrael, and then My children would be just like the other nations. Therefore, the text of the Torah will be committed to writing, but the rest of the Law will be transmitted orally, so that the Bnai Yisrael will always be unique'" (Yalkut Shimoni #405—see also Tosafos, Gittin 60b).

The Midrash tells us that the only reason the oral law was not written down was to ensure the enduring uniqueness of the Bnai Yisrael.

The Beis Halevi poses a question regarding this assertion from a statement in the Gemara (Eruvin 54a). The Gemara says that if the first Tablets had never been broken (i.e., if the sin of the golden calf had never taken place) no nation would have been able to exercise dominion over the Bnai Yisrael—they would have been invincible.

The Gemara proves this point from the *pasuk* in Shemos (32: 16), which relates that "[the writing] on the Tablets was engraved (*charus*)." An exegetic alteration of the Masoretic punctuation of the verse renders it, "[the writing] on the Tablets was able to bring freedom (*cheirus*)."

At the time that the Torah was originally given, it was not yet Israel's destiny to become subjugated by the nations of the world. What then, was the reason that Hashem did not write down the oral law? The reason given in the Yalkut should not have applied. Since the Jews were not destined to become subjugated to the other nations, the oral law could have, in fact, been given to them in written form!

It must be, concludes the Beis Halevi, that the first Tablets contained the *entire* body of Torah Law, and not only the written law. It is only with reference to the *second* set of Tablets—the ones which were not broken—that the Yalkut asserts that the oral law was not written down. At the time of the writing of the second Tablets it had already been decreed that Israel would be undergoing subjugation by the nations!

It might be asked, how is it possible to imagine that the entire body of Jewish Law—oral and written—was written on just two Tablets. This is really not difficult, however, when we remember that the Tablets were "the work of G-d" and the writing on them was "the writing of G-d" [Shemos 16]. The entire matter of the words inscribed on the Tablets was miraculous, as the Gemara [Shabbos 104a] points out (albeit in a different context).

III

The Beis Halevi brings some convincing textual proofs for his thesis that the first Tablets, unlike the second ones, contained more than just the "Ten Commandments."

Textual support for non-identical sets of Tablets

In Devarim 9:10 we read (concerning the first Tablets), "Hashem then gave me the two stone Tablets that were written by the finger of G-d, and *upon them* were *all* of the words that Hashem spoke to you on the Mountain." It should be recalled that it is the use of the word *all* that prompted the Yalkut to say that the entire body of Torah—written and oral—was related to Moshe on Mount Sinai. If so, we may similarly derive from the *pasuk* in Devarim that the entire Torah was *written* on the Tablets!

The Gemara (Megillah 19b) does, in fact, explain the word *all* in this verse as referring to *all* sections of Jewish Law, right down to the later institution of the reading of the Megillah Esther on Purim. Although the Gemara does not specifically say that all of this was written down on the Tablets, such a conclusion would seem inevitable, when the Gemara's words are seen in the context of the *pasuk.* The *pasuk* is, after all, describing what *appeared* on the Tablets. (A similar *drush* on this verse can be found in the Yerushalmi Peah 2:1.)

In reference to the second Tablets, however, the Torah repeats several times that what was written on the Tablets was simply "the ten utterances,"—see Shemos 34:28 and Devarim 10:4. This description is never given for the first Tablets.

The first Tablets indeed had more on them than the Ten Commandments, the second ones were very different in this respect—they had nothing on them but the Ten Commandments given to us on Mount Sinai.

Actually, the Beis Halevi was preceded in the above two observations by the great Torah commentator Hakesav Vehakabala, c. 1850, who wrote a similar comment to Devarim 10:4. Several other indications may be shown to support the Beis Halevi's thesis.

In Shemos 24:12 we are told, in reference to the first Tablets, "Hashem said to Moshe, '...I will give you the...Torah and the commandments that I have written to direct them.'" The Gemara (Berachos 5a) says that this *pasuk* implies that the entire body of Jewish Law—including the Torah text, Mishnah, Talmud, etc. was given to Moshe. Yet the verse says, concerning the above words, "...that I have written," implying that this entire body was indeed committed to writing in the first Tablets.

In the Yalkut Shimoni (#405) we are taught that although the first Tablets were written by the finger of Hashem (Shemos 31:18), when Hashem gave the second Tablets, He told Moshe, "You write!" (Shemos 34:27). (Note: Although the Torah seems to state explicitly that *Hashem* Himself recorded the Ten Commandments on the second Tablets, and not Moshe—see Shemos 34:1, Devarim 10:2—nevertheless, Moshe apparently committed to writing the *remainder* of the written Torah on parchment—see Ramban's comment to 34:28. The Yalkut here is apparently referring to this document.—MK)

The Yalkut Shimoni, #392, points out another contrast between the two sets of Tablets. The first Tablets were readable from both sides and were "the work of G-d" (Shemos 32:15-16)—the Tablets themselves were of a miraculous nature. The second Tablets, on the other hand, were hewn by Moshe himself from ordinary rock (Shemos 34:1). Based on the Beis Halevi's thesis, the need for these differences can be easily explained.

The first Tablets—which contained a vast amount of information—had to be made of a supernatural substance, and had to be written in a miraculous handwriting. The second Tablets, which contained only the ten statements, could be written on ordinary hewn stone, and Moshe himself could easily inscribe the written law alone in his own hand. Miracles were, therefore, unnecessary in the material and inscription of the second Tablets!

IV

The Beis Halevi uses this thesis to explain the meaning of another Midrash.

The flying letters

"When Moshe saw the Bnai Yisrael sinning with the golden calf, he looked at the Tablets and saw the words begin to fly off from them. At that point the Tablets became heavy in his hands and they fell down to the ground, shattering" (Yalkut Shimoni #393).

Once the Bnai Yisrael sinned, their entire destiny changed. It was at this point that it was decreed that Bnai Yisrael would one day become subjugated to the nations of the world, as explained earlier. At this time, then, it became impossible to have both components of the Torah—the oral law and the written law—in writing. Thus Moshe saw the words of the oral law "flying off" from the Tablets at this time. Hashem had decided not to commit the oral Torah to writing, and He removed that part of the miraculous engraving from the miraculous Tablets. These were the "words flying off" from the Tablets!

Moshe knew that it would be impossible for anyone to interpret the written Torah properly without the guidance of the oral law (and the idea of teaching the oral law orally was not yet introduced by Hashem). The Tablets "became heavy in his hands"—that is, Moshe realized that it was no longer possible for them to be given as an independent entity. Without the oral law to go with them, the Tablets would be "too heavy to bear." This is what the Midrash means when it relates that the Tablets became heavy in Moshe's hands, and fell to the ground.

According to this Midrash, the Beis Halevi continues, we can understand an expression of the Torah in Shemos 34:1 and Devarim 10:2. The Torah says that what was written on the second Tablets was that which was "written on the first Tablets *which you* [Moshe] *broke.*" Most of the material that had originally been engraved on the first Tablets had already "flown off" as soon as the sin of the golden calf took place.

By the time Moshe broke these Tablets, the only writing left on them was the "Ten Commandments." Only these ten statements that were on the Tablets "when you broke them" were reproduced on the second set of Tablets!

V

Our loss of the written record of the oral Torah is what the Midrash was alluding to by "leftover ink." When it was time for Moshe to write the second set of Tablets, he wanted to make a complete replica of the first Tablets—i.e., he wanted to put down in writing *all* aspects of the Torah, written and oral. However Hashem explained to Moshe that this was no longer possible, as the Bnai Yisrael were now destined to be exiled among the other nations, as the other Midrash (#405) mentions.

The leftover ink

This, explains the Beis Halevi, is what is meant by there being "extra ink" which was left over after Moshe finished writing the Torah. There was another section of Torah which was left to be written, but yet could not be written! The "extra ink" from this unwritten part of the Torah—the oral law—was then dabbed onto Moshe's head.

The Midrash (Shemos Rabbah 41:6) tells us that Moshe struggled to learn the Torah for the entire forty days that he was in heaven, but he could not succeed in mastering it completely until Hashem gave it to him "as a gift." Hashem implanted the ideas of the Torah into Moshe's mind so that they would be firmly and clearly entrenched there, as symbolized by the smearing of the ink of the oral Torah on his head.

This "ink"—the inculcation of the oral Torah into Moshe's mind—was what caused Moshe's radiance. There was now no one in the world who had access to the entire body of Torah Law except for Moshe, for only he knew the secrets of the oral Torah. Becoming the personal bearer of the oral Torah gave Moshe a unique status among mankind. It left its mark on him, causing his face to shine. "For a mitzvah is a candle and the Torah is light!" (Mishlei 6:23).

PARSHAS VAYAKHEL

Shabbos: Time Out For Torah

"Throughout the entire Torah there is not a single section which begins with the convening of an assembly except for this one, which begins, 'Moshe assembled the Bnai Yisrael,' and continues with a discussion of the laws of Shabbos. Hashem meant to tell Moshe, 'Make large assemblies [on Shabbos] and expound before them publicly on the laws of Shabbos in order that future generations should learn from you. They too should make large gatherings on every Shabbos in their *batei midrashos* [houses of Torah study] in order to teach the laws of the Torah publicly, so that My great Name may be praised among My children' " (Yalkut Shimoni #408).

The role of the Shabbos

"We find in a Midrash that the Torah complained before Hashem, saying, 'When the Bnai Yisrael enter the Land of Israel, everyone will become preoccupied with their agricultural pursuits—what will become of *me* then?' Hashem answered her, 'I have an excellent mate for you—the Shabbos. On that day, the Jews are not busy with their work, and they will be free to occupy themselves in studying you.' " (Tur Orach Chayim #290—see also Tana Devei Eliyahu Rabbah, chap. 1)

Mishnah: "Why should one not read from the Kesuvim [the Hagiographa, the third section of the Scriptures] on Shabbos? Because it may lead people to absent themselves from the *beis midrash* [house of Torah study]."

Rashi: "The Rabbi used to give a lesson for laymen on Shabbos, during which he would elaborate on many important halachic points. The Kesuvim are interesting and tend to draw one's attention. Reading the Kesuvim was therefore banned on Shabbos, out of the fear that one would become involved in them and forget about the Rabbi's lesson, which was more important than the study of the Kesuvim."

"How I love Your Torah; it is my speech all of the day" (Tehillim 119:97). The *pasuk* does not say "it is my speech all day," but rather, "it is my speech all *the* day." *The* day refers to a specific unique day, the Shabbos. On Shabbos, David dedicated himself completely to the joy of the study of the Torah" (Rabbeinu Bachye on Shemos 20:8).

We are used to viewing the Shabbos as the day of rest. The above citations, however, uncover a new aspect of the sanctity of the Shabbos day. Six of the seven days of the week we are busy, concentrating our energies on earning a livelihood. How will a hard-working laborer find time to study the Torah and learn the details of its mitzvos?

The Torah itself presents us with the solution. Every seventh day we are commanded not to do any manner of work. This allows us to pursue the study of Torah for an entire day, without any distractions! Shabbos is to be dedicated to the study—and hence the preservation—of the Torah and its mitzvos.

(Perhaps this is the reason the Torah always precedes the command to rest from work on the Shabbos with the statement, "You may work six days of the week"—a point the Ohr Hachayim discusses in the beginning of Parshas Vayakhel. The Torah may be telling us the *reason* that it is necessary for us to rest on Shabbos. Because "you may work six days of the week," it may be hard to find the time that we need for the study of the Torah, therefore, "on the seventh day you shall rest!"—MK)

II

This new aspect of Shabbos observance helps to explain a number of other statements of Chazal.

Associations of Torah and the Shabbos, in the Talmud

In Shabbos 86b the Gemara records an argument regarding whether the giving of the Torah took place on the sixth or the seventh day of the month of Sivan. However, the Gemara emphasizes, both sides agree that the day of the *week* that the Torah was given was Shabbos. What is the significance of this? Perhaps it is to intimate to us that Shabbos holds the secret for perpetuating the Torah amongst us. On the Shabbos day, when we are free from our daily, mundane responsibilities, we are given the opportunity for spiritual renewal through the study of the Torah!

In Bava Kama 82a we are taught that Ezra the Scribe instituted a custom that the Torah be read in the synagogue on Shabbos afternoon. This was done, we are told, because of the *yoshvei keranos* (lit., people who sit in shops). Rashi explains that the *yoshvei keranos* referred to here are people who sit in their stores all week and have no opportunity to hear or study the words of the Torah. In addition to the regular reading of the Parsha during the Shabbos morning services, an extra Torah reading was instituted at the afternoon prayer, similar to the reading of the Monday and Thursday morning services. This would allow even the very busy shopkeepers, who missed the Monday and Thursday readings in their hurry to get to work, the opportunity to hear the weekly readings. Again, Shabbos has been utilized for teaching the words of the Torah to the working masses.

III

The Midrashim quoted above tell us that the free time granted to us by the Torah on Shabbos was intended to be used for productive Torah study. It would stand to reason that the same could be said of the other times that we are freed from the mundane, physical obligations of earning a livelihood.

Shabbos and the other work-less seasons

We indeed find in the Midrash (Tanchuma Beshalach 20) that "the Torah could only have been given for exposition to those people who had the manna to eat, for they had no need to engage in labor or commerce." Having a supply of food delivered to their doorsteps every day enabled the Bnai Yisrael to free themselves completely from the worries of supporting themselves and their families. It enabled them to devote all of their time to the mastery of the newly-given laws, and the inculcation of its values into their daily lives.

On the Yomim Tovim [major holy days, holidays when most work is prohibited] of the five *Moadim* [biblical holidays], we are forbidden from engaging in work just as we are on the Shabbos. Perhaps we can apply a similar motif to the prohibition of labor on these days. Indeed, in the Yerushalmi (Shabbos 15:3—quoted by Beis Yosef in the beginning of Orach Chayim #288) we find the statement: "Shabbos day and Festivals were given to us for the sole purpose of engaging in Torah study."

On Chol haMoed [the intermediate days of Pesach and Sukkos], some types of work are permitted, but most kinds of labor and commerce are forbidden. There too, the Yerushalmi (Moed Katan 1:1) tells us that "there was no reason for the prohibition of labor on Chol haMoed other than to enable people to eat, drink and occupy themselves with Torah study."

Perhaps we can extend this idea to relate to the *Shemittah* [sabbatical] year, during which agricultural work—the predominant occupation of the Bnai Yisrael for many centuries after their conquest of Israel—was forbidden. Inevitably, this led to a large amount of free time for farmers during the year of *Shemittah*.

When laws of the *Shemittah* year are detailed, the Torah makes a point that those laws were given "on Mount Sinai" (Vayikra 25:1). Rashi (ad loc.) poses the famous question, "What does *Shemittah* have to do with Mount Sinai?" Perhaps we may suggest an answer with the concept that we have developed here. The Torah was given on a Shabbos day, as explained above, to demonstrate that Shabbos provides the key to the Torah's preservation. So too, the Torah in Parshas Behar may be emphasizing that what was given on Sinai would be preserved throughout the ages thanks to the mitzvah the Torah is about to describe—the mitzvah of *Shemittah*. The *Shemittah* year, with all of the free time that it provided, was the perfect opportunity for the working Jew to study the Torah and intensify his mastery of its wisdom and commandments!

IV

It may be further suggested that the converse of this concept is also true. If not for the added opportunity to study the Torah that the Shabbos offers us, the mitzvah of Shabbos would not have been given altogether. Why is that?

Born to toil

In Iyov 5:7 we are told that "Man was born to toil." What, then, is the point of having a day on which we are commanded *not* to toil and exert ourselves—namely Shabbos? The answer is that Shabbos is not a day when there is no toil. The struggle to confront the challenge of Torah also qualifies as toil! The Gemara (Sanhedrin 99b) proves exegetically that the verse in Iyov that attributes such a prominent position to toil in man's life is not referring to physical toil at all. Rather, the *pasuk* refers to the "verbal," spiritual toil of learning Torah. Shabbos, then, is a day when the daily challenges of life are transferred into a different sphere—into the non-material, spiritual domain.

With this in mind, we can understand the Gemara in Masseches Sanhedrin. In Sanhedrin 58b we are told that a non-Jew is not permitted to take a weekly day of rest for himself. (He simply can take a vacation when necessary; without a predetermined pattern.) Rashi adds that this is in order that the non-Jew should not be idle from work—probably alluding to the verse in Iyov that we mentioned.

The obvious question is, why may a Jew be idle from *his* work, if a gentile may not? The answer is, perhaps, to be found in the Gemara's next statement in Sanhedrin—that a non-Jew is also not permitted to engage in Torah study. (Note: Of course he may study laws that apply to gentiles [Sanhedrin ibid.]. Similarly, if a non-Jew is planning to become a proselyte, he may learn the laws that will apply to him upon conversion [Yevamos 47b; see also Maharsha, Shabbos 31a s.v. "*Amar Leh*"].) Since a non-Jew is not permitted to study the Torah, it follows that taking a day of rest for himself would not be in keeping with the verse in Iyov. As the verse states, our purpose in life is to toil. The Jew uses his Shabbos day to "toil" in the study of Torah. For a non-Jew, who may not study the Torah, there can be no "day" of rest.

PARSHAS PEKUDEI

Play It Again...

In Parshas Terumah and in Parshas Tetzaveh, Hashem instructs Moshe Rabbeinu to build a Mishkan. Every detail of the Mishkan's construction is carefully outlined, from the vessels of the sanctuary to the Mishkan's walls and surrounding curtains. Even the clothing that the priests were to wear while doing their work in the Mishkan is meticulously described.

In Parshas Vayakhel and Parshas Pekudei, the Bnai Yisrael carry out Hashem's commands. We are told how Betzalel takes all the materials donated by the Bnai Yisrael and fashions them into the Mishkan proper, its vessels, and the majestic priestly garments. As Betzalel does this, the Torah describes every detail of his work—again we are told the exact measurements and physical characteristics of every part of the Mishkan.

Even the casual reader of these Parshiyos cannot help but wonder at the amount of seemingly unnecessary repetition involved in the description of these events.

Repetition in the construction of the Mishkan

What is the reason that the Torah—usually terse in its discussion of even the most weighty subjects—suddenly becomes verbose and repetitive? Would it not have sufficed to simply say, "Betzalel and Moshe did all that Hashem had commanded them," as we find elsewhere in the Torah (see Bereishis 6:22, Shemos 17:6, and Bamidbar 17:26)?

Ramban (Shemos 36:8) and Rabbeinu Bachye (ibid. 35:1 and Bamidbar 8:19) discuss this issue. They explain the uncharacteristic repetitions by citing a Midrash which points out a similar anomaly in Bereishis 24. After giving a detailed description of Eliezer's (Avraham's servant) expedition to Charan and his successful search for a bride for his master's son, Yitzchak, the Torah quotes at length how Eliezer recounts the entire story of his trip for the bride's parents. Couldn't the Torah have said simply, "And Eliezer told Besuel and Lavan all about his journey and mission?" The Midrash (quoted by Rashi ibid. 24:42) notes this anomaly, and remarks, "The casual conversation of even the servants of the Patriarchs is more beloved to Hashem than the Torah laws written for their descendants, for the story of Eliezer is told twice in the Torah, while many of the most important laws of the Torah were written so that they could only be derived through allusion." The reason the Torah repeats the story of Eliezer then, says Ramban and Rabbeinu Bachye, is that Hashem wanted to show how beloved Eliezer's master, the Patriarch Avraham, was to Him.

The same idea can be invoked in reference to the Mishkan, the Ramban and Rabbeinu Bachye add. The Torah uses repetition in order to show the great love Hashem feels for His people, who built Him the Mishkan.

II

We can use this concept to explain some other examples of seemingly unnecessary repetition in the Torah. In Parshas Naso (Bamidbar 7), the Torah discusses the offerings brought by the *Nesi'im* [the leaders of the twelve tribes], on the occasion of the dedication of the Mishkan. The offerings the *Nesi'im* brought were all identical. Yet the Torah, when describing them, repeats all the details of the offering (five verses worth) twelve times, verbatim! Furthermore, at the end of this description the Torah gives a sum total of the items donated—twelve silver plates, twelve silver bowls, twelve golden spoons, etc. Surely all this repetition could have been avoided.

Repetition in the leaders' offering and in the Jewish nation's travels

The Chasam Sofer (new edition, Parshas Chayei Sarah) uses the idea mentioned above to explain that Hashem wanted to show how beloved the actions of the *Nesi'im* were to Him by reviewing the details of their offering again and again.

In Parshas Masei (Bamidbar 33) we are given a list of all the encampments made by the Bnai Yisrael on their journey from Egypt to the land of Israel. The Torah had already described most of these places, and the events that transpired there, during the recounting of the Exodus, from Shemos 12:37 to the end of Bamidbar. Why was it necessary to repeat this list of place names now?

Rashi (Bamidbar 33:1, quoting from Midrash Tanchuma) explains this repetition with a parable. There was once a king [Hashem] who had to take his sick son [the Bnai Yisrael, still flawed in their trust in Hashem] on a distant journey [the trip through the desert to Eretz Yisrael] to seek medical help. On the return trip [after the 40 years of wandering], after the son was healed, the father would fondly remark, "This is where we stopped to sleep, this is where you didn't feel well, this is where we stopped to eat, etc." This may be understood as yet another example of the idea developed above. by recounting all the details of their journey, the father is expressing his intense love for his son, and his joy over his recovery. So too, Hashem showed His profound love for the Jewish people by reviewing all the various stops they made along the long, arduous journey that was now about to come to a successful end.

We have thus discovered four instances where the Torah uses the instrument of repetition to reveal Hashem's intense love for a particular person, or group of people, at a particular time: the story of Eliezer, the description of the Mishkan, the detailing of the Mishkan's inauguration-offerings of the leaders of the tribes, and the reviewing of all the stops of the Israelite camp during the journey to Eretz Yisrael.

III

Some explanation is still in order. Why is it only in these particular four instances that Hashem expressed His love for the Patriarchs and their children? After all, the Torah certainly does not repeat *everything* that happened to our forefathers. Just these few narratives are repeated. What is unique about these instances?

Repetition in the Eliezer story: A sign of love

" 'Hashem is your shadow, by your right side.' This teaches that Hashem is like a person's shadow (or reflection). When A person smiles, his reflection smiles back at him; when he cries, his reflection cries back at him; when he shows a sad face, his reflection also shows the same to him. So too with Hashem—whatever attitude you (the people of Israel) show towards Him, He reflects the same attitude back to you." (Midrash, quoted by Rav Meir Ibn Gabbai in his *Avodas haKodesh* and the Sh'lah in *Sha'ar haGadol, os lamed.*)

In Yeshayah 41:8 Avraham is described as the "lover of Hashem." This was one of the unique characteristics exemplified by the Patriarch Avraham —his passionate love for Hashem. In return, Hashem showed His love for Avraham. In Bereishis 18:19 we read that Hashem says of Avraham, "I have *endeared* him (see Rashi), because he will command his children and his household after him to keep the ways of Hashem, to do righteousness and justice...." This *pasuk* similarly makes it clear that Avraham made certain not only to love Hashem himself, but to imbue all the members of his household with this sense of love and dedication.

We find that Avraham's servant Eliezer served him with tremendous devotion. Perhaps this too was a lesson he had learned from his master. Since Avraham served *his* master with an outpouring of love, his servants learned from him not only to serve the Creator, their ultimate Master, with dedication. They also learned to serve their direct master, Avraham, with dedication.

The trait of devotion and dedication to one's master by a servant is perhaps illustrated nowhere better than in Eliezer's journey to Charan to find a prospective bride for his master's son. We are told in Bereishis 24:10 (according to Rashi there) that Eliezer traveled with such determination, that he arrived in Charan, with Divine assistance, on the same day he left Canaan. Eliezer prayed to Hashem that He show him on that same day the proper choice of a bride through a particular test that the girl would pass. Hashem responded to his fervent request by sending the proper bride to him immediately. When speaking to the girl's parents to obtain their consent to the marriage, they requested a delay of a few months. Eliezer responded, "Do not detain me, when Hashem has granted me success with my mission!" and he left Charan on that same day.

The devotion of a servant to his master

From these details we can see how devoted Eliezer was to his master and to the fulfillment of his wishes (despite the fact that Eliezer wanted Isaac to marry his own daughter, according to the Midrash quoted by Rashi in 24:39). It was this trait of thorough dedication to following the wishes of the beloved master, which was the hallmark of Avraham, and which had been imbibed by Eliezer, that aroused Hashem's love for Avraham. Avraham's love for Hashem caused Hashem to "reflect" that love back to him. It is for this reason that at this particular place in the Torah Hashem chose to illustrate His love for the "casual conversation" of the servant of the Patriarch, by repeating the details of Eliezer's mission. This section illustrates better than any other the root cause of Hashem's love for Avraham—his own trait of love and selfless devotion to Hashem.

IV

We can similarly explain the repetitions employed by the Torah in the other examples noted above.

Repetition accounted for

In Shemos 25:2 and 35:5, when donations to the Mishkan from the populace are discussed, the expression "he whose heart aroused him" is used to describe those who donated their riches towards the building of the Mishkan. The Chasam Sofer explains this peculiar choice of words in the following manner. In reality it is not possible for a human being to "donate" to Hashem of his possessions to build a Temple —"Mine is the silver and Mine is the gold, says Hashem!" (Chaggai 2:8). The only thing a person can render unto Hashem is his heart —to channel his sentiments and emotions toward devotion to Hashem. Thus, explains the Chasam Sofer, the Torah, when describing the donation of material objects for the construction of the Mishkan, emphasizes that what made these donations meaningful was not their monetary worth, but the fact that they were given by people "who were aroused by their hearts" to participate in this undertaking. The Chasam Sofer is obviously alluding to the Gemara in Sanhedrin (106b) that tells us, "Hashem desires man's heart, thus it says (in I Shmuel 16:7) 'Hashem sees what is in the heart.' "

The donations towards the building of the Mishkan were thus tokens of the love and devotion the people felt toward Hashem. It was not the physical beauty of the Mishkan that brought Hashem's presence to rest there. Rather, it was the outpouring of love that went into the construction of the Mishkan, that found favor in the eyes of Hashem. Support for this suggestion can also be found in Shir Hashirim 3:9-10: "A Temple [Rashi says this is referring to the Mishkan] was made for the King of Peace [Hashem]...inside, it was paved with love by the daughters of Jerusalem [the Bnai Yisrael]." The Bnai Yisrael built the Mishkan not with material wealth, but with love.

It is thus fitting—bearing in mind what was explained above—that upon describing the collection of the donations for the Mishkan and there being fashioned into the articles and components of the Mishkan, that Hashem would "reflect" this love back, through the vehicle of "repetition."

The *Nesi'im*, who brought their offerings for the dedication of the Mishkan, also acted with great feeling and devotion. Rashi in Shemos 35:27 quotes a Midrash to the effect that the tribal leaders were so anxious to play a leading role in the Mishkan's inauguration that they made sure they would be the first ones to bring offerings on that occasion. Thus, Hashem reflected this enthusiastic love by repeating the exact makeup of those offerings several times.

In Yirmiyah 2:2 we read: "Thus said Hashem: I remember for you the compassion of your early days, the love of your nuptials, when you followed Me into the desert, into an unsown land." The fact that the Bnai Yisrael left Egypt and headed into a completely desolate desert, without taking any provisions along, is considered to be a consummate act of love and devotion by Hashem.

Thus, we may again apply the theory developed above to explain the repetition found in Parshas Masei, when the details of all the stations of the travels of the Bnai Yisrael are repeated. Bnai Yisrael's act of total devotion to Hashem was mirrored by an identical reaction from Hashem Himself, which is expressed by the repetition of the details of that devotion.

Thus, in all four instances we see the same concept at work: whenever the Bnai Yisrael showed an extraordinary outpouring of love for Hashem, Hashem reciprocated by showing His love for them, as represented by a seemingly "superfluous" act of repetition of the details of their act of love!

PARSHAS VAYIKRA

Lessons Learned From A Lessened Letter

"Hashem called (*vayikra*) Moshe and spoke to him from the *Ohel Moed* [the Mishkan, or Tabernacle], and asked Moshe to tell the Jewish people [the details of the various sacrifices]" (Vayikra 1:1).

In the very first *pasuk* of the book of Vayikra, Hashem calls Moshe, telling him to enter the *Ohel Moed* for the first time. According to the *mesorah* some letters of the Torah are written larger or smaller than others (see Shemini essay, section IV, p. 125). One of the most famous examples of such anomalies is the letter *alef* at the end of the word *vayikra*, at the beginning of this week's Parsha. This *alef* is written about half its normal size.

Traditionally, just as the words and even the letters of the Torah are meant to teach us the Divine Will, so too, we can learn from the physical appearance of the letters in the Torah. Every aspect of the Torah is Divinely inspired. What understanding can we glean from the miniaturization of the letter *alef* of *vayikra*? Numerous answers have been suggested throughout the ages. Let us examine some of these answers.

A small alef

II

"Why is the *alef* of the word *vayikra* traditionally written smaller than the other letters in the Sefer Torah? To demonstrate that although Hashem Himself called to Moshe, and although He showed Moshe tremendous respect by constantly speaking to him, even so, Moshe constantly 'lessened' himself before Hashem and before the Bnai Yisrael" (The Tosafists, in Pane'ach Raza to Vayikra 1:1 see also

Tosafos haRosh ibid.).

The Torah's intention here is to hint at Moshe's characteristic modesty by spelling the word *vayikra* with a small *alef*. Why did the Torah hint at Moshe's modesty in this particular word? Apparently, Moshe expressed great modesty at this point. It's unclear, however, in what way Moshe's modesty was expressed in this instance?

1. A hint at Moshe's humility

Raza d'Meir (a commentary on the Pane'ach Raza) offers a suggestion based on a Midrash. The Midrash tells us:

"Lower yourself until you are requested to rise to your proper status, rather than rising before you are called, lest you be told to lower yourself.... We find that Moshe...at the *Ohel Moed*, stood at the side until Hashem said to him, 'Why do you continue to lower yourself? It is your turn to rise now!' " (Vayikra Rabbah 1:5).

According to this Midrash, the reason Hashem had to *call* Moshe was that Moshe was humbly waiting to be called before entering the *Ohel Moed*. It is therefore appropriate for the Torah to hint at Moshe's unrelenting modesty through one of the letters of the word *vayikra* (Hashem "called").

We may add to this that, as we have shown on other occasions (Chayei Sarah essay, p. 19), when tradition dictates a variant spelling of a word in the Torah, both the *word* and the *letter* that is changed have lessons to teach us. In the example of the word *vayikra*, we have explained why a part of the word *vayikra* was written in miniature. It remains to be explained, however, why specifically the letter *alef* of *vayikra* was the particular letter minimized. Perhaps *alef*, the letter in the Hebrew alphabet with the lowest numerical value, connotes humility. Minimizing it therefore symbolizes the epitome of humility, and as the verse states, "Moshe was more humble than any man who ever lived" (Bamidbar 12:3).

III

Rav Yaakov Baal Haturim [author of the Tur, 15th century Spain] offers another explanation for the small *alef*.

2. Hashem "chanced" upon him

Moshe wanted to write *vayikar* in the Torah (spelled the same as *vayikra*, but lacking the concluding *alef*). *Vayikar* is the word used to describe the manner in which Hashem appeared to the gentile prophet Bilaam (Bamidbar 23:4). Moshe meant to say that Hashem appeared to him only by happenstance ("*kara mikreh*" see Rashi, Vayikra 1:1). However, Hashem insisted that Moshe write the *alef* (making it *vayikra*). Moshe wrote it, but made it smaller than usual [that was his compromise]. (Baal Haturim loc. cit. see also the words of his father, the Rosh, ibid., which apparently serve as a source for the words of the Baal Haturim.)

It is clear, according to Baal Haturim, why specifically the *alef* was minimized. The letter *alef* defines the difference between *vayikra* and *vayikar*. We may add, that it is not by chance that it is the letter *alef* that makes *vayikar* into *vayikra*. As we once pointed out (see Chaye Sarah essay, section II, p. 20), the letter *alef* hints at Hashem, the *Aluf* of the world. It is the degree to which the Divine Presence of Hashem rests upon the prophet that makes *vayikar* into *vayikra*.

The words of the Baal Haturim would seem difficult to accept. How could Moshe have planned to write *vayikar*? Didn't Moshe know that Hashem did *not* appear to him just "by chance," the way he appeared to Bilaam!

Before answering this question, let us examine an enigmatic Midrash. The Sifri (end of Parshas Vezos Haberachah), explains that the verse, "No other prophet who arose among the Jews was comparable to Moshe" means that among *the Jews*, no similar prophet arose, but among the gentiles there arose such a prophet. Who was that prophet? Bilaam son of Be'or!"

The Sifri's words are truly perplexing. In what way could the wicked Bilaam's prophecy possibly be compared to that of Moshe? (See the continuation of the Sifri loc. cit., which makes it appear that Bilaam sustained an even *greater* level of prophecy than Moshe did!) Perhaps the intention of the Sifri is to compare one particular aspect of Bilaam's prophecy to that of Moshe.

We find that Moshe, due to his unique level of prophesy, separated from his wife. This, of course, was not required of every Jewish prophet. Moshe himself chose to do this, and Hashem supported his decision (Shabbos 88a). The reason behind Moshe's unusual behavior is explained by Rashi. While other prophets had to prepare themselves in advance in order to receive the Divine Word (cf. I Shmuel 10:5, and Metzudos David), Moshe did not because he had to be ready to receive G-d's word without any prior warning. Thus, Moshe did not want to remain in a state of ritual impurity for any length of time (Rashi Bamidbar 12:4, see also Rambam Yesodei haTorah 7:6).

This may be the quality that Bilaam shared with Moshe. Bilaam, too, received the word of Hashem even though he had not prepared himself for it previously. Bilaam did not need to elevate himself to the proper level of spirituality in order to prophesy, rather, Hashem granted Bilaam the ability to prophesy although he *never* would be on the spiritual level required of a prophet. Prophecy was granted to Bilaam solely as a means of proving to the nations of the world that no other nation could match the Jewish People (Rashi, Bamidbar 22:5).

This, then, may be the implication of both the *vayikar* of Bilaam, and the *vayikra* of Moshe. Had the Torah used the word *vayikar*, it would have meant that Hashem abruptly appeared to Moshe, as if by chance (*kara mikreh*), i.e., without any warning. *Vayikra* also means that Hashem called, and instigated the contact, as opposed to Moshe first preparing himself to "invite" prophecy (as the simple *vayedaber* would have denoted).

The difference between the two terms, however, is that *vayikar* ("Hashem chanced upon him"), has the connotation of a one sided affair. This denotes that the recipient of the prophesy was caught unaware, and wasn't fully prepared to welcome the Divine Presence.

"*Vayikra*" ("Hashem called him"), with its implication of give and take (someone was being *called* to respond), carries the opposite connotation. The prophet was fully able and prepared to receive Hashem's word. It was only necessary for Hashem to call him and the prophet would respond.

Now we can understand Moshe's attempt to describe his encounter with Hashem as *vayikar*. Due to his extreme modesty, Moshe didn't consider himself fully prepared to receive the word of Hashem. Therefore, he felt that his meeting with Hashem should truthfully be described as "*vayikar*," as was Bilaam's. Hashem, however, insisted that Moshe write "*vayikra*," since Hashem said that Moshe was as prepared for prophecy at any given moment as was humanly possible. Moshe consented, but he wrote "*vayikra*" with a small *alef* as if to declare that, in his opinion, it wasn't entirely appropriate to add that *alef*.

IV

According to the two approaches that we have seen so far (Pane'ach Raza and Baal Haturim), the small *alef* indicates the extent of Moshe's modesty. Earlier, Midrashic sources, however, seem to find in the small *alef* an indication of Moshe's shortcomings.

3. The "gate of understanding" that Moshe lacked

Midrash Osios Ketanos, which is attributed to the sage Rabbi Akiva, notes that the *alef* of *vayikra* is small...to denote the difference between the manner Hashem calls the angels and the way Hashem called Moshe.

The Midrash tells us that the *alef* of *vayikra* is smaller than usual in order to show that a man of flesh and blood cannot possibly witness the presence of Hashem to the same extent as the angels.

In a similar vein, the Midrash haZohar learns from the small *alef* that Hashem didn't reveal Himself to Moshe in His full glory. Why was that? Because Hashem appeared to Moshe only in the Mishkan (as opposed to the Holy Temple) and in a foreign land (as opposed to in Eretz Yisrael). (Zohar 1:239a)

Rav Chaim Yosef David Azulai, in *Chomas Anach,* quotes a similar explanation from the school of the great 16th century Kabbalist of Safed, Rav Yitzchak Luria, known as the Arizal. The Arizal cites a Gemara (Rosh Hashanah 21a) that tells us there are 50 "gates to understanding" [i.e., levels of appreciating G-d's truth] in the world. Moshe attained all but one of them. This is the meaning of the small *alef*. *Alef*, the first letter of the Hebrew alphabet, has a numerical value of one—signifying that one gate to understanding was still lacking in Moshe.

These Kabbalistic approaches would seem to clearly contrast the first two approaches (Pane'ach Raza; Baal Haturim). While the first two explanations used the small *alef* to underline Moshe's humility, the approaches of the Kabbalists seem to understand from the small *alef* Moshe's shortcomings as a prophet. A friend of mine, however, haRav Arye Leib Reich of Jerusalem, suggested another understanding of the Kabbalistic approach which actually complements the words of the Pane'ach Raza and Baal Haturim.

V

If Moshe did not "open" one of the 50 gates to understanding, the *alef* would not be minimized. It ought to be left out altogether! (See *Chomas Anach*, ibid.)

Knowing what one knows not

The Divrei Yechezkel (Rav Yechezkel of Shinov) suggests a novel explanation (for the Gemara in Rosh Hashanah) that discusses the 50 gates to understanding, which may be used to answer this question. An oft-quoted phrase of the ancients goes, "Who is a wise man? One who knows that he really knows nothing!" This is certainly true of the 50th gate to understanding Hashem. It is inconceivable for a human being made of flesh and blood to conceptualize the being of the Creator. Humans acquire the greatest appreciation for their Creator when they understand why His ways are unimaginably distant from comprehension. *This* is the 50th gate to understanding. And this, too, was revealed in its full enigma to Moshe. Rav Yechezkel of Shinov says, "the Gemara should be read, "There are 50 gates to understanding in the world, and *all* of them without exception were revealed to Moshe. Even the 50th gate, which represents the lack of understanding, or the realization that one really *cannot* understand the Creator, was attained by Moshe. Because Moshe lacked it he truly attained it." In short, *not* understanding Hashem *is* the ultimate level of understanding.

We may apply the same thought, said Rav Reich, to the small *alef* of *vayikra*. As we saw in the first two explanations, the small *alef* demonstrates Moshe's humility. It shows that Moshe did not consider himself properly prepared to receive the Divine Word. Moshe understood that he really did *not* fully appreciate how a human being could relate to the Divine Presence. Moshe felt that he completely lacked the 50th level of understanding. And it is this, actually, which is the greatest proof that he *did* acquire the highest level of understanding humanly possible. This is the reason that the *alef* representing Hashem, or the 50th gate to understanding, as *Chomas Anach* pointed out *is* written in the word *vayikra*. It was specifically *because* Moshe felt that the *alef* should be left out, that the *alef* was written. The minimized *alef* thus speaks for itself, testifying to the fact that Moshe had reached the ultimate in spiritual heights!

PARSHAS TZAV

Passover: Why Is This Night Different?

"It once happened that Rebbi Eliezer, Rebbi Yehoshua, Rebbi Elazar ben Azariah, Rebbi Akiva and Rebbi Tarfon were celebrating the seder in Bnei Brak, and they discussed the Exodus from Egypt throughout that entire night (*oso halaylah*)" (Passover Haggadah).

In Hebrew, nouns are either masculine or feminine. Masculine nouns must be qualified by masculine adjectives or pronouns, and feminine nouns are qualified by feminine modifiers. Although there is no fixed rule to determine the gender of a particular noun, one principle always holds true: When a noun ends with the vowel *kamatz* followed by the silent letter *heh*, this word is feminine.

The Sh'lah, in his commentary *Matzah Shemurah* on the Passover Haggadah, asks why the Haggadah's author uses the masculine form of the pronoun for night (*oso*) in the above selection. The word for night (*laylah*) has the *kamatz-heh* ending; thus it should be considered a feminine noun and be preceded by the feminine form of the pronoun—*osah*.

To answer this question, the Sh'lah quotes a Midrash (Shemos Rabbah 18:11) that says that in the Messianic era night will be as bright and light as day. Perhaps, suggests the Sh'lah, the night of our redemption from Egypt, too, was lit up as bright as day. During this time of miraculous redemption, night "became day." In order to allude to the unusual quality of that night, the word *laylah* [night] is treated as if it were *yom* [day], a masculine noun. (See also Gan Raveh to Parshas Bo, Shemos 12:42.)

The Vilna Gaon, in his commentary on the Haggadah, expresses a similar thought in connection with the most famous of all Passover questions: "Why is this night (*halaylah hazeh*) different from all other nights?" The Hebrew word for night, the Vilna Gaon points out, is feminine. But why would the night (i.e., of Passover) be modified by the word *zeh*, a masculine pronoun. Should it not be referred to as *halaylah hazos*, with the feminine pronoun?

The Vilna Gaon explains that by its very nature, nighttime is feminine. This is why, he explains, many positive commandments ("Thou shalt...," as opposed to negative commandments—"Thou shalt not...") must be performed exclusively during the daytime. (Examples of these are: blowing the shofar on Rosh Hashanah, holding the four species on Sukkos, wearing tzitzis and tefillin, etc.) This is in accordance with the "feminine" nature of the night. Just as women are exempted from fulfilling these positive commandments (see Mishnah Kiddushin, 29a), so too, the night, in its role as "female," is "exempted" from all those mitzvos. The exceptions to this rule are the mitzvos performed on the seder night: the eating of matzah, marror [bitter herbs] and (in former—and future—times) the paschal lamb; and relating the story of the Exodus. The Torah earmarks these commandments to be performed *exclusively* at night. (It may be noted that the mitzvos of the night of Pesach apply to women as well, even though holiday-related positive commandments generally do *not* apply to women.—MK)

Thus, we can understand, says the Vilna Gaon, the deeper meaning of the Haggadah's question: Why is this night (*halaylah*) "masculine" (*hazeh*) in its properties—i.e., laden with positive mitzvos—whereas all other nights are feminine in nature and bereft of positive mitzvos? (The four questions can be seen as corresponding to the four positive mitzvos of Pesach night—see the Mishnah's version of this in Pesachim 116a.—MK)

If this is the intention of the Haggadah's question, then what is the answer? The Gaon does not elaborate. Perhaps the answer given by the Sh'lah could be applied here as well. The night of Pesach is imbued with a masculine character because it commemorates the night of the Exodus, which was lit up as bright as day (Zohar Bo, 2:38a; see also Gan Raveh Parshas Bo). This is why the Torah, which usually assigns positive mitzvos to the daylight hours, makes an exception here. On this night, the Torah designates nighttime for the performance of such mitzvos.

II

A question of proper grammar

As profound as these insights may be, Hebrew grammarians will be perplexed by the comments of these great sages. The word *laylah* appears hundreds of times in the Bible, and it is *always* treated as a masculine noun (*balaylah "hahu," belaylah "echad," "sheloshah" laylos*, etc.). It is well known as the sole consistent exception to the *kamatz-heh* rule that we mentioned at the beginning of this essay. How can the theory be advanced that only the *laylah* of

Pesach is treated as a masculine noun?

This problem is raised by the Torah Temimah in his Haggadah commentary, among others, and it has long puzzled talmudic researchers. It should be pointed out that the Vilna Gaon was a grammarian of note, and even wrote a treatise on Hebrew grammar. It is impossible that this is a mere oversight on his part. In fact, I would like to suggest that the true intention of the Vilna Gaon does not involve any grammatical discrepancies.

III

When one reads the Vilna Gaon's commentary carefully, it is clear that he is dealing with a much more profound issue. Let us first review what the Vilna Gaon told us about the "femininity" of nighttime. The Gaon observed that positive commandments often do not apply during the nighttime. The Gaon revealed to us that the reason for this is that nighttime has a feminine character. What makes the night feminine? Is it simply that the Hebrew word that describes it has a *kamatz-heh* ending? Perhaps there is more to it than that. Let us try to gain a broader understanding of night's femininity.

The Vilna Gaon's theory

A source for the Gaon's words that the night is feminine can be found in a Midrash haZohar. The Zohar (Bereishis 20b) asserts that daytime is when men are typically actively providing for their family's livelihood, as the verse says, "The sun shines...and men go out to do their work until evening" (Tehillim 104:22-23). Women, on the other hand, traditionally provide for their families at night, as it is written, "She arises while it is still night, and she prepares sustenance for her household..." (Mishlei 31:15) (During the daytime, while the children are awake, she presumably doesn't have the time to do so.—MK) In the Zohar's words, the man "rules" during the daytime and the woman "rules" during the nighttime.

Undoubtedly, a basic understanding of the concepts of Kabbalah is needed before the deeper messages of this passage can be appreciated. Nevertheless, perhaps we can attain at least a simple, non-Kabbalistic understanding of the Zohar's words.

The Gemara in Yevamos 77a tells us that it is characteristic of women to be less conspicuous than men. Several Biblical sources are adduced to show that it is proper for a woman to remain, whenever possible, withdrawn and private. This is, perhaps, why the Zohar is asserting that "the woman rules during the nighttime." Nightime is the time when her activities are less conspicuous. For the same reason, the night itself, hiding every action in a cloak of blackness, can be seen as feminine. During the nighttime, objects and events are hidden and obscured.

With this in mind we can take a new look at the Gaon's words. Perhaps, when the Gaon noted that the word *laylah* should be modified by the feminine *zos*, he was not referring to the word *laylah* mentioned in the Passover Haggadah. Perhaps he was referring to *every* appearance of the word in the Torah! According to the Gaon, the question of the *Mah Nishtanah* is: Why is *laylah* consistently given masculine modifiers? The word *laylah* should be treated as a feminine noun, not only because of its *kamatz-heh* ending, but also because it is feminine by nature!

Why is this question being asked on this particular night? There is no need to discuss Hebrew grammar at the Pesach table! The answer can be deduced from the continuation of the *Mah Nishtanah*: "On all other nights we eat chametz and matzah, but on this night we eat only matzah." On the night of Pesach, we find four positive commandments designated to be performed specifically at night—in contrast to nighttime's usual feminine character. What makes this night so "masculine?" Intuitively, we realize that this evening's masculine character must somehow be related to a much broader question. Why does the word *laylah*, in general, exhibit duality? What makes "night" so androgynous? On one hand, it has the feminine *kamatz-heh* ending, yet on the other hand, it is consistently associated with masculine modifiers.

How, then, do we answer the questions of the *Mah Nishtanah*? What gives this night its androgynous nature? According to the Haggadah, the solution is, "We were once servants of Pharaoh's in Egypt, and Hashem freed us from there...." What does this have to do with anything?! According to the Gaon's reading of the four (or actually five) questions, we may suggest the following explanation for the Haggadah's answer.

IV

The Talmud likens the world that we live in at present—rife with sorrow and suffering—to the night, while the radiant, joyful life of the World-to-Come is compared to the day (Chagigah 12a etc., see also Yeshayah 21:11, Zecharyah 14:7). This is a very apt metaphor. In the present world, we are often blind to Hashem's presence and control of the world. We see injustice and suffering where tranquillity would appear to be called for, and vice versa. Our perception of Hashem's hand guiding the world is blurred—it is as if Hashem is "hiding His countenance from us" (Devarim 31:17).

The Haggadah's answer

As we have demonstrated above, objects are concealed and inconspicuous during the night. It is therefore justified to compare the world we now live in to the night because Hashem's presence is elusive and often hidden from view. In the Messianic era, however, Hashem will make His majesty clear for all to see. All of the events that have taken place in this world will finally be understood to be only for our own benefit (see Pesachim 50a). Hashem's intervention in everything that takes place in this world will be clearly witnessed by everyone. The presence of Hashem will be "clear as day" (see Sukkos essay, section II, p. 268).

Similarly, just as the word for night in Hebrew has the feminine suffix, this world is considered "feminine," in comparison to the World-to-Come. As the Midrash tells us: "All the songs of praise of this world are referred to as *shirah* [song], in the feminine form...while the song to be sung at the future redemption is called *shir*, in the masculine form" (Mechilta, to Shemos 15:1).

"Just as a woman who delivers a child is bound to suffer the pains of labor and delivery with the birth of the child that follows, so too, are all the salvations of this world followed by new periods of suffering and anguish. In the future, however, there will come a final salvation, after which we will no longer endure suffering.... Upon this salvation we shall sing to Hashem the 'song of the male' " (Tosafos, Pesachim 116b).

Now we often have trouble discerning Hashem's guiding hand. Nevertheless, it is with us all of the time. All the troubles and misfortunes that befall us are intended exclusively for our benefit. (We will discuss some of the benefits of exile and suffering in the Tazria-Hachodesh essay p. 129 and the Metzora essay, p. 133.)

At the dawn of the Messianic era, Hashem's guiding hand will become self evident. In retrospect, we will be able to appreciate all that Hashem has done for us throughout history. This is the meaning of the statement we quoted above (in section I), that in the future redemption, night will become day. The tribulations of the Exile—which conceal Hashem's presence as if in a cloak of darkness—will be revealed as having been clearly wrought by the Hand of Hashem.

On the night of the Exodus from Egypt we caught a glimpse of this phenomenon. Night turned to day, as we understood that our enslavement to the Egyptians was necessary for becoming the dedicated servants of Hashem.

The night has the potential to be day

This is what makes the night of Pesach different from all other nights. On Pesach night, we realize that night itself has the potential to become day. The inconspicuously "feminine" presence of Hashem gives way to the clear manifestation of Hashem's presence. This is why, on the anniversary of the Egyptian Exodus, we were given positive commandments to perform in the nighttime. In fact, it is only in reference to the evening of the Exodus—or to the night of the Final Redemption—that we find night referred to as *layil*, without the usual *kamatz-heh* ending! (See Shemos 12:42; Yalkut Shimoni II, end of #418; Targum to Yeshayah 16:3; Rashi, Sanhedrin 94a s.v. *Shomer*; Yeshayah 30:29.)

The lesson, however, does not stop there. Even when we return to our daily lives, and the Divine Presence once again "fades into obscurity," we take with us what we have learned at the Passover Seder. We remind ourselves that although the "night" (the Divine Presence in this world) appears feminine, if we look at it from the proper perspective, its true masculine (i.e., clearly visible) nature can be observed—just as it was on that special night of the Exodus from Egypt!

The very grammar of the word *laylah* directs us to this conclusion. It has the *appearance* of being feminine, but is in reality masculine. We are sometimes under the impression that our Exile is "feminine," that the conduct of Hashem is hidden and inexplicable. But the truth is that it is plainly visible. This is how "We were once slaves of Pharaoh's..." explains the grammatical anomaly of "*laylah*."

May we soon merit to witness the ultimate manifestation of Hashem's Glory and to reveal the underlying "masculinity" of the long, bitter night of Exile!

PARSHAS SHEMINI

A Count Of The Letters Of The Torah

"The Early Torah sages were called *sofrim* [scribes or those who count] because they were able to count all the letters of the Torah. They used to say, 'The letter *vav* of the word *gachon* (Parshas Shemini, Vayikra 11:42) is the half-way point of the Sefer Torah....' " (Gemara Kiddushin 30a).

The mid-point of the Torah: four theories

"Rav Yosef asked, 'Is the *vav* of *gachon* the last letter of the first half of the Torah, or the first of the second half?' Abaye answered him, 'Let us bring a Sefer Torah and count the letters, to find out! Didn't Rabbah bar bar Chanah say that when a similar question was raised in the past, the sages did not move until they brought a Sefer Torah and counted?' Rav Yosef replied, 'Those sages were experts in *chaseros v'yeseros* [what must be written lacking and what must be written in a supplemented manner] while we are not experts in this matter. [Thus, our count will not be reliable in determining the central letter of the Sefer Torah]' " (Gemara Kiddushin 30a).

The Gemara in Kiddushin clearly establishes that the letter *vav* of the word *gachon* is the middle letter of the Torah. The Beraisa in Sofrim (9:2) states that for this reason the *vav* of *gachon* is actually written in a larger than normal size—to denote that it marks a unique position in the Sefer Torah.

However, if one actually counts the letters of the Torah, one discovers a problem. According to modern counts, there are in fact 304,805 letters in the Torah. The *vav* of *gachon* is not located at the midpoint letter—#152,403—but rather nearly 5,000 letters later, at letter #157,336!

Admittedly, Rav Yosef said that we are not expert at determining *chaseros v'ye-*

seros. The simple understanding of *chaseros v'yeseros* is that some words can be spelled both with and without the letters *vav*, *yud*, *alef*, or *heh*, as these "supplementary letters" are written to aid the recognition of vowels, but are not themselves always pronounced. Rav Yosef is then saying that in our Sifrei Torah, there might be a few words written without *vavs* or *yuds* that should have been written with them, or vice versa. However, it would seem bizarre to consider that 5,000 (!) letters were added or are missing in our Sifrei Torah. Even when we take into consideration all of the known *mesorahs* for writing Torah scrolls, from all the various Jewish congregations around the world, there are still only *nine* inconsistencies in spelling (Harav Moshe Sternbuch in *Mitzvas Hayom*, p. 34). Clearly, the missing 5,000 letters cannot be attributed to incorrect spelling of words.

Theory one: grammatical re-spelling

Furthermore, the halacha states that if even a single letter is added or missing in a Sefer Torah, the entire Sefer Torah is invalid (see Tosafos Menachos beg. 30a). Is it possible that Rav Yosef was challenging the validity of every Sefer Torah that existed in his time?

Rav Eliyahu Posek answers (Piskai Eliyahu, part 3:1) that perhaps the *sofrim*, who counted the letters, meant the following: Many words in the Torah should be written with or without a *vav* or *yud*, yet the Torah deletes or adds those letters for exegetical purposes. If one were to compile a list of all the *vavs* and *yuds* that the Torah excluded or included when it should not have, grammatically, the *vav* of *gachon* would be located at the middle of the list (it is assumed that *gachon* should really be written without a *vav*).

We would then explain the Gemara as follows: Rav Yosef asked whether the *vav* of *gachon* is the last letter of the first half of this list of letters, or the first letter of the second half of the list.

In order to determine this answer, it was recommended that all the letters that are included or excluded when they ought not have been, should be counted. Rav Yosef responded that since they lacked the grammatical expertise necessary to determine in which words the *vav* and *yud* would serve as extra letters and in which words they were part of the actual word, they would not know which letters to count. (See article by R. Yitzchak Zilber in *Shma'atsin* vol. 43 for a similar explanation.)

II

"There is a tradition that the Bnai Yisrael in any given generation never number less than 600,000 people" (Rabbeinu Gershom, Erchin 32b).

"There are 600,000 letters in the Sefer Torah just as there are 600,000 souls in the twelve tribes of the Bnai Yisrael" (Zohar Chadash, Shir HaShirim, page 74, column 4).

"The soul of everyone in Yisrael stems from one of the six hundred thousand letters in the Torah. The name 'Yisrael' can be seen as an acronym for the words ***Y**esh **s**hisim **r**iboe **o**siyos **l**aTorah* (There are six hundred thousand letters in the Torah)" (Megaleh Amukos, Vaeschanan #186).

600,000 letters for 600,000 Jews

We also find in the Kabbalah that the Bnai Yisrael can never number less than 600,000 people, since at its root Bnai Yisrael consists of six hundred thousand souls just as the Sefer Torah consists of 600,000 letters. Each member of the Bnai Yisrael is somehow connected to one of the 600,000 letters of the Torah.

Clearly this is problematic. As was noted previously, our modern day count find only 304,805 letters in the Torah. Why does the Zohar say that there are 600,000 letters—which is nearly double the apparent number! The answer of Rav Eliyahu Posek, cited above, obviously cannot explain the whereabouts of the missing 295,000+ letters. His solution does not provide for missing letters at all!

III

A number of other explanations, though, have been suggested which are able to explain both how the *vav* of *gachon* is the middle letter of the Torah, and how there are 600,000 letters in the Torah.

Second theory: Zohar Chadash: Spell out the letters

The Zohar Chadash suggests that when counting the letters of the Torah, we must not count each letter as a single letter. Rather, each letter must be counted according to the number of letters it comprises when its name is spelled out. For instance, the word *alef* is counted as *alef, lamed, pheh*, in other words three letters. The word *beis* is spelled *beis, yud, saf* making this word, too, three letters. *Gimmel*, is *gimmel, yud, mem, lamed*, or four letters. If all the letters of the Torah are counted in this manner, the Zohar explains, there will be six hundred thousand letters in the Torah!

The Zohar's counting method may also explain how the *vav* of *gachon* actually marks the halfway point of the Sefer Torah. The number of letters preceding this *vav* may equal the number of letters following it, if we count them in the above manner. Rav Yosef, in pointing out his lack of expertise in *chaseros v'yeseros*, may also have been explaining why he was not able to duplicate the Zohar's method of counting. Many letters of the *alef-beis* can be spelled with or without supplementary *vavs* and *yuds* to aid in their pronunciation. For instance, *beis* can be spelled *beis, yud, saf*, or *beis, saf. Vav* can be spelled *vav, yud, vav*, or *vav, vav*, etc. As a result, our ignorance regarding the spelling of many of the Torah's Hebrew letters prevents us from properly counting how many letters precede and succeed the *vav* of *gachon*!

Rav Shneur Zalman of Liady (the author of *The Tanya*, and first Rebbe of the Lubavitcher dynasty) provides another answer (Likutei Torah, Behar page 43, column 4). In order to count 600,000 letters in the Torah, he writes, one must add to every vowel that lacks supplementary letters, those letters. For instance, it is possible to add an *alef* or *heh* after every *patach* or *komatz* vowel that is not followed by them (see Rashi, beg. of Kesubos 69b, end of Makkos 7b). A *vav* can be added after every *cholem* or *kubutz* vowel, and a *yud* after every *chirik* or *tzarei* vowel. If all these additions are made, there will be 600,000 letters in the Torah!

Third theory: Likutei Torah explains we must add letters after open vowels

This, too, would explain Rav Yosef's statement in Kiddushin. The *vav* in *gachon* is the middle letter in the Torah after we supplement all the vowels lacking supplementary letters. However, Rav Yosef explains we lack expertise regarding which vowels can support an extra letter without changing the word's meanings and which vowels cannot. As a result, we do not know which of these unwritten supplementary letters to count!

According to both of these answers, obviously, the validity of our Sifrei Torah is not questioned. What is written in the Torah is all properly accounted for. Rav Yosef's doubts were only in regard to counting what is *not* written in the Sefer Torah itself!

IV

Both of the above answers, however, are difficult to understand. If we follow the formula of the Zohar Chadash and all letters were written out as two, three, and even four letters, there would be more than 600,000 letters in the Torah—there would be at least 800,000 letters!

Fourth theory: we must count letter-widths

If the formula of the Likutei Torah were followed, and all the unsupplemented vowels were written in supplemented form, there would still be far less than 600,000 letters, since many vowels of the Torah are already written in supplemented form and thus would not receive additional letters! (See R. Reuven Margoliot, *Hamikra Vehamesorah*, chapters 4 and 12, for a compilation of various other answers. R. Margoliot raises difficulties with all these other answers and then offers his own answer—which is itself difficult. See also *Torah Shelemah*, vol. 27, pp. 286-9, *The Handbook of Jewish Thought* by Rav Aryeh Kaplan, ch. 7, footnote #108; and Rav Tzadok Hakohen's *Peri Tzaddik*, beginning of Shemos.)

Perhaps we might approach both the question of the displaced *vav*-of-*gachon*, and that of the missing 300,000 letters, in a different manner. There is a tradition that at the beginning of every new Parsha-section in the Sefer Torah, a space, the width of nine letters, must be left blank (Rambam, Hilchos Sefer Torah 8:1). The Beis Yosef (Yoreh Deah 275 s.v. *Ul'inyan Shiur*) points out that the letters of the Torah are of different widths, so the size of a space nine letters wide will depend on which letters are used as a model.

The Beis Yosef writes that since the tradition does not specify which letters to use, nine widths of the smallest letter in the Hebrew alphabet—the *yud*—will suffice.

We can now understand how the *vav* of *gachon* is the middle letter of the Torah and how there are 600,000 letters in the Torah. According to the Beis Yosef, an unspecified letter does not refer to an average sized letter, but to the smallest letter. When counting the letters of the Torah, perhaps we should *not* count each character as a single letter. Rather, letters which must (halachically) be written the width of two *yuds*, count as two "letters." A large letter, such as *shin*, counts as three letters since its width is as wide as three *yuds* (the *shin* is comprised of three *yuds* extending from a base). In fact, if we allow another bit of space to separate each of the *yuds* of the top of the *shin* from each other, the *shin* is two bits *more* than three *yuds* wide.

Simple calculation reveals that there are only four letters that are one *yud*'s width wide: *vav*, *zayin*, *yud*, and *nun sofis* (final nun). There are two letters a *yud* and a half wide—*gimmel* and *nun* (due to their bases). Fifteen letters are two *yud* widths wide, five letters are two plus-a-bit *yud* widths wide, and one letter is three plus-two-bits *yud* widths wide. This just about doubles the number of letters in the Sefer Torah! Therefore, if each letter is counted by its *yud* widths, there will be 600,000 letters in the Torah, instead of 300,000!

This suggestion can also explain Rav Yosef's statement that inexpertise concerning *chaseros v'yeseros* prevents us from ascertaining that the *vav* of *gachon* is at the Torah's midpoint Perhaps *chaseros v'yeseros* does not refer to *vowels* and *words* that are lacking or expanded with supplementary letters. Rather, it refers to *letters* that are lacking or supplemented in their widths. Massoretically, certain letters in the Sefer Torah are written in one place either smaller (lacking) or larger (supplemented) than in other places. For example, the *alef* in the word *vayikra* (Vayikra 1:1) is written smaller than usual, and so is the *yud* in the word "*teshi*" (Devarim 32:18). The *beis* of the first word in the Torah, "*Bereishis*," is written larger than normal, as is the *vav* in *gachon*.

When the *sofrim* stated that the *vav* of *gachon* is the Torah's midpoint, perhaps they meant that if all the letters of the Torah were to be counted by their *yud* widths, this *vav* would be the center of the Torah! When Rav Yosef commented that we cannot confirm this statement due to our lack of expertise in *chaseros v'yeseros*, he may have meant that we do not know positively which letters to enlarge or shrink, or how much to enlarge or shrink them, due to an uncertainty in the *mesorah*. Nevertheless, this uncertainty would not render a doubt as to the validity of today's Sifrei Torah.

The Rambam states explicitly (Hilchos Sefer Torah 6:9) that if a letter is made larger or smaller than its true Massoretic size, it does not invalidate a

Sefer Torah! Our own Sifrei Torah can now be seen as having 600,000 letters, and the *vav* of *gachon* may truly be the central character of those 600,000 letters!

(After this D'var Torah was publicized, a friend showed me Rav Yaakov Kaminetsky's, zt'l, book *Emes L'Yaakov* where he uses a nearly identical approach to explain how there are 600,000 letters in the Torah. I thank Hashem for leading me in the path of such a great Torah scholar. Rav Yaakov even calculated the total number of letters, based on this hypothesis, and came out with 576,000 letters, still 23,000 letters short. However, Rav Yaakov didn't count the extra "bits" in the six letters that I mentioned. Also, as my friend haRav David Lichtman suggested, we ought to add nine letter-widths for each new Parsha in the Torah. [The halacha requires that at least a nine-letter space be left between Parshiyos.] If each of the extra "bits" are taken to be equal to the width of one half of a letter, we find that there are approximately 597,000 letter-widths in the Torah! [The numbers of times that each letter appears in the Torah can be found at the end of the Torah Temimah chumashim and in the new Concordance. The figures in the two sources vary slightly. See also Rav Kaplan's footnote in *Menashe ben Yisrael: The Conciliator* (Hermon Press: N.Y., 1972, Part 1, page 250).]

PARSHAS TAZRIA

Parshas Hachodesh—Shabbos Rosh Chodesh
Rosh Chodesh: The Woman's Holiday

"Women who refrain from work on *Rosh Chodesh* are following an established custom" (Yerushalmi Taanis 1:6). In numerous Talmudic sources we are told about the custom of women refraining from work on *Rosh Chodesh*. In fact, the Be'ur Halacha (Orach Chaim 417) informs us that it is not simply a custom—women are *obligated* to make *Rosh Chodesh* different from a normal working day. It is even preferred for women to abstain from simple work on *Rosh Chodesh*, but the obligation is to at least differentiate between *Rosh Chodesh* and a normal working day.

What is the meaning of this unusual Yom Tov uniquely celebrated by women? The Pirkei d'Rabbi Eliezer (quoted in part by Rashi and Tosafos Megillah 22b), tells us the source of the *Rosh Chodesh* holiday:

A holiday for women

"When the Jews asked Aaron to make them a golden calf, Aaron said to them, 'Remove the rings that are in the ears of your wives' (Shemos 32:2). The women, however, did not agree to give their jewelry to their husbands. Rather, they said to them: 'Should we make a calf which is an abomination and has no power to save us? We will not listen to you!' Hashem rewarded women in this world that they should keep *Rosh Chodesh*. He also rewarded them in the *Olam Habba* [World-to-Come] that they will be renewed like the *Roshei Chodoshim*, as the verse says: 'Your youth shall be renewed to be [as light] as an eagle' (Tehillim 103:5)" (Pirkei d'Rabbi Eliezer, Ch. 45).

The Midrash tells us that Jewish women merited this special holiday because they did not join the rest of the Bnai Yisrael in the sin of the golden calf.

The sin of the golden calf, however, occurred on the 17th of the lunar month of

Tammuz, which is nowhere near the first of the month. Why, then, did Hashem reward women specifically with the holiday of *Rosh Chodesh*?

II

Why Rosh Chodesh? Two explanations: The Tur and The Prisha

The Tur (Orach Chaim 417) offers an explanation for the above Midrash in the name of his brother, haRav Yehudah. On the three *Regalim,* [pilgrimage festivals]—Pesach, Shavuos, and Sukkos—all of the Bnai Yisrael went to Yerushalayim to offer *korbanos* [sacrifices] in the Beis Hamikdash. These holidays were given to Bnai Yisrael, haRav Yehudah explains, in the merit of the three forefathers: Pesach for Avraham, Shavuos for Yitzchak, and Sukkos for Yaakov. Similarly, the twelve *Roshei Chodoshim* were to be given as holidays in the merit of the twelve tribes. However, when the twelve tribes committed the sin of the golden calf in the desert, they lost these holidays. The women, who refrained from sinning in conjunction with the men, were rewarded with at least a remembrance of these forfeited holidays.

The Prisha (ad loc.), brings another answer in the name of his Rebbi, Rav Heschel. Rav Heschel explains that the real reward given to the women for their refusal to partake in the sin of the golden calf is found at the end of the above quoted Pirkei d'Rabbi Eliezer. Pirkei d'Rabbi Eliezer tells us that in the World-to-Come women will become youthful again. *Rosh Chodesh* hints to this future reward because after disappearing, the moon becomes "youthful" again at the beginning of every month, when it reappears and begins to grow anew. Therefore, it is appropriate for the women to be granted *Rosh Chodesh* as a holiday, which alludes to their eventual reward of regaining their youthfulness.

However, Rav Heschel's suggestion requires further explanation. Why did Hashem choose to reward the women specifically by returning them to their youthfulness? We may suggest the following: Had the sin of the golden calf never been committed, there would be no death in the world and the Bnai Yisrael would have enjoyed eternal life and youthfulness (Gemara Avoda Zara 5a). As the women abstained from transgression, they will in return receive that same eternal youth in *Olam Habba*. The women's renewed youthfulness will be identical to the condition of the Bnai Yisrael before the sin of the golden calf—a state of eternal life and youth.

III

Perhaps another approach may be mentioned concerning why the women were rewarded with the holiday of *Rosh Chodesh*. Let us begin by asking another question: What do we celebrate when we see a new moon?

The Gemara tells us in Eruvin 54a that if the Bnai Yisrael had not committed the sin of the golden calf, they never would have been sent into *galus* [exile]. Only after this sin, was their destiny to be a nation in exile. There is another side to this punishment, though. Although *galus* is clearly meant as retribution, it is also a means for the Bnai Yisrael's continued existence. Why is that?

Galus as an opportunity for atonement

When the Bnai Yisrael committed the sin of the golden calf, Hashem wanted to wipe them out—"Let my anger flare up against them and I shall annihilate them!" (Shemos 32:10). But Moshe Rabbeinu pleaded with Hashem to refrain from punishing the Bnai Yisrael with sudden and total destruction. Hashem then agreed to mete out punishment slowly over many generations: "Now, go and lead the people to where I have told you...[but] each time the Bnai Yisrael sin in the future, I shall bring this sin to account against them [along with their other sins]" (Shemos 32:34). This is the purpose that exile serves. Although *galus* is a punishment, it also holds the key to our continued existence. If the Bnai Yisrael had not been granted *galus* as an opportunity for atonement, Hashem would have annihilated them in the desert!

This second role of *galus* is brought out in many Talmudic sources—see, for example, Sanhedrin 37b, "*Galus* is an atonement for everything," Taanis 16a, "We have been exiled, may our exile be an atonement for us." Although *galus* has negative aspects, it is at the same time a vehicle for Jewish survival.

IV

The Midrash states that Esav and Yaakov are, respectively, compared to the sun and moon:

The waxing of the moon: Yaakov's return from galus

"Hashem created...the greater luminary [the sun] to rule by day, and the lesser luminary [the moon] to rule by night" (Bereishis 1:16).

"It is appropriate for the greater [older] brother to base his calendar on the greater luminary, and for the lesser [younger] brother to base his calendar on the lesser luminary. This is why Esav's calendar is based on the sun, while Yaakov's calendar is based on the moon.... Esav counts his days by the sun, which is the greater luminary. The sun rules only by day and not by night, and so too, Esav has a portion only in this world, but not in the World-to-Come. Yaakov counts his days by the moon, which is lesser. Just as the moon can be seen by day and by night, so too, Yaakov has a portion both in this world and in the World-to-Come" (Bereishis Rabbah 6:3).

Perhaps, then, the phases of the moon can be construed as representative of Yaakov's fate. The moon shrinks, getting smaller and smaller until it reaches its smallest point. This alludes to *galus*, a punishment which necessarily involves the reduction and weakening of the Bnai Yisrael. Afterwards, however, the moon again waxes, increasing in size until it becomes full. This represents the other side of *galus*—the eventual strengthening and redemption of the Bnai Yisrael.

This, then, may be the reason for the joy experienced upon seeing the moon at the beginning of the month, when the moon has just begun to return after its disappearance. We are celebrating the return of Yaakov and his children to their former glory. In fact, when we recite the blessing on the new moon, we say, "David the king of Israel is alive and continues to be!" (see Gemara Rosh Hashanah 25a).

The Gemara in Chullin would seem to support this interpretation: "First we are told that Hashem made 'the two great luminaries,' implying that the two were equally large. Later we are told of 'the greater luminary...and the lesser luminary!' (Bereishis 1:16). The explanation of this discrepancy is that originally the two luminaries were indeed equal. However, the moon spoke before the Hashem saying, 'Ruler of the World, is it possible for two kings to share the same crown?' Hashem replied, 'Go and make yourself smaller!' The Moon retorted, 'Because what I said was correct, I must reduce myself?' Hashem comforted her, saying, 'Go and rule both by night and by day' " (Chullin 60b).

The Gemara implies that because of the moon's unwarranted grievances Hashem punished her and shrank her. This made the moon both less luminous than the sun, and subject to phases, during which it "shrinks" for half a month (see Chizkuni Bereishis ad loc.). It would appear that the Gemara is detailing the punishment of the moon for speaking up arrogantly before its creator. But how can this be true—the moon, lacking mind and free choice, has neither the ability to speak nor the capacity for sin!

We may explain this strange Aggadah in light of the comparison drawn above between the moon and *galus*. The moon represents the Bnai Yisrael. It is the Bnai Yisrael who complain to Hashem that Hashem created Esav as the twin of Yaakov, thereby granting them equal power. If Esav, who is conspiring to do evil instead of the will of his creator, is granted strength equal to Yaakov's (two kings sharing the same crown), then there is no guarantee that Yaakov will prevail. Instead, as we see with the sin of the golden calf, it is possible that Esav and the forces of evil will prevail over Yaakov and the legions of good.

Hashem responds by saying to the Bnai Yisrael "Make yourself smaller!"—hinting, as we have suggested, that due to their eventual sin, the Bnai Yisrael will be punished with exile. The moon then counters that her complaint was valid—it is Esav who should be minimized, to prevent the triumph of evil! What good will be accomplished by shrinking the moon? Reducing the power of the Bnai Yaakov will only make matters worse! Now, not only is it possible for evil to prevail over good, evil has been granted the upper hand in the battle! Hashem replies, "Rule by day and by night!" Hashem assures the Bnai Yisrael that instead of making the situation more difficult for them by sending them into *galus*, He is ensuring their survival and their eventual victory. Due to the expiatory effects of the *galus*, they will eventually rule both "by day and by night"—in this world, and in the World-to-Come, as seen in the previous Midrash. (See also Maharsha Chullin ad loc., Zohar Chadash 15b.)

V

With this in mind, we may perhaps answer the question with which we began—why were women rewarded with the holiday of *Rosh Chodesh* because of their restraint from sin? We may now suggest the following:

The celebration of the women, in light of the above

On the one hand we find that the shrinking of the moon represents the exiles and the punishments for the transgressions of the Bnai Yisrael. The moon's waxing, on the other hand, represents Hashem's promise that this reduction and weakness is only temporary. It demonstrates that *because* of our trials and tribulations, we will be able to survive as Hashem's nation, and merit the final redemption.

The men who committed the sin of the golden calf, do not deserve to celebrate the waxing of the moon. After all, if the men had not sinned, there would have been no need for a *galus* to guarantee the survival of the Bnai Yisrael. The men, therefore, have nothing to celebrate when the moon waxes. Women, however, did not sin, and therefore did not deserve to be punished. Women, thus, can rightfully celebrate the waxing of the moon, rejoicing in Hashem's promise to preserve the Jewish nation (despite their sins) by sending them into *galus*!

PARSHAS METZORA

Measure For Measure In Loshon Hara

METZORA

"This is the law of the *metzora* [a *metzora* is someone afflicted with *tzaraas*, a skin disease similar to leprosy, which imparts ritual impurity to the afflicted party] (Vayikra 14:2)—this verse may be read homiletically as 'this is law of the *motzi-shem-ra* [slanderer]'" (Erchin 15b).

"He who guards his mouth and tongue, guards himself from *tzaros* [misfortune]" (Mishlei 21:23). Do not read the word as *tzaros*, but rather (homiletically) as *tzaraas*" (Midrash Tanchuma, Metzora, #2).

The punishment of the slanderer

"The primeval serpent mentioned in Bereishis 3:5 slandered his Creator; therefore he was punished with *tzaraas*. How did he slander his creator? ...He told Adam and Chavah, 'those who practice a certain trade are naturally hostile to their peers' (intimating that Hashem prohibited the Tree of Life to Adam and Chavah, because He didn't want them to become His "competitors," see Bereishis 3:5). ...The rough scales on the skins of today's snakes are the manifestation of the serpent's *tzaraas*" (Midrash Tanchuma, Metzora, #2).

In many places Chazal tell us the severity of the sin of *loshon hara* ["the evil tongue", or speaking ill of a fellow Jew in the presence of others]. Not only is it forbidden to speak *loshon hara*, it is forbidden for the person hearing *loshon hara* to accept it as true. The statements of the Rabbis quoted above make it clear that the disease of *tzaraas* is considered a punishment for transgressing this very serious prohibition.

The Midrash comments that the primeval serpent, the archetypical speaker of *loshon hara*, was stricken with *tzaraas*, as can be recognized in the scaly skin of its descendants. In fact, the snake is one of the only large animals to regularly shed its entire skin, akin to *tzaraas*, a disease which causes the human skin to deteriorate and peel. The connection between *loshon hara* and *tzaraas* is alluded to in the Torah. We are told that Miriam contracted *tzaraas* immediately upon slandering her brother Moses (Bamidbar 12:10).

There is a general rule that whenever Hashem metes out a punishment for a particular sin, there is some connection between the offense and the penalty (*middah keneged middah*). This allows someone to deduce from the punishment what he is being punished for, so that he can find the path to repentance. What is there about *tzaraas*, then, that makes it an appropriate punishment for the sin of *loshon hara?* What is the connection between the two?

II

When one speaks *loshon hara*, it can cause emotional, monetary, or even bodily harm to the person being spoken about. The Rabbis tell us that the effects of this sin go even further than that:

Loshon hara kills

"Death and life are in the hand of the tongue" (Mishlei 18:21). The Gemara explains (Erchin 15b): Does a tongue then have a hand? Rather, this expression is used to convey the idea that just as one's hand can kill, so can a one's tongue.

"'A spear, a sword and a sharp arrow—such is one who bears false testimony against his fellow man' (Mishlei 25:18). Note that *loshon hara* is compared to these three weapons of killing, because it can cause just as much harm" (Yalkut Shimoni, Mishlei, #961).

The Rabbis make it clear that slandering someone is tantamount to actually killing them. The Rambam in Hilchos Deios 7:1 elaborates on this idea further: The Rambam says that one who speaks maliciously of another person transgresses a negative commandment of the Torah. This is a grave sin and causes the loss of many lives among the people of Israel. It is for this reason that the prohibition against *loshon hara* is juxtaposed in the Torah against the verse "Do not stand by at the shedding of your neighbor's blood" (Vayikra 19:16). You can see this illustrated by the story of Doeg the Edomite in I Shmuel 22:9.

The comparison of *loshon hara* to murder may be understood in two ways. Firstly, as the Rambam's example of Doeg illustrates, *loshon hara* can lead to the actual killing of the people implicated in the malicious slander of the tale bearer. Alternatively, even if the harm caused by the hearsay that was spoken is only emotional, we are taught that when someone embarrasses a friend in public, it is as if he has killed him (Gemara Bava Metzia 58b). Thus, *all loshon hara* may be understood as having caused, in a certain sense, a loss of life.

III

In Nedarim 64b we are taught that a *metzora* is described as "dead." This may also be understood in two ways. In the advanced stages of disease, the *metzora* may completely lose feeling in one or more limbs. These parts of his body have, in effect, died. Alternatively, the "death" of the *metzora* may be explained in a different sense. The *metzora,* in general, would be quarantined. Halachically, a *metzora* is forced to live "in solitude, outside the camp" (Vayikra 13:46)—he may not go inside any walled city. This enforced isolation obviously causes him extreme humiliation (see Berachos 5b), and this humiliating situation, as we have seen above, is comparable to death.

Tit for tat

Based on this understanding of the *metzora*'s plight, we can understand why the punishment of *tzaraas* is appropriate to the sin of *loshon hara.* The slanderer causes death—physically and emotionally—to the victim of his gossip, so he is punished by being killed, in a sense, both physically and emotionally.

IV

With what we have established, we can perhaps shed light on another aspect of the laws of the *metzora.*

We know that under certain circumstances, the Torah imposes a punishment for bringing about someone's death, even it was done without malicious intent (unintentional manslaughter). This punishment is *galus,* or exile from the perpetrator's home town to a "city of refuge," (see Bamidbar, Chap. 35). Since the unintentional killer "uprooted" a person from the world, he himself must suffer by being uprooted from his physical surroundings and leaving his home and his family for a strange city.

Exile & loshon hara

In Mishnah Kelim 1:7 we find that the *metzora* must leave any walled city in Israel. He, too, is effectively exiled from his city. The similarity between the punishments of the killer and the *metzora* may be explained in light of what was discussed above. The *metzora,* like the actual murderer, has brought about the loss of life of another human being through his destructive and disgracing slander. He must therefore suffer the penalty of exile, just as the murderer. It is interesting to note that the *loshon hara* of the primeval serpent also led to exile—the most famous and far reaching exile of all—the banishment of the serpent along with Adam and Eve, from the Garden of Eden!

May we all learn from this the importance of keeping our tongues from speaking anything negative about our fellow human beings, and may we thereby merit to see an end to our own lengthy exile, and the rebuilding of the Beis Hamikdash!

PARSHAS ACHAREI MOS

Keeping One's Distance

"Hashem spoke to Moshe after the death of Aharon's two sons, who had died when they approached before Hashem" (Vayikra 16:1).

"Aharon's sons, Nadav and Avihu, each took their shovel, put incense in it and brought a fire that was not sanctified before Hashem—which He had not commanded them to bring. A fire went forth from before Hashem and devoured them."

" 'A fire went forth'—Rebbi Eliezer explained: Aharon's sons died because they made a halachic decision [to bring their own fire to the altar] without first asking their master, Moshe. Rebbi Yishmael said: [They were killed] because they entered the Mishkan while under the influence of alcohol" (Vayikra 10:1-3, and Rashi).

Too many sins

Aharon's sons were dramatically killed in an episode which took place during the Mishkan's inauguration ceremony. A heavenly fire flashed out of the Holy of Holies, claiming their lives while leaving their bodies intact (Sanhedrin 52a). The verse clearly reveals to us the sin of Nadav and Avihu. They were punished for bringing an unsolicited fire to the Mishkan upon which they offered an incense offering (either in the Holy of Holies or on the altar of the courtyard, see Tosafos Eruvin 63a).

In the Midrash (see Vayikra Rabbah, 20:6-10, Sanhedrin 52a), however, we unexpectedly find a long list of purported causes for the death of Aharon's children. Even more confusing is that many of the reasons listed in the Midrash seem entirely unrelated to the explicit description of their sin found in the Torah text! Aside from Rashi's comment (that they either made a halachic decision on their own, or entered the Mishkan in a drunken state) we are also told that Nadav and

Avihu refused to marry and bear children.

Furthermore, the Midrash says, they were heard to comment, "When will these old men [Moshe and Aharon] pass on, so that we may be the nation's new leaders!" Another Midrash tells us that they sinned by entering the Mishkan without donning a *me'il* [the high-priestly robe]—an altogether cryptic suggestion since they were *not* high-priests and thus were not required to wear this robe.

Tosafos (Yoma 53a) notes the confusion raised by the Midrash on this issue, but he does not offer any insights for resolving the various Midrashim. What do all of these sins have to do with bringing an unsolicited fire to the altar? Also, does a common thread run through the various suggestions of the Midrash? Let us attempt to attain at least a partial understanding of these peculiar Midrashim.

II

First, let us analyze yet another comment made by the Midrash (ibid.) involving the deaths of Nadav and Avihu. At the end of Parshas Mishpatim (Shemos 24:9-11) we are told that when we were given the Torah, Moshe and Aharon took Nadav, Avihu and seventy elders up to Mt. Sinai. There, they "beheld Hashem and ate and drank." Rashi (loc. cit.), based on the Midrash, explains that Nadav and Avihu beheld Hashem haughtily, while satiated with food and drink. Rashi tells us further:

Reaching too high

"[Nadav and Avihu and the elders] beheld Hashem and gazed at Him more than was permitted to them. A punishment of death was decreed upon them [and they ought to have died right then and there], but Hashem did not want to dampen the joy of the Giving of the Torah. On the day of the inauguration of the Mishkan, Nadav and Avihu were dealt their punishment..." (Rashi ibid.).

Why did Hashem choose the inauguration of the Mishkan for Nadav and Avihu's retribution? Perhaps Rashi is teaching us that Nadav and Avihu's sin at the inauguration ceremony brought to mind their former sin. The two sins were rooted in the same basic misconduct. How were these sins connected?

Nadav and Avihu's sin at Mt. Sinai is described quite clearly. Hashem revealed Himself on Mt. Sinai to an extent that He had never done before. Hashem appeared in His awesome majesty in order to give His chosen nation the Torah and reveal to them His Divine Will. It was to this display of the Divine Presence that Moshe brought Nadav and Avihu and the seventy elders at the end of Parshas Mishpatim. However, the sons of Aharon were unprepared for the encounter.

When Moshe ascended Mount Sinai to encounter the Presence of Hashem and receive the two Tablets of the Law, Moshe abstained from food and drink for forty days (Shemos 34:28). Nadav and Avihu, however, did not display the requisite awe for this momentous occasion. Perhaps they believed that they *were* spiritually prepared to behold the Divine Presence. But the Torah reveals that they were still entrenched in the physical world of eating and drinking. "Their hearts were dense with food and drink" (Rashi). They did not realize how stringently one must separate oneself from the world of material pleasure in order to approach Hashem in an intimate manner. They "peered" at the Divine Presence a bit too intensely for their particular level of spirituality.

It was this same attitude that brought Nadav and Avihu to enter the Mishkan with their fire at the inauguration of the Mishkan. Nadav and Avihu, according to the Midrash, offered incense on their own in the Holy of Holies on the day that Hashem first rested His Presence there. Since they were chosen to serve in the Mishkan as Kohanim, they considered themselves to be on a high enough spiritual level to enter the Holy of Holies and behold the Divine Presence uninvited. They repeated the mistake that they had made at Mt. Sinai—and this time they suffered the grievous consequences.

III

Armed with this insight, we may begin to make sense of the confusion in the Midrashim that discuss Nadav and Avihu's sin.

A second look at the midrashim

As we quoted earlier (section I), one Midrash states that Nadav and Avihu died because they commented, "When will Moshe and Aharon pass away, so that we may become the nation's new leaders?" Nadav and Avihu were not power hungry. Rather, as is clear from their behavior at Mt. Sinai, they considered themselves to be spiritually on par with—perhaps even greater than—Moshe and Aharon. Just as Moshe was granted "unlimited access" to the Holy of Holies (Toras Kohanim, Acharei, Parshesa 1:6) and remained always in a state of preparedness to prophesy (Rashi Bamidbar 12:4) so, too, Aharon's sons felt that they were fit to serve before Hashem with similar "familiarity." Since they were Kohanim (and unlike Aharon were not involved in the sin of the golden calf), they felt that they would be more appropriate leaders.

Even though Moshe was chosen to take the Jews out of Egypt, in the Mishkan's era, they believed that the Kohanim who served in the Temple would make better leaders. If Moshe still remained at the helm, they felt it was only in recognition of his past accomplishments.

The Midrashim also tell us that Nadav and Avihu refused to marry and bear offspring. Because Moshe had to always be ready to receive Hashem's word, he separated from his wife, Tzipporah (see Rashi Bamidbar 12:4). Nadav and Avihu felt that they had attained similar spiritual heights. They, too, abstained from marriage.

This is also why they decided for themselves the halacha (about bringing fire to the altar) without asking their master, Moshe. They felt that they were as competent as Moshe in matters regarding Temple decorum.

The verse that begins this week's Parsha tells us that Nadav and Avihu died simply because they *approached*—that is, they came too close before Hashem. They did not hold themselves at an appropriate distance from the Divine Presence. This, too, is why the verse refers to their offering as an *eish zarah*, or a non-sanctified fire—a fire that was inappropriate for the holiness of the environment. It truly may have been appropriate to bring a fire to the altar on this occasion (see Sukkah 21b). Nevertheless, coming from Nadav and Avihu, who were *not* spiritually prepared to bring it, this fire was deemed a "strange fire."

IV

Intoxicated & lacking a me'il

The Midrash tells us further that Nadav and Avihu entered the Mishkan while under the influence of intoxicating drinks. The mind is our most spiritual part. We can become spiritual beings in this world, if we allow our intellect and reason to dominate our physical, worldly desires—not vice versa. Full control of one's physical desires is the goal of a servant of Hashem. Nadav and Avihu did not yet fully attain this lofty goal. They entered the Mishkan in a mindless, drunken state—i.e., their reason did not yet retain full control over their worldly impulses.

Finally, the Midrash criticized Nadav and Avihu for entering the Mishkan without the high-priestly *me'il*. The *me'il* had woven bells dangling from its hem that tinkled gently as the high-priest walked. The Torah tells us that the purpose of the bells was "that their sound may be heard as [the high-priest] enters the Holy before Hashem...that he may not die" (Shemos 28:35). As the Ramban (ibid.) explains, the bells were meant to announce the high-priest's arrival. One who enters a king's chamber suddenly, without prior invitation, is liable to punishment by death. The bells of the *me'il* denote that the high-priest would only enter before his Master's presence, as it were, after having been granted permission. It is meant as well to remind its wearer to prepare himself for the service of the King.

The sin of Nadav and Avihu was that they did not wait for permission to enter the Mishkan. They entered the Mishkan to bring their incense offering before reaching the spiritual level demanded by such a service. They did not first request "permission" to enter. This is what the Midrash means by asserting allegorically that they were not wearing the *me'il*—even though they were not high-priests they did not learn the lesson that can be gleaned from the high-priest's *me'il*! In short, all of the Midrashim that discuss the sin of Nadav and Avihu are leading to the same conclusion. Nadav and Avihu were acting in a manner befitting a spiritual level which they had not yet fully attained.

PARSHAS KEDOSHIM

Love Of The Mitzvos

"One should not say, 'I am disgusted by pig's meat; I have no desire to wear clothing containing *shaatnez* [a mix of wool and linen threads].' Instead one should say, 'I would like to do these things, but what can I do? My Heavenly Father has forbidden me from doing them!' How do we know that this is the proper attitude? Because in Vayikra 20:26 it states, 'I have separated you from the other nations to be Mine.' This implies that our separation from these other nations should be solely for Hashem's sake. One should refrain from the forbidden act in such a manner that one accepts the yoke of Heaven upon himself" (Rashi, quoting from Sifra).

Rashi tells us that it is *not* proper to try to inculcate within ourselves disgust and disdain for things prohibited by the Torah. To the contrary—it is actually better to retain a desire for these forbidden objects and strive to overcome this desire.

In the Rambam's introduction to Pirkei Avos [known as Shemoneh Perakim], ch. 6, the Rambam mentions that the famed philosophers of old believed the opposite to be true. These philosophers maintained that it is more virtuous for someone to completely excise any desire for forbidden behavior from his mind than to foster such desires and strive to overcome them. Rambam notes that this position seems to be borne out by Biblical verses: "The soul of the wicked desires evil" (Mishlei 21:10); "Doing justice is a joy for the righteous, but it is a dread for evildoers" (ibid. 21:15).

Two classes of mitzvos: Rambam

How, then, can the outlook of the Rabbis—that our separation from these other nations should be solely for Hashem's sake—be reconciled with that of the philosophers (and the Tanach)? Should one strive to make hatred of sin a part of one's psyche, or is it preferable to have a desire for sin and successfully conquer this desire?

The Rambam points out that both approaches are actually correct, depending upon the situation. Torah prohibitions considered "ethical" and "logical," such as murder, theft, cheating, etc. are obviously to be eschewed even if the Torah had not told us so openly. Thus, it is better for us to develop within ourselves a strong aversion to these actions.

For Torah prohibitions which are "non-rational"—i.e., have no independent logical basis other than that they are the Torah's commands, such as the dietary laws, wearing *shaatnez*, etc.—we are told that we should not condition ourselves to despise these acts, but rather we should refrain from them solely for the sake of Heaven.

The distinction which the Rambam makes may be explained as follows: Hashem instilled in humans the tendency to feel noble and virtuous when performing a morally correct deed and to feel guilty when acting dishonorably towards others. There is an authentic "good feeling" that one experiences as a result of performing such mitzvos. This physical feeling of pleasure, then, stems from the *spiritual* desirability of the act. The element that makes the deed a mitzvah—its moral correctness—is the same element that gives us pleasure in its performance. A sense of aversion toward dealing dishonestly thus does not interfere with one's intent to serve the Creator through refraining from dishonesty.

With "non-rational" mitzvos, however, there is no such natural exalted feeling when these acts are performed. A distaste for the meat of non-kosher animals stems only from the meat's physical flavor, an entirely mundane experience. Developing a physical loathing towards these prohibitions would therefore detract from one's purity of intent to serve Heaven alone. This is why the Rabbis said that our separation from these other nations should be solely for Hashem's sake.

II

Two classes of mitzvos— The Maharal

The Maharal (*Tiferet Yisrael*, chaps. 7-8) carries the statement of the Sages quoted by Rashi one step further. Not only should one not say, "I am disgusted by pig's meat," but neither should one claim, "I believe that eating pig's meat is unhealthy."

We should avoid assigning *any* logical, physical benefit to the Torah's prohibitions. The Maharal reasons that it is absurd to think that we should receive a heavenly reward for serving our own physical best interest! Therefore, establishing physical grounds for the mitzvos detracts from one's purity of intent in the service of Hashem.

The Maharal develops this theme further. He states that it is even incorrect to keep the mitzvos on the grounds that they teach us moral behavior.

Although ethical conduct is certainly a praiseworthy spiritual goal, it is not the purpose of the prohibitions of the Torah. For example, the prohibition of not slaughtering a calf and its mother on the same day (Vayikra 22:28) was not meant to instill in us compassion. This is evidenced by the fact that the prohibition applies only to domestic animals—not to animals of the wild, such as deer. Also, one is permitted to slaughter the mother even one minute after its child, provided that the sun sets during that minute.

Obviously, says the Maharal, the reasons Hashem gave us the "non-rational" mitzvos are more esoteric than we think. A true understanding of the Torah's rationale is attained only by a few of the greatest scholars. (This sounds like a hint to a Kabbalistic derivation of the mitzvos.—MK) Since the mitzvos obviously weren't given exclusively to such scholars, Hashem could not have intended that we perform the mitzvos for their *real*, deeper reasons. Hashem must have intended that we perform the mitzvos simply because they are His will in this world, without understanding why. *Any* other motivation for keeping the mitzvos would detract from the purity of our intent.

Textual support for the Maharal's explanation can be found in the Midrash itself. The Sifra quoted above ends off by saying, "One should refrain from the forbidden act in a manner that he accepts the yoke of Heaven upon himself," implying that *any* motive one may have for performing a mitzvah, other than to show submission to Hashem, is to be discouraged.

The words of the Maharal in no way contradicts the Rambam's dichotomy between the different types of mitzvos. According to the Maharal's interpretation of the Midrash, the distinction between "ethical" and "non-rational" mitzvos ought to be explained as follows: When the Torah commands us not to murder, steal, act deceitfully, etc., it is clear that the Torah intends these rules for the benefit of society. They are not designed to be a medium through which we show our subordination to Hashem. But those commandments which are not based on rational, pre-existing notions, are designed to bring us to the realization that we must submit our will to Hashem. We must learn to obey the Divine word even when we have no idea of the reason behind a particular command. Assigning other explanations for the performance of mitzvos undermines the essential function of this class of mitzvos—to teach us that we must submit ourselves totally to Hashem's will.

III

Reasons behind the mitzvos?

The principle laid down by the Maharal thus states that at least for the "non-rational" mitzvos, it is undesirable to assign meanings and motives to the commandments of the Torah. As we have pointed out above, Maharal's theme is reflected in the words of the Midrash itself. However, as we well know, many chapters of the Rambam's philosophical treatise *Moreh Nevuchim* are dedicated to establishing reasons for all the mitzvos of the Torah (see especially sec. 3, ch. 26 and on)! Hundreds of other rabbis, ancient and modern, have devoted a great deal of effort into similar quests to find the meanings behind all the mitzvos. The Torah itself seems to suggest the validity of such an approach: "The Torah will make you look wise and knowledgeable in the eyes of all the nations. They will hear these laws and say, 'This great nation is truly wise and knowledgeable!' " (Devarim 4:6, see also Ramban on Devarim 6:22).

How can this be reconciled with the Sages' statement in the Sifra quoted above? Aren't all rationales and physical explanations incorrect and to be shunned? Conversely, if so many reasons *have* been found over the ages to explain the mitzvos, why does the Sifra insist that the reasons for the mitzvos are irrelevant? Why can't we base the performance of the mitzvos on some of these suggested reasons?

IV

Generalities and specifics

Perhaps an answer to these questions may be suggested, bearing in mind the Rambam's important qualification in *Moreh Nevuchim* (3:26). All the various reasons offered for the mitzvos, the Rambam says, only explain the general theme of the mitzvos. The details and minutiae which accompany all mitzvos usually cannot be accounted for by referring to these reasons.

For example, let us assume that the reason the Torah prescribes its particular method of slaughter of animals is to minimize the pain to the animal. We find, nevertheless, that a calf that emerges from its mother's womb after the mother was slaughtered is considered to be already slaughtered itself. This calf may be killed and eaten in *any* manner, since, halachically, *shechitah* was already performed on it. Theoretically, it may even be killed in a cruel manner! If the Torah instituted the law of *shechitah* in consideration of the animal's pain, why not apply the law to this calf as well?

Another example is mentioned above—a calf and its mother may be slaughtered one minute apart, as long as they are separated by the halachic start of a new day—sunset. Obviously, the rationale offered to explain a mitzvah in the Torah applies only to the general commandment and not to the many details attached to it.

My father-in-law, Harav Gedalyah Rabinowitz, augmented the statement in *Moreh Nevuchim*. The reasons for the mitzvos, he explains, are learned from the manner in which the mitzvos are presented in the *written* law—i.e., the *appearance* of the mitzvos as they are recorded in the Torah. Only the broader, more general view of the mitzvos appears there. Hashem recorded the mitzvos in the Torah in such a manner that clear, moral lessons can be learned from each and every one of them. However, the details outlined in the *oral* law, which affect the actual performance of the mitzvos, are not necessarily explained by the reasons that have been offered for the mitzvos. (Perhaps there is a need for clear-cut halachic categories and guidelines when it comes to performance of mitzvos. This sometimes makes it necessary to define the law for certain situations in a way counter to the mitzvah's general objective.—MK)

We may now suggest the following: Every mitzvah has important lessons to teach us, or meaningful values to convey. The lessons, however, are learned from the mitzvah as it is *described* by the written law, i.e., from the *general* structure of the mitzvah. It is these lessons to which the Torah refers by saying "The Torah will make you look wise and knowledgeable in the eyes of all the nations."

The Midrash that says one should *not* seek ulterior, logical reasons for the mitzvos, on the other hand, was discussing the *performance* of the mitzvos. Whatever reasons may be offered for the mitzvos—and there are many—they will not be able to account for all details of the performance of the mitzvos. If pig's meat is prohibited for health reasons, why is putrid cow's meat permitted? The only way to explain the "non-rational mitzvos as they are performed"—i.e., with all of the details gleaned from the oral law—is to understand these mitzvos as a means by which we can show our subordination to Hashem's will. This is what the Midrash means by telling us to "refrain from the forbidden act solely for My sake"!

V

The Rambam's dichotomy between rational and non-rational mitzvos may be used to answer another question. It is well known that the mitzvos may be divided into two categories: those between a human being and G-d, and those between two people.

Two classes of mitzvos with regards to blessings

Before we perform any mitzvah of the first category we recite a blessing: "Blessed is Hashem...Who has sanctified us through His mitzvos and commanded us to eat matzah, don tefillin, separate challah, etc." Why is there no blessing for mitzvos done between two people? Why do we not praise Hashem for sanctifying us by commanding us to give charity to the needy, to visit the sick, attend to the dead, etc.? The Rashba (in a responsum, vol. 1 #18) suggests that a blessing cannot be said in these cases because the recipient of the favor may refuse the act of kindness. Since kindness is thus *not* an absolute obligation, we cannot apply to it the phrase, "Who has *commanded* us to ...."

According to what was outlined above (in section II), however, a different answer may be suggested. The "ethical" mitzvos were given to inculcate in us the values that they teach, while the "non-rational" mitzvos remind us of G-d's mastery. Announcing that we are dealing kindly with another person "because we were commanded to do so," would diminish the mitzvah!

We should follow these mitzvos because we yearn to do them, because we have conditioned ourselves to value such behavior. It is only with the "non-rational" mitzvos that we are expected to declare that we are doing them because, and only because, Hashem "sanctified us through His mitzvos and commanded us to...."

May we all merit to serve Hashem with all our hearts, and to love each other with all our feelings!

PARSHAS EMOR

Seven Days; Seven Holidays

"Hashem spoke to Moshe, saying, 'These are the holidays of Hashem, which you shall declare as holy; these are My holidays. Six days work may be done, but on the seventh day there is a total Shabbos, a holy day; no work may be done...These are the holidays of Hashem, which you shall declare in their set times. On the fourteenth of the first month, in the afternoon, it is Pesach unto Hashem...' " (Vayikra 23:1-5).

In this week's parsha, we find a listing of the Jewish holidays. Beginning with the above quote, the Torah describes all of the year's holidays. There is, however, an obvious problem. The Torah says that it is about to list all the holidays (*Moadim*) of the year (v. 2). Why does it begin with a description of Shabbos? Shabbos, which comes every week, can hardly be described as a *Moed*! It seems to be completely misplaced. Many of the classical commentators have dealt with this question.

A strange interlude in the list of holidays

The Vilna Gaon suggested a brilliant, novel solution. He proposed that the "Shabbos" mentioned in verses 2-3 does not refer to Saturday, the weekly Shabbos described numerous other times in the Torah. It refers instead to the Holy Day of Yom Kippur. Like Shabbos, Yom Kippur is also referred to in the Torah as *Shabbos Shabbason* (translated here as "a total Shabbos")—see Shemos 31:15 and Vayikra 23:32. Yom Kippur is also certainly one of the *Moadim*.

But if the "Shabbos" referred to in this verse is Yom Kippur, then what are the six other days mentioned here? The Gaon explains that these are the other six Yomim Tovim: Rosh Hashanah, the first and eighth days of Sukkos, the first and seventh days of Pesach, and Shavuos. The meaning of the verse is thus, according to the Gaon's interpretation: "On the [other] six days [mentioned in this section, certain types of] work may be done [i.e., the cooking and preparation of food, which is permissible on festival days], but on the seventh day [of the holidays under discussion], there is a total Shabbos, a holy day; *no* work [i.e., not even cooking, etc.] may be done...."

Instead of describing the six *days of the week* which culminate in Shabbos, the verse is actually referring to the six *festivals* during which some work is permitted, which culminate in the "total Shabbos" of Yom Kippur! The Torah thus introduces the description of the holidays with a statement about the *Moadim* in general, indicating that one of the seven days under discussion is holier than the other six.

(The comparison of the seven holidays to the seven days of the week—without mention of our parsha—can also be found in the Maharsha, Chidushei Aggados, Yoma 2a.)

II

The seven holidays and the Passover mnemonic

Following through on this theme, we may suggest that the seven holidays of the year are equal not only in number to the days of the week. They parallel *in content* the seven days of the week as well—as we shall soon explain. There is, in fact, another context where the various holidays are presented in the context of consecutive days of a week, and that is in the Tur's discussion of the Jewish calendar (O.C. 428). The Tur points out that if one knows which day of the week Pesach begins in any given year, one can determine the day of the week the other holidays will occur in that coming year. This is accomplished through a mnemonic based on *at-bash*, as follows:

At-bash is a system in which each letter of the Hebrew alphabet is paired up with the letter on the "opposite side" of the alphabet. The first letter *alef* is associated with the last letter *taf*. The second letter *beis* with the second to last letter *shin*, etc. Each consecutive day of Pesach is assigned a letter from the beginning of the alphabet *alef*, *beis*, *gimmel*, etc. The Tur demonstrates that the first day of Pesach, which would be assigned *alef*, will always fall out on the same day of the week as the holiday whose name begins with the last letter of the alphabet—*taf*—Tishah b'Av. The second day of Pesach—*beis*—falls out on the same day as the holiday that begins with *shin*—Shavuos. The third day—*gimmel*—becomes *reish*, for Rosh Hashanah. The fourth day—*daled*—becomes *kaf*, for Krias haTorah, which refers to the holiday observing the start of the new cycle of the reading of the Torah—Simchas Torah.

Note: This one only works in the Diaspora; in Israel, Simchas Torah falls out on the same day of the week as the *third* day of Pesach. Finally, the fifth day of Pesach—*heh*—which corresponds to the letter *tzadi*, predicts the day of the week of *Tzom* [the Fast of] Kippur.

[Actually the Tur continues to say that the sixth day—*vav*—determines the day of the week for the Rabbinic holiday of *peh*, which is Purim, but this refers to the *previous* Purim, *not* to the coming Purim. Modern-day pundits add to the Tur's list that the seventh day of Pesach—*zayin*—matches the day of the week of the pseudo-holiday of *ayin*—which is *etzim* (in English "trees"—referring to Tu Bishvat (this works only in non-leap years); or Tu b'Av, day of the *korban etzim* wood offering celebration.]

Thus every one of the *Moadim* is accounted for by this system. As noted above, this mnemonic system only works for the Diaspora (perhaps because the fixed lunar calendar was only instituted after the main population of the Jewish nation had shifted to the Diaspora). It should also be noted that when the end of a holiday is pinpointed, the very last day of the holiday is used, and *not* the day before last, although it is more significant. Thus the *ninth* day of Sukkos (Simchas Torah) is marked, and not the more substantial *eighth* day.

If we look carefully at the arrangement of holidays in this *at-bash* mnemonic, we see that not only are all the holidays accounted for, but they are arranged in perfect chronological order, beginning with the first holiday of the year—Pesach itself!

Take note: (1) The *alef* is the day of the week on which the first holiday of Pesach falls, obviously. (2) That same *alef* also shows the day for the *last* day of Pesach (in the Diaspora), for that is the same day of the week as the first day. (3) The *beis* sets the day of the week for Shavuos, as the Tur demonstrated. (4) The *gimmel* determines which day Rosh Hashanah will come. (5) Sukkos always falls on the same day of the week as Rosh Hashanah, so this is also determined by the *gimmel*. (6) The *daled* shows the day of the week for Simchas Torah. (7) The *heh* corresponds to the day of the week for Yom Kippur. The order of holidays determined by the days of Pesach is thus: First day Pesach, last day Pesach, Shavuos, Rosh Hashanah, Sukkos, Simchas Torah [i.e., the last day of Sukkos], Yom Kippur. This represents the exact order these holidays occur during the course of the year—except that Yom Kippur, which is out of chronological order, is number seven.

The Rabbis apparently arranged the present calendar so that each consecutive holiday would fall on a consecutive day of the week [where possible, and on the same day as the previous one where it was not], and so that all these holidays would alphabetically correspond to the days of Pesach. Yom Kippur was the exception to show that it is the seventh day, the culmination—in terms of degree of holiness—of the seven-day holiday cycle. This system obviously parallels the Gaon's interpretation of the verse in our Parsha—that the six other holidays are the "weekdays" that precede Yom Kippur, just as the six days of the week precede Shabbos!

III

Upon further examination, it can be seen that the Vilna Gaon's comparison between the six holidays and the six days of the week goes even deeper. Each one of the consecutive holidays, beginning with the first—Pesach—can be shown to parallel its corresponding weekday.

A day by day comparison

1. The first day of Pesach parallels the first day of creation, the day called by the Torah *yom echad* [the day of the one]. Rashi explains that it is referred to in this way (based on the Midrash), because this was the only day that Hashem was truly the only Being in the Universe since even the angels were not created until the second day.

On Pesach, too, we find that Hashem Himself, without any Heavenly Agent, went forth to strike at the Egyptians and free His people from their bondage.

"Thus says Hashem: 'At midnight I am going out into the midst of Egypt, and every firstborn in the land of Egypt shall die...' (Shemos 11:4). 'I' and not an angel; ...'I' and not a *seraph*; ...'I' and not a messenger" (Passover Haggadah).

Such Divine intervention was actually necessary for the Plague of the Death of the Firstborn. Only Hashem could distinguish between children who were actually firstborn to their fathers and those who weren't (Gemara Bava Metzia 61b). Thus, on Pesach eve Hashem demonstrated to the world His oneness, since He performed an act that only He alone—not even an administering angel—could have done.

Furthermore, on the first day light was created. An element of this primordial light was judged to be too Divine for this material world. It was "hidden away," reserved for a time when Hashem would reveal Himself to the righteous (Rashi Bereishis 1:4). On the night of the Exodus, however, the Divine light of the first day of creation shone bright (Zohar 2:38a, see also Tzav-Passover essay, p. 116).

2. On the second day of creation the "firmament" [*rakia*] was created in order to "divide between the one water and the other water."

There is an obvious parallel here to the second of the *Moadim*—the seventh day of Pesach—which commemorates the splitting of the Red Sea into two, as the Rambam in fact points out in his commentary to Pirkei Avos 5:6. (See Rashi Megillah 31a, s.v. *Vayehi*.)

3. The third day of creation saw the origin of fruit-bearing trees (Bereishis 1:11).

According to the Gemara (Rosh Hashanah 16a) Shavuos—the third of the *Moadim*—is the day on which Hashem passes judgment on the quality of the fruit harvest of the coming year. It is for this reason that Shavuos was also the first day on which *bikkurim,* or first-fruit offerings, were allowed to be brought to the Temple.

Furthermore, the Torah is known as the "tree of life" (Mishlei 3:18) and was given on Shavuos to the Israelites at Mount Sinai. Moreover, the third day of creation is distinguished by being the only one of the days of creation on which the phrase "*ki tov*" [it was good] was declared twice. According to the Gemara, the Torah is often referred to as *tov* [the good]—see Mishlei 4:2, Berachos 5a.

4. On the fourth day of creation, the heavenly bodies were created—the sun, the moon, the stars, etc. It marked the beginning of the lunar and solar cycles.

Rosh Hashanah, the fourth *Moed,* marks the beginning of our yearly cycle (Gemara Rosh Hashanah 2a—see also Rosh Hashanah essay, p. 259).

5. The fifth day of creation has a thematic connection with Sukkos, which is the fifth *Moed.* On the fifth day the water "issued forth crawling living things and birds to fly in the heavens" (Bereishis 1:20). All of that day's creations issued from the waters (ibid.). One of the major themes of the Sukkos holiday is the supplication for rain at the beginning of the rainy season. It is at this time that Hashem passes judgment regarding the amount of rain which will fall during the coming year (Rosh Hashanah 16a). Sukkos is the holiday during which special libations are performed and prayers are recited (and branches waved) in order to beseech Hashem for an adequate supply of water, the life-giving elixir that will preserve all creatures of the world during the coming year.

The Torah gives special mention to one sea creature that was created on the fifth day—the *leviasan* (Bereishis 1:21 and Rashi). As we are told, at the onset of the Messianic era Hashem will "make a *sukkah* out of the hide of the *leviasan* for the righteous" (Bava Basra 75a).

6. The sixth day of creation is the day on which the human being was created.

Rashi, in Bamidbar 29:35, tells us that the entire theme of the Shemini Atzeres holiday (of which Simchas Torah is a part) is the uniqueness of the People of Israel. On Simchas Torah we celebrate having received the Torah and the observance of its mitzvos, since it is the Torah and its observance which distinguished the people of Israel from other nations. The Torah makes us a spiritual people. It is on this holiday that we celebrate the creation of the "spiritual man."

All the other days of creation are called "*a* second day," "*a* third day," etc. Only the sixth day is called "*the* sixth day." Rashi comments that this alludes to the fact that the Torah would be given on the *sixth day* of a month (Sivan) many centuries later. Rashi explains that it was as if Hashem stipulated with all of creation that its existence was conditional upon the acceptance of the

Torah by Israel at Mount Sinai. If so, it is fitting for the sixth holiday of the year to be dedicated to celebrating our possession of the Torah.

7. There are several parallels between Shabbos, the seventh day, and Yom Kippur. Yom Kippur is the only one of the holidays during which *all* manner of work is forbidden (i.e., even work relating to the preparation of food is prohibited). This cessation of creative activity mirrors the laws of the Shabbos, the day that Hashem "rested" from creating the world.

Furthermore, it was on the seventh day that Hashem forgave Adam for eating the forbidden fruit and allowed him to live. This was the first, and hence the archetypal, case of atonement for sin. The Midrash tells us that it was Adam who composed the "Psalm for the Shabbos Day" (Psalm 92), unconventionally translating the opening verse as "It is good to *confess one's sins* before Hashem" (Midrash Socher Tov, ad loc.). Similarly, Yom Kippur was the first time that Hashem granted forgiveness to Israel as a nation. As Rashi tells us (Devarim 9:18), this was the day Hashem forgave Israel for the sin of the golden calf—which is why Yom Kippur was singled out as a day of atonement for all times.

IV

The "spiritual week"

Perhaps the idea underlying the parallelism between the holidays and the days of the week is the following—the seven *Moadim* represent seven aspects of the formation of the spiritual world, just as the seven days of the week represent seven stages in the creation of the physical world. Perhaps through the observance of these seven holidays, we can elevate the mundane, material world of the seven days of creation to a higher, more spiritual plateau.

May we merit to observe the Torah's *Moadim* properly, and create a unique, spiritual dimension in our lives!

PARSHAS BEHAR

Then He Is To Break Down The Door...

"If a man sells a house in a walled city, its redemption period shall be for a full year. If it is not redeemed [by the seller] by the end of the year, the house in the walled city shall become a permanent possession of the one who bought it, for all his generations. It shall not be subject to release in the *yovel* year" (Vayikra 25:29-30).

Two ways of viewing the redemption of a house in a walled city

There is a general rule that any land that is sold in Israel reverts to its original owner in the *yovel* [jubilee] year. However, the Torah makes an exception for houses located within walled cities. Houses in walled cities may be redeemed by their original owner for up to one year. During that year, the buyer of the house *must* agree to return the house to the seller, if the seller offers to refund the money. If, however, the seller does *not* redeem his house within the first year, he loses it forever. The house does not even return to him in the *yovel* year.

We can view this forced restitution of purchased property within the first year in two ways. On one hand, we can say that the Torah enforces an implicit stipulation for any sale of a house in a walled city, that if the seller refunds the money, the sale is annulled *retroactively.* If so, the buyer's money—which had been in the possession of the seller for several days or months—is considered, in retrospect, a loan.

Another way of looking at this halacha is that the original sale is never annulled. The house is simply *repurchased* by the original owner when he refunds the money to the buyer. The original sale was unconditionally valid, but the Torah imposes upon the buyer an obligation to make a *new* sale upon being reimbursed by the original owner.

Two of the most well-known commentators on the Choshen Mishpat section of the Shulchan Aruch—the Ketzos Hachoshen and the Nesivos Hamishpat (both of 18th century Poland) took up the two opposite sides of this debate. In Choshen Mishpat 55:1, the Nesivos assumes the first of the two alternatives, while the Ketzos prefers the second side of the argument.

(A careful survey of the topic reveals that among the earlier authorities—Rashi and Tosafos in Erchin 31b, Rashba in Gittin 75a—the view that the sale is annulled *retroactively* is prevalent. However, there is at least one early source for the latter view as well, namely, Rabbeinu Gershom [10th century Germany] in his commentary to Erchin 31b.—MK)

R. Yosef Rosen of Dvinsk, known as "the Rogatchover Gaon" (because of his birthplace in Russia, d. 1936), discusses this issue in *Tzafnas Pane'ach*. He says that not only is the original sale not annulled, but when the original owner gives money to the buyer to buy back his house, he is actually performing two acts: He is fulfilling the condition that the Torah stipulates in order for a person to redeem his property—namely, to return the money to the hands of the buyer. In addition, he is performing a bona fide *kinyan* [act of acquisition] which officially transfers the title of the house to him. (In order for any item to change hands, a *kinyan* must be performed. The four *kinyanim* applicable to acquiring real estate are: payment of money; handing over of a bill of sale; making an improvement or change in the state of the property [*chazakah*]; and symbolic barter [the "exchange" of an object, usually a handkerchief, for the property]. In this case, payment of money is being used as the *kinyan*.) If this is the case, says the Rogatchover, we can now offer an explanation for a difficult passage in a Mishnah in Erchin.

II

"Break down the door"

If a buyer of a house did not want to be forced into selling the house back he would hide from the original owner on the last day of the year of purchase (so that the original owner would not be able to give him back the money, in case he hadn't done so yet). This way he could ensure that the house would become permanently his. Hillel then enacted a law that the money could be deposited in a certain office on the Temple grounds, where it was available to the purchaser to retrieve whenever he wanted it. Thereafter the original owner was to "break down the door and enter the house" (Mishnah Erchin 31b).

Hillel did this as a way of forcing the purchaser to "receive" his money even against his will. The money would be deposited by the original owner in a certain place, and would thereupon be considered the money of the uncooperative buyer. But what is the point of "breaking down the door of the house?" If the Mishnah had said "He *may* thereafter reclaim possession of his house, by force if necessary"—then we would have understood the intent. But the way the Mishnah is in fact worded, it sounds as if the "breaking down of the door" is somehow a part of Hillel's enactment. It seems to say that in order to complete the terms of the enactment, the original owner had to break down the door of his house. What is the logic of such a strange requirement?

The Rogatchover explains this enigmatic statement of the Mishnah based on what was stated above, as follows:

In Gittin 75a there is a discussion concerning whether giving an object to a person against his will constitutes a valid act of "giving." If a man, for instance, says to his wife, "I consent to divorce you, but only on the condition that you give me 200 shekels," and he subsequently refuses to accept the payment in order to invalidate the divorce, may she give the money to him against his will? Is this considered a valid fulfillment of the condition?

The Rashba (Spain, 13th century) asserts that even if we were to decide that payment by coercion is acceptable, it would only be acceptable as an act of *giving*, but would not be considered as though the other party has *received* what was given. Thus coercion will only help when it is not necessary for the recipient to take acquisition of what has been given. Nobody can be forced to *receive* an object (i.e., to acquire it through a *kinyan*) against his will, so the recipient—in our case, the divorcing husband—will not acquire the money that has been thrust upon him. Nevertheless, it can be said that the woman has "given" him the money, and fulfilled the condition, since making something *available* for another person to take can also be called "giving".

In the case of the divorce, the Rashba explains, the condition was for the woman "to give" 200 shekels to the man. To fulfill this condition, it suffices for her to make the money *available* to her husband. Even though the money does not become the property of the husband, i.e., he did not "receive" it, nevertheless, by making it available to him, the woman has "given" it to him.

If so, we may conclude that after Hillel's enactment that one must pay the buyer of the house against his will (which the Gemara in Gittin ibid. compares to the divorce case), the money is considered as having been "given" by the original owner when he throws it into the specially appointed office and makes it available to the one to whom he is returning it. However, the recipient—the one who bought the house—does not own that money as long as he does not wish to *receive* it.

III

The Rogatchover follows this line of reasoning to its logical conclusion. According to the second opinion quoted above (that of the Ketzos, which the Rogatchover also prefers) we explained that the original sale of the house is never annulled. In order to receive his house back, the original owner must (a) return the money that he received from the buyer and (b) make the house his property once again through a new, bona fide, act of *kinyan.*

Payment to an unwilling recipient

Putting the money in the designated office against the buyer's will may suffice for the "giving" back of the money to the buyer (a) since giving forcefully is also classified as "giving". However, based on the Rashba's premise, the money does *not* come into the possession of the purchaser of the house. Therefore the payment cannot constitute a proper *kinyan* of "payment of money," to allow the original owner to regain acquisition of the property. (b) In order for this *kinyan* to work, the money must be *received* by the seller, not just made available to him. Only then, when one party receives the money, can the other party receive the land in return.

Thus in order for the original owner to have his house returned, he must still perform a legal act of acquisition on that property before the year's end. Until this act of *kinyan,* the house will *not* become legally his again. The *kinyanim* of "payment," "barter" and "transferal of deed" are obviously not operable in this case, where the other party in the sale is unwilling to cooperate. The only option left is for the original owner to make a *kinyan* of *chazakah* on his house by making an improvement or change in the state of his property. The Mishnah (Bava Basra 42a) describes the classical *chazakah* as "locking up a door or breaking down a locked door."

We can now better understand the Mishnah in Erchin. The Mishnah states that the process by which the original owner gets his house back is not complete with just depositing the money—the original owner must also "break down the door" to his house. He must break down the door in order to make a *kinyan* of *chazakah* on the house. Only by making a formal act of acquisition (i.e., a *kinyan*) before the year's end, will the house return to his possession! (Tzafnas Pane'ach, in *Kuntrus Hashleimah* p. 4—see also *Ishim Veshitos,* Rogatchover, 2:15. A similar explanation of the Mishnah in Erchin is attributed to the Brisker Rav by R. Shmuel Rozovsky in his *Shiurim on Kesubos* 3a.)

PARSHAS BECHUKOSAI

Two Ways To "Cease"

"If you go in the ways of the Torah...I will bring peace to the land, and you will lie down without fear I will cause dangerous animals to cease (*'vehishbati chayah ra'ah'*) from the land, and war will not pass through your land" (Vayikra 26:6).

" 'I will cause dangerous animals to cease from the land'—Rabbi Yehudah says this means, 'I will eliminate them altogether.' Rabbi Shimon says it means, 'I will curb their dangerous behavior, so that they do no damage'—but they will still be in existence in the land. Rabbi Shimon said, 'Which is more of a praise for Hashem—that there be no dangerous animals at all, or that there be dangerous animals who, against their nature, do no damage? You must admit that it is the latter that is a greater praise for Him' " (Toras Kohanim, ad loc.).

The Tannaim disagree on the interpretation of the verse "*vehishbati chayah ra'ah*"—which is one of the blessings reserved for those who follow Hashem's ways.

The opinions of R. Yehudah and R. Shimon from Toras Kohanim

Literally, the verse can be translated as "I will cause dangerous animals *to cease.*" But how will Hashem cause dangerous animals to "cease" when Israel is deserving of His blessing? What specifically is meant here? The complete elimination of the animals—or their preservation but a transformation of their vicious natures? Rabbi Shimon and Rabbi Yehudah have opposing opinions.

At first glance this seems to be a difference of opinion concerning only a technical grammatical point, without any practical bearing on any halachic issue. However, several recent commentators have suggested that this argument is based on a much broader issue which does have significant halachic implications.

II

Rav Yosef Rosen of Dvinsk (d. Russia, 1936—known more commonly as "the Rogatchover Gaon," after his place of birth), proposes that the opinion of Rabbi Yehudah in our Midrash is perhaps based on Rav Yehudah's own opinion in a different context.

Rabbi Yehudah: cease equals obliteration

In Pesachim (21a) there is a Mishnah that states the following: "Rabbi Yehudah says the disposal of chametz (in preparation for the Pesach holiday) must be carried out by burning it. But the other Sages say that one may even crumble it and scatter it in the wind or throw it into the sea." According to the Sages, any method of disposal which renders the chametz inedible is enough to be considered "disposal" of the chametz.

The Gemara (ibid. 27b) quotes the Sages as defending their position by quoting the verse "By the first day [of Pesach] you shall cause all chametz to cease (*tashbisu*) from your houses" (Shemos 12:15) The Sages claim that this implies that any method of "causing to cease" suffices. Crumbling the chametz and dispersing it makes it "cease to exist," since it can no longer be used as a food. The words of the Sages clearly imply that if the *quality* of the chametz, i.e., its defining characteristics, have changed, then it has "ceased to exist."

Rabbi Yehudah, however, rejects this argument. He apparently interpreted the word *tashbisu* in a more limited sense. It may be suggested that Rabbi Yehudah read the word to mean a complete, total destruction of the item in question—i.e., an obliteration of the actual "quantity" [presence] of the chametz, and not simply a change in its defining qualities.

The words *tashbisu* (in reference to chametz) and *vehishbati* (in reference to the dangerous animals) are two conjugations of the same root. Since Rabbi Yehudah interpreted the word as implying total destruction when it concerned chametz, he interprets the word in this way in our context as well—that dangerous animals will cease to exist in Eretz Yisrael altogether. Rabbi Shimon, however, must have been one of the "other Sages" who interpret *tashbisu* as causing an object to become nonfunctional. He therefore explains the word similarly in our Parsha. The animals will be there, but they will not act viciously!

III

Rav Meir Simcha Hakohen, a contemporary of the Rogatchover Rav in Dvinsk, explains in his Torah commentary *Meshech Chochmah*, that Rabbi Shimon, too, is basing his interpretation on an opinion that he expressed elsewhere.

The Gemara (Berachos 35b) mentions a disagreement concerning the interpretation of a passage in the second paragraph of the *Shema* (Devarim 11:14). When listing the blessings reserved for those who hearken to Hashem's mitzvos, the Torah states, "I will send the rain in its time...and you will gather your grain, grape and oil crops." Since the Torah tells us that we will gather our own crops, Rav Yishmael infers that although we are bidden to study the Torah "day and night" (Yehoshua 1:8), the Torah allows us to pursue our livelihoods in a normal fashion as well. It is therefore totally acceptable for even an outstanding scholar to indulge in agricultural pursuits.

Rabbi Shimon: no compromises

Rabbi Shimon bar Yochai (ibid.), however, protested: "If someone plowed during plowing season, sowed during sowing season, harvested during harvest season, etc., what would become of Torah study!"

Rabbi Shimon says that the second paragraph of the Shema speaks of a situation where people are *not* completely dedicated to Hashem's will and are thus are still tilling the soil. They can be rewarded for "hearkening to Hashem's mitzvos" when they act in this manner, but they are not yet considered as having reached the *highest* level of divine service. When they have attained the loftiest of spiritual heights, all material pursuits will be abandoned. In return Hashem sends others to perform their labors so that they may remain free to engage in Torah study. Rav Yishmael's "compromise" of toiling while studying Torah is not an acceptable one, in Rabbi Shimon's extremist view. (See Eikev essay, p. 235.)

Rabbi Shimon bar Yochai's opinion is evident elsewhere in the Gemara. In Shabbos 33b a story is told about how Rabbi Shimon, upon seeing people plowing and planting their fields, exclaimed in disbelief, "These people are forsaking eternal life (Torah study) for transient life (pursuit of a livelihood)!" (Whenever the name "Rabbi Shimon"—without any further description—is quoted in Talmudic literature, the reference is to Rabbi Shimon bar Yochai). We find in Shabbos 11a that Rabbi Shimon did not pray, in order not to take off precious time from his study of Torah. The Gemara (ibid. 10a) reasons that even involvement in prayer can be called "forsaking eternal life for transient life," when we pray for Hashem to grant us a livelihood and our other physical needs (Rashi ad loc.).

IV

We find that when a person becomes devoted to Hashem and His service on the highest level, Hashem protects this person from even the natural dangers posed by vicious animals. Daniel, for example, was thrown into a pit full of hungry lions (Daniel 6), yet he was on such a lofty spiritual level that miraculously the animals left him unharmed.

Stepping "above" nature

The Gemara (Berachos 33a) speaks of Rav Chaninah ben Dosa, who used his foot to cover the hole of a poisonous snake, inciting the animal to bite him. Instead of the scholar being harmed, it was the snake who died from the bite! As Rav Chaninah ben Dosa termed it, "It is not the viper that kills; it is the sin that kills!" When a person is without sin there is no way that he can be hurt by even the most dangerous animal.

In Makkos 11a the prophet Eliyahu [Elijah], similarly, reprimands Rav Yehoshua ben Levi, saying that if he was on the proper spiritual plane no wild animals would harm him. Not only that, but they would harm no one else in his entire region!

It is for this reason that the prophet Yeshayah tells us that in the Messianic era "a baby will play by the viper's hole." (Yeshayah 11:8). At that time there will be no more sin and people will reach the highest spiritual levels (ibid. 1:9). In this situation wild animals would be rendered harmless.

However, Hashem bends the rules of nature only to protect the righteous during moments when the righteous people are involved with otherworldly concerns (see Shabbos beg. of 30b, Makkos 10a). When the righteous are preoccupied with their spiritual growth, they are "freed" from the physical travails of this world, as though they are temporarily transported to the spiritual realm on which their minds are dwelling. However, even the righteous are subject to the daily laws of nature when their minds are involved with their physical needs.

All the magnificent rewards promised in this week's parsha to the Jewish people if they follow the Torah's commandments, were clearly meant to be given only if they reached the *optimum* level of doing Hashem's will (see Rashi 26:2, Ramban 26:6).

According to Rabbi Shimon, then, the Bnai Yisrael will only receive these benefits if they abandon all physical and mundane pursuits in their never-ending quest for attaining spiritual heights. To such people, says the *Meshech Chochmah*, it is possible to promise that, although dangerous animals will *not* completely disappear from the land, they will present no physical threat. Since such perfect people would use every waking moment to attain spiritual growth, they would never be vulnerable to the dangers of vicious animals. Therefore, Rabbi Shimon can interpret the word "*vehishbati*" to mean that, although the animals will be present, they will be rendered harmless.

However, according to Rav Yishmael, even when the people are engaged in mundane activities, they may be considered to have achieved the highest level of doing Hashem's will. They are eligible for the blessings listed in this week's Parsha even if they tend to their fields and otherwise earn their bread during part of the day, since they can still be described as maximally performing the will of Hashem. For such people, though, it would be hazardous to coexist with wild animals. If they are confronted by a lion during the non-physical part of their day, while they delved into the laws and ways of the Torah, they would certainly be free from harm—but what would happen if they were attacked while tending their fields? They would then be subject to the mundane "laws of the land," and be at risk from physical dangers. Thus, according to Rabbi Yishmael, the blessing would necessarily be that no harmful animals in the land would exist at all. If Rabbi Yehudah of the Toras Kohanim accepted Rav Yishmael's opinion, it is clear why he interpreted *vehishbati chayah ra'ah* the way he did!

In short, the Rogatchover Rav explained why Rabbi Yehudah had to interpret *vehishbati* the way *he* did. The *Meshech Chochmah* added that only Rabbi Shimon was able to explain the word the way *he* did!

PARSHAS BAMIDBAR

Shavuos—Preparing For The Ultimate Interrogation

As codified in the Mishnah, the oral law of the Torah is divided into six sections. These six sections are derived from the written Torah. Perhaps this is why the Gemara (Bava Basra 25b) uses the Beis Hamikdash's golden menorah to symbolize the Torah since the menorah consisted of six branches emanating from a central shaft. The six divisions of the oral law similarly emanate from the central pillar of the written Torah.

The source for the Mishnah's subdivision into six sections is found in the Gemara: "What is the meaning of the [very enigmatic] verse, 'And *wisdom* and *knowledge* shall be the *stability* of your *times*, and *strength* of *salvation*: the fear of the Lord is his treasure' (Yeshayah 33:6)? Reish Lakish said: The six Hebrew words (the translation of which is here italicized) at the beginning of the verse refer to the six sections into which the Mishnah is divided...but after all is learned, the most important point remains that 'the fear of the Lord is his treasure.' Rava said: A man is asked six questions when he is brought before the heavenly court when his life on earth is finished—(1) Did you conduct your business affairs honestly? (2) Did you arrange set times for Torah study? (3) Did you bring children into the world? (4) Did you long for the coming of the Final Salvation? (5) Did you analyze wisdom? (6) Did you draw conclusions based on that analysis? Even after these six questions are asked, in the final analysis if 'the fear of the Lord is his treasure' he is judged favorably, and if not, not" (Shabbos 31a).

The six sections of the oral law

Reish Lakish derives the division of the Mishnah from the verse in Yeshayah, while Rava apparently offers an alternate interpretation of the same verse. The connection between each word and the corresponding subdivision of the Mishnah is left vague in the Gemara and is explained further by Rashi. The connection between each word and the corresponding question to be asked by the heavenly tribunal is more obvious. However, we will not discuss how these associations are made. Instead we will turn our discussion to a different point.

II

The six questions of the Day of Judgment

First of all, we must clarify some of the terms mentioned in the context of the six questions. What is meant by the question, "Did you analyze wisdom?" How does it differ from the question that follows it: "Did you draw conclusions based on that analysis?"

In Tehillim (111:10) we read that "The foundation of all wisdom is the fear of Hashem." It is thus logical to assume that when the Gemara mentions "analyzing wisdom," "wisdom" here refers to attaining the fear of Hashem, and understanding that everything that happens in the universe is under Hashem's control. This is accomplished by analyzing the world around us and noting the symmetry and beauty of Hashem's creations, and His kindness to us. The next question, referring to "drawing conclusions based on that analysis," may then mean allowing this realization to express itself in one's actions.

It is interesting to note that the six questions fall into two even categories. The first three questions deal with man's productive contribution to the world: first (1) between man and his fellow, then (2) between man and Hashem, and finally (3) between man and himself—reproduction. The last three concern man's recognition of his Creator. (4) Waiting for salvation implies a belief that Hashem's power will eventually be witnessed by all—if not now, then at a future date; (5) analyzing the fear of G-d means finding His presence—even its hidden state, such as in the present day; and finally, (6) acting on that understanding. It may be concluded that these six questions outline Judaism's six most fundamental purposes of life. And this is why one is faced with these questions when it comes time to account for one's life on this earth.

III

The six sections of the Law vis-a-vis the six questions of the Day of Judgment

At first glance it seems that the interpretations of Rava and Reish Lakish are two distinct, unrelated approaches to explain the cryptic verse in Yeshayah. However, upon more careful consideration we may find that the two issues—the six divisions of the Mishnah and the six questions asked on "judgment day"—are really closely interrelated. We could even say that the reason the Sages divided the Mishnah into the present system of six subdivisions is to teach us how to appreciate and understand the six fundamental questions which concern a Jew.

Each division of the Mishnah is set up to enable us, through studying that division, to favorably answer one of those six questions. This is especially evident in the "flagship" tractate, which begins each section of the Mishnah. (See the Vilna Gaon quoted in *Kol Eliyahu*, Shabbos 31a where it seems that the Gaon is hinting at such a correlation between the Mishnah and the six questions, although he does not say so explicitly. The source for the quote in *Kol Eliyahu* is a comment of *Maharatz Chayos* to Shabbos, ad loc.)

IV

The first section of the Mishnah is called Zeraim ("Seeds") and discusses all the various laws of the Torah relating to the produce of the land, such as tithes and the blessings to be recited before and after eating.

The first section of the Mishnah: Zeraim

More than any other laborer, the farmer is shown that the amount of time and effort put into his work is not necessarily connected to the volume of his yield. After all the farmer's work is done, in the face of the elements he remains powerless. Without the necessary amount of rain, the crops will not mature. If winds carry locusts or blight to his field, there is little he can do to protect his crops.

There are numerous tithes and other offerings that farmers must give from their harvest. These are intended to inculcate within farmers the understanding that their crops are not simply the products of their own efforts. They are granted by Hashem's grace.

When this realization becomes instilled, an individual would never consider trying to attain money dishonestly. Even that which is earned honestly are only gracious grants from Hashem, so how could he even think of "extending" his share of wealth through deceitful means! As the Gemara (Beitzah 16a) puts it, "The amount of a man's sustenance is determined each year on Rosh Hashanah." There can be no altering of one's predetermined share.

When the Jews left Egypt, they subsisted on the manna that fell from heaven. Although each person went and gathered as much manna as possible, nevertheless, when each person returned home each one's share was found to be exactly equal! This, too, was to demonstrate [to that generation and to future generations] that it is not one's efforts that grants one his livelihood, but rather Hashem's good will.

Clearly then, the division of Zeraim, [with its multitude of laws regarding tithing and thanking Hashem for his bounty,] makes us aware that our earnings are bestowed upon us by Hashem's blessing. Zeraim prepares us to face the question, "Did you conduct your business affairs honestly?" This lesson is brought out most clearly in the opening tractate, Berachos, which discusses the various blessings that we say in acknowledgment of every gift that Hashem endows us.

The second of the Mishnah's sections is Moed ("Holy Days"), which deals with the various restrictions and observations of the Shabbos and the holidays, etc. The reason such restrictions on mundane activities and labors were given for the holy days is to ensure that we have free time to be used for learning Hashem's Torah and for otherwise attaining spiritual growth. (This idea was discussed at length in the Vayakhel essay, p. 102.) Moed drives home the importance of setting aside time for Torah study. Moed also readies us for the second question, "Did you arrange set times for Torah study?"

The second section of the Mishnah: Moed

Although work is prohibited to a certain extent on all of the Moadim, the most encompassing prohibitions apply to the Shabbos day. Shabbos is more absolutely dedicated to the lesson of setting aside time for Torah study than other holidays. Therefore, it is Shabbos that appropriately is the opening tractate of Moed.

Nashim ("Women") is the third section of the Mishnah. This section is concerned with aspects of marriage and responsibilities of the spouses. A husband and wife's relationship is considered to be one of the most sacred relationships in human experience.

The third section of the Mishnah: Nashim

The word used throughout the Talmud for the start of the marriage process is *kiddushin*, which actually means "sanctity" (see Kiddushin 2b).The Gemara (Sotah 17a) tells us that when husband and wife live in harmony, the Presence of Hashem (the *Shechinah*) dwells with them. In fact, according to the Gemara (Niddah 31a), three partners are involved in the conception of a human being: the woman, the man and Hashem. Reproduction is not supposed to be a physical, worldly pursuit, but rather a venture of the highest spiritual order.

When man is asked, "Did you bring children into the world?" (the third question) the real question is, "Did you realize the importance and significance of reproduction, and therefore attempt to bring children into the world?" If one refrains from marriage or childbearing because one feels that this is not a noble undertaking, or because one does not consider it important enough to allow it to "cramp his style" of living, he will not be able to answer this question in the affirmative when the time comes. The way we may arrive at the fullest realization of the Divine [and highly spiritual] nature of this endeavor is through the study of the Nashim section of the Mishnah.

This lesson is evident in the laws of *yibbum* [levirate marriage], discussed in this section's opening tractate. If a man dies without children, the brother of the deceased is instructed to marry the widow so that children can be brought into the world "on behalf" of his deceased brother (Devarim 25:5-10). So far-reaching is the importance of bringing children into the world!

Fourth, is the section known as Nezikin ("Damages"), which deals with the laws of damages and other monetary responsibilities of one person toward another. It also discusses the workings of the court system and the various forms of punishment incurred by transgressing the numerous prohibitions of the Torah. By studying the laws of damages one realizes the importance of maintaining peaceful relationships between people. In order that all people may be at peace with one another, stringent laws of compensation are applied for even slight damages. Certain actions, for instance, are prohibited in one's own property, for fear that they may bring damage or discomfort to a neighbor. Such sensitivity towards the rest of humanity will undoubtedly bring one to yearn for a time when there will no longer be hatred, when peaceful coexistence will be the norm. This is the period referred to as the "End of Days," the Messianic era of the Final Redemption. "When Elijah comes (to herald in the Messianic age) his purpose will be...simply to bring peace to the world" (Mishnah Eduyos, 8:7).

The fourth section of the Mishnah: Nezikin

Furthermore, by learning about the punishments ordained by the Torah for various transgressions, one realizes that all of the trials and tribulations faced by the Jews in their long and bitter exile are *not* natural occurrences, but rather are the result of a Divine decree designed as a punishment for our wrongdoings. When this is understood one will pray to Hashem to have mercy and bring an end to this situation, and direct hope towards Hashem, asking Him to bring about the future redemption to our exile. Studying the laws of damages thus imbues within us the desire to see the coming of the Messianic era, and prepares us to deal with the fourth of the questions: "Did you eagerly anticipate the coming of the Final Salvation?"

Nezikin's first tractate begins with a description of the four primary categories of damages upon which the whole system of Jewish laws of torts is based. These are often seen homiletically as representing the four periods of subjugation and exile that the Jewish people have undergone through the ages—the time [spent] in Babylonia, Persia, Greece and Edom (i.e., Rome, including the nations and religions of today that are based on Roman culture)—see Maharsha to Bava Kama 3b, Vilna Gaon Haggadah on Chad Gadya [Art Scroll edition, p. 133], and in the Selichos for the ten days of repentance. This is certainly an appropriate start for the section that bids us to long for the end of all exiles.

Kodshim ("Consecrated Items") is the fifth section of the Mishnah. This section deals with all the laws of the Temple and its sacrificial service. A mitzvah in the Torah obligates us to take ten percent of our produce and bring it (or its cash value) to the "place that Hashem will choose [Jerusalem, the site of the Beis Hamikdash]" and eat it there with great rejoicing (Devarim 14:22-23). The Torah tells us we must do this so that we may "learn to fear Hashem your G-d all the days." Tosafos (Bava Basra 21a) explains how a person will learn to fear Hashem by visiting Jerusalem. Tosafos quotes a Midrash which

The fifth section of the Mishnah: Kodshim

states that when a person witnesses the magnificence of the Temple service in Jerusalem, and beholds the Kohanim ministering before Hashem in holiness and purity, he becomes so awe-inspired that he is overcome with powerful feelings of fear for Hashem. Thus, a study of the intricacies of the sacrificial rite in the Temple imbues one with a profound sense of awe and fear of G-d. According to this, it is clear that studying the details of the Temple sacrifices is an excellent way for one to prepare oneself for a favorable reply to the fifth question: "Did you investigate wisdom (i.e., fear of G-d)?"

This is especially evident in the first tractate of this section, Zevachim, which discusses the various animal sacrifices. The Ramban, in his interpretation of Vayikra 1:6, explains the underlying theme behind animal sacrifice. A penitent who brings his offering, is meant to witness the slaughtering and burning of the animal and reflect that "it is really I who am deserving of slaughter, etc. for my sin." This certainly is a direct lesson in fear of G-d.

The last of the six divisions: Taharos

The last of the six divisions of the Mishnah is Taharos ("Purity"), discussing the intricacies of the laws of *tumah* [ritual impurity] and *taharah* [ritual purity]—that is, under what circumstances food or objects or people are considered to be rendered unfit for sanctified use. These laws, then, deal not with the Temple service itself, but with how we must conduct ourselves when dealing with sanctified objects. We are, in effect, extending the conclusions we have learned from Kodshim into actions.

Although the laws of Taharos should only have been in use when dealing with sanctified objects or places, nevertheless, it was common practice for people to observe (as an extra stringency) the rules of *tumah* and *taharah* even for non-sacred purposes. They would refrain from eating *any* food which had been rendered ritually impure. The practice of these laws can be seen as an extension of the exclusively Temple-dependent laws of Kodshim into our everyday lives. We are demonstrating that even in daily, mundane events we discern sanctity. Hence, the study of Taharos inculcates within us the *practice* of our fear of Hashem, preparing us for the last of the questions: "Did you draw conclusions based on that analysis?" which means, as we explained earlier, "Did you translate your fear of Hashem into deeds?"

Perhaps the best illustration of this concept is given by the tractate Kelim, which discusses every imaginable type of household utensil and whether or not it is susceptible to the rules of *tumah* and *taharah*. Even the most mundane objects are discussed and put into the framework of the most sublime forms of worship of Hashem—the Temple service. It is therefore a most appropriate opening for the sixth section, Taharos.

May Hashem help us to accept upon ourselves to master both the Mishnah and its moral lessons, that we may not be ashamed of ourselves when confronted with the six questions on the day of judgment!

PARSHAS NASO

Shimshon's Years: Twenty-Twenty

This week's Parsha lays down the laws of the *nazir*—a man or woman who chooses to accept certain additional strictures in order to attain a higher level of sanctity and closeness to Hashem. Perhaps the most famous *nazir* of all times was Shimshon [Samson], whose story is related in Shoftim (Judges 13-16), from which Naso's Haftorah is excerpted.

Shimshon's story, as recorded in Shoftim, supplies a prime example of how careful one must be when studying Tanach not to be tempted to suggest textual emendations to "correct" our present day Masoretic text.

"He led Israel for 40 years": A missing verse

Shimshon was one of the later *shoftim*, or leaders of Israel, in the pre-monarchy period. He was a man of extraordinary—even supernatural—strength, who rose to save his people from the oppression of the Philistines, who then ruled over substantial parts of Eretz Yisrael. Shimshon once single-handedly killed a thousand Philistines, armed with only a donkey's jawbone (Shoftim 15:15). The Philistines finally succeeded in overpowering Shimshon with the help of his infamous wife, Delilah. His eyes were gouged out and he was imprisoned in the Philistine capital of Gaza. One day Shimshon was brought out of his cell to be humiliated and perform for the crowds. The Philistine crowds had assembled in their huge temple at a celebration in honor of their god. Shimshon, however, situated himself between the two main pillars of the temple and literally "brought down the house," killing thousands of Philistine spectators along with himself. In the Talmud Yerushalmi we find the following comment concerning Shimshon's years of leadership:

"One verse says, 'He [Shimshon] led Israel for forty years,' while another verse

(Shoftim 16:31) says, 'He led Israel for twenty years.' How can this be resolved? Rav Acha said: This teaches us that the Philistines feared Shimshon for twenty years after his death just as they feared him for twenty years during his life" (Yerushalmi Sotah 1:8).

Concerning the first of the two contradictory verses, Tosafos notes: "The Talmud seems to be in disagreement with our texts of Tanach.... The Talmud Yerushalmi quotes a verse saying, 'He led Israel for *forty* years.' In all of our texts of the Tanach the reading is '*twenty* years' (Shoftim 15:20, 16:31)" (Tosafos Shabbos 55b, s.v. Maavirim).

Thus we see that the contradiction pointed out by the Yerushalmi is, according to our texts, non-existent! Tosafos is led to the conclusion that the Sages of the Talmud apparently had a variant reading for this verse.

This presents a difficulty: If the Sages of the Talmud had a different reading—and we always follow the rulings of the Talmud—why should we not admit our "mistake" and emend our texts to correspond to the Talmudic version? (See the words of the Gaonim in *Teshuvos Gaonim Kadmonim* #78 regarding textual integrity in cases where the Talmud apparently presents a different reading of the text.)

II

Perhaps we should not be quick, however, to doubt the authenticity of our texts of the Tanach. A different reading of the Yerushalmi may remove the necessity of tampering with either the Tanach *or* Yerushalmi text.

Two verses are as good as one

In Shoftim 13:1 we read, "The Children of Israel continued to do what was wrong in the eyes of Hashem, and Hashem delivered them into the hands of the Philistines for forty years." The Tanach then tells the story of Shimshon's conception and birth. Although the simple reading of the verse implies that Shimshon was born after the Israelites had already been subjugated for forty years by the Philistines, this cannot be the case, as the commentators point out. Some, or all, of the forty years of Philistine domination must overlap with the years of Shimshon's leadership of Israel—otherwise there would be more than the requisite 480 years between the Exodus from Egypt and King Solomon's Temple as recorded in I Kings 6:1.

According to the Yerushalmi, for forty years Shimshon prevented the dominating Philistines from attacking Israel. Since the Philistines only subdued Israel for forty years, we may conclude that Chazal understood that *all* forty years of the Philistine domination of Israel coincided with Shimshon's tenure as leader.

Perhaps this is alluded to in the promise the angel made to Shimshon's mother shortly after his conception, "Your child will begin to save Israel from the hands of the Philistines." It states, however, that Shimshon would *begin* to bring salvation when the Philistine rule began, and would *continue* to be their nemesis for *as long as* the Philistines retained power over Israel. Shimshon would prevent the Philistines from overburdening Israel throughout their entire period of rule over Eretz Yisrael.

If Chazal understood this to be the angel's intent, then they have a clear source in Tanach to demonstrate that Shimshon indeed led Israel for *forty* years—i.e., for the entire period that they were subjugated to the Philistines.

Perhaps this, then, is the verse that the Yerushalmi cites to show that Shimshon led Israel for forty years. If so, the exact wording of the verse is not "He led Israel for forty years," as the Yerushalmi quotes. Rather, there are two distinct verses: "Hashem delivered them into the hands of the Philistines for forty years," and "[Shimshon] will begin to save Israel from the hands of the Philistines." It is possible that the Yerushalmi did not intend to cite a verbatim quote at all—the Yerushalmi may have really meant to paraphrase the two above-mentioned verses. Such combining of verses is not uncommon in the Talmud, as Tosafos himself points out in Megillah 3a (s.v. Vayyalen) and in many other places.

No verse, then, openly states that Shimshon led Israel for forty years. However, there are verses that *imply* it, and it is to these verses that the

Textual evidence

Yerushalmi is referring. There is no need to assume that the Yerushalmi had a variant reading of the verse, nor is there a need to tamper with the text of the Yerushalmi! (See also Maharsha to Sotah 10a, who offers a similar explanation to reconcile the Yerushalmi with our texts. All of the following commentators independently reached the same conclusion as the Maharsha: *Tzion Yerushalayim* to the Yerushalmi loc. cit.; Rashash to Bamidbar Rabbah 14:9; *Hamikra Vehamesorah* by R. Reuven Margulies, essay #2. The way that they present it, however, it is still necessary to make extensive emendations in the text of the Yerushalmi.)

It is interesting to note that the conclusion of the Yerushalmi—that Shimshon's reign spanned two distinct twenty-year periods—can be corroborated by another piece of textual evidence. The Yerushalmi based its conclusion on the insinuation that Shimshon humbled the Philistines throughout the entire forty years that they held a position of power in Israel. The Midrash to this week's Parsha comes to the same conclusion based on the *repetition* of the verse that describes Shimshon's twenty-year tenure as leader.

"On the tenth day...the leader of the tribe of Dan brought his offering: ...two bulls" (Bamidbar 7:66, 71)—These two bulls represent the two times, in connection with Shimshon [who was from the tribe of Dan], that it is said 'He led Israel for twenty years' (once in Shoftim 15:20, and once in Shoftim 16:31). The phrase was repeated in order to teach us that the Philistines feared Shimshon for twenty years after his death just as much as they feared him for the twenty years of his life" (Bamidbar Rabbah 14:9).

III

Twenty two years?

We may now shed some light on an even more perplexing passage in the Babylonian Talmud [Talmud Bavli]. (Just before Shimshon toppled the Philistine temple, he called out,) "My Lord Hashem, remember me and strengthen me just this once, O G-d, and I will avenge myself on the Philistines the revenge for one of my two eyes." (Shoftim 16:28)—Rav said: This is what Shimshon said before Hashem: "Master of the Universe! Remember for me the twenty two (sic) years that I led Israel, during which I never asked any one of them to so much as bring me my walking stick."

First question

When reading this quote we are immediately struck by the words "twenty two years". As we have seen, the verse clearly stated that Shimshon's reign lasted *twenty* years! The Rashba (13th century Spain), in his responsa (1:88), was asked to explain this Gemara. He said that the word "two" must be a copyist's error and should be deleted from the Talmudic text! Several centuries earlier, the Gaonim grappled with this problem and offered no solutions (*Teshuvos Hagaonim*, Liek 1864, end of #45).

Second question

Another difficulty with this excerpt is that Rav's comment seemingly has nothing to do with the verse quoted to introduce his statement. What is the connection between Shimshon's prayer "Remember me... revenge for one of my two eyes" and Rav's comment that Shimshon was recalling his years of faithful service to his nation? Where did Rav see this motif in the verse quoted? (Both Rashi and Maharsha, who were also bothered by this problem, offer rather forced suggestions.) Perhaps, based on what we have explained, we may suggest a new interpretation for this passage.

IV

Two eyes & two periods of leadership

Perhaps the Talmud Bavli was also bothered by the problem with which the Midrash and the Yerushalmi dealt—why does the verse count *two* twenty-year periods during which Shimshon guided Israel? However, the Bavli rejected the resolution suggested by the Midrash and the Yerushalmi—that posthumously Shimshon frightened away the Philistines for an additional twenty years. After all, why should the Philistines continue to fear someone who is dead, no matter how mighty and fierce he was alive? (Some commentators explain that, according to the Yerushalmi, the Philistines were not certain that Shimshon was dead, since his body was spirited out of the wreckage by his brethren.)

The Bavli may have understood instead that the two periods of Shimshon's leadership were the twenty years during which Shimshon judged, and another twenty years during which he was *imprisoned* by the Philistines. (The Tanach, in fact, does *not* record how long Shimshon was in prison before he was brought out to perform for the crowds. It may well have been for a lengthy period.) If so, it would be entirely understandable that the Philistines feared Shimshon during the latter twenty-year period. They were afraid that Shimshon would burst out of his shackles, even though he had been bound and blinded. Only after twenty years did they have the audacity to publicly taunt him (and we all know what happened to them then....) If so, the end of the forty-year Philistine rule coincided with Shimshon's dramatic martyrdom. Perhaps Shimshon brought about the downfall of the Philistines by destroying their temple and their leaders at the time of his death!

We may now suggest that the original reading of the Gemara was "the two twenty years that I led Israel," ("*shenaim esrim shana*"). Shimshon was asking Hashem to remember for him the two twenty-year periods during which he led the Jewish nation! Since the phrase "two twenty-years" seems at first glance to be meaningless, it was "corrected" by copyists to "twenty two years," which is, of course, erroneous! (See Maharsha Sotah 10a, who proposes a similar emendation of the text of the Bavli.)

Answer to first question

We now understand the connection between Rav's teaching and the verse from which it was derived. Perhaps Rav saw in the word "eyes" an allusion to "leadership." In Bava Basra 4a the Gemara tells us that the words "the *eyes* of the congregation" (Bamidbar 15:24) refer to the *leaders* of the congregation. Thus, "one of my two eyes" may be homiletically interpreted as meaning "one of my two periods of leadership." From this verse, Rav derives further support for the thesis that Shimshon led Israel for *two* twenty-year periods. Shimshon was now asking Hashem to reward him for at least one of his periods of leadership in this world, by allowing him to bring about the fall of his captors!

Answer to second question

We saw before that the Yerushalmi and the Midrash found two separate hints in the verses of Shoftim to Shimshon's "double-term" as spiritual leader. The Talmud Bavli now adds a *third* source for that contention!

PARSHAS BAHAALOSCHA

Hillel And The Wager, Revisited

"Miriam and Aaron spoke against Moshe.... They said, 'Is it only with Moshe that Hashem has spoken? Didn't He speak with us as well?'—and Hashem heard it. And the man Moshe was very modest, more than any other man in the world" (Bamidbar 12:1-3).

Moshe's sister, Miriam, spoke badly of Moshe for having separated from his wife (see Rashi's comment on verse 1). Moshe had decided that the separation was halachically necessary and Hashem verified the appropriateness of Moshe's decision (Shabbos 87a)—Miriam apparently was unaware of this. Hashem punished Miriam for her insolence by afflicting her with *tzaraas.*

Moshe's modesty

After Miriam's criticism of her brother, the Torah tells us that Moshe was the most modest person in the world. But how is Moshe's modesty relevant to Miriam's criticism? It would have been more logical for the Torah to say that Moshe was exceedingly righteous and thus could be blamed in no way for divorcing his wife. His *modesty,* however, seems irrelevant in this context.

Rebbi Natan in the Sifri, explains that Miriam slandered Moshe in Moshe's presence. Although insulted to his face, Moshe displayed extraordinary modesty and did not react. Hashem had to intervene to defend Moshe's honor. We thus find that Moshe's trait of modesty *was pertinent* to the incident described, since it was Moshe's modesty that enabled him to overlook Miriam's criticism.

Moshe's lack of reaction was truly remarkable. The Gemara (Gittin 36b) pays tribute to people who show such exceptional restraint: "People who are insulted but do not insult others, who hear disparaging remarks yet do not return them, who act with the love of Hashem and are happy with any hardships that may come their way—they are the ones referred to in the verse 'Those who love [Hashem] shine like the sun in its full intensity' (Shoftim 4:31). Perhaps for this reason, we find that 'the face of Moshe was like that of the sun' " (Bava Basra 75a).

II

The wager

Unfortunately people who show such restraint and modesty are few and far between. (How many of us can admit that we react in such a manner on a regular basis?) There is one particular sage from Mishnaic times, however, who was well-known for his embodiment of this trait—Hillel, the Nassi [spiritual and temporal governor over Israel during the period of Roman rule, c. 30 BCE].

The Gemara (Shabbos 31a) tells us the following narrative: "A person should always be modest, like Hillel... Once there were two men who made a wager, saying that whoever could anger Hillel would receive four hundred *zuzim* [silver coins]. The men wagered on a Friday, and Hillel was washing his hair for Shabbos. One of the men went to the door of Hillel's house and asked, 'Is Hillel here? Is Hillel here?' Hillel put on his robe and greeted the man. He sat him down and asked, 'What do you want, my son?' The man replied, 'I have a question I must ask.' Hillel replied, 'Ask, my son, ask.' The man asked, 'Why do Babylonians have elongated heads?' Hillel replied, 'You have asked a good question, my son! It is because their midwives are not well-skilled [and their heads become misshapen at birth].'

[No sooner had Hillel returned to his shower, when the man again rudely interrupted him,] 'Why are the eyes of Tarmudians so narrow?' Hillel replied, 'You have asked a good question, my son! It is because they live in a sandy environment (see I Kings 9:18—MK) [and they are always squinting because of the sand that often blows into their eyes].'

[Shortly afterwards the man returned, this time to ask,] 'Why do Africans have wide feet?' Hillel [left his shower again and] replied, 'You have asked a good question, my son! The answer is that they live in marshy areas [and they must therefore go about barefoot, which causes their feet to become flat and wide].'

The man then said, 'I have many more questions to ask—but I am afraid that you will become angry at me.'" Hillel wrapped himself in a garment and sat down before the man, saying, 'Ask all the questions you wish to ask!' The man said to him, 'Are you the Hillel whom they call Nassi?' Hillel said, 'Yes, I am.' The man retorted, 'If you are he, then may there not be many others like you in Israel! It is because of you that I have lost four hundred *zuzim*!' Hillel scolded him, saying, 'Mind that you don't act so impulsively! Better that many times four hundred *zuzim* be lost through Hillel, than that Hillel should become angry!' " (Shabbos 30b-31a).

This man's insolence is remarkable. Everything he did, from the timing of his visit, to the contemptuous tone with which he addressed the venerable sage ("Is Hillel here?"), to the petty nature of his questions and his insistence of urgency, were designed to upset Hillel. Yet Hillel responded with extraordinary humility, leaving his bath and getting dressed three times for this disrespectful young man, giving him as much time as he desired.

Hillel's humility is even more impressive if we remember that Hillel himself was from Babylon (Pesachim 66a, Sukkah 18a). The question, "Why do Babylonians have elongated heads?" thus directly insulted Hillel's physical appearance! Yet, like Moshe, Hillel was able to retain his composure even when subjected to such extreme humiliation.

III

Elongated heads

The main point of this story obviously demonstrates the extent of Hillel's humility. However, one wonders about the nature of the specific questions that the man posed. Of all the inane subjects he might have chosen why did he choose these odd questions? And Hillel, for all his modesty, could have simply said, "I am sorry, my son, but I am a rabbi and I don't specialize in these areas. Perhaps you have another question which I am more qualified to answer." Why did Hillel answer these questions so earnestly? And did Hillel really believe that the shape of the Babylonian's heads was a product of poor midwifery? Perhaps there is more to this lesson in humility than meets the eye.

If we further contemplate the man's questions, they may be seen to have a deeper significance. Perhaps the man was not talking about the *physical* condition of the Babylonians' heads, but about what is *inside* their heads. What he meant to say was, "Why is it that while we Israelis have a conventional, straightforward manner of thinking, you Babylonians have an 'elongated,' or lopsided, manner of thinking? How do you dare take your crooked, Babylonian methods of thought and rule over sages whose background is much more intellectually sound than yours, when you are not even a proper rabbinical scholar!"

This was meant to be a particularly harsh insult to the man who was the spiritual leader of the nation. (The insult is seen to be particularly vicious when we bear in mind that Hillel was granted his lofty post through proving himself more worthy than the Israeli scholars in an intellectual challenge—Pesachim 66a.)

To this disparaging remark Hillel replied modestly, "You are right. Perhaps our minds are not as keen as those of the people of Israel. But even if that is so, we are not to be blamed. It happened due to a lack of professional 'midwives.' I.e., the people who brought us into the world of Torah and nurtured our development were not as learned as the great rabbis of Israel. (See Rashi to Gittin 6a, who says that until many years after Hillel there was never more than one Yeshiva in Babylon, while in Israel there were many Yeshivos.) If you believe that my intellectual capabilities are inferior to my colleagues, it is due to a flaw in my early education."

Both the question and the answer should be understood metaphorically. The man was leveling a low insult at Hillel, and Hillel responded to the slight in an extremely humble manner.

IV

The connection of the question about "Babylonian heads" to Hillel now may be understood, but can the other two questions also be of deeper metaphorical significance? It is possible that these two questions were also designed to incite Hillel's anger. If there is one thing that can upset a Jew more than a direct personal insult, it is a disparaging remark about his Rabbi or mentor!

Squinty eyes and flat feet

Hillel's mentors—from whom he was very proud to have learned (Pesachim ibid.)—were Shemayah and Avtalyon, the two great sages of Babylon of the previous generation (Avos 1:10).

The Gemara (Gittin 57b, Eduyos 5:6) tells us that Shemayah and Avtalyon were actually converts to Judaism—descendants of none other than the evil Sancheriv (who destroyed the Northern Kingdom of Israel, driving the ten "lost" tribes into exile): The Gemara does not specify to which nationality they belonged, but the Rambam (*Perush haMishnayos*, Eduyos, 1:3) says that they had difficulty pronouncing various Hebrew sounds—in their homeland they had been totally unfamiliar with the consonants of the Hebrew language. This intimates that they did not come from lands of major Jewish settlement such as Babylon, where Jews and the Hebrew consonants were familiar, but from a remote land where there were few, if any, Jews. Perhaps we can speculate that the land of origin of one of Hillel's teachers was none other than Tarmud. (See Yevamos 16a, "Chaggai the prophet said...that it is permitted to accept Tarmudian converts," and Rashi ad loc.) The other sage may have hailed from Africa. If so, it is easy to see how the second and third questions were aimed at angering Hillel—they insulted his mentors! Let us take another look, now, at the latter two questions.

"Eyes" or leaders

"Eyes" is a term often used to represent "leaders". By asking why Tarmudians squint, the man was implying that people from Tarmud are unsuitable as proper leaders —they can't "see" (lead) properly. But, despite the provocation, Hillel did not lose his temper. He answered the taunt humbly by explaining that the Tarmudians lived in a "desert land"—that is, a land devoid of spirituality and morality. The sand of this "desert" affects the eyes of its inhabitants—a metaphor for the deleterious effects that such unwholesome surroundings can have on all who live there. If the leaders hailing from Tarmud are any less qualified, then this is why. Even after one has uprooted oneself from a wicked environment, and subsequently attained great spiritual heights, the "sand" may have affected one's ability to be a proper spiritual leader ("his eyes").

"Feet," too, can easily be understood as representing the leaders of the people, since leaders walk before the people and guide their steps. When the man asked Hillel why Africans have wide feet, he implied that African "feet," or leaders, are "deformed"—i.e., inferior, unworthy of leading.

"Feet" or leaders

Hillel did not let the intended insult to his teacher "get under his collar." Hillel humbly answered that the Africans live in swampy areas. Swamps and quagmires are also often used as metaphors to depict evil, idolatrous influences (see Tehillim 69:3). Once again, Hillel explained, it is not an African's fault if he shows poor leadership skills, for he is unalterably affected by the habitat where he was raised. The "swamplands" (that is, the idolatrous, immoral conduct rampant in that area) take their toll on the "feet" (i.e., leadership capabilities) of everyone born and raised there.

According to this analysis we can see that Hillel's patience was tested in a way similar to that of Moshe's. Like Moshe, Hillel passed the test without batting an eyelash! In the words of one gentile who converted to Judaism under the guidance of Hillel—"Hillel, the humble! May many blessings come upon your head, for your conduct has enabled me to recognize the Divine Presence and become one of His people" (Shabbos 31a)!

PARSHAS SHELACH

In Search Of The Lost Chilazon

"The Bnai Yisrael shall put on the tzitzis of the corners [ritual strings that hang from the corners of four-cornered garments] a string of *techeles* [wool dyed with a certain blue dye]" (Bamidbar 15:38).

"*Techeles* is only kosher if it is made from the *chilazon*; if it is not made from the *chilazon* it is invalid" (Tosefta Menachos 9:6, Beraisa in Masseches Tzitzis).

The *techeles* (or Biblical blue) dye is mentioned dozens of times throughout the Tanach, usually together with another dye named *argaman* (royal, or tyrian, purple). In the ancient world these two dyes were worth many times their weight in gold. Clothing dyed with these pigments were reserved for royalty, or at least for high ranking nobles. In Parshas Shelach, the Torah gives every Jewish man the right—even the obligation—to wear a string of this royal *techeles* on his garments.

Royal colors

Unfortunately at some point in history the art of the manufacture of *techeles* was lost, and its use discontinued. This is already apparent in the Midrashim (Bamidbar Rabbah 17:5; Tanchuma, end of Shelach) which mention that the *techeles* has been hidden away (*nignaz*). It is conjectured that the production of *techeles* ceased in the seventh or eighth century, perhaps as a result of the devastation and upheaval caused in the year 683 by the Arab conquest of Israel.

What exactly is this *chilazon* from which the *techeles* dye is extracted? Is it possible to reconstruct the long-lost art of *techeles* production? What is the nature of the *techeles* that some men wear today on their tzitzis? Let us take an excursion into the world of the *chilazon* and the *techeles* dye and see if we can unravel some of the mystery that pervades this fascinating subject.

Before we start, it must be pointed out that in the field of *techeles* research a great debt of gratitude is due to the former chief Rabbi of Ireland and later of Israel, Rav Yitzchak Isaac Herzog, who at age 24 did a study on the topic for his doctoral thesis. Rav Herzog combined his exceptional scholarship in eight different disciplines and 12 languages, not to mention a tremendous erudition in Judaic sources to complete his thesis. To this day his thesis remains *the* basic, authoritative work on the subject, from both a scholarly and a Talmudic standpoint. The Hebrew version of his thesis was recently reprinted in full in the book *HaTechelet* by Rav Menachem Burstein (Jerusalem, 1988, pp. 352-437), an excellent work which sums up all of the *techeles* research which had been done until that date.

II

The Radziner techeles

What color is the *techeles* dye? Here we have clear, specific information. The Gemara in Bava Metzia 61b says that (Clue #1) the color of *techeles* is indistinguishable from that of indigo (*Kala Ilan*—see Sefer Ha'Aruch). When it comes to the *chilazon*, though, the information we are given is sketchier.

From where does the *chilazon*—the source of the *techeles* dye—come? In Yechezkel 27:7 we read that (clue #2) the most professional production sites of *techeles* were to be found in "the islands of Elisha," since identified as either Italy (see Targum, ibid.) or Cyprus. The Talmud tells us in several places that (clue #3) the only place *techeles* was to be found in Eretz Yisrael was in the territory of the tribe of Zevulun, which was along the Mediterranean coast from Haifa and northward to Tyre (Shabbos 26a, Megillah 6a).

Let us now turn to the identity of the *chilazon* itself. What sort of creature is it? The only explicit source about this question is the following:

"The body of the *chilazon* (clue #4) resembles the sea (alternate reading: resembles the sky), and (clue #5) its body is similar to that of a fish. It comes up once every seventy (alt. reading: seven) years (clue #6). (This may be an exaggeration employed to emphasize the scarcity of the species.—MK) The *techeles* dye is obtained from its blood [secretion], and it is therefore very expensive" (Menachos 44a; Beraisa in Masseches Tzitzis).

In the late 19th century a talmudic researcher named Yehudah Levisohn proposed in his work *Talmudic Zoology* (p. 284-5) that the *chilazon* was a type of squid known as the cuttlefish. Levisohn based his conclusion on an inference from a statement of the Rambam in Hilchos tzitzis 2:2. Shortly afterwards, a brilliant Chassidic Rebbe, Rav Gershon Henoch Leiner of Radzin, came to the same conclusion. He carried the conclusion one step further though, actually developing a process whereby the sepia [inky secretion] of the cuttlefish, which normally produces a dark brown dye, was transformed into a blue dye! The dye turned out to be identical, chemically, to a common synthetic light-blue dye invented in 1704, known as Prussian blue.

The Radziner Rebbe authored three large volumes intended to prove that he had indeed re-discovered the long-lost *techeles*, and set up a factory where the dye was produced. His followers adopted his opinion and began wearing the new *techeles* string in their tzitzis. With the exception of the Breslover Chassidim, however, the innovation was not accepted by the rest of the Jewish world, and his movement was met with a substantial amount of opposition.

Unfortunately, there are a number of technical difficulties with the *techeles* produced according to the Radziner method. Firstly, (clue #7) *techeles* was known to be absolutely indelible (Menachos 43b), the Radziner *techeles*, however, can fade (a process called "bleeding") when washed with common detergents (see *HaTechelet* p. 179). Furthermore, in the land of Zevulun there is no greater amount of squid than anywhere else in the Mediterranean. The only place squid can be found in particular abundance is in the area of Italy (*HaTechelet* p. 178)!

Perhaps the strongest objection to the Radziner *techeles*, though, is (clue #8) that the word "*chilazon*" is used in numerous places in Chazal as a general term meaning a snail or a snail-like object. The *chilazon* mentioned in Shir HaShirim Rabbah (4:11), is clearly a creature that lives inside a shell which grows along with it—which is not true of a squid. (The Radziner Rebbe's comments on this are recorded in *HaTechelet* p. 174.)

III

The relationship between *argaman* and *techeles*

But which of the many species of snails is the one which produces the *techeles* dye? *Techeles* is often mentioned in conjunction with *argaman* (in fact, in the Talmudic literature the term "*techeles*" is often used to refer to either of the two). In the middle of the 17th century an English naturalist named Thomas Geig wrote that he found a snail which contains within it a liquid which becomes a purplish dye after being extracted and exposed to sunlight. At around the same time, Saul Bochart (*Hierozoicon*, 1663) proved from ancient sources that *argaman* was produced from snails. Shortly afterwards, researchers put the two facts together, concluding that Geig's snail was indeed the source used by the ancients to produce *argaman* (*HaTechelet* p. 252, 371, 418).

Archaeologists have, in fact, uncovered numerous ancient dye-producing factories all along the Mediterranean coast (mostly in the north-eastern area, "from Haifa to Tyre"), with large heaps of snail shells alongside them. These shells have been identified as belonging to three distinct species of snails: *Purpura haemastoma*, *Murex brandaris* and *Murex trunculus*. That these snails were the source of Tyrian purple—*argaman*—has become accepted as a historical fact. These snails are, in fact, much more numerous along the northern coast of Eretz Yisrael than along the southern coast, with their population steadily increasing as one goes north. South of Haifa, the snails are few and far between. This corresponds nicely with the description of the *chilazon*'s distribution presented by Chazal.

The identities of these snails were well-known to Rav Herzog when he wrote his work on *techeles*. And, as he himself pointed out, it seems clear from several Biblical and historical sources that the Jews and the gentiles extracted their blue dyes from the same creature (*HaTechelet* pp. 426-7. See also Shabbos 26a, and Rashi ad loc. "*U'Lyogvim*"). Nevertheless, Rav Herzog rejected the idea that one or all of these species may be the true *techeles chilazon* for several reasons. First of all, the color of their shells is white, which contradicts the Gemara's description (quoted above) that the *chilazon*'s body "resembles the sea," i.e., is of a bluish hue. Furthermore, and more importantly, the dye extracted from these creatures is purple, not indigo. The above-mentioned snails were clearly the source of *argaman*, or "purpura" in Latin. However, *techeles*, referred to in Latin by Josephus and Philo as "*hyakinthos*," may have been produced from another snail altogether!

IV

Rav Herzog's techeles

Rav Herzog suggested that there was another snail, distinct from the above-mentioned snails, from which *techeles* was derived. The snail Rav Herzog chose is known as *Janthina pallida Harvey*. It is found in the Mediterranean, and has a beautiful violet-blue shell. When excited, it discharges a secretion of the same color. It is quite rare and lives in colonies. The colonies experience population explosions every four to seven years, and large numbers of them are washed ashore! All the pieces of the puzzle seem to fit now! (*HaTechelet* p. 427.)

However, there are several problems with identifying the *chilazon* as the *Janthina* snail. For one thing, as with the cuttlefish, it is no more common along the shore of Zevulun than anywhere else in the Mediterranean. For another, as Rav Herzog himself points out, no *Janthina* shells have ever been discovered in any archaeological site, nor is it mentioned anywhere in the Greek or Roman literature that discuss blue dye. It thus appears not to have been in use in the ancient world.

V

A contemporary of Rav Herzog's, Alexander Dedekind of Vienna, suggested in his work *Archeological Zoology* (Vienna, 1898, p. 467) that the blue dye of *techeles* actually did come from the snails found near the ancient dye vats. He differentiated between the *techeles* and the *argaman* snails,

Modern techeles

singling out *Murex trunculus* (known in modern Hebrew as "*argaman keheh kotzim*," for "short spiked *Purpura*") as the source of the blue *techeles*. In contrast, the other two species were used exclusively for the production of *argaman*. Alexander Dedekind based this distinction on the fact that not far from Sidon an ancient dyeing site was discovered which had near it two separate piles of shells. In one pile the shells of *Purpura haemastoma* and *Murex brandaris* were mixed together, while in the other only shells of *Murex trunculus* were found (*HaTechelet* p. 421). This certainly seems to support the idea that *Murex trunculus* was used for a different purpose than the other two snails. In fact, the *M. trunculus* produces a slightly "bluer" dye than the other two.

Although he personally favored his *Janthina* theory, Rav Herzog himself reluctantly admitted that "the logical conclusion would certainly appear to be that the blue pigment produced by the *chilazon* was obtained using the *Murex trunculus* dye…it is highly unlikely that the *techeles chilazon* was not the *Murex Trunculus*" (*HaTechelet* p. 421). The evidence seems to point overwhelmingly to *Murex trunculus* as the source of *techeles*. Is there any way to overcome Rav Herzog's objections (mentioned above) to identifying the *chilazon* as *Murex trunculus*?

The first question can be answered easily. Rav Herzog pointed out that the shells of *Murex trunculus* were white and not "similar to the sea." However, his conclusion was based on the color of the centuries-old shells found by archaeologists or by museum samples. As a matter of fact, though, when the snail is first removed from the sea, it does indeed have a bluish-purple tinge to it, produced by sea-fouling. (On the *Murex* shell that I have in my possession, I can clearly discern a pronounced purplish-bluish tint.—MK)

The other problem raised was that the secretion of *Murex trunculus* turns purple and not blue. Rav Herzog himself raised the possibility that "there might have been some scheme known to the ancients for obtaining a blue dye out of this secretion" (*HaTechelet* p. 423). Sure enough, recent research has shown that when the secretion is exposed to bright sunlight immediately upon being extracted from the snail, the sunlight breaks down a certain chemical bond in the liquid and it subsequently forms a blue dye. In fact, the resulting dye consists mostly of components bearing the exact same chemical makeup as indigo! Although this is true of all three of the snails mentioned before, *Murex trunculus* yields this blue color much more readily than the others. *M. trunculus* does not require a lengthy exposure to the sun in order for the chemical reactions to take place. (Credit for this discovery goes to the late Otto Elsner of the Shenkar Institute of Fibers in Ramat Gan, Israel, whose essay on this subject can be found in *HaTechelet* p. 299-302—see also p. 423, note 39). It has recently been discovered, that cooking the dye in boiling water after it is extracted, also makes it take on a much bluer tint.

In the practical realm, we must acknowledge the work of a scholar in Jerusalem named Rav Eliyahu Tevger (author of *Kelil Techeles*). Although faced with many technical difficulties and high costs, he undertook the project of locating and collecting enough of the *M. trunculus* snails, then mastering the technique of transforming their secretion into a high-quality blue dye, and applying the dye to wool—all this despite the general antipathy of the scientific community.

Nine years ago, his initiative first saw success, and he used his product to dye wool threads, according to halachic requirements, which were made into *techeles* for tzitzis for the first time in fifteen centuries! Along with three others who have dedicated themselves to this endeavor—Joel Guberman, Ari Greenspan and Baruch Sterman—Rav Tevger has formed the *Petil Techelet Society*, which can be reached through e-mail at tekhelet@virtual.co.il. In 1993 the *Petil Techelet Society* started to mass produce their *techeles.*

Although, for various reasons, Torah authorities have decided that there is no halachic obligation to wear the present version of *techeles*, the almost mystical reappearance of the *chilazon* and the *techeles* during the past decades is certainly an exciting development!

PARSHAS KORACH

Pidyon Haben: The Trials And The Holiness Of The Firstborn Son

"You shall redeem the firstborn...and his redemption should be given when he is thirty days old, five shekels..." (Bamidbar 18:15, 16).

Firstborn sons had been chosen to be Israel's religious leaders and officiators. Later they lost this right due to their part in the sin of the golden calf (Bamidbar 3:11-13; Bamidbar 8:14-19). Instead, the Kohanim—the sons of Aharon—were given the privilege of serving in the Beis Hamikdash.

Today, the father of a firstborn son must give five shekels to the Kohanim to "redeem" his son. Symbolically, this reminds us that Hashem chose to transfer the holiness of the firstborn son to the Kohanim.

The unique status originally afforded to a firstborn son in the Temple service requires further analysis. Why was it that Hashem decided to grant them this special status in the first place? The most obvious answer is that "on the day that I struck down all the firstborn in Egypt [but spared those of Israel] I sanctified the firstborn of Israel to Myself" (Bamidbar 3:13). This does not, however, really address the question at the core—it only moves it over to a different plane.

Why were the firstborn sons of Egypt singled out for death on the night of the Exodus? In order to answer this, let us first take a look at what is entailed in the Temple service.

A king's power and glory are manifested more in the king's palace than in any other location in his kingdom. Similarly, Hashem's power and glory are more evident in the Beis Hamikdash than anywhere else (see Tosafos Bava Basra 21a, s.v. Ki MiTzion). It is a place where Hashem's pride and omnipotence are demonstrated. This may be the reason the Temple is referred to as the "pride" of your power (*gaon uzeichem*) in Yechezkel 24:21.

This may also be the reason we are taught (Bava Basra 4a) that the Sages felt it appropriate for the walls of the Temple to be embellished in a style that would evoke the waves of the sea. Hashem's "pride" (*gaavah*) is said to be seen in the power of the waves of the sea—"You rule over the 'pride' of the sea" (Tehillim 89:10); "Hashem reigns; He is clothed in 'pride'...he is known to be mighty on high through the crash of the great waters" (ibid. 93:1-4).

When the Jewish people sang to Hashem after He split the waters of the Red Sea they declared, "I will sing to Hashem because He is extremely 'proud'...in Your great 'pride' You destroy Your enemies." The pattern on the walls of the Temple was designed to recall Hashem's pride and power—the theme of the entire Temple structure (see also Tetzaveh essay, section II, p.93).

It is therefore fitting that a person who ministers to Hashem should have a degree of pride and self-assuredness himself. Otherwise, how can he feel worthy of serving the King Who appears in all His might? This man must have the trait found in the righteous King Yehoshaphat: "His heart was 'proud' in the ways of Hashem" (II Divrei Hayyamim 17:6). A firstborn son naturally has a higher sense of self-regard and pride. This is a natural effect of the pride parents show in their firstborn son. It is perhaps because of this sense of pride and self-esteem that firstborn sons were originally chosen to serve Hashem in His Temple.

II

Pride vs. arrogance

On the other hand, the pride that is prevalent among the firstborn can lead to outright arrogance. This can lead to denial, rather than service, of Hashem. If the firstborn's pride is not channeled to serve his Maker but rather to an overconfidence in his own attributes, he is bound to fail. "Lest you eat and become satisfied and build nice houses and live in them...and your heart become proud, and you forget Hashem...and think, 'My own strength and power have acquired these riches'" (Devarim 8:12,14,17). This is the reason the Gemara (Sotah 4b) says that "anyone who has arrogance in him—is as if he worshipped idolatry... and it is as if he has denied the existence of Hashem." Haughtiness is one of the pitfalls that can lead to an outright denial of Hashem's mastery over the world.

The Gemara (ibid.) compares an arrogant person to an *Ashera* tree, an object of worship in the ancient world. According to the Torah, this tree must be chopped down and destroyed. The arrogant man is liable to not only *worship* idolatry. In his own eyes his arrogance may make him become an object of worship ! A firstborn has a tendency toward pride and egoism, and thus is especially liable to fall into this trap.

The Egyptians were known for their arrogance. "As for Egypt...I say of them, 'They are arrogant'" (Yeshayah 30:7). The firstborn sons of the Egyptians certainly did not channel their extra dosage of pride toward the service of their Creator. They allowed their pride to lead them completely astray, causing them to deny Hashem totally, and even to deify themselves. This is the reason Hashem slayed the firstborn Egyptian sons on the night of the Exodus. When Hashem demonstrated His uniqueness and His superiority by destroying all of the Egyptian idols (Rashi, Shemos 12:12), He struck down the firstborn males as well. The Torah says, "I will pass through Egypt on this night and I will strike down all the firstborn in Egypt and I will enact judgments against all the gods of Egypt." The slaying of the firstborn and the enacting of judgments against the Egyptian deities were not two *separate* acts—the firstborn themselves were slain for their role as gods!

When the father of a firstborn son gives a five shekel "ransom" to the Kohen to redeem his child, it is intended to remind the father that the Egyptian firstborn sons were killed while the Jewish firstborns were spared (Shemos 13:15). The father here is thus being reminded to be careful not to teach the wrong kind of pride to his son.

It is natural for a father to feel proud of his first son, which, in turn, makes the son feel proud of himself. When the father reminds himself of the death of Egypt's arrogant firstborn, he will stop short of feeling "my own strength and power have acquired" for me this child. If the father has these feelings about his child, it invariably influences the boy to express his own pride in a similar style, and as the Egyptians fell, so will he. (See *Chinuch*—mitzvah #91—who gives a similar rationale for the mitzvah of *bikkurim.*)

III

The firstborn tribes

Perhaps we can find a hint to the dangers of being a firstborn son in the personalities of the firstborn among the tribes of Israel themselves. There were three tribes who renounced their portions in the Land of Israel proper, opting instead to take their share of land on the East Bank of the Jordan (see Bamidbar 32). These tribes were: Reuven, Gad and Menashe. It is interesting to note that all three were their mother's firstborn sons—Reuven was Leah's firstborn, Gad was Zilpah's and Menashe was Joseph's firstborn, who in turn, was the firstborn of Rachel. The reason they chose the East Bank of the Jordan over Israel proper was because they were led astray by their great riches and their large holdings in livestock (see Bamidbar Rabbah 22:7, Rashi Bamidbar 32:16). Perhaps this was the pride of the firstborn at work again. Instead of using their pride for positive purposes, they allowed themselves to be cut off from the main body of the Jewish people.

What of the firstborn of Bilhah—namely, Dan? We find that Dan encamped on the northern extremity of the camp during the Israelites' travels in the desert (Bamidbar 2:25). Rabbeinu Bachye points out that north (of the celestial equator) is the only direction where the sun never can be found (in the northern hemisphere, which is where Egypt and the Wilderness are), and the north thus represents darkness. (In fact, the Hebrew word for north—*tzafon*—has a connotation of "something that is hidden" for this reason.) The tribe of Dan was positioned there, says Rabbeinu Bachye, because it was Dan's tribe who "darkened the eyes of Israel" through adopting idolatry. It was also the Danites who accepted upon themselves the infamous idol of Michah, which remained the Danites' focus of worship for many centuries (Shoftim 18:30-31). As the Gemara in Sotah pointed out, arrogance—which, as we have seen, is the bane of the firstborn—can all too easily lead to idolatry!

CHUKKAS

PARSHAS CHUKKAS

Jewish Pet Care

In this week's Parsha we read how Moshe miraculously extracted water from a rock for the thirsty Israelites. The Torah tells us that the water was to give drink "to the congregation and their cattle." The wording implies that water was provided first to the populace and later to their animals. However, the Gemara in Gittin clearly teaches us that the Torah enjoins us to always see to our animals' sustenance before feeding ourselves!

"Rav Huna and Rav Chisda were once sitting together when Genniva passed by...They said to him, 'Why don't you have a bite with us?' He replied...'It is forbidden for a person to even taste food (*lit'om*) until he has fed his animal, as it says (Devarim 11:15), 'I will put grass in your fields for your *animals*, and *you* will eat and be satisfied'—first your animals should eat, and only afterwards may you eat'" (Gemara Gittin 62a).

The difference between eating and drinking

Similarly, in the story of Avraham's servant Eliezer, we read that when Eliezer traveled to Charan, Rivka offered Eliezer a drink and afterwards attended to his camels. This, too, contradicts Rav's rule! Why didn't Rivka pour the water for the camels first? And why didn't Eliezer delay his own drinking until his camels had finished drinking?

These discrepancies were noted by Rav Yehudah haChassid (14th cent. Germany) in his *Sefer Chasidim* (*Book of the Pious*). "When it comes to *thirst*, a man should be served first, and then his animal, as it says, 'When [Rivka] finished giving [Eliezer] to drink she said, 'I will also draw [water] for your camels, until they have finished drinking.' And it says furthermore, 'Bring out water from the rock for them, and give drink to the congregation and their cattle.' But when it comes to *eating*, animals come first, as it says (later in the same story of Rivka and Eliezer—Bereishis 24:32-33), 'Rivkah's brother gave straw and fodder to the camels and only then he placed food before Eliezer to eat,' and as it also says, 'I will put grass in your fields for your *animals*' and only afterwards, 'and *you* will eat and be satisfied' " (*Sefer Chasidim* #531).

Sefer Chasidim solves the apparent contradictions pointed out above by differentiating between eating and drinking. Rav's rule in Gittin that "animals come first" applies *only* for eating, not for drinking. Since both of the contradictions to Rav's rule concern cases of drinking, our problem seems solved!

II

Sefer Chasidim's explanation requires further examination. Is there any logical reason for this seemingly arbitrary distinction between eating and drinking? After all, what is the reason for the requirement of tending to one's animal's needs before his own? The apparent rationale behind the requirement is that an animal is helpless and dependent on its master for sustenance. In order to ensure that owners of animals will not neglect them, the owner is required to give the needs of his animals precedence over his own needs. This rationale is borne out in Rambam's words (at the very end of *Hilchos Avadim*): "The sages of old were always accustomed to feed their animals and servants before feeding themselves." By extending the rule to servants as well as animals, the Rambam makes it clear that this principle is related to being dependent on someone else for sustenance, and *not* with the physical nature of animals as opposed to that of humans.

Why distinguish between eating and drinking?

However, this reasoning applies equally to drink and to solid foods. What, then, is the basis for the *Sefer Chasidim*'s distinction between eating and drinking? Several later commentators have indeed attempted to explain the reasoning behind the *Sefer Chasidim*'s words. However, most of the explanations offered are forced (see Gan Raveh in section *Divrei Chanoch* to Parshiyos Noach and Behar; Pardes Yosef, Bereishis 24:19; *Mekor Chesed* by Rav Reuven Margoliot, to *Sefer Chasidim* ad loc.).

Perhaps we may offer the following explanation. There is a rule (Shabbos 9b; Shulchan Aruch O.C. 232) that one should not begin to eat a meal in the afternoon before one has said the Minchah prayer. This is because the meal may become drawn out and one may forget altogether about Minchah. Taking a *drink* before Minchah, however, is *not* forbidden. This is because it is unusual for someone to become preoccupied with drinking. It is the nature of food, not drink, to cause one's attention to be diverted from other matters.

This may offer an understanding of the *Sefer Chasidim*'s words concerning feeding animals. The distinction made by Rav Yehudah haChassid between eating and drinking does *not* have to do with a difference between an animal's eating and drinking habits, but rather with a human's eating and drinking habits. One should not begin to eat before attending to one's animals, because eating can become drawn out and lead to neglecting the animal. However, one may drink before giving one's animal something to drink, since a drink is not likely to divert one's attention from the animal's needs. (According to this, perhaps drinking wine or other alcoholic beverages may indeed be forbidden before attending to one's animals, as these may lead to negligence of an animal's needs.)

Another difficulty remains, however, with the words of *Sefer Chasidim* . The Gemara which stated Rav's rule about "animals first" said, "It is forbidden for a person to even taste food (*lit'om*) until he has fed his animal." The Gemara in Shavuos (22b) states that the word *lit'om* (lit., to taste or have a snack) covers *both* eating and drinking! If so, since Rav said that one should not *lit'om* before feeding his animals, how can R. Yehudah haChassid say that this applies only to eating and not to drinking! (Note: The words of Tosafos in Shavuos loc. cit., s.v. *lit'om*, may offer a solution to this problem.—MK)

III

A number of commentators offer alternate solutions for the difficulty posed by the two verses (Bereishis 24:19 and Bamidbar 20:8) which seem to put man's needs before his animal's—in contradiction to Rav's rule.

Hosts and guests are different

Eliyahu Rabbah (O.C. 167) suggests that the "animals first" rule is applicable only with regard to the owner of the animal, and not to another party. Thus when a person is entertaining a guest who has an animal, it is unnecessary for the host to serve the animal before the human guest.

This is a logical distinction for two reasons. Firstly, the host has no obligation to feed this animal since this animal is not dependent on the host for sustenance. Secondly, although the concept of showing concern for animals is an important moral lesson, A slight to a guest's feelings is an even more important consideration.

Of course, one may still question this answer. Although it is proper for the host to *offer* food or drink to his guest before offering something to his guest's animals, the guest should follow Rav's rule and decline the food (or drink) until he attends to his animal. Since a host is permitted to offer food to his guest before offering it to his guest's cattle, that guest should, in the interest of civility, accept it and then afterwards see to his animal. (See also Pri Megadim O.C. 167; Chasam Sofer—in *Toras Moshe* on Parshas Chayei Sarah, and quoted in Teshuvos Ksav Sofer, O.C.32; She'elas Yaavetz, #110—who all suggest the same approach as the Eliyahu Rabbah.)

In any event, the distinction suggested by Eliyahu Rabbah also solves both difficulties. In Rivka and Eliezer's case, it was someone other than the owner of the animals who was providing the drink, and it was thus proper that Eliezer was served first.

In the case of Moshe and the congregation, too, Moshe was told to "give drink" to the congregation. Since Moshe was serving them, it was completely permissible for *him* to offer the congregation something to drink before considering their cattle.

A glitch to this approach

There is, however, a glaring difficulty with this approach. The case described in Gittin in connection to which Rav's rule was applied, involved a third party offering food to the owner of an animal! How, then, can the Eliyahu Rabbah (et al.) say that Rav's rule does *not* apply when the giver of the food is not the animal's owner?!

Furthermore, as *Sefer Chasidim* pointed out, when Eliezer came to Rivkah's house, the camels were fed before food was given to Eliezer. According to the Eliyahu Rabbah this was improper in this situation! How can the difference between Rivkah's feeding of Eliezer first, and her brother's feeding the camels first, be accounted for—unless *Sefer Chasidim*'s distinction between food and drink is true?

IV

Extreme discomfort is an exception

The commentators offer another explanation as to why in these two situations (Bereishis 24:19 and Bamidbar 20:8), we find that people were attended to before their animals. This approach is developed by the Ohr Hachayim (Rav Chaim Ibn Atar, Israel, 17th century), in his commentary to both Chayei Sarah and this week's Parsha. The Ohr Hachayim asserts that the rule that animals come first is not ironclad. If a person is in extreme discomfort and suffers from intense hunger or thirst, he may see to his own needs before those of his animals. It is only when a person is about to eat a regularly scheduled meal, i.e., under normal circumstances, that Rav's rule was meant to be applied.

The logic behind this distinction is obvious. We are instructed to feed our animals before ourselves *not* because animals are more important than humans, but rather to ensure that we do not ignore the animals while indulging our own appetites. However, if a person is in pain or discomfort, human needs come before animal needs. We are always more interested in humans' well-being than in that of animals! Showing concern for one's animals is therefore subordinate to meeting an urgent human need.

When Eliezer met Rivka, he had just arrived from a lengthy journey from the land of Canaan. He was undoubtedly in great discomfort when he begged for a cup of water from the local water-drawers. Rivka was thus justified in quenching his thirst before that of his animals. Later on, however, when Eliezer was invited to Rivkah's house, his weariness from the journey had already been addressed. His camels were thus fed before him.

Similarly, when Moshe supplied water for the congregation, they were severely tired and drained from their travels in the desert. The sudden loss of their water supply threatened them with death from thirst (Bamidbar 20:4). In this situation it was thus also appropriate for Moshe to give them water before their animals!

We may add that perhaps the Ohr Hachayim's approach is not in contradistinction to *Sefer Chasidim*, but is in harmony with it. Perhaps when *Sefer Chasidim* distinguished between food and drink, these were only used as examples. He actually had Ohr Hachayim's approach in mind. Even when someone is extremely hungry, the hunger that he feels can usually be kept out of his mind until a more appropriate time arises. Extreme thirst, however, tends to be a more urgent need—it can cause fainting or loss of consciousness. Thus, when *Sefer Chasidim* said that Rav's rule applies not to drink but only to food, it was meant that the rule applies only to cases of moderate need (as hunger for food usually is), but not to cases of great urgency (as thirst for drink usually is)—just as the Ohr Hachayim maintains! It is common for a person to become weak or faint from dehydration, but how often have we heard of a person "fainting from hunger" because he delayed his meal?

Such an understanding of *Sefer Chasidim* is even suggested in the wording of Rav Yehudah heChassid's thesis. He does not say "When it comes to liquids (or drinks) a man should be served first," but rather, "When it comes to *thirst....*" The word "thirst" (*tzimaon*) implies a situation of urgent need.

If we understand *Sefer Chasidim* in this way, the difficulty we mentioned before is also resolved. We showed that *lit'om* includes both eating and drinking, and asked how *Sefer Chasidim* could limit Rav's prohibition to eating only. Now we are suggesting that *Sefer Chasidim* agrees that Rav's rule applies to both eating and drinking. It is only when someone is thirsty *to the point of major discomfort* that this rule does not apply!

V

Various commentators point out other discrepancies with Rav's rule that can be found in the Torah. In Vayikra 25:6 we read that "the sabbatical produce of the land (in the seventh, sabbatical year) shall be for you to eat—for *you*...and for your *animals* and the beasts of the field." First you, and then the animals!

Another exception: leftovers

Similarly, in Bereishis 6:21, Noach is instructed to take food into the ark in order that "it should be for *you* and for the *animals* to eat"—again in the wrong order! (The first question is posed by the Yitav Lev, ad loc., while the second is asked by the Pardes Yosef quoted above.)

An answer to the first of these questions is found in Gan Raveh (in the name of Yalkut Gershuni), and in Pardes Yosef (in the name of the Gerer Rebbe). The two great commentators point out that the verse that instructs us to feed our animals before ourselves, refers to feeding the animals animal fodder ("grass in your fields for your animals"). It does not mention feeding them *human* food.

Indeed, it is generally not permissible to degrade food fit for human consumption by "wasting" it on animals (Taanis 20b). If one has only human food available, it stands to reason that one must eat this first. Only leftovers—no longer designated for human use—can be used to feed his animals.

In Vayikra 25:6 the Torah refers to "the produce of the field," which is to be eaten by people and animals. Accordingly, it is the people who must eat first, until the produce no longer has a function for humans at which point animals may eat from it. (See also Rambam in *Hilchos Shemittah* 5:5, he clearly understands the verse to be referring to human food. The words of the Torah in Shemos 23:11 also seem to bear out this interpretation: "The poor of your people shall eat of the produce [during the sabbatical year], and then the beasts of the field will eat *what is left over.*")

The same approach can be used to answer the second question (regarding Noach's ark) as well. When Noach was commanded to take into the ark all kinds of food, foods fit for human consumption were included in the command. When these rotted, they would be fed to animals that thrive on decay, for example, rotten fruits for insects and worms, etc. Thus, it was entirely appropriate that at times the humans in the ark would eat before the animals—that is, when the food in question was first fit for human consumption, and only afterwards became suitable for animal consumption!

VI

Further exception: animals of the wild

Gan Raveh, in the name of Levias Chein, points out yet another difficult verse: "God said [to Adam], Behold, I have given over to you all the vegetation, which grow seeds...and all trees which have fruits with seeds in them, for you to eat. And for all the beasts of the field and all the birds of the heavens and all the creeping creatures...all the green vegetation for eating" (Bereishis 1:29-30). God seems to provide food for Adam, the first man, before providing food for the animals of the earth!

The question is compounded further by the fact that *Sefer Chasidim* (in the continuation of the section cited above) quotes this verse to show that one should feed his animal *before* himself! Where did he see anything in this quote to suggest that animals come before people, when the order mentioned in the verse is the exact opposite of this? The commentators on *Sefer Chasidim* have a difficult time indeed with this "proof"!

To the first question, we may suggest the following simple solution. Rav's rule applies only to animals that one owns and is responsible for, as explained above. Rav certainly did not mean that a person must put out a bowl of food for all the wild cats of the neighborhood, or bread for all the pigeons in town, before beginning his own meal! The verse quoted here specifically mentions the "beasts of the field" and the "birds of the heavens"—wild animals, who do not depend on any human being to supply them with their needs. These animals certainly are not fed before man! Thus, the verse is totally irrelevant to Rav's rule, and does not constitute a contradiction to it.

As to how the *Sefer Chasidim* can "prove" from here that animals come first, we may suggest the following. When the Torah describes man's food in this verse, it speaks of vegetation (*esev*). This word is in fact usually used in connection with animal fodder—for example, "I will place vegetation in your field for your *animals*" (Devarim 11:15—see also Torah Temimah, Bereishis 3 note #26.) If so, why does Hashem say that He will give vegetation to *man* to eat? Perhaps the verse refers not to the food that *man* is to eat, but to the food that he is to use for feeding his *animals*. The phrase "Behold, I have given over to you all the "vegetation" which grows seeds..." refers to food Hashem grants man to use for his *animals*. The continuation of the verse, "And all trees which have fruits with seeds in them, for *you* to eat," refers—as it says explicitly—to food to be *consumed* by man. The next verse adds a third category of food: "for all the beasts of the field and all the birds of the heavens and all the creeping creatures...all the green vegetation for eating." This third category deals with *wild* animals, and is irrelevant to the discussion of Rav's rule, as explained above. From the first two categories of food discussed in the verse, however, we see that the food used by man to feed his animals is mentioned before food used for his own consumption. Hence, *Sefer Chasidim* saw in these verses a further proof for Rav's rule—"animals first!"

Incidentally, this new reading of the verse solves another difficulty which Rashi points out later in Bereishis. In Bereishis 3:18, Rashi asks, in what way could Hashem's pronouncement that Adam would have to eat "the vegetation of the field," be considered a curse? Wasn't this Adam's designated food all along, as it says in the verse we were just discussing (1:29)?

According to our interpretation of verse 1:29, Rashi's question is answered. When Hashem gave to humans "the vegetation of the field," it was not in order to be used as man's own food. It was to be used as fodder, for feeding his animals. Adam was later cursed to eat the same food as his animals!

In either case, our reading of the verse clearly supports the conclusion of Rav. When sitting down to eat, remember—pets first!

PARSHAS BALAK

The Wrath Of G-d

The evil Bilaam raised his voice in prophecy and proclaimed, "These are the words of Bilaam son of Be'or...the words of he who hears the speech of G-d and knows the mind of the Most High!" (Bamidbar 24:15-16).

In Avoda Zara 4a-b it says that " 'G-d becomes enraged every day' (Tehillim 7:12). How long does G-d's rage last? It lasts just one moment (*regga*). No human being in the world knows when that moment is—none, that is, but the wicked Bilaam of whom it is written 'he knows the mind of the Most High.' "

"Did Bilaam really know the Almighty's plans? If he did not even know the mind of his beast (Bamidbar 22:23-31), how could he claim to know the mind of the Most High?! What he meant to say was that he was able to determine the moment of Hashem's wrath. [He would take advantage of this knowledge by cursing people at the moment of Hashem's wrath, thus directing the anger of the Almighty at those he cursed.] How long does Hashem's 'moment' of anger last? The amount of time it takes to pronounce the word *regga*."

Bilaam's curse

"If the moment of Hashem's anger is so brief, what curse could Bilaam have pronounced during that time span? He wanted to utter the word *kallem* (annihilate them). However, G-d reversed the letters of this intended curse, as it says (Devarim 23:6) 'Hashem your G-d did not consent to listen to Bilaam, and He *reversed* the curse, transforming it into a blessing.' Instead of *kallem* (spelled *kaf, lamed, mem*), Bilaam said *melech* (spelled *mem, lamed, kaf,* which means "king"). It is for this reason that we find in Bilaam's prophetic vision (23:21) the word 'king'—'The *King's* love is always with the Bnai Yisrael.' " (Tosafos;

in Avoda Zara 4b s.v. "*regga*," and in Da'as Zekenim to Bamidbar 23:8)

Bilaam wanted to prevent the Bnai Yisrael from successfully completing their forty-year journey in the wilderness and their triumphant entry into the Land of Israel. Bilaam planned to pronounce a curse on them during Hashem's "moment of anger." This curse would presumably arouse Hashem's anger against His people and persuade Hashem to annihilate them.

This requires further explanation. Doesn't Hashem grant every person due process? How can a curse—regardless of who utters it—persuade Hashem to bring calamity upon someone who does not deserve it?

We may also ask why Bilaam would have intended to utter specifically "*kallem*." He could just as well have said "kill them" (*hargem*) or "eradicate them" (*abdem*) or several other such synonyms, all of which can be expressed in one two-syllable word in Hebrew. What is the significance of *kallem*?

II

To understand what exactly Bilaam was trying to accomplish, and analyze what a curse in general is able to achieve, let us examine the concept of Hashem's "wrath" (in Hebrew, *af*).

Our weak point

One of the descriptions of Hashem's mercy is "*maarich af*" (Yeshayah 48:9) or "*erech appayim*" (Shemos 34:6), which means "deferring wrath." Rashi (Shemos ad loc.) explains this attribute of G-d to mean that He "postpones his wrath and does not administer punishment immediately, giving the sinner time to repent." "Deferment of wrath" is interpreted to mean granting a grace period to allow for penance. Thus, we may infer that the "wrath" of G-d indicates a situation where He *does* bring punishment promptly, without allowing a period of grace. It is not that Hashem punishes someone undeservedly, but that the *deserved* punishment is meted out without delay.

Hashem's anger cannot be aroused through a curse unless there has been a sin committed to which the curser wishes to call Hashem's attention. If the sin is brought up for reconsideration at the "opportune" moment, when Hashem is not "deferring wrath," the ensuing wrath aroused by the sin can bring the Almighty to promptly collect his due in full. This was the tactic that Bilaam attempted to use to the Bnai Yisrael's disadvantage.

But what sin could Bilaam find to bring punishment to the entire nation of Yisrael as one? Undoubtedly, the sin of the golden calf (Shemos 32), for which Hashem had already threatened to annihilate the entire nation! When Moshe prayed to Hashem to forgive His people for that incident, Hashem agreed, but stipulated that "On the day that I punish them, I will punish them for [this] sin too" (ibid. 32:34). Rashi explains this to mean, "I have agreed to your request for now, but from now on, continuously, whenever I bring punishment upon them for some other matter, I will include punishment for the golden calf as well." The effect of this sin was thus never fully eradicated, but has lingered on throughout Jewish history. Apparently, full punishment was never meted out, Hashem instead deferred the implementation of His wrath. If Hashem's wrath were to be aroused against Israel for that sin, G-d forbid, no one would survive.

In fact, Hashem Himself alludes to this idea in the aftermath of the golden calf incident: "You are a stubborn people; if I go among you, in one instant (*regga*) I could annihilate you" (ibid. 33:5). Rashi explains (ad loc.) that Hashem's mention of "one instant" was a reference to the *regga* of His wrath which occurs daily. Hashem was saying that if this grave sin were to be brought before Him during that ill-fated *regga*, it could bring about the annihilation of His people!

Similarly, when the people rose up against Moshe during the Korach rebellion, Hashem said, "Separate yourselves from this evil congregation, and I will annihilate them in a *regga*" (Bamidbar 16:21). In the next incident of insurrection, Hashem again says "I will annihilate them in a *regga*" (ibid. 17:10).

As the Meshech Chochmah (Rav Meir Simcha of Dvinsk, d. 1932) points out, these are clear references to the *regga* of Hashem's wrath that the Gemara was discussing in Avoda Zara. Hashem was saying that since the Bnai Yisrael were angering Him with their actions, they would bring about their annihilation during the daily *regga* of Hashem's concentrated anger. Perhaps their new sins once again aroused the sin of the golden calf, which could cause their annihilation during the *regga* of wrath. The sin of the golden calf always lurks in the background, waiting for the right "*regga*" to arrive—"When I punish them, I will punish them for this sin too." It is the Achilles' heel of the Jewish nation.

III

Perhaps Bilaam intended, then, to take advantage of this *regga* of Hashem's anger by recalling before him the sin of the golden calf. In fact, from the Parsha it seems that this is exactly what Bilaam had planned. As Rashi explains:

The implications of kallem

"Bilaam said, 'Whether or not He wants to curse them, I will mention their sins and the curse will take effect automatically.' This is why the verse continues, 'and he turned his face toward the desert'—that is, as Targum translates, 'toward the sin of the golden calf that was committed in the desert.' " (Rashi, Bamidbar 24:1)

Furthermore, in the beginning of the Parsha, the Moabite king, Balak, describes his fear of the Israelites as follows: "Now this congregation will lick up all our surroundings as an ox licks up the grass in a field" (ibid. 22:4). The Chasam Sofer explains that with this strange metaphor, Balak was intimating the possible avenue of attack against Israel—i.e., using Israel's sin of the golden calf (described in Tehillim (106:20) as "a grass-eating ox") to agitate Hashem into annihilating Israel.

Now we can understand why Tosafos says that it was specifically the word *kallem* [annihilate them] that Bilaam had in mind to utter. This is precisely the word that Hashem Himself used when describing the potential punishment for the sin of the golden calf (Shemos 32:10): "My wrath will burn against them and I will annihilate them (root: *kalleh*)." And again in 33:5: "In one instant (*regga*) I could annihilate you (root: *kalleh*)." (The same root is used in the references cited above, section II, from Parshas Korach.) Since Bilaam's entire plan was to allude to the sin of the golden calf, he naturally chose a word that described Hashem's anger over that event—the word Hashem actually used in that connection.

IV

Stopping the curse of kallem

At the end of the Parsha we find that Bilaam, after failing in his assignment to curse the people, suggests an alternate plan to King Balak. He proposes that Balak send Moabite girls into the Israelite camp to incite the Israelite men to sin with them promiscuously. The sin of Jewish men consorting with heathen women would certainly arouse Hashem's anger against them.

The ruse worked, and Hashem inflicted a plague on the camp, in which 24,000 people died (Bamidbar 25:1-9, and Rashi). It is interesting to note that the three Hebrew letters which spell the word *kallem*—*kaf, lamed, mem*—have the numerical values of 20, 30 and 40, respectively. The product of these three numbers is 24,000! The curse of *kallem* did indeed have an effect against the people!

This is also what is meant when Hashem said to Pinchas (the one who brought a stop to the plague), "Pinchas...turned away My wrath from the Bnai Yisrael...so that I did not *annihilate* (root: *kalleh*) the Bnai Yisrael in My vengeance" (ibid. 25:11).

As Tosafos pointed out, instead of carrying out Bilaam's intended curse of "annihilation," Hashem transformed the curse into a blessing of "king." True, many Jews lost their lives in the plague which was brought about through Bilaam. Nevertheless, the remainder of the nation was not "annihilated" in the desert, but lived to enter Israel. Their "King" (Hashem) remained amongst them. Perhaps that is why Bilaam declared (verse 23:21, see Rashi), "Hashem doesn't look at the sins of Yaakov, nor at the wrongdoing of Yisrael (the sin of the golden calf), He doesn't budge from their midst (by allowing me to pronounce on them *kallem*); the King's love (the reverse of *kallem*) is always with them!"

PARSHAS PINCHAS

What's In A Name?

In Gemara Avoda Zara 10b there is a moving account of Ke'tia bar Shalom's defense of the Jews. "There was once a Caesar who hated the Jews. He asked his advisers, 'If someone has dead flesh in his foot, should he cut it off and become healed or should he leave it and suffer?' They answered, 'He should cut it off and become healed.' (The Caesar was referring to the Jewish people in his empire, whom he saw as a source of frustration.)

Ke'tia bar Shalom: his story and his name

"Ke'tia bar Shalom, one of his advisers, then interjected, 'First,' he said, 'you will never be able to kill all of them, for they are dispersed throughout the four corners of the world...and they are as important for the continued existence of the world as the winds. (Therefore other monarchs who have a greater appreciation for the indispensability of the Jews in *their* kingdoms will foil your plans.—MK) Furthermore, if you execute all the Jews of your kingdom, your reign will go down in history as a bloody one!

"The king responded, 'You have argued cogently. However, there is a rule that whoever outwits the king must be buried alive in a house full of dirt' (I.e., form of execution—Rashi. Alternate reading: thrown into a fiery furnace—Rabbeinu Chananel). As they were taking Ke'tia away, a Roman matron called out, 'Woe to the ship that travels without paying its dues!' (Rashi says this means "what a pity! You are giving up your life for the Jews, and you haven't even been circumcised so that you may join their ranks in the World-to-Come.") Ke'tia immediately circumcised himself, exclaiming, 'I have paid my dues—now I may pass through freely!'

"As they were throwing him to his death Ke'tia cried out 'All my property is granted to Rebbi Akiva and his colleagues!' A heavenly voice was heard saying, 'Ke'tia bar Shalom is destined for the Hereafter!' "

This moving account of Ke'tia bar Shalom's defense of the Jews serves as an inspiring testimony to Hashem's protection of His nation. The selfless Ke'tia was in just the right place at the right time to counter the murderous plotting of the evil Caesar.

Let's examine the story more carefully now. The fact that, specifically, Ke'tia bar Shalom stood up in defense of the Jews, is even more striking than is at first apparent.

In the Gemara (Berachos 7b) we are told that a person's name holds within it a clue to his future destiny. In Gemara Yoma 83b we find that Rav Meir acted warily with a stranger solely on the basis of an inference from the man's name.

In this case, it is immediately obvious that the name Ke'tia is intricately intertwined with the seminal event of Ke'tia's life (as pointed out by R. Reuven Margoliot in his *Lecheker Shemos VeKinnuyim BaTalmud*, #1, letter *lamed*). When the Caesar asked about "cutting off" the dead flesh, the word used is *yikte'ena* (root: *kata*, the same root as that of Ke'tia). When Ke'tia objected that killing the Jews would result in a bloody reign, the Hebrew words he used were *malchusa ke'tia*. And the word used to describe his circumcision is *kat'ah* (root: *kata*). The same root from which his name was derived described the problem with which he was faced (Caesar's challenge), his solution to the problem, and his dramatic circumcision, whereby he merited a share in the Hereafter.

Even Ke'tia's surname, or father's name, is appropriate in the context of this story. (*Bar*, in Aramaic—as in bar Shalom—and *ben*, in Hebrew, literally mean son of. However, they are often used in a broader sense, meaning from or of.) Bar Shalom would mean son of peace, and indeed Ke'tia guaranteed the peace of the Jewish people. Furthermore, he acquired for himself eternal peace (shalom), as the Hereafter is described in Yeshayah (57:2): "He who goes on the straight path [in his lifetime] will attain *peace* and will rest in his place of repose." Ke'tia's very name was replete with references to his most outstanding achievement!

II

"There is nothing that is not hinted at somewhere in the Torah" (see Gemara Taanis 9a, Zohar 3:221). Even the names of people who will be living in future generations are hinted at in the Torah (see Bava Metzia 86a, about Rav Ashi and Ravina). In fact, the Ramban found hints in the Torah to the names and accomplishments of the Rambam (Shemos 11:9) and the Rambam's student, Rav Avner (Devarim 32:26, see Kav Hayashar ch. 23.) The Gaon of

Ke'tia bar Shalom in the Torah

Vilna found his own name and accomplishments in the Torah (Devarim 25:15 see *Emunah Vehashgacha*, the section of collected insights of the Gaon's), and so forth. Can we find an allusion to the story of Ke'tia bar Shalom in the Torah?

As a matter of fact, we can find such an allusion right in this week's Parsha! In Parshas Pinchas we are told that Pinchas saved the Bnai Yisrael from annihilation. He fearlessly slayed one of the sinners—a distinguished member of the tribe of Shimon—in public. Pinchas' reward from Hashem for his heroism was: "Behold, I am giving him My covenant of peace (shalom)" (Bamidbar 25:12). In Kiddushin 66b the Gemara tells us that the Hebrew letter *vav* of the word "shalom" should be written "broken," i.e., in two disjointed pieces.

As the Gemara puts it, "The *vav* of shalom is *ke'tia* [cut up]." This broken letter *vav* (which is, incidentally the *only* instance of this phenomenon in the entire Torah) is thus a Ke'tia of shalom—or Ke'tia bar Shalom! This is clearly a hint to the events related in the above story from Avoda Zara! (This idea was first called to my attention by Rav Chaggai Preschel, presently Rosh Yeshiva of Yeshivas Shvut Ameinu in Moscow. I later saw that Rav Reuven Margoliot [ibid., footnote #17] alludes to this as well.)

But why should the Torah choose this particular letter in this particular location to bear a clue to Ke'tia bar Shalom? Is the context of the section in which it appears related to the episode of Ke'tia and the Caesar?

In fact, there are several parallels between the episode of Pinchas and that of Ke'tia. 1. Both men saved the Jews from situations which threatened them with total annihilation. ("Pinchas son of Elazar turned back My wrath from the Children of Israel, so I did not annihilate them..."—(Bamidbar 25:11). 2. Both men acted with selfless dedication, risking their very lives for the welfare of the Jewish people. (The Gemara [Sanhedrin 82a] points out that Zimri, the Shimonite executed by Pinchas, would have been completely within his rights to turn around and kill Pinchas in self defense.)

Finally, the Sages tell us that Pinchas and the person referred to in Kings as Eliyahu Hanavi [Elijah the Prophet] are one and the same (Bava Metzia 114b, and Rashi ad loc. s.v. "*Lav*"; Yalkut Shimoni, beginning of Parshas Pinchas). As a reward for the zealousness he displayed, Eliyahu was awarded a place of honor, a "chair of Eliyahu" at every circumcision ceremony throughout the generations. (Pirkei d'Rabbi Eliezer, end of chap. 29). This was what Hashem meant when He gave Pinchas (Eliyahu) a "covenant (*bris*) of peace." (Bris is commonly used to refer to the Covenant of Circumcision.) Thus, the ultimate rewards of Pinchas and Ke'tia also bear a similarity to each other. Both of their rewards involved circumcision—Pinchas became an eternal witness to circumcision, and Ke'tia was himself circumcised.

III

Here is another interesting example of the significance of a name:

"They once asked R. Eliezer: How far does the mitzvah of honoring one's parents extend? He answered: You can learn from what a certain non-Jew named Dama ben *Nesina* of Ashkelon once did for his father. The treasurers of the Temple once offered him 600,000 dinar coins for a precious stone (the *yashfeh* stone, according to the Yerushalmi Kiddushin 1:6) that they needed in order to complete the breastplate of the Kohen Gadol. At the time, however, the keys to the jewel's box were under the pillow of Dama's father, who was sleeping! Dama decided not to disturb his father, and he passed up the deal.

Dama ben Nesina: his story and his name

(The Yerushalmi continues the story: Dama told the treasurers that he would not be able to sell them the stone. They thought that he was dissatisfied with their offer, so they raised their bid to ten times the original price—but Dama still refused to disturb his father's rest. After a while the father woke up and Dama contacted the Temple treasurers and told them that he was now willing to conclude the deal. He insisted, however, on taking only the amount of money *originally* offered to him, since he did not wish to derive any benefit from the rise in price that occurred solely as a result of his respect for his father.)

The following year, Dama's cow gave birth to a red heifer. The Temple treasurers wanted to buy it from him for the ritual of purification (Bamidbar 19). He told them, 'I know that you would be willing to pay all the money in the world for this heifer. However, I will ask you only for the money which I declined in last year's gem transaction!'" (Gemara Avoda Zara 23b, Kiddushin 31a).

In this story, too, the name of the main character ("Dama") is intertwined with the story told about him. The word that the Gemara normally uses for "money" is "*damim.*" Sleeping is expressed by the word "*damich,*" in the Yerushalmi's version of the story. And the word for *red* heifer is "*adumah.*" All three of these words are built around the core letters of DaMa.

Note also, that the stone Dama sold to the Temple representatives was the *yashfeh* (as mentioned by the Yerushalmi). Rabbeinu Bachye, in his commentary to Shemos 28:15, mentions that this particular stone has in it a power to control excess bleeding (blood = *dam*). Thus, there is a further parallel between Dama's name and the stone that he was so famous for selling.

Dama's surname (or father's name), ben Nesina, is also appropriate to the story, for *nesina* means "giving over," and that is precisely what Dama did with his precious possessions, as the Yerushalmi relates. Here too, the man's virtuous deed related to "Dama ben Nesina" (refusing to take money—*damim*—or to wake his sleeping father—*damich*; he gave—*nesina*—the gem for the original price).

Dama was also rewarded with a "Dama ben Nesina" (a red—*adumah*—heifer, which he received as a compensation for his giving—*nesina*). (See also Maharal in *Chidushei Aggados*, Kiddushin end of 31a, for another reading into Dama's name.)

IV

Can an allusion to the story of Dama ben *Nesina* also be found somewhere in the Torah? Let's take a close look at the following section, from Parshas Toldos:

Dama in the Torah

"Yaakov was cooking lentil soup (lentils are traditionally eaten by mourners, and Yaakov was making it for his father Isaac, who had just suffered the loss of *his* father, Avraham—Rashi). Meanwhile, Esav returned from the field, exhausted. Esav said to Yaakov, 'Give me some of that red stuff (*adom*), I'm completely drained!' (this is why Esav became known to all as Edom [red]). Yaakov said, 'Sell me your birthright (the right to officiate at religious sacrifices, which was reserved for the firstborn son in those days—Rashi).' Esav answered, 'Here I am about to die, what do I care about the birthright?'...and he sold his first-born rights to Yaakov. Yaakov gave (*nasan*) Esav bread and lentils...and Esav disgraced his birthright. (Bereishis 25:29-34)

Esav was called Edom because his desire for the red lentils was so strong that he traded his birthright in exchange for it. Perhaps this is the hint to Dama ben Nesina. *Adom* (*alef, daled, mem*) is spelled with the same letters as *Dama* (*daled, mem, alef*). The red lentils ("*adom*") which were given over ("*nesina*") could be said to be the "Dama ben *Nesina*" of the Torah! (Alternatively, Esav ("Edom") who gave away ("*nesina*") his first-born rights for a dish of lentils, was the Dama ben Nesina of the Torah.)

But what does the story of Esav have to do with that of Dama? The Sages (Yerushalmi, ibid.) tell us that Esav outstandingly performed the mitzvah of honoring one's parents. Rabban Shimon ben Gamliel, the Nassi (spiritual and temporal leader of Israel), declared that in all his years of serving his father, he did not do for him even one percent of what Esav did for his father! Dama, who was a Roman general according to the Gemara (ibid.) and thus a descendant of Esav (see Rashi Bereishis 27:39, 36:43), also excelled in the performance of this mitzvah.

Why is this particular event in Esav's life chosen to contain the hint to Dama's noble behavior? As the Torah itself says (Bereishis 25:34), Esav acted contemptuously by displaying such a cavalier attitude toward the birthright, which included the right to personally participate in the service of Hashem in the Holy Temple. On the other hand, there was a positive side to his actions as well. Yaakov, who was obviously more suited for the position, was enabled to become the one who would officiate in the service of Hashem. Because of this positive outcome, Esav was blessed with the righteous Dama as one of his offspring. Although it was already many generations later, Esav, through his descendant Dama, was given a chance to rectify his sin of spurning the sacrificial service of Hashem.

A sin is considered rectified and proper repentance is considered to have been done, if the sinner later faces the same temptations as he did when he first sinned, but succeeds in overcoming them (Rambam Hilchos Teshuvah 2:1). On a broader scale, perhaps such repentance can be accomplished even on the time scale of generations. The descendant of a sinner can "set the record straight," to a certain extent, by not falling into the same trap as his father, when confronted with the same situation that his father had originally faced.

In the case of Dama be *Nesina*, when the Temple representatives were looking for the components necessary to carry out the Temple service, the means to supply these objects fell into Dama's hands. Esav, the "grandfather," had shown his disdain for the Temple service in his exchange. Dama, on the other hand, showed respect for the Temple's needs. He was able to "support" the continuation of the Temple service, by supplying the Sages with the missing stone. Secondly, while Esav was willing to "sell" the service of Hashem in order to satisfy his uncontrollable desires for physical pleasure, Dama turned down the huge financial gain he was offered for the stone that he gave for use in the Temple services.

It is also interesting to note that just as Esav received something red—red lentils—in return for his sale, so too was Dama granted the *red* heifer as a reward for his.

V

A fourth parallel may also be drawn. As Rashi pointed out, lentils are traditionally eaten by mourners. Why? Rashi explains that just as lentils have

The one who had a mouth

no "mouth" (*ein lahen peh*—lentils, unlike other beans, are perfectly round, and have no indentation), so, too, a mourner has no "mouth." A mourner is forbidden to exchange greetings with other people (see also Bava Basra 16b).

Each of the twelve stones on the Kohen Gadol's breastplate represented one of the twelve tribes of Israel. The *yashfeh* stone was inscribed with the name of Binyamin, as it represented that tribe. Rabbeinu Bachye explains the connection between Binyamin and the *yashfeh* stone:

"Binyamin knew that his brothers had sold Yosef into slavery, yet he did not reveal their shameful deed to their father, Yaakov. Although Binyamin had misgivings about whether he should withhold this information from his father, he overcame his desire to reveal the secret. *Yashfeh* may also be read, by rearranging the vowel marks, as *yesh peh*—there is a mouth. Even though Binyamin was able to tell his father about his brothers' conduct—he, in fact, had a mouth—he refrained from doing so." (Rabbeinu Bachye, Shemos 28:15—his source is Midrash Bereishis Rabbah 71:5)

Thus, the *yashfeh* (has a mouth) stone may be said to be the opposite of lentils (have no mouth).

Esav *took* for himself the "mouthless" lentils. Symbolically, what Yaakov sold to Esav eternally *closed Esav's mouth* from singing to Hashem in the Holy Temple. Dama, on the other hand, *gave away* the stone with a mouth. This may be seen to symbolize that he inspired the Sages, through this sale, to *tell* his story throughout the ages as a demonstration of how much one must respect one's parents!

PARSHAS MATTOS

Mine Is The Silver And Mine Is The Gold... The True Source Of Wealth

"The sons of Reuven and the sons of Gad had an extremely large amount of livestock, and they saw that the land of Yazer and the land of Gilead was a place for grazing.... They said (to Moshe) ...'Let this land be given to your servants for their portion; do not bring us across the Jordan.'" (Bamidbar 32:1,5)

The children of Reuven and Gad chose to live outside the boundaries of the sanctified Land of Israel as delineated in the Torah (see Bamidbar 34:1-15). They did this because they coveted the abundant grasslands that were available for their livestock east of the Jordan river. Chazal looked askance at the decision of these two tribes (see Korach essay, p. 185). They had already been told that the Promised Land was the choicest of lands for serving Hashem. In the interest of finding an easy livelihood, they ought not to have passed up the opportunity to live there. They should have trusted that Hashem would provide for them all that they would possibly need in His land, too.

It is perhaps for this reason that the Midrash Rabbah on this week's Parsha goes into a lengthy discussion of what the proper attitude towards one's livelihood and source of support should be.

"It is not from the east or from the west, nor from the desert mountains (*harim*)" (Tehillim 75:7).

"It is not from the east or from the west"—this means it is not from traveling from east to west that one becomes wealthy. Even if someone travels to the most remote deserts and mountains, it will not make him rich.

"Nor from the desert mountains"—Rebbi Abba of Romania said: All mention of the Hebrew word *harim* in the Tanach should be translated as "mountains," except for this mention, which should be understood as "to raise up." This verse signifies "nor does traveling in the desert raise oneself up [make one rich and honored]" (Bamidbar Rabbah 31:7)

The theme that one's fortune is not necessarily related to the efforts put into attaining it occurs frequently in the words of Chazal. The Mishnah at the end of Masseches Kiddushin tells us:

"Rebbi Meir says: [Rather than teaching one's child the most lucrative business in the market,] a person should try to train his son in an honest and simple vocation and he should pray to Him to Whom all wealth and possessions belong. There is no trade that does not have both wealthy and poor practitioners. It is not the *career* that gives a person wealth or poverty, rather a man's wealth is granted to him according to his merits" (Kiddushin 82a).

When choosing a career, Rebbi Meir advises us, not to look for the field that appears to be most lucrative. There is no guarantee that it will bring one wealth. We are also advised not to take for granted that a trade that involves more effort will bring greater profits. We are told to simply seek a trade which one can pursue simply and honestly, and trust in Hashem. That is the best way of ensuring a proper livelihood.

We can find this lesson hinted at in the story of the manna that rained from heaven for the Bnai Yisrael during their stay in the desert. The Torah tells us that no matter how much of the manna one tried to accumulate, every person ended up with an equal amount (Shemos 16:18). Perhaps this was intended to accent to the Bnai Yisrael the important theme mentioned above. A person's sustenance and livelihood are not functions of the amount of effort he invests in earning money. Rather, they are blessings bestowed upon him by the One above. (See also Bamidbar-Shavuos essay, section IV, p. 163.)

II

A direct gift from Hashem

The reason that the extent of one's earnings is not relative to the amount of effort one puts into it is obvious. All monetary gain is a direct gift from Hashem. No amount of effort will give one more than what Hashem has allotted. As the verse from Tehillim (quoted above) concludes: "It is not from the east or from the west, nor from the desert mountains—"for Hashem is the Judge; He lowers one person and raises up another one." This theme is brought out in many other places in the Talmud as well:

"Every day, for three hours, Hashem sits and involves Himself in ensuring that every creature on earth gets the food it needs to survive—from the smallest bug to the largest beast" (Avoda Zara 3b).

"Hashem sits at the top of the universe, dispensing food to every living creature" (Pesachim 118a).

Chazal thus portray the gift of life and sustenance as coming directly from Hashem Himself.

Of course, *all* that befalls us is a Divine edict (see Gemara Chullin, bottom of 7b, etc.). Why, then, do our Sages stress the Divine involvement in the provision of food more than the hand of Hashem in any other dispensation? Also, what do the Rabbis mean by attributing so much of Hashem's time towards feeding His creations?

Perhaps the Gemara means to impress upon us how wondrous is the fact that every creature of the earth finds a means of sustenance. An honest reflection on this phenomenon can lead to only one conclusion: Someone from above must be sitting and tending to the needs of all of His creatures. Miracles are happening day by day, not only to humankind, but in the animal kingdom as well! The Talmud is conveying to us that we can *feel* Hashem's presence in the ecological balance of the world. The success of the food chain relies on such perfect coordination between the various organisms, that it is in fact miraculous!

The Midrash Rabbah in our Parsha tells us:

"Wealth is a bountiful gift from Hashem, enabling a person to have everything he wants in this world. But when is this so? When it is granted to a person from Heaven, in the merit of studying and observing the Torah. But the wealth of a human being is nothing at all" (Bamidbar Rabbah 22:7).

What does the Midrash mean when it distinguishes between riches that "come from Heaven" and those that "come from a human being?" Are there really two kinds of wealth? Doesn't *all* monetary earning come from Hashem? "Mine is the silver and Mine is the gold, says Hashem, Lord of Hosts!" (Chaggai 2:8).

What the Midrash means is that there are some people who acknowledge the fact that all that they earn is a gift from Hashem. Their riches "come from Heaven," and are a wonderful gift, helping them serve Hashem. However, others feel that they have "worked hard for what they have," and do not acknowledge Hashem's part in granting them their riches. Their wealth is referred to as money that "comes from a human being." Such wealth is not a benefit to its owner. It will just cause him to become arrogant and rebel against his Creator, as we are told in the Torah (Devarim 8:12-18).

III

Fixed allotments

We have seen that all of a person's efforts to earn money are to no avail if Hashem has judged him unworthy of this money. The Gemara explains this further, "All of a person's income is determined for him yearly, on Rosh Hashanah" (Beitzah 16a). On Rosh Hashanah, a person's livelihood for the entire coming year is determined. Any "extra" earnings a person may receive during the year will just bring his year's supply of income to an early end.

In Bava Basra we are taught that not only the amount to be *earned* in a given year is predetermined, but also the amount of *losses* a person will sustain during that year is decided. The Gemara illustrates this idea with a story:

"Rebbi Yochanan ben Zakkai saw in a dream that his sister's children were going to lose seven hundred *dinarim* during the coming year. He prevailed upon them to give a great deal of money to charity, and managed to have them donate 683 *dinars* that year. When the day before Yom Kippur arrived, a representative of the Caesar came and collected 17 *dinars* for a tax!" (Bava Basra, 10a).

The theme of fixed allotments in life is borne out in another story as well:

"Rebbi Chaninah ben Dosa's wife once said to him, 'How much longer will we go on suffering from poverty? Why don't you pray that we should have some money?' He prayed, and a hand appeared from Heaven which handed him a golden table leg! That night, his wife saw in a dream a vision of the righteous eating in the World-to-Come at golden tables of three legs, while she and her husband were eating at a golden table of only two legs. When she told her husband of her dream, he asked her, 'Are you willing to accept that everyone else will eat at three-legged tables in the World-to-Come, and we will eat at a two-legged table?' She answered, 'Pray again, that the golden leg be taken away from us!' He did so, and the leg was taken away" (Taanis 25a—See also Shemos Rabbah 52:3, for some similar stories).

Here, too, we see that a person has a set amount of prosperity. If one gets more than that which was originally decreed for him, it can only come at the expense of his portion in the afterlife. He will be "eating from his portion of the Hereafter."

How is it possible to "use up" ethereal reward in this physical, mundane world? One way of understanding this idea is the following: The lot that Hashem grants a person is in accordance with what the person needs in order to accomplish his particular mission in this world. By refusing to accept his financial lot, the person is also refusing to achieve his unique goal in this world. This, in turn, will necessarily lessen his portion in the World-to-Come.

IV

Wealth often changes hands

Until now we have shown that a person cannot exceed the amount of fortune that has been set for him. However, there is yet another point to be made in this regard. Even when a person does receive his rightful share of wealth, it is not always intended that he should be the one to benefit from it. As King Solomon put it, "[Hashem] arranges that a sinner gathers and collects a great deal, only to give it over to one who is good in His eyes." Haman, for instance, managed to amass a great fortune, but in the end, "Esther placed Mordechai over Haman's house" (Esther 8:2). Even the wealth that Haman was allotted by Hashem was not meant for him, but rather for someone truly deserving of it (Megillah 10b).

This thought, too, is borne out in many places in the words of Chazal:

"Not everyone who is rich today is rich tomorrow, nor is everyone who is poor today poor tomorrow, for Hashem raises some people up and lowers other people, as it says, 'Hashem is the Judge; He lowers this one and raises that one' " (Shemos Rabbah 31:3).

"A certain Roman matron once asked Rebbi Shimon ben Chalafta, 'How many days did it take God to create the world?' 'Six days,' was the answer. She then asked him, 'If so, what has He been doing all the time since then?' He replied, 'He creates ladders, by which He raises up some people and lowers others, as it says, 'Hashem is the Judge; He lowers this one and raises that one' " (Bamidbar Rabbah 22:8).

"Do you know why property is called *nechasim* in Hebrew? Because it becomes covered up (*nichsim*) from one person and discovered by another! And why is currency called *zuzim* in Aramaic? Because it moves (*zazim*) from one person to the next. Why is money called *mamon*? It stands for *ma moneh*—"Why bother counting it?" It's not worth the effort! ...And you can similarly explain [the other names for money in this manner] (Ibid.).

There is a fixed amount of wealth in the world at large. When one person gets money, it is usually because someone else somewhere in the world has lost it. And the situation is always fluid—right now the wealth is in one person's hands, tomorrow it may very well be in someone else's hands, as the various Hebrew terms for "money" seem to suggest. (Perhaps we could add that the English word "money" should also be read as *ma ani* [what am I worth?]. "Dollar" may be seen as an abbreviation for "*dal, ra*" [poverty and evil]. "Pound" would be "*po, nad*" [it's here, but it moves]. "Rand," is "*ra, nad*" [it's evil, and it moves], etc.)

V

Perhaps this theory of the "conservation of wealth in the world," is what the Gemara had in mind in the following selection:

Life's ups and downs

"Man's sustenance is as miraculous a feat for Hashem as the splitting of the Red Sea"(Pesachim 118a). (A person must take this to heart when he prays for sustenance.—Rashi)

What does making a living have to do with the splitting of the Red Sea? At the Red Sea, although the Israelites experienced a great salvation, the Egyptians were all drowned. The good fortune of the Israelites came as a direct result of the ill fortune of the Egyptians. So too, when a man seeks sustenance from Hashem, he is asking Him to take money from someone else and bring it to the supplicant—one man's benefit is another man's loss!

Perhaps this interpretation can be used to explain yet another passage in the Gemara:

"Matchmaking between men and women is as miraculous a feat as the splitting of the Red Sea" (Sotah 2a).

What is the meant by comparing finding a suitable mate to the splitting of the sea? The Gemara limits the truth of this maxim to second marriages. (First marriages are preordained in Heaven, and finding the perfect match comes easily. See, however, Meiri ad loc. and Arizal in *Sha'ar haPsukim*, for novel interpretations of what is meant by a "second match.") In a second marriage, while there is a gain for the new couple there is a loss for the ex-wife or ex-husband, who had to lose their spouse in order for this marriage to take place. Just as the splitting of the Sea involved one party benefiting at the expense of another, so too is this the case with second marriages!

Support for this interpretation of the Talmudic analogies to the splitting of the sea can be drawn from the Midrash. In Bereishis Rabbah (68:4) the story of the Roman matron appears in a slightly different form. According to Bereishis Rabbah, Rebbi Yossi ben Chalafta was asked, "What has Hashem been doing since He finished the creation of the world?" The Midrash then presents *two* versions of Rav Yossi's answer. Some say that he answered, "He occupies Himself with finding mates for men and women…which is as hard as splitting the Red Sea." Others said that Rav Yossi's answer was, "He arranges the rise and fall of men's fortunes" (as in Bamidbar Rabbah, quoted above). The implication is that this, too, is as hard as splitting the Red Sea, and that is why it takes up so much Divine time. If so, it is clear that the interpretation we have suggested above is correct. The specific point that makes man's sustenance as hard as splitting the Red Sea is the necessity to "raise one man while causing another to fall!"

The above selection from Bereishis Rabbah also provides proof for our explanation of the difficulty of matchmaking. After quoting Rav Yossi's answer—that matchmaking is as hard as splitting the Red Sea—the Midrash proves its point from a verse in Tehillim: "God brings people to their home; and He brings out prisoners in a fitting manner (*bakosharos*)" (Tehillim 68:7).

The Midrash suggests that the beginning of the verse means that Hashem *Himself* is the one who brings man and wife together to a common home. The Midrash adds that the word *bakosharos* at the end of the verse can be read as "*bechi veshiros*"—with crying and rejoicing. The Midrash says that the intention of the verse is that "the one who is satisfied with the match rejoices, while the one who is not, cries" (Midrash ibid.; see also Sanhedrin 22a).

What does the Midrash mean by this? Who is unhappy about the match? And who is the "prisoner" that had been "taken out" of prison, according to this reading of the verse? Perhaps the Midrash, like the Talmud, is referring to second marriages. The spouse of the first marriage [the prisoner] has been freed of their commitment [taken out of bondage], in order to become a match for another person at the expense of their first spouse! If so, it is the spouse from the first marriage that is sad, while the spouse from the second marriage rejoices!

The Midrash presents its reading of the verse in Tehillim as proof that matchmaking is as hard as splitting the Red Sea. It thus lends support to our contention that the splitting of the sea is equated with matchmaking because they both involve one person's gain at the expense of another's!

(Some of our explanation of the analogy to the splitting of the sea can be found in the work *Yefe To'ar* on the Midrash Bereishis Rabbah. I later found more proof for this interpretation in the Midrash haZohar to Bereishis 73b. The Zohar discusses how "hard" it is for Hashem to remove one person from the world in order to give his mate to another person, citing the story of King David and Batsheva as an example—Shmuel II, Ch. 11.)

PARSHAS MASEI

A Punishment That Fits The Crime

"You shall prepare for yourselves cities to be cities of refuge, so that a killer—someone who has taken a life unintentionally—may flee there. These cities will be a safe haven for the killer from the relatives of the victim" (Bamidbar 35:11-12).

The Torah administers a unique punishment to a Jew who unintentionally kills another Jew. The killer must undergo forced exile (*galus*) to one of six or, in a broader sense, 48 cities which were chosen for this purpose. While living in one of these "cities of refuge," the unintentional killer is safe from the next-of-kin of the murdered person, who may seek to avenge a relative's blood. If, however, the killer ever steps out of the city a relative may kill him with impunity (ibid., 35: 26-27).

When a person deliberately commits an act of murder, he is given the death penalty, (when there is a *sanhedrin*—supreme Jewish court—which convenes on the grounds of the Beis Hamikdash). However, this is only if the perpetrator was given a full, clear warning (*hasra'ah*) of the consequences of his act immediately prior to the crime. If a person has committed intentional murder without first receiving a proper warning regarding the sin and its consequences, he is not executed.

One would think, however, that, at the very least, the punishment prescribed by the Torah for manslaughter—exile—should be enforced in this case. After all, deliberate murder is certainly more serious than unintentional murder and ought to be punished at least as severely.

The surprise is that this is not the case. The Mishnah (Makkos 9b) tells us that an intentional murderer acquitted on technical grounds (such as the lack of a prior warning) is *not* sent into exile. Rather, he goes unpunished. The intentional murderer is thus better off than the unintentional murderer! What is the logic behind this ruling?

The Gemara (Makkos 2b) notes that an intentional killer is not punished with *galus* so that he will not receive any atonement for his sin and would thus not be exempt from future punishment.

A killer's forced exile atones for his sin and also protects him from harm. In cases involving intentional murder, the Gemara tells us, the crime is too severe to merit salvation from the next-of-kin through *galus*. It is thus a *stringency* (lack of opportunity to escape from the next-of-kin) imposed upon the murderer by *not* punishing him with *galus*, and is not, in fact, a leniency. (See also Rambam, Hil. Rotzeach 6:4-5.)

II

A similar line of reasoning may be used to explain some other halachic paradoxes.

Food products that grow in the land in Israel may not be eaten until certain tithes and offerings have first been removed from them. The first of these offerings is called *terumah*, and, in the times when it was known who was a true Kohen, it was given to a Kohen. No non-Kohen may eat *terumah*. If a non-Kohen eats *terumah* unintentionally, he must repay the Kohen who owned the *terumah* its full value, and add a 25 percent "fine" on top of that. Surprisingly, however, if a non-Kohen eats *terumah intentionally*, he does not have to pay the 25 percent fine! What is the logic behind giving a greater punishment to someone who commits a crime unintentionally and a lesser punishment to someone who commits a deliberate crime?

Other halachic paaradoxes

The Rambam (beginning of ch. 7 of Mishnayos Terumos) explains this anomaly by invoking the principle presented above. A 25 percent fine is considered to be a means of "atoning" for the sin committed. In fact, the Kohen to whom the fine is paid cannot waive this fine. It is not his personal money to pass on, but rather a means of granting forgiveness to the person paying the fine. This atonement is prescribed by the Torah only for the sin of eating *terumah without* intent. Eating *terumah* knowingly is a more serious sin, so the Torah does not wish to offer the sinner a way of acquiring atonement.

Some commentators take this principle even further. According to Torah law, in cases of perjury, the false witnesses receive the punishment that they attempted to administer to their victim. If the perjury took place in the context of a trial for a capital offense, where the punishment is death, the false witnesses are themselves executed. The Gemara tells us, however, that this punishment is only carried out if the perjury was detected *before* the victim is punished for his alleged crime. If,

Punishment for purjury

however, the witnesses misled the court until the defendant was killed for his alleged crime, the witnesses are *not* killed for their perjury (see Ki Setzei, essay, p.251).

What could be the logic behind this? Certainly it is more grievous to *succeed* at framing someone than to *fail* in the attempt!

The Meiri (Makkos 2b) and the Kesef Mishneh (to Hil. Edus 20:2) invoke the above-mentioned principle to explain this law. Whenever a Jewish court administers the death penalty for a particular sin, and the criminal willingly accepts the Divinely prescribed punishment, he is absolved of his crime. (See Mishnah, Sanhedrin 43b. The same applies to other forms of punishment in court, see Makkos 23a.) Serious offenders who have killed their victim are not entitled to be given an opportunity for atonement through execution by the court.

Applying the "no-atonement" principle to this case takes the principle another step further. The penalties of *galus* and the 25 percent fine for eating *terumah* are thus clearly to be regarded as forms of atonement. They were not intended to be preventative measures to deter others from following the sinner's example—after all, these penalties are administered in cases where the offender committed his sin unintentionally.

The punishment for perjury, however, could be intended as a deterrent: witnesses who know that they could receive as punishment what they hope their victim will be given may think twice before becoming entangled in any such schemes. (Although it is true that execution by a Jewish court of law *also* effects expiation for one's crime, this is seemingly only a secondary, peripheral effect of the punishment's implementation, and not its main goal.)

It would seem appropriate to punish the sinner even when the punishment will not atone for his sins, simply in order to prevent others from following in the sinner's ways. Apparently, though, this is not a viable option. A punishment is considered to be just, if its execution fully absolves the sinner from his crime (should he willingly accept his punishment out of true repentance). Thus, a Torah punishment must be perfectly molded to fit its crime. It cannot be too harsh, or it will over-punish, and it cannot be too lenient, or it will offer the sinner an easy way to escape the retribution that he deserves.

The Gemara (in Makkos 5b) notes the puzzling nature of the rule that the punishment for perjury is only administered if the perjury is detected *before* the victim's sentence has been carried out. In reference to this law, the Gemara cites a general principle which states that one may not take a punishment prescribed by the Torah in one case and apply it to another case through logical deduction. Even if the second case is a more serious infraction than the first, it may be exempted from the punishment of the first. This principle is known in Hebrew as *ein ohnshin min hadin* (lit., "we do not punish because of logic").

It is not difficult to see that the logic we have used to explain the laws of perjury may be extended to explain the general principle of *ein ohnshin min hadin*: We can never apply the punishment for a lighter crime to a more serious crime because it is inappropriate to offer such "simple" atonement to the more serious criminal. This is, in fact, exactly what the Maharsha suggests (in Sanhedrin 64b).

III

There is, however, another way to understand the principle that physical punishment is not administered based on the dictates of logic. The human mind cannot possibly grasp *all* of the ramifications of a given act. What seems to us to be more sinful may actually be less sinful in Hashem's eyes. Therefore, only Hashem defines punishments. As the verse states, "Justice is for Hashem to administer" (Devarim 1:17). If Hashem does not specify a punishment in the Torah for a particular sin, it is not because He expects us to deduce the punishment by ourselves, but rather because that sin is *not* punishable.

Physical punishment is not based on the dictates of logic

As an example of the role that Divine considerations may play in jurisprudence, let us again consider the case of perjurers. Earlier, we invoked the no-atonement theory to explain why the punishment for perjury is not applied after the victim has been executed. The Ramban suggests another possible explanation. If Hashem would have wanted to stop an innocent man from being killed, Hashem could have done so. Therefore, if Hashem did *not* intervene to save the victim, obviously this man was deemed deserving of death by "due process" in the Heavenly court. (See Ki Setzei essay, p. 251, where this matter will be discussed at length.) This is why witnesses are *not* punished if they succeed in executing their victim. Similarly, when it comes to administering any other punishment not explicitly prescribed by the Torah, Divine considerations which man cannot possibly speculate upon may be involved.

This explanation for not punishing based on logic is offered by *Halichos Olam* (Sha'ar 4, p. 25b—see also Rashi, Sanhedrin 73a s.v. *Hekesha*; Zevachim 106b, s.v. *Atia*).

IV

These two views of the logic behind the principle of not punishing on logical grounds alone (*ein ohnshin min hadin*) may perhaps help us to better understand a dispute between the early Talmud commentators involving that principle.

A dispute

In addition to the sins that carry the death penalty in court (murder, incest, adultery, etc.), the Torah mentions several sins punishable by death by the hand of Heaven or by the related punishment of *kares* (excision). Does the principle of *ein ohnshin min hadin* apply to these sins as well? According to Tosafos (Chullin 115b, s.v. *Mah*) and the Shittah Mekubetzes (Bava Kama 2a s.v. *haTzad haShaveh*), heavenly punishments are also subject to this rule—we cannot assume that a more serious case will necessarily have the same heavenly punishment as a less serious case. According to the Rosh (Tosfos haRosh, Kiddushin 57b, s.v. *Iy Mah*), however, heavenly punishments are an exception to the rule, and we may use logic to extend a punishment from one case to another.

Perhaps this dispute may be explained in light of the two theories mentioned above. If the reasoning behind *ein ohnshin min hadin* is that a punishment offers an opportunity for atonement, this rule should not apply to heavenly punishments. Punishments such as *kares*, when administered by the heavenly court, are obviously the ultimate retribution for one's sins. They are not a means for acquiring atonement and "exempting" oneself from Divine retribution. Therefore, a worse sin certainly ought to carry a worse heavenly punishment.

If, however, the reasoning for the principle of *ein ohnshin min hadin* involves our ignorance—what seems to us to be a more corrupt act is actually a *less* corrupt one in the eyes of the Creator—then the principle still holds true regarding punishments administered by the heavenly court. We cannot fathom Hashem's wisdom in order to predict what punishments the heavenly court will or will not mete out, unless the Torah specifically spells it out for us. This is why Tosafos and the Shittah Mekubetzes insist that we *cannot* assume that Hashem will punish a sinner in the heavenly court based on the dictates of our own logic!

Punishments that may seem illogical to us have their own logic that only Hashem knows. In summary, when a ruling of our Sages seems illogical to us, we should nevertheless treat it with respect. Sometimes, human logic alone will not suffice to fathom the laws of the Creator.

PARSHAS DEVARIM

Tishah b'Av: Days Of Doom; Days Of Joy

"Five events befell our ancestors on the 17th of Tammuz and five events befell them on the ninth of Av (Tishah b'Av)... On the ninth of Av: 1. It was decreed that our ancestors, in Moshe's time, would not enter the Land of Israel (Bamidbar 14:29-31); 2. The First Temple was destroyed (by the Babylonians, circa 420 BCE); 3. The Romans destroyed the Second Temple (circa 70 CE); 4. The stronghold city of Betar was captured and destroyed by the Romans (circa 135 CE); 5. The Romans razed and plowed over Jerusalem" (Tur, Orach Chayim #549) (Mishnah, Taanis 4:6).

Why did so many tragedies befall us on the very same date? Are there some days less auspicious or "unluckier" than others? The Gemara (Shabbos 146a) states clearly that the Bnai Yisrael's fortunes are governed neither by luck nor by astrological influences. What then can be understood from the coincidence of so many tragic events on one day?

The Talmud says: "Reward is saved for a day of merit, and destruction is saved for a day of guilt" (Taanis 29a). Because, in the times of Moshe, our ancestors committed such a terrible sin on the ninth of Av, this day became one reserved for destruction. Every year, when that day arrives, the sin of our ancestors is brought back to light. Since we have not yet fully corrected our ancestors' misdeeds, Hashem may not extend to us His usual loving-kindness on that day, leaving us vulnerable to impending adversity. The ninth of Av has thus become a "weak link" in the chain of Jewish history. (A similar reasoning can be extended to the 17th of Tammuz, as we shall soon see.)

Ninth of Av: A day reserved for punishment

The Sages of the Talmud (Sanhedrin 90a) tell us that whenever Hashem punishes someone it is always done so that the punishment corresponds to the sin that was committed (*middah keneged middah*). A classic example of this is the Egyptians' punishment.

The Egyptians persecuted the Israelites through water, by drowning Jewish babies in the Nile river (Shemos 1:22). Their ultimate punishment was that they themselves were drowned in the Red Sea (ibid. chap. 14, see Rashi on Shemos 18:11. See also Metzora essay p. 133, for more on this theme.)

As we have pointed out, the catastrophic events of the ninth of Av were all precipitated by the sin of Moshe's generation. Here, too, it can be shown that the specific events that transpired on these days were all clearly wrought with the theme of *middah keneged middah*—measure for measure.

II

Ninth of Av: Measure for measure

Let us first consider our ancestors' sin on Tishah b'Av. The Jews sent spies to scout out the Land of Israel prior to what they believed was their imminent entrance into the land. These spies toured the land for forty days, and returned with a depressing account, preaching the hopelessness of ever wresting the land from its current inhabitants. Instead of trusting in Hashem and His appointed leaders, the people rallied rebelliously behind the sinful spies—"The people wept all through that night" (Bamidbar 14:1).

This sin, the Mishnah notes, took place on Tishah b'Av. "That night that the people wept was the eve of Tishah b'Av. Hashem said to them, 'You wept on this day for no good reason; I will establish this day as a day of weeping for all generations'" (Taanis 29a). The tragedies that befell the Jews throughout the generations were apparently further punishments for the original sinful act committed by the generation of the Exodus.

Now let us review the five punishments of Tishah b'Av:

A review of the five punishments of Tishah b'Av

1. The Torah tells us that the punishment meted out immediately to those who allied themselves with the spies was that they would have to wander in the desert for forty years—"one year for each day" of the spies' excursion (Bamidbar 14:34). The Torah makes it clear that the punishment of forty years in the desert was "measure for measure"—forty for forty. Can we say the same of the latter-day punishments—the four tragedies listed in the Mishnah in Taanis? A closer examination reveals that, in fact, we may.

2, 3. The sin of the Bnai Yisrael was that they rejected the Land of Israel. They were willing to pass up possession of the Promised Land, without even trying to conquer it, even though Hashem had already told them of its unique virtues.

The destruction of the Temples that took place centuries later was more than just a loss of opportunity to perform the sacrificial rite ordained by the Torah. It was the event that, symbolically and actually, spelled the end of organized Jewish settlement in Israel. The destruction of the Temple and the concept of exile are always considered to be two sides of the same coin by our Sages (see for example Berachos 3a, Chagigah 5b).

The Torah itself seems to make this connection in Vayikra 26:31-2: "I will destroy your Temple...and will scatter you among the nations." It is clear that the punishment of the destruction of the Temple—tantamount to exile of the population—is closely correlated to the Jews' sin on the original Tishah b'Av. Because on Tishah b'Av the Bnai Yisrael expressed an unwillingness to accept the gift of the Land of Israel, on that very same date they eventually lost the Land of Israel.

4. Betar was the central stronghold of the Bar Kochva rebellion against Rome (Eichah Rabbasi 2). Some sixty years after the second Temple was destroyed, the Jews, led by the charismatic and courageous Bar Kochva, tried to throw off the Roman yoke. They even succeeded to some degree in establishing an autonomous Jewish state for several years in Israel (132-135 CE). When the Bar Kochva uprising was finally quelled by the Romans with Betar's fall, it effectively represented the end of any Jewish hope to sovereignty in the Land of Israel for the foreseeable future. This, too, then, is clearly an appropriate punishment for the sin of the spies and Israel's rejection of the Land of Israel.

5. The last of the five events of Tishah b'Av can be interpreted along the same lines. The final razing of Jerusalem was designed to end any hopes among the Jews for a restoration of their sovereignty, or even of their ability to dwell in the city. Once again, on the very date which marked Bnai Yisrael's original spurning of Eretz Yisrael, Eretz Yisrael was showing its own scorn for them.

III

We have shown how the events of subsequent Tishah b'Av reflected the nature of the sin that had taken place on that day. Can the incidents that occurred on the 17th of Tammuz be explained in a similar manner? Do these events also show a measure-for-measure relationship to some primordial sin?

17th of Tammuz: Measure for measure

On the 17th of Tammuz:

1. The Tablets of the Ten Commandments were shattered (Shemos 32:19);

2. The daily (*tamid*) sacrifice of the Temple was discontinued in the days of the Second Temple;

3. The walls around Jerusalem were breached during the Roman siege (in

70 CE);

4. The Greek ruler Epistemos publicly burned the Torah scroll;

5. Menashe, a king of Judea in the First Temple period, erected an idolatrous image on the Temple grounds (II Kings 21:7). (Mishnah, Taanis 4:6)

Now let us take a closer look at these five punishments:

A closer look at these five punishments

1. Let us examine the original sin of Tammuz the 17th. The Bnai Yisrael, disoriented by what they considered Moshe's tardiness in coming down from Mount Sinai at the end of the prescribed forty day period, assumed Moshe to be dead. They decided to create a golden calf to take his place. "Get up and make a god for us, for we do not know what happened to this man Moshe who took us out of Egypt" (Shemos 32:1). Later, they declared this golden calf to be their new god. They worshipped the calf and sacrificed to it (ibid. 32:4-6). While still encamped before Mount Sinai, they rejected the Almighty Who had taken them out of the land of Egypt, led them through the desert, and given them the Torah! As it says in Tehillim (106:20): "They exchanged their Glory (Hashem) for an image of a grass-eating ox." It was as a reaction to this disgrace that Moshe threw the Tablets from his hands and shattered them (Shemos 32:19).

2. With this in mind, we can understand how the punishments of the 17th of Tammuz through the ages correspond to the original sin of that day. The easiest to explain of the four punishments listed is that related to Menashe's sin of placing an idol in the Beis Hamikdash. By doing so, he prevented the Jews from serving Hashem in the Beis Hamikdash, and replaced the worship of Hashem with that of an idol directly in Hashem's Holy Temple! This was an appropriate punishment for the Bnai Yisrael, who had done the same centuries earlier with the worship of the golden calf in front of Mount Sinai.

3. The daily *tamid* sacrifice personified the service of Hashem in the Temple. When this was discontinued, the situation paralleled the discontinuation of the worship of Hashem by the Jews who worshipped the golden calf at Mount Sinai.

Furthermore, we are told in the Gemara (Bava Kama 82b) that the discontinuation of the Tamid took place during the civil war between the rival brothers Aristobulus and Hyrcanus. Jerusalem was under siege and no goods could be transported into or out of the city. Every day, however, people standing outside the city wall brought two sheep, which were then hoisted over the wall and used by the Kohanim in the Temple for the *tamid* sacrifice.

One day, this operation was terminated by the sieging party. When the Kohanim hoisted up their daily "catch," they were horrified to discover that it was a pig that had been sent instead of a sheep! It is interesting to note that pigs were offered by the Romans to their god Jupiter (see Megillas Antiochus and secular historical sources—perhaps this is why the verse "The pig of the forest chews on them" [Tehillim 80:14] is interpreted by the Midrash [Vayikra

Rabbah 13] to be a reference to the Roman persecution of the Jews).

The element of "substitution" is apparent in this story as well. Not only was the *tamid* sacrifice stopped, but the sheep of the *tamid* was supplanted by an impure pig. The sacrifice unto Hashem was replaced by an animal used for idolatrous sacrifice.

There is another opinion that the discontinuation of the *tamid* sacrifice (to which the Mishnah refers) happened *not* during the war of Aristobulus vs. Hyrcanus, but rather during the time of the Roman siege of Jerusalem, prior to the destruction of the Temple. After the Romans destroyed the Temple, it is documented that they used the site for their idolatrous pig-sacrifices. The glory of Hashem in the Beis Hamikdash was again exchanged for that of idolatry.

4. The burning of the Torah by Epistemos paralleled the sin of the golden calf in a different way. As has been mentioned, when Moshe saw that his people had committed such a terrible sin he shattered the Tablets. As a punishment for bringing about the destruction of Hashem's Tablets of the Law, the Jews of a future era had Hashem's Torah burned before them by a blasphemous ruler.

5. The breach in Jerusalem's walls may also be shown to parallel the original sin of the 17th of Tammuz. The Gemara (Bava Basra 7b) tells us that just as a city wall provides protection to all members of a community, so do the righteous people and Torah scholars of the generation provide protection. For this reason, the Talmud says that scholars do not have to contribute to the expense of building defensive ramparts around their home towns—their Torah study is their share in the city's defense. As the Gemara expounds on a verse from Shir Hashirim [the Song of Songs]:

"I am a wall, and my breasts are like towers" (Shir Hashirim 8:10).

"I am a wall"—refers to the Torah, which affords protection to its people. "My breasts are like towers"—refers to Torah scholars (Bava Basra 7b).

When the Bnai Yisrael rejected the leadership of Moshe and chose a golden calf to lead them instead, they were showing disdain for the ultimate scholar of the Torah. Their sin, in addition, caused the shattering of the Tablets of the Torah. Since Torah and Torah scholars are compared to city walls, a fitting punishment for this sin was that in a future generation the Jews of Jerusalem would have their protective wall breached on the anniversary of the original sinful deed.

IV

The continuation of the "Tishah b'Av" Mishnah in Taanis goes as follows:

"There were no greater celebrations for the Bnai Yisrael than those that were held on the 15th of Av and on Yom Kippur" (Mishnah Taanis 4:8).

What is the relevance of this fact to the fasts of the 9th of Av and the 17th of Tammuz—or to anything else in Tractate Taanis? It seems to be completely out of place!

Let us examine the reasons that Yom Kippur and the 15th of Av were established as days of celebration. Yom Kippur is a joyous day because it is the day when Hashem told Moshe that He forgave the Bnai Yisrael for the sin of the golden calf, and He promised to forgive the sins of Israel throughout the generations (see Rashi to Taanis 30b and Shemos 33:11).

15th of Av & Yom Kippur: days of Joy

The 15th of Av is considered a day of celebration because this was the day that the Bnai Yisrael realized that the forty-year punishment of death and wandering in the desert had drawn to a close (Taanis 30b). It was thus the day of the expiration of the punishment for the sin of the spies. In fact, according to one of the Tosafists (Rabbeinu Tam), that day did not just mark the *completion* of their forty year punishment. On the 15th of Av, Hashem *forgave* the sin of the golden calf, leaving those who had not yet been punished to live and enter the Holy Land! (Tosafos in Gemara Bava Basra 121a).

If so, it is very clear what these two joyous days have to do with the previous topic of the Mishnah. The Mishnah had just described the two days of mourning and fasting—the 17th of Tammuz, whose sad events were precipitated by the sin of the golden calf; and the 9th of Av, whose events were brought about by the sin of the spies. The Mishnah then explains that the days of greatest celebration were the days commemorating the abatement of Hashem's anger for these two sins. On Yom Kippur, Hashem's anger over the sin of the golden calf abated, and on the 15th of Av, Hashem exonerated us from the sin of the spies!

In Zecharyah (8:19) we read: "The fasts of Tammuz and Av and Tishrei and Teves will become times of happiness and rejoicing for the house of Yehudah." Usually we understand this verse to mean that there will come a time when mourning over the destruction of Jerusalem and the Temple will become obsolete, since they will be rebuilt in Messianic days. However, according to the approach developed above, the verse could be interpreted to mean that even now, in our days, there is a certain element of the transformation of the fasts of Tammuz and Av into days of celebration! (See also Radak, beginning of Yechezkel.)

In any case, it is clearly not "poor fortune" that causes calamity to befall our people on certain days. It is our own sins. And when our repentance for those sins will be complete, those days will too become days of joy!

PARSHAS VAESCHANAN

Unveiling The Secrets Of The Decalogue

The Decalogue, or Ten Commandments, is recorded twice in the Torah. The first time is during the narrative of the giving of the Torah on Mount Sinai (Shemos 20:2-14). The second account appears in the form of a review of those events, in this week's Parsha (Devarim 5:6-18).

Surprisingly, the texts of the two accounts are *not* identical—there are in fact twenty-two differences between the two versions. Many of these discrepancies are minor, such as the addition of the letter *vav* [and] seven times and its omission twice, in the second version. The order of the words in one commandment is also reversed. There are several more significant inconsistencies as well. In six places words are *added* in the second version, and in six other places, completely different words are *substituted* for those used in the first version of the commandments.

The question we must ask then is why should there be *any* differences whatsoever between the two accounts? After all, don't they describe the same exact set of events? Many commentators have discussed this. The consensus is that when Moshe reviewed the Decalogue for the people, he added his own explanatory comments to the original wording. The Vaeschanan Decalogue is Moshe's rewording of the Ten Commandments. (Ibn Ezra Shemos 20:1, Ramban Shemos 20:8, etc.). This seems to be the understanding of the Talmud as well (Shavuos 20b).

Two sets of tablets or one?

Elsewhere, however, the Talmud seems to have a completely different explanation of the differences between the two presentations of the Decalogue. In Bava Kama (55a), the Gemara points out that in the Shemos version we are told to honor our parents "in order that you should live long days." In Devarim, the incentive given is "in order that you should live long days" and so "that you shall have good." Why is this extra phrase omitted in the first record, yet mentioned in the second? The Gemara explains that Hashem knew that the first Tablets would be shattered, and He did not want the promise of "that it should be good for you" to be "shattered" along with the Tablets. Were that to happen, there would, G-d forbid, be no more goodness for the Jews.

The implication of this aggadic interpretation is clearly that goodness could only be written on the second set of Tablets, which were given on Yom Kippur (see Shemos 34) and were never broken. If so, the Devarim version of the Decalogue must be the version engraved on the *second* Tablets, while the Shemos version represents the text engraved on the *first* Tablets—the original ones, later shattered by Moshe when he witnessed the sin of the golden calf. This explains very simply why there are so many differences between the two versions. The two accounts of the Decalogue do *not* represent the oral delivery of the original revelation at Mount Sinai. Instead, they represent the written texts—and oral deliveries—of two completely different sets of Tablets!

The same conclusion may be drawn from a statement of the Pesikta Rabbasi (beginning of Parsha 23), addressing the fact that the first account of the Decalogue says "Remember (*zachor*) the Sabbath Day," and the second account says "Keep (*shamor*) the Sabbath Day."

The Pesikta explains that the word "keep" was used to intimate that the Bnai Yisrael were being instructed that only through "keeping" the Shabbos would they succeed in "keeping" the second Tablets from being lost as the first tablets were. Here, too, the insinuation is that the Devarim account of the Decalogue records the text of the *second* Tablets, while the Shemos account records the text of the *first* Tablets.

However, the assertion that the Decalogue of Vaeschanan is actually the text of the *second* Tablets, given on Yom Kippur, seems to be contradicted by the context of the narrative. The Decalogue of Vaeschanan is introduced with the words: "Hashem spoke to you face to face on the mountain, from the midst of the fire. I stood between Hashem and you...to tell you the word of Hashem" (Devarim 5:4-5).

This clearly seems to be a description of the oral delivery of the first Tablets, amidst the spectacle of thunder and lightning and loud blast of the shofar, in the presence of the entire congregation of Israel (see Shemos 20: 14-17). Neither fanfare nor public address can be found accompanying the delivery of the second Tablets, which Moshe himself brought down for the Bnai Yisrael (see Shemos 34:28-29 and Devarim 10:4-5). How, then, can these two citations from the sages imply that the Decalogue quoted in Devarim 5 is a description of the address accompanying the second Tablets?

II

Actually, even according to the first approach mentioned above—that the Decalogue of Devarim contained the text of the *first* Tablets along with Moshe's explanatory addenda—some further explanation is in order. Why did Moshe need to add explanatory remarks? If the people understood the Ten Commandments the first time, why would they require more explanation forty years later? Besides, what explanation is added by the numerous changes Moshe made?

It takes 40 years to fully understand

In this week's Parsha we are told that upon the Bnai Yisrael's awe-filled reaction to his revelation Hashem said to Moshe, "Who would make it possible that the Bnai Yisrael would fear Me like this and keep all of my commandments all the days? Then they and their children would have good forever!"(Devarim 5:26).

The Gemara in Avoda Zara (5a) tells us that had the Bnai Yisrael immediately responded to Hashem's remark by exclaiming, "'You' make it possible for us," Hashem would have done just that. Hashem had offered them a cue so that they would declare their desire for Him, strengthen their resolve and weaken their evil inclination, but they missed the hint.

Why did Moshe decide to mention Hashem's comment at this point, recognizing that it is not recorded in the context of the original story of the revelation on Mount Sinai in Shemos? The Gemara explains that it was only forty years after the revelation, that Moshe realized that Hashem gave this opportunity to the Bnai Yisrael. As the Gemara puts it, "A student does not fully understand the intent of his master's words until forty years after he has heard them."

Perhaps such an explanation may be extended to our situation as well. Hashem was offering the Jewish people veiled advice as to how to face the trials that awaited them—but they missed his intimations.

III

Let us begin with a *mashal* [allegorical story]. Once there was a father who was sending his son off to school in a distant city. They had a relative in that city who was involved in illegal activities. The father suspected that the relative would try to lure his son away from learning an honest livelihood by enticing him with offers of "easy money." Naturally, the father wanted his son to avoid this relative at all costs. However, he knew that it would be counterproductive for him to give explicit instructions to his son to refrain from meeting this man, as this would only arouse the boy's curiosity concerning the relative. The young man, suspecting some secret family feud, might even acquaint himself with the villain rather than shun him. Furthermore, the son might feel insulted

Hashem's hidden advice

that his father showed such lack of confidence in his own judgment, making him unreceptive to his father's sound advice.

Instead, the father offered his son several general, indirect suggestions: Do not keep company with a person whose integrity is in doubt; do not be eager to accept monetary offers from strangers; do not become taken in with seemingly easy schemes for making large amounts of money, for they usually backfire; etc. Hopefully, through this kind of indirect counsel, the son would realize when the time of temptation would arrive, that he should keep his distance from the offensive relative.

Let us apply this parable to the circumstances of the Bnai Yisrael at the time of the giving of the Torah. Hashem knew that His children would soon be facing challenging situations, and that their loyalty to Him would be tested. In fact, the incident of the golden calf took place right at Mount Sinai only 40 days after the Torah was given. It was this incident that caused the loss of the first Tablets of the Law, and was destined to cause the Jews much future suffering and misfortune (see Rashi to Shemos 35:34; Balak essay p. 194 and Devarim-Tishah b'Av essay p. 217). And, as the Mishnah says, "'Everything is foreseen [by Hashem]' (Avos 3:15)—the past present and future are one to the Creator."

With this in mind, perhaps we may suggest that Hashem wanted to give His people veiled warnings of the test that awaited them. This way, when the pitfall of the golden calf presented itself, perhaps the Jews would reconsider before sinning, realizing that Hashem had cautioned them to beware of falling into such a trap. The Giver of the Law therefore implanted several tacit hints into the wording and nuances of the Ten Commandments. Unfortunately, the intent of these hidden messages was lost on the people. Even Moshe himself did not grasp these subtle allusions until forty years later—in hindsight, after the people's infamous sin at Sinai was already history.

It took the great Moshe forty years to understand that the people had forever lost their opportunity to declare "*You* make it possible for us not to ever sin!" At the same time, Moshe realized that Hashem had been trying to give them the advice they would need to avoid the notorious pitfall of the golden calf. Now, while Moshe was delivering his farewell address of admonishment and warning to the Bnai Yisrael, he pointed out the several gentle warnings that Hashem Himself had provided in the Ten Commandments.

IV

The two versions of the Decalogue: A side by side comparison

Let us now examine the differences in the wording of the two versions of the Decalogue and see how they can be explained according to our theory that hints to the pitfalls of the golden calf are contained in the first Decalogue:

A) In the second commandment of the Shemos version we read that Hashem does kindness to those who keep "*mitzvosai* [My commandments]."

Three warnings not to serve a calf's form: First warning

In the Devarim version (8:10), the word is "*mitzvaso* [His commandment]"—singular. (*Mitzvaso* is the way the word is written [*kesiv*]. The word is, in fact, pronounced [*kri*] *mitzvosai*, in consonance with the Shemos version. Nevertheless, the change in spelling ought to be addressed.)

In Chullin 5a we are taught that one sin is equal in gravity to all the other sins of the Torah combined—idol-worship. "If someone worships idols, it is as if he has transgressed the entire Torah; and when someone renounces idol-worship it is as if he has fulfilled the entire Torah." Moshe saw that at the end of the second commandment—the commandment against idol-worship—Hashem promised to bestow kindness to "those who keep My commandments." Moshe understood that Hashem was hinting that the observance of this one precept was tantamount to "keeping My commandments"—*all* the commandments of Hashem. Thus, when Moshe reviewed the contents of the Decalogue in Devarim, he underscored the fact that in reality *one* particular commandment was being discussed here by using the singular word *commandment* or *mitzvaso*. Moshe was implying that they had been warned with this subtle cue to be cautious when it comes to idol-worship, and avoid falling into the trap of sinning with the golden calf.

B) In the Shemos version of the second commandment it says, "Do not make for yourself a sculpted image *nor* any likeness of anything in the heavens above and on the earth below...."

Second warning

In Devarim (8:8) it says, "Do not make for yourself a sculpted image, a likeness of anything in the heavens above and on the earth below...," with the word *nor* omitted. In Shemos the prohibition seems to be divided into two separate components, while in Devarim it is worded as one long prohibition. How can this discrepancy be explained?

The Ramban (Shemos 32:1) explains that the reason the people chose the form of a calf as their object of worship is because, as described in Yechezkel 1, the form of an ox's head formed part of the image of Hashem's Divine chariot—the "Throne of Hashem's Glory." The four heads of creatures that appear on the Divine chariot represent four ways in which Hashem exerts control over what happens in this world. The Bnai Yisrael wanted an object that would evoke the powers and protection of Hashem, and they found this in the image of the calf.

When Hashem warned against making "a sculpted image, nor any likeness of anything in the heavens above and on the earth below," Moshe realized that the reference was not just to a general sculpted image of an imaginary creature. It was a warning not to create a sculpted image that is a specific *likeness*, that of a creature which was to be found *both* in the heavens above and the earth below—i.e., one of the figures of the Divine chariot, such as an ox! Moshe now knew that Hashem meant this sentence to be understood as one long subtle warning against making a sculpture *of* any likeness of that which is in the heavens above and the earth below. Therefore he omitted the *nor*, to accentuate this point.

C) Another reference to the golden calf can be found in the fourth commandment. In the Shemos version, the fourth commandment enjoins us to refrain from all labor ("*melacha*"—better translated as "constructive act") on the Sabbath day—"you, your servant, your maidservant and your animals." In Devarim, this is rephrased as "you, your servant, your maidservant, *your ox, your donkey and all* your animals" (Devarim 5:14). Why the addition of these several animals?

Third warning

The reason that Hashem told the people to extend the Shabbos rest to their animals, Moshe now realized, was that the people may have an inclination to accord a revered status—or perhaps some element of divinity, as is done in India—to some animals, thus exempting these animals from participating in Hashem's ordained day of rest. For this reason Hashem stressed that animals, too, must rest. In order to emphasize this, Moshe now rephrased this sentence to explicitly equate the *ox* with all other animals, as far as the day of rest was concerned. As Moshe explained, Hashem was hinting that we should not venerate any animal, particularly the ox which Hashem knew would shortly become a snare for the people.

There are a number of noteworthy changes in the final commandment of the Decalogue. In the Shemos version, the last commandment says, "Do not covet your friend's *house*; do not covet your friend's *wife*, nor his servant nor his maidservant, *nor* his ox nor his donkey nor anything that belongs to your friend."

The concluding commandment

In Devarim (8:18) it says, "**Do not covet your friend's 'wife'**; **Do not 'desire'** (instead of covet) **your friend's 'house'** (it reverses the order of house and wife), **'his field'** (added word) **nor his servant nor his maidservant, his ox** (leaves out 'nor') **nor his donkey nor anything that belongs to your friend.**"

We have pointed out four discrepancies:

A. The order of "friend's house" and "friend's wife" are interchanged in the two versions.

B. In Shemos the same verb (*sachmod*—covet) is used both times, in Devarim, however, the commandment begins with *sachmod* ("covet") but then switches to *tisavveh* ("desire").

C. The Devarim version adds the words "his field," to the commandment, which are not in the original version.

D. The word "nor" before the words "his ox" is omitted in Devarim.

We may suggest that all of these changes can be explained in light of the theme developed above.

A. "Your friend's wife" may be understood to have an allegorical meaning in addition to its simple connotation. The Hebrew word *re'a*, which literally means friend, is sometimes used to refer to the Creator. This is how the word is to be understood in Mishlei 27:10 (according to Rashi Shabbos 31a): "Do not forsake your 'friend' and the 'friend' of your father." Perhaps we can understand the word *re'a* in this light in our verse too. What would be the meaning of "your friend's [Hashem's] 'wife' (or 'woman')?"

As previously mentioned (#1B), images of the heads of four creatures appear in Hashem's Divine Chariot (see Yechezkel 1), each one representing another of four attributes that Hashem uses in administering the world. The figures (*chayos*) which bear these images making up the Chariot, or Throne of Hashem, are referred to as "women" (Yechezkel 1:9, 23). Thus the "woman" of Hashem that we are told not to covet may be one of the figures of the Divine Chariot—a figure bearing the head of an ox! We were thus being warned not to try to "use" such a figure for our own benefit.

As we shall see, the entire commandment against coveting may have been directed towards warning the Jews against sinning with the golden calf. However, the mention of the "woman of *re'acha*" may be the most explicit hint to that incident. Moshe, realizing the implication of this expression, moved it to the top of the list of things not to covet, in order to make his point that the tenth commandment cautioned against the sin of the calf.

B. As noted above, in the second Decalogue we are told not to "desire" our friend's house. In the original version we are told not to "covet" our friend's house. The root "*ivva*," for "desire" is used in connection with the Jew's eagerness to worship idols by the incident of the golden calf—"They desired (*ivvu*) for themselves many gods" (Rashi Shemos 32:1, Sanhedrin 63a). This is why Moshe, when he reviewed the Decalogue to the Bnai Yisrael, expressly used the word "desire" instead of "covet" which was used in Shemos. Moshe intended to bring out that this prohibition was directed towards golden-calf-like sins.

C. The Gemara (Gittin 52a) tells us that the word "field" may be used to mean "ox," since in many countries throughout history an ox performed most of the labors in the field. Here too, Moshe added the word "field" (without any conjunction to separate it from the preceding word, "house") to intimate that when Hashem spoke of "your friend's house" He meant not only the house in its most limited sense, but also the area around the house—its "field". This, in light of the Gemara in Gittin, was a veiled reference to the ox—"Do not covet the ox of the Divine Chariot!"

D. By omitting the conjunction ("nor") before the word "ox" Moshe also helped stress the connection between the "field" and the "ox" which appears two words later. The word, "ox," is, after all, only a "clarification" of the less explicit word "field," since the word for field can also mean "ox," as we have shown. The ox of the verse is not an "additional" piece of property.

"**Do not** (a) **murder 'and' do not** (b) **commit adultery 'and' do not** (c) **steal 'and' do not** (d) **give false testimony regarding your friend 'and' do not** (e) **covet**..." (Devarim 5:17,18). In the Devarim version, the last five commandments are joined together with the constant repetition of the word "and." In Shemos this conjunction is omitted, giving more of an impression of five distinct commands. How can this difference be accounted for?

Four extra "and"s

Moshe realized that the last five commandments were intended to represent one long progression of sins (which would lead up to the sin of the golden calf), and not five *unrelated* transgressions. Hashem was warning the people not to become ensnared in one sin, which would bring on another, and another, and eventually to the infamous sin of idolatry. How so?

(a) Before Moshe ascended Mount Sinai he left Aharon and Aaron's nephew Chur in charge of the people (Shemos 24:14). Chur, however, is never heard from again, despite the budding leadership role he seems to have played in the past (see Shemos 17). What ever became of Chur? The Gemara (quoted by Rashi to Shemos 32:5) tells us that he was murdered by the rabble when he refused to cooperate in the construction of the golden calf. Thus, the first sin to be transgressed in the progression of events leading up to the sin of the golden calf was the sin of murder.

(b) The Gemara (Sanhedrin 63b) explains that the Bnai Yisrael were not stupid—they had already experienced G-d's worship, and knew that molten gods could not possibly have any divine powers. The only reason they ever indulged in idol worship, the Gemara asserts, was as an excuse to engage in licentious behavior. If Hashem could be renounced and a new form of deity instituted, the people would be free to follow the basest of their instincts with impunity. In fact, we find that after they built the golden calf "they arose to amuse themselves" (Shemos 32:6). Rashi explains that this means they engaged in immoral behavior—behavior which the words "amuse himself" refer to in Bereishis 39:14.

(c) When Aharon was confronted with the people's demand to make a god for them, he told them to bring him all of their wives' golden ornaments. It is these ornaments that he intended to melt down to mold into an image. As Rashi explains, Aharon knew that the women would not easily part with their jewelry, and he hoped that the delay would give Moshe enough time to return from the mountain's summit.

In fact, as Pirkei d'Rabbi Eliezer (chap. 45) points out, Aharon was right. The women refused to surrender their ornaments (see Tazria-Hachodesh, essay p. 128). But this did not stop the men from executing their plan—they took the jewelry by force! Thus, the sin of the golden calf was made possible only through the prior sin of theft.

(d) As explained above (#2A), the Hebrew word *re'a* [friend] is sometimes taken as a reference to Hashem. Thus the ninth commandment—not to give false testimony about one's "friend" (*re'a*)—may also be taken as a prohibition to utter falsehoods about "Hashem." This was a veiled warning to the Bnai Yisrael not to fall into the trap that would lead them to declare "This (the golden calf) is your god, O Israel!" (Shemos 32:4).

(e) The last commandment is "Do not covet." Rashi (to Shemos 32:1), quoting the Gemara (Sanhedrin 63a), points out that when the Bnai Yisrael accepted the golden calf upon themselves they had a strong "desire" to make molten gods, like the other nations had (see above, #2B). It was this "coveting" that brought them to sin.

We have thus shown that the episode of the golden calf involved much more than the "mere" sin of idolatry, but also comprises the sins of murder, immoral behavior, theft, false testimony and covetousness. By juxtaposing these sins in the Decalogue, Hashem was conveying a veiled description of what would happen if the people were not careful. Moshe understood this implied hint and by adding the conjunction "and" between the last five commandments was pointing it out to the people. This made it clear that the last five commandments were intended to be warnings about the golden calf disaster.

The phrase "**As Hashem had commanded you**" is found twice in the second Decalogue—in the fourth and in the fifth commandment, referring to the Shabbos (verse 12), and to honoring one's parents (verse 16). This phrase does not appear at all in the first version. Since Moshe was paraphrasing the words that Hashem used when He gave us the Torah, the words "as Hashem had commanded you" must mean that Hashem had commanded these two laws prior to the Revelation at Mount Sinai. As related in Shemos 16:25, the Bnai Yisrael were indeed given a series of laws at Marah several weeks before they arrived at Sinai. The Sages tell us that the Sabbath and honoring one's parents were among these laws (Rashi ad loc.). But why did Moshe see fit to remind the people of the episode at Marah?

As Hashem commanded you...

Moshe now realized that the reason Hashem chose to give these two specific mitzvos Before He gave the Torah, was because He wanted the people to become accustomed to them even before they arrived at Mount Sinai. These two precepts would, more than any others, enable them to better withstand the test that would face them there. How so?

The mitzvah of keeping the Sabbath, we are told, is considered as important as the keeping of all the other mitzvos combined. The same is said for the mitzvah of refraining from idolatry (Eruvin 69b). The reason for this emphasis on the Sabbath is that Shabbos observance constitutes a declaration that one believes in Hashem as the creator of the universe.

Similarly, the Gemara (Yevamos 5a) tells us that honoring one's parents is tantamount to honoring Hashem Himself. (Recognizing one's indebtedness to one's parents for having brought one into the world will undoubtedly bring one to recognize the other Factor involved in his or her creation —Hashem.) In fact, the Gemara (Berachos 35b) tells us that "father" and "mother" may sometimes be taken to mean "Hashem" and "the Congregation of Israel," respectively. Thus the commandment to honor one's father, if expanded to its broadest scope, will bring one to show honor to Hashem as well.

At any rate, the two mitzvos of Shabbos and honoring one's parents had it in their power to strengthen the Jews' trust in Hashem. According to Rashbam, this is why these are the only two positive mitzvos included in the Ten Commandments. The only positive mitzvos included in the Commandments were those that involved accepting upon ourselves the yoke of the service of Hashem. That must have been the purpose of the mitzvos of observing the Shabbos and honoring one's parents also (Rashbam, Shemos 20:7).

Moshe now realized that these two mitzvos were given to the people "ahead of schedule" because of the important lesson they were supposed to impart concerning the honor we must give to Hashem. In fact, our Sages tell us that if the Jews had kept their first Shabbos properly, they would never have been exiled from their land (i.e., they wouldn't have sinned with the calf, causing their eventual exile—see Ki Sisa essay p. 97). The Gemara adds that even the worst idol-worshippers are absolved, if they keep the Sabbath day (Shabbos 118b).

Moshe now understood that the Jews were given an early start in these two mitzvos for the same reason that specifically these two positive commandments were chosen to be included in the Big Ten. This is why in the second version of the Decalogue Moshe mentioned the words, "As Hashem (previously) commanded you."

The purpose of keeping the Shabbos

Perhaps the most glaring discrepancy between the two presentations of the Decalogue is the description of the mitzvah of Shabbos. In Shemos we are told to remember the Shabbos to commemorate the fact that Hashem created the universe in six days and ceased His creation on the seventh. In Devarim, however, we are bidden to keep the Shabbos in order to remember the fact that **we were slaves to the Egyptians and that Hashem took us out of their bondage.** How could Moshe *completely* change the entire basis upon which the mitzvah of Shabbos is founded from what Hashem Himself said?

The commentaries explain that the mitzvah of Shabbos actually contains within it two distinct precepts—refraining from doing labor and experiencing a day of rest. Cessation from work commemorates the fact that we once were forced to labor for the Egyptians and were subsequently freed; observing a day of rest is to recall that the Universe was created in six days. But why did Moshe stress only one of these aspects, while Hashem Himself stressed the other?

Many commentators ask why the Ten Commandments begin with the declaration "I am Hashem...Who took you out of Egypt." Would it not have been more powerful to have said "I am Hashem Who created heaven and earth?" Many commentators say that Hashem chose this as His introductory declaration because the people had just recently experienced the Exodus from Egypt. It would be much easier for them to relate to Hashem's having performed all the miracles that they had witnessed than to relate to Hashem having created the Universe, as august as is that concept.

Here too, although the primary purpose of Shabbos observance is to commemorate the Creation, and that is why Hashem mentioned the Creation in the Decalogue, Moshe brought in the other aspect of Shabbos because of its greater relevance to the people at the time of the giving of the Torah. Through appreciating Hashem the Liberator, the Jews could come to realize the greatness of Hashem the Creator. Moshe in effect was reprimanding the people for not using this tool (i.e., of recalling the miracles of the Exodus) to help themselves substantiate the belief in Hashem as the Creator—which would have prevented them from sinning with the golden calf.

V

A re-examination of the "Two Decalogue" Midrashim

Now that we have explained the differences between the two versions of the Decalogue, we must return to the question with which we started with at the beginning in section I. How can the Gemara and the Pesikta Rabbasi maintain that the Ten Commandments found in Devarim represents the text engraved on the second tablets (received on Yom Kippur), if the context of the story in Vaeschanan surrounding that text clearly discusses the revelation at Mount Sinai?

Let us examine the statements in question more carefully. The Gemara said that the reason the words "so that it will be good for you" (mentioned in the fifth commandment referring to honoring one's parents) did not appear on the first tablets was so that this promise for goodness to be bestowed by Hashem would not be broken along with the tablets. The implication is that these words *did* appear on the second tablets. But perhaps this is not what the Gemara meant to say. Perhaps the Gemara meant that although the lessons of "so that it will be good for you" were implicit in the text of the Ten Commandments (i.e., meriting the eternal good), as

Moshe himself pointed out in his "revised version" of the Decalogue, they were not stated *explicitly* in the Tablets, for if they had been—and the people would have sinned in spite of the explicit warning—they would never again have any "goodness." Their sin would then have been so grave that they would have lost any chance of ever attaining the ultimate good.

The Pesikta said that the word used for Shabbos observance in Devarim is "Keep (or 'be careful of') the Shabbos day," to imply that the Bnai Yisrael should "keep" these Tablets and not lose them as they lost the first ones. Perhaps this may be explained in a similar fashion. It is not that the second Tablets actually contained the words "keep the Shabbos day." Rather Moshe, when he recounted what was written on the *first* Tablets, pointed out to the people *why* the commandment of observing the Shabbos day was included in the Tablets. "Keeping" [observing] the Shabbos was the key to "keeping" the Torah permanently. Moshe used the word "keep" when he retold the story of the first Tablets to drive this message home to the Bnai Yisrael. Observe the Shabbos properly, he said, and you will never again come into a situation where the Torah will become lost to you!

We have illustrated our approach to only a few of the inconsistencies between the accounts of the Decalogue. However, even those discrepancies that we have not discussed here may be explained similarly. The key to the differences between the accounts is that Moshe was admonishing the Jews to pay closer attention to the nuances of their Master's words.

PARSHAS EIKEV

Torah Or "Avoda?"

"If you carefully obey My commandments that I command you today...I will grant you the rains of your land on time...and you shall gather in your grain, your wine and your oil. I will make grass grow in your fields for your animals, and you will eat and be satisfied" (Devarim 11:13-15).

In Gemara Berachos 35b this verse is examined: "What is the meaning of the verse 'You shall gather in your grain, etc.'? In another verse we read, 'The words of the Torah shall never depart from your mouth; you shall contemplate the Torah day and night' (Yehoshua 1:8). One might think that this verse is to be taken literally (i.e., that we are expected to learn Torah to the exclusion of all other occupations). The Torah says, 'You shall gather in your grain, etc.,'—to indicate that we should study Torah in the framework of the everyday necessities of life. This is Rebbi Yishmael's opinion."

The reward of those who obey Hashem's will

"Rebbi Shimon bar Yochai, however, said: 'Should a man really plow during the plowing season, sow in the sowing season, harvest during the harvest season, etc.? What then would become of Torah study? Rather, when Israel does the will of Hashem their labors are done by others,' as it says, 'Foreigners will come and tend to your flocks...' (Yeshayah 61:5). It is when the people of Israel do *not* do the will of Hashem that they must do their own labor, as our verse states, '*You* shall gather in your grain' (Devarim 11:14). And that is not all—they will even be forced to do the labors of others, as it says, 'You will work for your enemies' (ibid. 28:48)" (Gemara Berachos 35b).

Rebbi Shimon bar Yochai presents us with a radical and far-reaching approach to Torah study: If someone trusts completely and unfalteringly in Hashem ("does the will of Hashem"), he ought not toil for a livelihood. Rather, he should trust that his physical needs will be taken care of by the One Who created him with those needs. (This is the ideal situation for which one should aspire; although, as the Gemara points out (ibid.), there are few individuals who actually have practiced Rebbi Shimon's strategy and succeeded. Apparently, half-hearted attempts to follow Rebbi Shimon's lifestyle are doomed to failure. Only those who are capable of abandoning all mundane pursuits with peace of mind, fully convinced that they will receive all that they need from the One Above, can succeed with Rebbi Shimon's attitude. See also Bechukosai essay, section III, p. 157.)

This, Rebbi Shimon tells us, is the background of our verse, "You will gather your grain." This verse is dealing with people who are not fully fulfilling Hashem's will. They are tending to their own grain, rather than waiting for others to do it for them.

Looking at the context of the verse, however, it is very difficult to understand how Rebbi Shimon can possibly interpret the verse in this manner. The paragraph begins: "If you carefully obey my commandments that I command you today...." How can the continuation of this paragraph possibly be taken to refer to people who are *not* properly fulfilling Hashem's words? (This question has perplexed many of the greatest commentators; see particularly Maharsha, Ahavas Eisan on the Ein Yaakov, Meshech Chochmah to Devarim 11:13, etc.) Perhaps we may suggest a novel approach to this problem.

II

Immediately after discussing the reward for those who follow the ways of Hashem the next verse in the Torah says:

Reward & punishment or cause & effect?

"Beware, lest your heart become tempted and you go astray and worship other gods...and Hashem becomes angry with you and holds back the sky so that there will be no rain..." (Devarim 16-17).

The simple understanding of the transition of ideas in this section is that after having been told of the reward for *following* Hashem's will, we are told of the punishment for *not* following His will. Thus there are two different themes discussed in this section: reward and punishment.

However, there may be another way of interpreting the flow of the verses. The Gemara tells us:

"A full stomach is one of the worst sins [i.e., it can lead to the worst sins], as it says, 'When they ate well they became satisfied, and when they became satisfied they became arrogant and forgot Me' (Hoshea 13:6). Rebbi

Nachman proved it from a different verse: 'Lest you eat and become satisfied and build elegant houses and live in them...and your heart will become arrogant and you will forget Hashem' (Devarim 8:14). The other Rabbis proved it from here: '[Israel] will eat and be satisfied and grow fat and turn to other gods' (Devarim 31:20). Alternatively, from here: 'And *Yeshurun* (Israel) grew fat and rebelled' (ibid. 32:15)" (Berachos 32a).

Material success and complacency lead to arrogance. Arrogance leads to the worst of sins. Based on this theme, we can suggest a new interpretation of the verses we are discussing. It is necessary to warn those who have merited blessings of prosperity not to allow their success to lead them *away* from Hashem. The verses are not a description of reward followed by a separate description of punishment. Rather, they are a description of reward followed by a *warning* not to *react* to the reward in a way that will cause us to sin.

As a support for this interpretation, it is interesting to note that the Torah does not introduce the second half of the paragraph with the words "If you do not obey My commandments, etc."—as it began the initial reward section with the words "If you carefully obey My commandments." Rather, it states, "*Beware* lest your heart become tempted...."

The Sifri, in fact, states quite clearly that this is the intent of these verses: "'...and you will eat and be satisfied; beware, lest your heart become tempted...'—Take care that you do not rebel against Hashem. Typically, it is only when a person is "satisfied" that he is prone to becoming rebellious" (Sifri ad loc., chap. 43).

III

How can this explain Rebbi Shimon's reading of the verses? According to what we have described, there are three parts to the section we are dealing with: (1) A description of the reward granted to those who keep the mitzvos, (2) a description of an improper reaction to this reward, and (3) a description of the punishment that will be brought upon one who reacts to the reward in such a manner.

Rebbi Shimon's reading of the verses

Exactly where in the paragraph is the transition from the discussion of the reward, to the description of the reaction to the reward? At first glance it would seem that vv. 13-15 (If you carefully obey...) constitute the description of the reward, while the end of v. 15 ("you will eat and be satisfied") warns of to what the reward may lead.

However, Rav Shimon, perhaps draws the line in a different place. It would seem that according to Rebbi Shimon, the description of the reward ends in the middle of v. 14, with the words "I will grant you the rains of your land on time, the early rain and the late rain." The continuation of that verse—"and you will gather in your grain, your wine and your oil"—is already the beginning of the objectionable reaction to the blessings of prosperity. If you will react to the blessings of Hashem by "gathering in your own grain,"—devoting more and more time to cultivating your abundant grains, rather than putting your trust in Hashem—and by "eating and becoming satisfied," then you must beware lest you completely rebel against Hashem!

If so, it is true that the section is dealing with the reward for those who *follow* the mitzvos of Hashem. Nevertheless, the verse that discusses "gathering in your grain" is not describing a positive deed. It is describing the *negative* reaction that may follow Hashem's bountiful blessings.

IV

Bearing this in mind, we can also gain a deeper insight into Rebbi Shimon bar Yochai's opinion.

The pitfalls of the working man

Why does Rebbi Shimon has such an unfavorable attitude towards earning a living? On the surface, it appears that his concern is that one should not spend valuable time that could be used constructively—i.e., in spiritual pursuits—in a "wasteful" way, on mere mundane matters. This would seem to be a rather extreme way of looking at life. If a person toils to earn a living with a positive, "healthy" attitude—i.e., that his money may be used to foster observance of the commandments and allow the peace of mind necessary for Torah study and closeness to Hashem, etc.—why should it be looked at as regretful? Isn't this kind of exertion also fulfilling a mitzvah of Hashem?

According to the theme developed above, however, there may be another reason behind Rebbi Shimon's somber view on working for one's living. The more time and effort one invests in making money, the more one will be tempted to take credit for one's successes. "[Beware,] lest you eat and become satisfied and build elegant houses and live in them...and your heart will become arrogant and you will forget Hashem...saying to yourself, 'It is my *own strength and the power of my hand* that have earned me this wealth' " (Devarim 8:12,14,17). If one, on the other hand, trusts totally in Hashem, completely refraining from any personal input into his earnings, this pitfall is obviously avoided. It will be unquestionable that all that he has received is simply a gift from Hashem. This may be one of the reasons behind Rebbi Shimon's assertion that the truest believers are justified in devoting all of their time to learning Torah, and letting Hashem provide for them.

There is also a difficulty in the wording of Rebbi Shimon's statement which may now be resolved. Rebbi Shimon, after telling us that it is of people who are not truly God-fearing that the Torah states "you will gather in your grain," continues and carries the thought one step further: "And that is not all—they will even be forced to do the labors of others, as it says, 'You will work for your enemies' (ibid. 28:48)." This statement seems to be irrelevant to his basic theme—that it is not Hashem's will that people should attend to their *own* livelihoods. It seems to be simply a description of an additional punishment meted out to those who do not follow Hashem's will. (See *Chidushei Gaonim* on the *Ein Yaakov* and others, who are bothered by this point.)

We can now propose an explanation for what Rebbi Shimon meant by adding this phrase. The words "And that is not all" imply a progressive deterioration. The wrongdoing won't stop with "gathering in their grain." The wrongdoing will worsen, until eventually the sinners will have to be punished by being slaves for others. Rebbi Shimon may have meant to emphasize exactly what we have just pointed out above. Why should "gathering in one's crops" be so frowned upon? Not necessarily because it is so terrible in and of itself, but rather because of its possible consequences. It may cause a person to become arrogant and leave the path of his Creator. He will eventually be punished "measure for measure" by being condemned to destitution and slavery, depending on others for his every need.

Secondly, by pointing out this imminent progression, Rebbi Shimon may be explaining how he understands the flow of verses in our Parsha. As we asked in section I, how can Rebbi Shimon explain that those who gather their crops are non-believers, when the paragraph is introduced with the statement, "If you carefully obey my commandments that I command you today?"

The answer, explains Rebbi Shimon, is as we have outlined above. "Gathering the crops" is *not* Hashem's blessing—it is a *reaction* to that blessing. The Torah is warning us that if we respond to Hashem's blessing by letting ourselves take credit for our successes, (cultivating and gathering in our grain), it may set off a progressive deterioration. This is why the Torah finds it necessary to immediately warn us, "Beware lest your heart become tempted and you go astray and worship other gods..."—don't cause Hashem to enslave you to others!

Rebbi Shimon's addition of the phrase "And that is not all..." thus reveals to us another rationale for his radical philosophy as well as shedding light on his reading of the verse at hand. Trusting in one's own physical prowess for earning a living may lead to arrogant smugness, and ultimately to apostasy, exile and slavery.

May we all merit to preoccupy ourselves with Torah and the fear of G-d, so that Hashem may fulfill for us the verse "Foreigners will come and tend to your flocks!"

PARSHAS RE'EH

Tzedakah [Charity]—The Surest Protection

Be careful to tithe (*"Asser Te'asser"*—lit., "Tithe, you shall tithe") all the produce of your seeds that comes out of the field every year (Devarim 14:22).

The Gemara (Taanis 9a) examines this verse: Rav Yochanan said: What is meant by the double expression "Tithe you shall tithe"? It should be read as "Tithe (*Asser*) so that you will become rich (*tisasher*)..."

R. Yochanan's nephew asked him, "How do you know that tithing makes one rich?" He replied, "Go and try it, and you will see for yourself!" "But," the nephew protested, "is one permitted to put Hashem to a test?" R. Yochanan answered, "I have a tradition from R. Hoshayah that in this one case it is permitted to test Hashem, as it says (Malachi 3:10), 'Bring all your tithes to the storage house, and test me by this—see if I do not open up the windows of the heavens and pour out upon you endless blessings!' " (Taanis 9a).

Rav Yochanan, based on two verses in the Scriptures, asserts that proper tithing bears with it the promise of monetary success. The verse in our Parsha in which this concept is alluded to is specifically referring to the *obligational* tithing of *agricultural* produce that was grown in Israel (see Shabbos 119a). Nevertheless, in various places the Sages reaffirm this promise of wealth as a dividend of any type of charity or gift to the poor. A person who gives charity, is guaranteed to be repaid even more than the amount he gave (see Tosafos ad loc.).

Tithe that you may tithe yet again

What is it that prompted R. Yochanan to interpret the phrase *"asser te'asser"* in a way which necessitates changing the letter *sin* into a letter *shin*? Is he really suggesting to change the Massoretic reading of the verse? Usually such emendations, even when purely homiletical in nature, are suggested by some compelling textual inference (see Ki Setzei essay, p.251).

Rabbeinu Chananel (in his commentary to the Talmud, loc. cit.) explains the logic behind Rav Yochanan's reading. Rav Yochanan did not derive his idea that "charity enriches" by changing the diacritical markings into *tisasher*. Rather, he is bothered by the double expression of "*asser te'asser*" (lit., "tithe, you shall tithe"). In explanation, Rav Yochanan suggests that the extra word was meant to imply that one who tithes his produce will be rewarded with the opportunity to give additional tithes—i.e., he will be blessed with increased prosperity. (Such interpretations of double verbs are not uncommon—see Rashi on Parshas Eikev—Devarim 11:13—and Bava Metzia 32a.) Rav Yochanan expressed this idea by transposing the characters of the verse with other, similar ones, producing the pun "Tithe so that you will *tisasher* [become rich]." He did not *derive* the thought, though, through that transposition.

II

In any case, the concept that giving charity makes one more wealthy can be used to explain a passage from the Gemara: "The word 'sowing' in Scriptures can sometimes be understood to mean 'giving charity'" (Bava Kama 17a, based on Hoshea 10:12).

Give charity, and you will become wealthy

What is the connection between sowing and charity that could suggest an interchanging of meaning between the two words? Perhaps in both cases a small amount of one's possessions is ostensibly "thrown away" and "wasted," only to produce an eventual yield of many more times the original outlay.

The theme that giving charity is represented by the word "sowing" is found elsewhere in the words of Chazal. In Bereishis 26:12 we read: "Yitzchak sowed in the land of the Philistines and he received that year [a yield of] one hundred times, for Hashem blessed him." The tract of land that Yitzchak cultivated was estimated to be able to produce "x" bushels of grain, and instead it produced "100x." But why did Yitzchak assess the expected yield of the field in the first place? Rashi (quoting Midrash Rabbah) explains that this was done in order to establish the amount of tithe necessary for that produce. Another Midrash elaborates on this theme:

Why did "Yitzchak sow"—by himself? [Didn't he have servants who could have done this labor for him, as stated in the following verse?] The verse should be understood as follows: Yitzchak "sowed" the *produce* of his fields, by tithing it and giving charity to the poor! (Pirkei d'Rabbi Eliezer, beginning of chap. 33)

According to this Midrash, the second half of the verse—"he obtained a yield of one hundred times"—corroborates Rav Yochanan's thesis. Yitzchak's charity was rewarded in kind by Hashem, with increased prosperity and bounty. His "spiritual" sowing was the cause of his unusual success.

This is also the meaning of a verse in Hoshea (10:12), which says, "Sow for yourselves tzedakah, and you will reap [Hashem's] kindness." This verse is another reaffirmation of Rav Yochanan's theme: "Sow charity by giving to others, and *you* will receive charity from Hashem in return."

A beautiful allusion to this idea is suggested by the famous Kabbalist, Rav Menachem Azarya of Pano (*Ma'amar Chikkur Din*, part 3, chap. 20). In Shabbos 104a the Gemara uses a code system known as *at-bash*, whereby each letter, according to its order in the alphabet, is interchanged with the letter in the corresponding place starting from the other side of the alphabet. Thus the first letter (*alef*) becomes the last (*taf*), *beis* becomes *shin*, etc. The tradition of the Sages tells us that secrets of the Torah and the Hebrew language can sometimes be brought to light by transposing letters according to the *at-bash* system.

Rav Menachem Azarya (The Rama, for short) of Pano points out that the word "tzedakah"—*tzadi, daled, kuf, heh*—when transposed into its *at-bash* equivalent comes out to be—tzedakah—spelled backwards—*heh, kuf, daled, tzadi*! This may be meant to demonstrate that any charity a person gives is bound to return to him in the opposite direction, as "charity" from Hashem!

III

Tosafos (Taanis 9a), however, seems to suggest a different approach to what it was that prompted Rav Yochanan to suggest his interpretation of the verse (as we quoted in section I). According to Tosafos, the key word in the verse is "*all* the produce of your seeds." Tosafos, it seems, read the verse as follows: "If you give your tithes you will be able to tithe *all* of your produce the *following year*." Your fields will not produce less in the future than they produced in the past. The implication of this reading is that in order to *remain* rich, you must take care to tithe properly. Tosafos (ibid.), in fact, quotes Midrashim to the effect that a person who does *not* tithe his produce, will end up producing only "that which comes out of the field every year" in tithes—that is, he will collect a yield of only ten percent of what the field used to produce. (Note: My reading of Tosafos is far from explicit in his words. It's my own interpretation of Tosafos' implicit intent.—MK)

Give charity, and Hashem will safeguard your wealth

This theme—that giving charity will increase a person's wealth, and withholding charity will cause the *loss* of wealth, is mentioned a number of times in the words of Chazal.

In Kesubos 66b a popular saying of the people of Jerusalem is recorded:

"The way to 'salt' (preserve) money is to diminish it (give charity)."

In Beitzah 15b the Gemara says, "Rav Yochanan...said: If someone wants to ensure that his property will remain his, let him plant an *adar* (lit., a type of cedar tree). What is an *adar*? As it says: 'Hashem is mighty (*addir*) on high'" (Tehillim 93:4).

Rabbeinu Chananel explains that the Gemara is interpreting Rav Yochanan's use of the word *adar* as a pun. He didn't mean that we should plant cedars, but that we should "plant" our money with the Mighty One on high (*addir*). Giving charity is like depositing your money in a celestial bank, where it is safe from worldly burglars or accidents. It is considered as if one has given his money to the Mighty One on high for safekeeping, as it says, "Charity (*tzedek*) peers out from the heavens" (Tehillim 85:12, see also Bava Basra 10a).

IV

Beyond granting monetary success and protecting one's possessions, giving tzedakah protects one's life.

Give charity, and Hashem will protect you

In Mishlei (10:2; 11:4) we read, "Tzedakah saves from death." The Gemara (Bava Basra 10a) explains that tzedakah saves a person from two kinds of death: from "death" (i.e., non-participation) in the World-to-Come, and from dying an unnatural death. In Shabbos 156b the Gemara extends the power of tzedakah to preventing (that is, postponing) death altogether. (See the Gemara in Shabbos ibid., which records some true stories illustrating this fact.)

It is for this reason that the Gemara (Rosh Hashanah 16b) tells us that before Rosh Hashanah a person should give charity. Charity, the Gemara tells us, is one of the three things that have the power to change an evil heavenly decree concerning a person's fate. Even if it has been decreed that a person is to pass away during the coming year, giving charity may change this decree and extend one's life.

Perhaps this is what the Gemara means when it says, "If a fast day is declared and tzedakah is not given on that very day, it is as if innocent blood had been shed" (Sanhedrin 35a). Why should withholding of charity be compared to bloodshed (see Rashi ad loc.)? According to what we have said, we may suggest the following explanation. A fast day called for by the prevailing rabbinic authorities is usually declared in the face of a current or imminent disaster. If a catastrophic heavenly decree is indeed in store for the people fasting, then by *not* giving tzedakah to prolong their own lives, it is as if they have shed blood—their own blood.

In Bava Basra 10a we learn that Rav Elazar used to set aside a small amount of money for charity before his prayers. The explanation for this practice is perhaps also based on this same theme. One asks one's Creator for health and long years to use for the service of Hashem when one prays. In order for these prayers to be effective, one must complement them with the life-giving effects of tzedakah.

V

We know that when Hashem grants a person a reward or punishment He does it according to the principle of *middah keneged middah*—i.e., there is always some sort of correspondence between the deed done and the recompense given (Sanhedrin 90a; see Tishah b'Av essay p. 217). There is an obvious connection between giving tzedakah and obtaining wealth—both have to do with the transferal of money. But what is the relationship between lengthening one's expected lifetime and giving charity?

Measure for measure in the reward for giving charity

Perhaps the answer to this is, as the Gemara says:

"Poverty is comparable to death itself, as it says (Shemos 4:19), 'The people who had sought your life are now dead.' We know that they were still alive, and only lost their power and influence. This indicates that one who has lost his money is considered as dead" (Nedarim 7b).

If losing one's money is tantamount (in some sense) to death, then it follows that giving a poor person money is tantamount to granting him life. Now we can understand that an appropriate reward for tzedakah is the lengthening of the giver's life in return!

This thought is actually expressed almost explicitly in the Midrash:

"Charity saves from death." This shows that a person is granted reward in accordance with his good deeds. By giving tzedakah, a person is resolved that the poor man should live and not die. Therefore Hashem sees to it that the benefactor should also live and not die (*Tana Devei Eliyahu Zuta,* ch. 1).

If so, perhaps we may extend this train of thought to lend new support to Rav Yochanan's derivation from the verse in our Parsha. Charity saves from "death," not only by adding years to the giver's life, but also by ensuring that a person's wealth will remain with him, thereby protecting him from the "death" of suffering poverty!

Let us see to it that we take care to tithe our income regularly, in order that we may preserve both our money and ourselves!

PARSHAS SHOFTIM

Absolved Through Murder

"If a dishonest witness gets up to testify falsely about a man...And the judges investigate thoroughly and discover that the witness is a false witness...then you shall do to him just as he had planned to do to his fellow, and you shall eliminate the evil from Israel" (Devarim 19:16-19).

The Torah prescribes an appropriate punishment for perjurers—they must be dealt the same fate that they had plotted against their intended victim. If their testimony would have led to the defendant's execution or to his being flogged, they themselves must be put to death or flogged. If they tried to frame the defendant into being charged money by the court, then they must pay that amount of money (to the defendant).

However, how is it possible to *prove* that a witness is testifying falsely? The testimony of two or more witnesses is considered to be the most authoritative evidence in Jewish jurisprudence. There is no stronger proof required for any question of law—not the testimony of three witnesses or even that of a thousand witnesses. Whenever there is a contradiction between sets of witnesses, both sets are disregarded. Neither group has the power to positively disqualify the testimony of the opposing witnesses, against whom their word stands.

How can witnesses be falsified?

Of course, if the judges themselves have some information which impugns the testimony of the witnesses, it is they who would realize that the witnesses have lied. This cannot be the case in the above verses, however, because the Torah says that the judges discovered the ploy by "investigating it thoroughly," implying that they were not acting on the basis of some previous knowledge that they had.

Self-incrimination on the part of the witnesses is also not a possibility, as under Jewish law one cannot recant one's testimony. A witness is not able to falsify his own testimony. Testimony that has been accepted by the court does *not* lose credence if the witnesses "back out." Instead, we just assume that the witnesses got "cold feet".

The Gemara (Makkos 5a) explains, on the basis of textual inference, that the Torah is indicating here that there is a way for a pair of witnesses to disqualify the testimony of a previous pair, proving them to be liars. This unique situation is to be found when a set of witnesses testify to the fact that the previous witnesses *could not have been present* at the scene of the supposed crime or incident at the time it was committed—because the two sets were actually *together* in an entirely *different* location at that very moment! It is only in this instance that the Torah prescribes its punishment of "tit for tat" to the first set of witnesses.

II

If they killed, they are absolved

Rashi points out on Devarim 19:19 (based on Makkos 5b, where the rule is derived from textual inference) that the prescribed punishment is meted out to the perjurers only when their attempted plot ended in failure. If they had succeeded in having the defendant executed by the court, however, they are no longer liable to that punishment. Instead, they are absolved from *all* punishment! As the gemara puts it, "If they killed, they are not killed."

This rule seems to be an enigma. If the Torah prescribes punishment for perjury when an *attempt* was made to incriminate someone, why should it exempt the perjurer when *actual* harm is done? The Gemara itself admits that this rule seems to run counter to logic, but the rule stands nonetheless, as it is derived exegetically from the Torah's words.

Over the ages commentators have tried to offer a rationale for this odd rule. Let us investigate some of the more intriguing of these suggested explanations.

III

The Ramban (to Devarim 19:19) proposes the following reasoning:

1. Ramban: Hashem's will has been carried out

Any God-fearing person knows that Hashem does not allow harm to befall someone unless that person somehow deserves that misfortune. If a person is framed by false witnesses and this is proven before any harm befalls him, Hashem has apparently decreed that the defendant is not deserving of the punishment in question. If, however, the evidence absolving the defendant was not brought to the fore until *after* he had already met his punishment, it is apparent that Hashem in His wisdom has decreed that this person was deserving of this particular punishment—even if he was innocent of the particular charge for which he was convicted. Since the punishment was presumed deserved in any event, the witnesses who brought this punishment are *not* held accountable for their deed, as evil as their deed may have been.

There seems to be a basic flaw to this reasoning, however. The Gemara (Berachos 7b) tells us that sometimes a wicked person is granted success and good fortune, and that in such times even the righteous may suffer at their hands—as our everyday experience suggests. Should these criminals be absolved on the grounds that all evil is preordained anyway?

Ramban adds the following point to perhaps address this question: It is specifically in this case that this line of reasoning is valid. Here, the punishment is not delivered directly by the wicked person, but through the agency of a divinely ordained court of law—"Hashem Himself stands in the courtrooms of the congregation of God" (Tehillim 82:1). In such a situation we may say that whatever punishment is administered by the *court* indeed represents the Hashem's will.

Rabbeinu Bachye raises an objection to the Ramban's reasoning. Even if the defendant, executed under false pretenses, is regarded as having deserved this punishment for some Divinely dictated reason, those who brought about his execution should nonetheless be culpable for their evil actions. They still testified falsely, violating in the process numerous biblical commandments! Perjury, when committed against a man who happens to be a murderer, *is* still perjury, and should be punished as such.

The Chinuch's addition: Killing a dead man

(The Mishnah—Makkos 6b—tells us, in fact, that even if the defendant's culpability is established on the basis of other, unrefuted testimony, witnesses who testified falsely against him are punished with the full severity of the law! See also Rambam's principle about the punishment of the Egyptian tormentors, in Hilchos Teshuvah 6:5; Nero's apprehension in Gittin 56a.—MK)

How, then, can the Ramban attempt to explain the absolution of a false witness on the grounds that the defendant "had it coming to him anyway"?

The *Sefer haChinuch* suggests an answer to Rabbeinu Bachye's question. In the Gemara (Erchin 6a) there is a rule stating that after a person has been sentenced to death in court, in a certain sense he is no longer considered to be a living human being. The Gemara tells us that if someone would murder this individual he would *not* be subject to capital punishment. It is considered as if he had murdered an already dead man. With this in mind, the *Chinuch* deals with Rabbeinu Bachye's question. When a man is executed due to the spurious testimony of a set of false witnesses, it is obvious that Hashem had been using those witnesses as a means of carrying out a Divine death sentence. In such a situation, it is considered (retroactively) as if Hashem had already pronounced a death sentence on the defendant when the perjurers presented their testimony in court. It is, therefore, a "dead man" who they have executed. Thus, witnesses cannot be punished for causing this execution to take place.

This explanation, however, is also problematic. It accounts only for the absolution from punishment of witnesses who brought about a man's *execution* through false testimony. It does not explain cases which do not involve capital offenses, such as if a defendant is sentenced not to death but to flogging, or to monetary payment, because of false testimony. Why should the perjurers be exempted in cases where they succeeded in only flogging or causing monetary loss to the defendant?

In fact, there is indeed an opinion that the rule of "If they killed, they are not killed" applies *only* to capital cases. If flogging or money is involved rather than execution, however, there is no absolution from punishment when the defendant's sentence had been carried out (Rambam, Edus 20:2). The *Chinuch* may, then, be presenting a logical basis for those that maintain this opinion. However, it must be noted that this opinion is rejected by nearly all the other commentators. (As for the Ramban, there may be an entirely different reading in his words that avoids Rabbeinu Bachye's objection. However, we cannot here deal with this possibility.)

V

2. Maharal: A punishment reflected

The Maharal (16th cent. Prague) suggests a different explanation (Gur Aryeh 19:19). Writing in typically cryptic terminology, he compares the testimony of the false witnesses to a ball. When the ball is in motion, it will rebound from a wall with the same force with which it was thrown against it. If the ball is at rest, however, it does not move at all. In other words, as long as the judicial process is in progress, the punishment can be deflected from the defendant onto the witnesses. Once the process has come to an end, through the carrying out of the defendant's sentence, however, the punishment is no longer existent. It can no longer be deflected from the defendant to the witnesses, the Maharal says.

Although this is an interesting parallel, the Maharal's explanation still needs elaboration. Why must a punishment be "deflected," in order for it to be inflicted on the witnesses? After all, there are many other punishments prescribed by the Torah, none of which involve a similar "rebounding." Perhaps the words of the Maharal may be understood along the following lines.

There are two different rationales for why Hashem would prescribe a punishment for sin in His Torah. One reason would be for the benefit of the offender himself—to "serve notice" to him that he has embarked on a sinful path, and that he should mend his ways, much as a father hits a child to teach a lesson for the child's benefit. Another reason for punishment is to discourage *others* from following the sinner's example, similar to a teacher who sometimes "makes an example" of one student in order to make an impression on the entire class.

The first rationale would seem more acceptable, since the one who is punished is himself the one who benefits from the punishment. This, then, ought to be the reasoning behind most of the punishments of the Torah. The second category, if anything, should be reserved for specific sins which could wreak havoc on society at large, if they are not kept in check. In such instances, it may be justified to take the drastic measure of making the sinner suffer simply to prevent *others* from following in his evil ways.

There is a rule (Makkos 2b) that the Torah administers no punishment for a sin that does not involve a physical action. If a transgression is committed through a person's inaction (such as not ridding his house of chametz before Pesach) or through his thoughts or speech, he is not punished by the court. The reason is that a person who allows his body to perform a forbidden physical act, can become accustomed—even, in a way, "addicted"—to such behavior. He is, therefore, in need of a physical punishment to prompt him to change his mode of behavior, and prod him back onto the path of life. A sin that does not involve a physical act, however, does not require such a drastic measure, since the sinner's body has not become "accustomed" to sinning. It is still easy enough for the sinner to stop in his tracks and sin no more.

The sin of perjury is a non-physical act (because "speaking words does not constitute an action"—see Makkos 4b, Sanhedrin 65b). Hence, a punishment of the first sort discussed above is not appropriate. Physical punishment is not necessary to enable one to change his ways. (The Maharal himself clarifies this point about the punishment of false witnesses in B*e'er HaGolah* ch. 2.)

If a physical punishment for perjury is nevertheless prescribed, it must be in order to illustrate to *others* that crime does not pay. When the reason for punishment is to discourage *others* from following the sinner's ways, we must not look upon how the sin affected the offender, but at the harm the sinner has caused to society. The fact that no physical action was involved may affect the level of sin for the individual sinner, but it does not mitigate the effect that this sin had on the unfortunate defendant.

This point, that the punishment the Torah prescribes for perjurers is intended to teach a lesson to society at large—as opposed to the sinner himself—is borne out by the Torah itself. After delineating the measure-for-measure punishment for perjurers, the Torah concludes, "You shall eliminate the evil from Israel, and those who remain will hear and be afraid, and will refrain from doing such a thing in your midst ever again" (19:19-20). This verse clearly indicates that the punishment of the false witnesses belongs to the second category of punishment, as we have proven above.

We have established that the entire point of the punishment of false witnesses is to make a demonstrative statement to others that "crime does not pay." Engaging in evil schemes risks that the schemes backfire on the schemer. "He who digs a trap will fall in it" (Mishlei 26:27). This lesson can only be taught when the plan that the witnesses intended in order to frame someone can be turned around ("rebound") and backfires on the witnesses themselves.

When the witnesses succeed in their evil plan, however, this lesson cannot be shown by punishing them. Rather than showing the futility of perjury, their punishment will publicize that perjurers have succeeded in doing harm. Even if the court were to mete out another punishment in return for the false witnesses' evil act, this would not undo the wrong that has been done. It will show others that the court *avenges* injustice—not that an evil plot is liable to *backfire.* Since revenge is itself inherently unjust, we will be adding wrongdoing to what has already been done wrong. People are liable to react saying, "Look, the court too takes revenge!" This will not accomplish our goal— that of teaching others that evil plans will not prevail. The harm that has been done cannot be corrected.

It is, perhaps, for this reason that the Torah limits its punishment of perjurers to situations where the punishment of the defendant has not yet been executed.

PARSHAS KI SETZEI

King Solomon's Wisdom

If there are brothers, and one of them dies without children, the wife of the deceased man may not marry "out," to another man. Her brother-in-law (that is, her *levir*, or husband's brother) must marry her and thus perform *yibbum* on her.... If the man does not want to marry her, she shall approach the elders and declare, "My brother-in-law refuses to establish his brother's name in Israel; he does not consent to perform *yibbum* on me".... Then she shall approach him in the presence of the elders and remove his shoe from his foot, and spit in front of him, and proclaim, "Such should be done to a man who would not build up his brother's house!" (Devarim 25:5,7,9)

What is yibbum?

The Torah describes in this week's Parsha the practice of *yibbum*, a rite which must be performed when a man who has a living brother dies childless. If this relatively uncommon situation occurs, the widow may not remarry unless one of two actions is taken—either she must marry the brother of the deceased, or she must be released from the obligation of marrying her brother-in-law by having him perform the *chalitzah* ["removing" of the shoe] ceremony. The details of *yibbum* are quite complex. An entire Tractate of the Talmud (Yevamos) deals at length with its various intricacies.

It is obviously uncomfortable for a woman to be "trapped" in this situation, under which she is subject to the will of another man. Her brother-in-law may not be locatable or compliant. Hence it was (and is) a common practice for a man who has no children (but has a live brother) to arrange a divorce for his wife, if he fears that he may die imminently. A woman who is divorced before her husband dies, is *not* required to practice *yibbum*.

In an interesting twist, the laws of *yibbum* may be used to provide the key to understanding a completely unrelated incident recounted in the Tanach—the story of the decision of King Shlomo [Solomon] regarding the infant.

II

Solomon's judgment

In the beginning of the book of Melachim (Kings), we read that when Shlomo was age twelve Hashem promised him that He would grant him great wisdom—he was to be the wisest man ever to live (Melachim I 3:12). As an illustration of the fulfillment of this blessing of immeasurable wisdom, the Tanach relates the following account of a case that was brought before Shlomo, and his wise judgment of the case:

Two women came to the King and stood before him. One woman said, "My lord: This woman and I dwell in the same house, and I gave birth while with her in the house. On the third day after I gave birth, this woman also gave birth. We live together; there is no outsider with us in the house; only the two of us were there. The son of this woman died that night, because she lay upon him. She arose during the night and took my son from my side while I was asleep, and laid him in her bosom, and her dead son she laid in my bosom. When I got up in the morning to nurse my son, behold, he was dead! But when I observed him (later on) in the morning, I realized that he was not the son to whom I had given birth!"

The other woman replied, "It is not so! My son is the live one, and your son is the dead one." But this one said, "It is not so! Your son is the dead one, and my son is the live one!" And they went on arguing before the King.

The King said, "This one claims, 'My son is the live one, and your son is the dead one,' and this one claims, 'It is not so! Your son is the dead one, and my son is the living one.' " So the King said, "Get me a sword!" and they brought a sword before the King. The King said, "Cut the living child in two and give half to one and half to the other."

The woman whose son was the live one turned to the King, because her compassion was aroused for her son, and she said, "Please, my lord, give her the living baby, and do not kill it!" But the other one said, "Neither mine nor yours shall he be. Cut!" The King spoke up and said, "Give her [the first one] the living baby and do not kill it; she is his mother!" (I Melachim 3:16-27)

Upon reading about this incident the reader is struck by an odd development in the story. The woman who was lying was obviously interested in taking the child for herself—otherwise the case would never have been brought before the court. But when the real mother offered to let the liar keep the child in order to spare its life, she refused, saying, "Neither mine nor yours shall he be. Cut!" What made her suddenly lose interest in having the child for herself? Furthermore, although it may be granted that Solomon's wisdom gave him the insight to foresee that one of the women would recoil when she heard of his intention to kill the infant, nevertheless, how could he possibly have predicted that the other woman would react the way she did—by insisting on complying with the grotesque "compromise?" Surely it was more likely the second woman would respond, "Yes, I am glad you have finally admitted that the child is mine. I see that although you are cruel enough to steal my child you are not ruthless enough to see him killed for your lie!" Then what would he have done?

A brilliant and original answer to these questions is offered by two 13th century commentators: Rav Yehoshua Ibn Shu'ib in his Drasha for Parshas Mishpatim, and Rav Menachem haMeiri in his commentary to Yevamos 17a. (Another Torah sage, the author of *Shemen Rokeach* and *Sha'ar Hachazakos*, arrived at the same explanation independently several centuries later.)

In order to understand their answer, an introduction summarizing several of the details of the laws of *yibbum* is called for.

III

Some of the laws of yibbum

(1) *Yibbum*, as mentioned above, is only applicable when a man dies childless. "Dying childless" includes cases where a man once had children, but these children were already dead at the time of his own death (Yevamos 87b).

(2) If the deceased man has no living children but he does have living *grandchildren*, he is not considered to be "childless." Therefore, there is no *yibbum* (ibid. 70a).

(3) The widow is only obligated to marry her husband's *brother*. If the deceased husband does not leave behind a living brother, his wife is free to marry whoever she pleases (ibid. 17b).

(4) If the deceased left behind any offspring at all, there is no *yibbum*—even if the offspring is only one day old. Not only that, but even if the offspring is still a fetus at the time of the husband's death, its mother is exempted from being bound to the living brother. This is only true, however, when the offspring is viable. If the fetus is aborted or stillborn, or even if it is born alive but dies or is killed before it has lived for thirty days, it is not considered to have ever been a viable offspring. *Yibbum* is therefore required (ibid. 111b; Shabbos 136a).

(5) If the brother of the deceased is a minor, the widow is still bound to him. In this case, however, she does not have the option of freeing herself through the *chalitzah* ceremony, since a minor is not able to perform a *chalitzah*. Instead, she must wait until the brother is thirteen years old, in order for him to be able to perform a *chalitzah*. Only then may she remarry (Yevamos 105b). (Even if she wants to marry this minor, and have him perform *yibbum*, she must wait at least until he is 9 years old—Niddah 45a.)

IV

Let us now return to Shlomo's judgment.

The Midrash (Koheles Rabbah 10:16) tells us that the reason both of these women were so desperate to have the living child declared theirs was that they were both potential *yevamos* [widows subject to *yibbum*; singular form is *yevamah*]. Neither of the two had any other offspring.' Whoever would be judged to be the childless woman would not only lose the infant, but would also be trapped in the unpleasant status of *yevamah*, being dependent upon her brother-in-law's good will.

The wily yevamah

There is another Midrash (Yalkut Shimoni 2:175), that asserts that the husbands of the two women were father and son. That is, one woman was the mother-in-law of the other.

The above commentators suggest that these two Midrashim may be complementing each other. The two women—the mother-in-law and the daughter-in-law—had just been bereaved of their husbands, and needed a live child to exempt them from the status of *yevamah*. Both gave birth to babies. However, these two babies were still less than thirty days old at the time that one of them died, as the verse indicates. The mother of the dead child would therefore be subject to the laws of *yibbum* (rule #4). This, then, was the lying mother's motivation for taking the other woman's child.

Now, if it were the mother-in-law's child who had died, she would have no reason to try to seize her daughter-in-law's child. Even though her son (husband of the daughter-in-law) had passed away *before* her husband had, and therefore *he* would not exempt her from *yibbum* (rule #1), nevertheless, she would be exempt from *yibbum* for another reason. The living child, if he was not her own child, was at least her *son's* child, and a grandchild is enough to exempt one from *yibbum* (rule #2)!

Only the daughter-in-law would have a motive to lie and try to claim (falsely) that the child was hers. If it was her baby who had died within 30 days of its birth, leaving her childless, she would indeed be bound to her husband's brother as a *yevamah* (rule #4). And who would that brother be? None other than the living baby, who was in fact her mother-in-law's child —i.e., her deceased husband's brother! Since her brother-in-law was a newborn, the daughter-in-law would have to wait thirteen years before this baby would be able to perform *chalitzah* on her and free her to marry others (rule #5)! (This baby was the only living brother of her husband. There could not have been any other, older brothers, because, as the Midrash points out, the mother-in-law was herself a potential *yevamah*. This means that she had no living children except for the baby in question.)

The youthful King Shlomo, in his wisdom, realized all of this. He suspected that since the only one with a strong motive to lie was the daughter-in-law, the child must really belong to the mother-in-law. In order to confirm this conclusion he ordered that the child be cut in half. What would that accomplish?

If the remaining child were to be killed, this too would free the daughter-in-law from her *yevamah* status—since the living baby was her only brother-in-law (rule #3). From the daughter-in-law's perspective, in fact, killing the child would be an even "better" solution. By just kidnapping the child she might convince the court that she was not a *yevamah*. However, she herself would know that the child was not really hers, and that she really was not permitted to remarry, halachically speaking, until *chalitzah* was performed. By having the baby killed, though, she would truthfully be released from the bonds of *yibbum*! This is the reason the daughter-in-law suddenly lost interest in keeping the child when she saw that Shlomo was ready to cut the child in half. This would serve her interests even more than if she took the child for herself. "Cut!" she insisted.

Shlomo had guessed that this would be the woman's reaction. By tricking her into making such a seemingly ludicrous statement, he revealed her true motives. In this manner, Shlomo demonstrated beyond doubt that the daughter-in-law was indeed lying!

PARSHAS KI SAVO

The Al Hamichyah Blessing

"You shall take the first of all fruit that is produced by your land...put it in a basket (*teneh*), and go to the place where Hashem will choose to have His Name dwell [i.e., the Beis Hamikdash]. You shall come to the Kohen who is serving there at the time and say to him, "I declare thanks on this day before Hashem, your God, for bringing me to the land that Hashem swore to...give us." Then the Kohen shall take the basket from your hand and put it down before the altar of Hashem, your God" (Devarim 26:2-4).

"How does one designate his *bikkurim*? He goes into his field, and when he sees a cluster of grapes or a pomegranate that is beginning to grow, he ties a string around it, and declares, 'These are hereby *bikkurim*!' " (Bikkurim 3:1)

Differences between the blessings of Al Hamichyah and Birkas Hamazon

The mitzvah of *bikkurim* consists of yearly bringing the first fruits from one's field to the Kohen in the Beis Hamikdash. The Kohen places these fruits at the southeastern corner of the altar's base (Mishnah Bikkurim 2:3). The owner then recites a specified declaration (verses 26:3,5-10), and the fruits are then given to the Kohen (Bikkurim 3:8; 2:11). The mitzvah of *bikkurim* applies only to the seven species for which Eretz Yisrael was praised (in Devarim 8:8)—wheat, barley, grapes, figs, pomegranates, olives and dates (Bikkurim 3:6).

(Although many other types of produce are now grown in Eretz Yisrael, these are the *only* species of produce truly indigenous to Israel. Other, "immigrant," species can be destroyed by drought or harsh weather, but these seven species will always be part of the land—a leading botanist has told me.—MK)

A look into the mitzvah of *bikkurim* may shed light on a puzzling choice of words in the blessings we recite after eating. After bread is eaten, the *Birkas Hamazon* grace, which consists of four blessings, is recited.

After eating food prepared from any of the seven species for which Israel was praised (enumerated above), an abridged version of this grace consisting of one blessing is recite, commonly known as *Al Hamichyah*.

We would expect that, since it is an abbreviated version of *Birkas Hamazon*, *Al Hamichyah* would include only ideas contained in *Birkas Hamazon* without new additions. Upon examination, however, we see that there are some added phrases found in the *Al Hamichyah* blessing that are not found in the "parent" blessings of *Birkas Hamazon*.

First, in *Birkas Hamazon* we pray for the restoration of "Jerusalem and Zion." In *Al Hamichyah* we pray for the restoration of these and *also* for the restoration of "Your altar and Your Temple (*mizbechecha*)." Also in *Al Hamichyah* and not found in *Birkas Hamazon* is the prayer that He may once again "bring us to [Jerusalem] and cause us to rejoice in its rebuilding...that we may praise You for [Eretz Yisrael] in holiness and purity." What is the nature of these two additions, and why were they included in the shorter *Al Hamichyah*, yet omitted from the longer, more inclusive, *Birkas Hamazon*?

I heard an answer to this question, given by the Brisker Rav (haRav Yitzchak Zev Soloveitchik, d. 1962), which I would like to present here (with a few embellishments of my own).

II

First of all, it should be noted that there is actually one other addition in the *Al Hamichyah* blessing not found in *Birkas Hamazon*. In *Al Hamichyah* we specify that Hashem gave us Eretz Yisrael so "that we may eat of its fruits, and be satiated by its bounty"—and we ask Hashem to return Eretz Yisrael to our hands for the same purpose. Why is our appreciation for Israel's fruits stressed in this particular blessing?

Al Hamichyah: Thanks for the seven species

The answer is obvious. *Birkas Hamazon* is recited after a meal consisting of *any* kind of food (provided it was eaten with bread). *Al Hamichyah*, however, was instituted to be recited only after partaking of one of the seven species of Israel. It is appropriate that we offer praise to Hashem that relates specifically to what we have just enjoyed (Berachos 40a). Therefore, after eating the fruits of Israel, we thank Hashem for giving us Israel with "its unique fruits and satiating bounty."

III

With this in mind, we can now answer our questions regarding the additions in the *Al Hamichyah* blessing. Why do we add a special prayer for the restoration of the *altar*? Perhaps it is because, aside from the enjoyment we derive from the seven fruits of the land, we also use these fruits to perform the mitzvah of bringing *bikkurim*, which must be chosen from the seven species (Bikkurim 3:6). The mitzvah of *bikkurim* entails placing the fruit-basket at the corner of the *altar*. Therefore, after partaking of these species we ask Hashem to:

Al Hamichyah: A prayer for the restoration of the mitzvah of bikkurim

(1) Return us to His land so that we may "eat again" of its special fruits, and (2) Rebuild "His altar," so that we may again bring those fruits as *bikkurim*!

A similar approach can explain the other addition found in *Al Hamichyah*. After eating any of the seven species, we ask Hashem to "bring us to Jerusalem," i.e., in order to fulfill the mitzvah of *bikkurim*. Bikkurim must be brought to Jerusalem and eaten there, as mentioned above in section I).

We also ask Hashem to "cause us to rejoice in its [Jerusalem's] rebuilding." What is meant by this? *Bikkurim* may only be eaten in Jerusalem when the city is rebuilt and its walls are restored (Bava Metzia 53b). When that condition is fulfilled, all the halachos of *bikkurim* apply. These halachos include bringing our *bikkurim* to Jerusalem, and "*rejoicing* in all the good that Hashem has given you" (Devarim 26:11). Therefore, in the *Al Hamichyah* blessing we pray that Hashem may cause us to *rejoice* (i.e., in the bringing of *bikkurim*) through the *rebuilding* of Jerusalem.

Next, we promise Hashem that upon the rebuilding of Jerusalem we will "praise You for [Eretz Yisrael] in holiness and purity." What does this statement mean, and what makes it specifically appropriate to the *Al Hamichyah* blessing? Perhaps here, too, we are imploring Hashem to allow us to bring Him *bikkurim* from the seven species of fruit whose after-blessing is *Al Hamichyah*. How is that?

When *bikkurim* were brought to the Kohen, its owner would say, "I declare thanks this day before Hashem, your God, for bringing me to the land that Hashem swore to...give us" (Devarim 26:3). Thus we use the *bikkurim* as a vehicle to thank Hashem for having given us Eretz Yisrael. This thanks is recited in the courtyard of the Beis Hamikdash—i.e., in an atmosphere of "holiness." "Purity" is also an appropriate adjective for the bringing of *bikkurim*, as entrance to the Temple grounds was permitted only to those who were ritually pure. Also, the *bikkurim* themselves (like *terumah*) must be kept in a state of ritual purity.

If so, the Brisker Rav explains, the terminology of the *Al Hamichyah* blessing is particularly apt. After partaking of the seven species, we implore Hashem to once again allow us to use these species for *bikkurim*, that we may praise Him for giving us the land that produces these fruits while in a state of holiness and purity!

(Heard from haRav Nasan Lesinger, of Jerusalem, as told by the Brisker Rav. A similar thought can be found in the *Brisker Haggadah*, p. 272.)

PARSHAS NITZAVIM/VAYELECH

Rosh Hashanah: What's So "New" About The New Year?

Besides being the beginning of the year in terms of the formulation of man's yearly destiny, the first of Tishrei is considered the first day of the year for other halachic purposes. It is the day on which the sabbatical and jubilee years begin, and it is the first day of the year in terms of calculating *ma'aser* (tithe) and *orlah* (see Vayikra 19:23). It is also the day on which the date for legal documents (nowadays the figure 5755 is used) goes up one notch (Rosh Hashanah 2a).

Given that the first of Tishrei is considered the "beginning of the year" in these regards, we may wonder why the first day of the *seventh* month is afforded "New Year's Day" status at all! What is there about this day that is essentially right smack in the middle of the Torah's yearly cycle that makes it the beginning of a new year?

How does Rosh Hashanah begin the year?

It is true that the autumnal equinox occurs at (or close to) the beginning of Tishrei, and that this point in time, when days and nights are equally long, may be regarded as a starting point in the yearly astronomical cycle. However, the vernal equinox at the beginning of Nissan (the *first* month), would seem to be at least as appropriate a starting place as its autumn counterpart.

Actually, the Midrash discusses this question:

"It was taught in Rebbi Eliezer's name: The creation of the world began on 25 Elul (six days before 1 Tishrei).... On Rosh Hashanah [man was created]...and in the tenth hour of that day he sinned (by eating the forbidden fruit)...in the eleventh hour of the day he was judged, and in the twelfth hour he was exonerated of his sin. Hashem said to Adam, 'This will be a sign for your descendants—just as you stood before me on this day and were exonerated, so too will they stand before me in judgment and be exonerated on this first day of the seventh month.' "(Vayikra Rabbah 29:1).

Solution #1: Rebbi Eliezer's opinion

According to this Midrash, the first of Tishrei was chosen to be the New Year since it is the anniversary of the completion of Creation, which brought with it Adam's sin and exoneration. The Midrash (ibid.) musters support for this idea from the Rosh Hashanah liturgy. In the Musaf prayer of Rosh Hashanah we say, "This is the day of the beginning of Your works; it is a remembrance of the first day [of history]." The first of Tishrei is the beginning of a yearly cycle which started on the first day of man's history.

This explanation, however, appears to be only a partial solution to our question. In the Gemara (Rosh Hashanah 8a and 27a) we are told that although Rebbi Eliezer (author of the above Midrashic excerpt) believed that the Creation of man took place in Tishrei, Rebbi Yehoshua disagrees with this. Rebbi Yehoshua states that it was in *Nissan* that the world was created. How can we account for assigning the first of Tishrei the role of "New Year's Day" according to R. Yehoshua? To make the question even more pertinent, it should be noted that Rashi and Tosafos both point out (in their commentaries on Rosh Hashanah 12a) that the halacha is in accordance with R. Yehoshua's view, and *not* with that of R. Eliezer!

Tosafos (Rosh Hashanah 27a) deals with this in part. Following through a point made by the Gemara there, Tosafos points out that it does not seem consistent that we should determine that the halacha is in favor of R. Yehoshua (i.e., a Nissan Creation), while still retaining the line "This is the day of the beginning of Your works..." in the Rosh Hashanah prayer books (which are read on the first of Tishrei). Tosafos suggests that the line in question may be interpreted in a slightly different light in order to accommodate R. Yehoshua's opinion. It should be understood as, "This is the day of the beginning of Your works *of judgment* of the world. In this sense the first of Tishrei is commemorative of the first day of history—since on this day it is being decided whether the world shall *remain* in existence or not."

The textual difficulty of the liturgy aside, however, we still must explain the nature of the holiday. Why should the first of Tishrei be assigned the status of New Year's Day in the first place?

II

A number of suggestions have been offered by various commentators to account for Rebbi Yehoshua's opinion:

1. The Ran (Rosh Hashanah 16a) points out that Rosh Hashanah comes out only nine days before Yom Kippur. Yom Kippur was designated as a day

of forgiveness for Israel throughout history, after the sin of the golden calf was forgiven on that very day in the Sinai Wilderness (Taanis 30b). Hashem therefore chose that day to be the day that the judgment of mankind is completed, in order that the mercy He arouses on that day would be utilized for judging His people in a spirit of pardon and grace. (This is very similar to the theme of Rebbi Eliezer's Midrash quoted here in section I, with regard to Rosh Hashanah).

Two suggestions for resolving the above according to the opinion of Rebbi Yehoshua

Since Yom Kippur is the day of the final judgment, a holiday was ordained in close proximity to that Day of Atonement to serve as a day of penitence and introspection in preparation for the great day of judgment just ahead of it. It is even possible, he adds, that Hashem's "change of attitude" that led to the exoneration of the Jews for the sin of the golden calf began on the 1st of Tishrei. If so, Rosh Hashanah is actually an anniversary of this historical rapprochement between God and his people. It is therefore an ideal day to designate as the Day of Judgment—and, mercifully, of exoneration—throughout the ages.

2. Rabbeinu Tam (quoted in Tosafos to Rosh Hashanah 27a, s.v. *kaman*) explains that even according to R. Yehoshua, who contends that the anniversary of creation is at the beginning of Nissan, Hashem had originally "planned" to create the world at the beginning of Tishrei—i.e., He wanted to place the world at a point in the course of its revolution around the sun that would correspond to a time six months earlier than the actual date of creation. (Why Hashem "changed His mind" and delayed the Creation is a topic for another occasion.) Thus, the first of Tishrei commemorates even more of a beginning than the beginning of Creation—it marks the *planned* beginning of Creation. (A similar idea may be found in Ohr haChayim's comments on Bereishis 1:1, #16.)

The Arizal (R. Yitzchak Luria, renowned Kabbalist of Tzefas, 16th century) used this thought to explain the expression used in the Rosh Hashanah liturgy—"Today was the *conception* of the world ('*haras olam*')." This day does not mark the *birth* of the world, but the *conception* of the world—i.e., the day that it was first conceived!

III

Perhaps we can add a suggestion or two of our own to those mentioned above to explain the choice of the first of Tishrei as a day of judgment:

1. Since Tishrei is the beginning of the rainy season in Eretz Yisrael (see Rosh Hashanah 16a and Taanis 2b), it may be regarded as the beginning of the agricultural year in Eretz Yisrael. Fields were sown during Tishrei in preparation for the first rains of the season. Crops grew and blossomed through the winter and began to bear fruit in Nissan (Shemos 23:15). Various

types of produce were gathered from the fields during the summer months (Rashi on Devarim 25:11). In Tishrei, a new cycle began. Since Tishrei is the beginning of the cycle of growth and flourishing for life-giving crops, it can also be said to be a more fitting occasion for the judgment of man's destiny for the year than the first of Nissan, which was the alternate choice for New Year's day, as mentioned in section II.

Two original suggestions explaining why 1 Tishrei is the start of the New Year

(One may still argue, of course, that the *appearance* and *ripening* of the year's produce would be a more suitable marker for the start of the yearly cycle. See R.S.R. Hirsch in *Horeb*, Soncino Press, par. # 166 and footnote.)

2. In Shemos 12:2 the Torah tells us: "This month (Nissan) shall be for you the first of months; it shall be the first of the months of the year." When counting the order of months we thus always consider Nissan to be the first, Iyar the second, etc. (see Tosafos Rosh Hashanah 12a, s.v. "*ella*"). The Ramban (ad loc.) interprets this verse as a positive commandment. We must always count our months from Nissan to commemorate the Exodus that took place in Nissan. (This is similar to how in Hebrew we refer to the days of the week according to their position in relation to Shabbos—*Yom Rishon* "First Day" = Sunday, *Yom Sheini* "Second Day" = Monday, etc. We do this so that we can constantly recall the Sabbath day throughout the course of the week, see Gemara Beitzah 16a.)

Accordingly, we may suggest that perhaps the first of Nissan is indeed a more appropriate time to fix as the first day of the year, according to Rebbi Yehoshua's opinion, since the first of Nissan was the day of the world's creation. However, making the first of Nissan a New Year's Day would have detracted from Nissan's status as the "month of the Exodus." If the year actually began in Nissan because of reasons relating to historical considerations (i.e., the creation of the world), people would not realize that it is only because of the *Exodus* that Nissan was chosen to be the first of the months. Hashem therefore "moved" the date of New Year's Day to the other equinoxal month, Tishrei. The peculiar situation of having the year begin in the *seventh* month would enhance, rather than diminish, the commemoration of the Exodus!

PARSHAS HA'AZINU

Yom Kippur—Yonah's Mission

Following the Yom Kippur afternoon Torah reading, we read the story of Yonah ben Amitai the Prophet. Yonah went to visit the Beis Hamikdash along with many other Sukkos holiday pilgrims. He rejoiced there with his fellow Jews in the special love that Hashem bestows upon the His people.

Yonah's adventure

The climax of the yearly celebration came during the *Simchas Beis Hashoeva*—The Celebration of the Water Drawing—an evening event, held daily from the second until the seventh day of the Sukkos holiday. During this ceremony, Yonah's joy reached ecstatic heights. Hashem's Holy word may rest upon one when one is rejoicing in the performance of a mitzvah, and that is exactly what happened in the case of Yonah ben Amitai. Yonah found himself overwhelmed by Hashem's Holy word. He became a divine emissary, appointed to warn the gentile population of Ninveh to repent (Yerushalmi Sukkah 5:1).

For reasons which will not be discussed here, Yonah balked at his assignment. He refused to accept his mission (see *Jewish Thought, A Journal of Torah Scholorship*, a publication of the Orthodox Union, vol. 3:1, p.7, for Rav Yehoshua Bachrach's discussion of this matter). Yonah tried to flee from Hashem's word by boarding a boat headed for Tarshish. When Hashem stirred up a storm that nearly sank the ship, Yonah publicly admitted his guilt in evading his duty. He advised the other passengers on the boat to throw him overboard. When they accepted his counsel and tossed him into the sea, the sea was immediately calmed (Book of Yonah, ch. 1).

The passengers on the boat were so inspired by what had transpired, that each of them vowed to bring *korbanos* to Hashem (*Targum Yonah*, end of ch. 1). In fact, the passengers on this boat became so convinced of the omnipotence of Yonah's G-d, that they all eventually became proselytes. In fact, we refer to proselytes such as Yonah's boat mates when we pray three times daily for Hashem to have mercy on "the righteous proselytes" *(Pirkei d'Rabbi Eliezer,* end of ch. 10).

Yonah was undoubtedly plagued by the nagging question, "Why me?" It is obvious, however, that if *he* was chosen for the mission, Hashem must have had good reason for the choice. Perhaps, after a careful look at Chazal's words, we can offer at least somewhat of an answer to this question, and gain a better understanding of Yonah's mission as well.

II

Zevulun's emissary

HaRav Chaggai Preschel, a good friend of mine and presently dean of Yeshivat Tikvat Ameinu, the Moscow Yeshiva High School, once shared with me an intriguing thought concerning Yonah and his mission.

As Chazal tell us, Yonah's father came from Zevulun's tribe (Yerushalmi Sukkah 5:1). It is for this reason that Yonah's first impulse, upon fleeing the word of Hashem, was to board a ship. The tribe of Zevulun were primarily traders who often sailed to distant parts of the world to sell their wares (Rashi, Devarim 33:18). It would therefore be natural for Yonah to feel safe and at ease when voyaging upon a boat.

On the day Moshe Rabbeinu died he blessed all of the tribes of Yisrael. Implicit in Moshe's words were many revelations about all the tribes' future destinies. Rashi describes Moshe's blessing for Zevulun in the following manner:

[The tribes of] Zevulun and Yisaschar made a partnership. Zevulun traded at sea. He then shared his profits with Yisaschar, who remained at home and studied the Torah...[it therefore can be said that] Yisaschar's knowledge of Torah, was to Zevulun's credit.

"Zevulun," Moshe Rabbeinu said, "you shall trade successfully, and rejoice in your success. Yisaschar—you shall succeed in your Torah studies, and rejoice in that. You shall master the intricacies of the lunar calendar, and dictate to the tribes of Yisrael when to gather at *Har Hamoria* [i.e., the Beis Hamikdash] for the yearly holiday pilgrimages."

Alternatively, the verse means that *foreign nations* will gather at the Temple Mount through Zevulun's tradings. When foreign traders crossed the seas to trade with Zevulun, they would say, "Since we have already come this far, we might as well visit Jerusalem and see what these people worship." When they arrived and saw all of Yisrael serving a single deity and eating a single diet, they would be so overcome with awe that they would become proselytes (Rashi, Devarim 33:18-19).

Rashi reveals to us the dual mission of the tribe of Zevulun. Through his support of Yisaschar, Zevulun plays a major role in bringing about the yearly pilgrimages. Through his foreign trade, Zevulun makes the G-d of the Jews known to the other nations of the world.

It is now evident why Yonah's prophesy came in the manner it did, and why Yonah was chosen for this prophetic mission. As a member of Zevulun's tribe, Yonah had a pivotal role in the pilgrimages and their associated festivities. (*Rejoice*, Zevulun, when you go out..."—Devarim ibid.) They were "his" mitzvah, so to speak. (The Gemara tells us that even Yonah's wife, who, as a woman was exempt from making the yearly pilgrimages, also went to Jerusalem three times a year, out of her love for the mitzvah—Eruvin 96a.) Yonah was therefore able to take full advantage of these mitzvos, and gain from them true spiritual growth—even unto prophesy.

The prophetic message he was entrusted with, however, was not directed towards, the Bnai Yisrael. Rather, his assignment was to go out to the nations of the world and bring them to repent and follow the just and moral ways of Hashem. When Yonah refused to do this, there was only one way for him to correct his wrongdoing. He had to be thrown into the sea! The miraculous end that this brought to the storm demonstrated clearly to the gentile passengers that Hashem is the true master of the universe.

III

I would like to add a further observation to what Chaggai has shown. Out of the entire tribe of Zevulun, it was *Yonah* who was chosen for this mission. This, too, was not by chance. It may well be that Hashem brought Yonah to this world solely for the purpose of fulfilling this mission. As we are taught in Gemara Berachos 7b, "A person's name decides his role in life."

Yonah, the dove

The Midrash draws a fascinating analogy between the Bnai Yisrael, and the bird known as the *yonah* [dove]:

[The Bnai Yisrael are compared to a *yonah* in a number of ways:]

1. Just as the *yonah*'s walk is a pleasure to behold, so too, the Bnai Yisrael's walk is a pleasure to behold when they come on their yearly pilgrimages.

2. Just as the *yonah* is modest, so, too, the Bnai Yisrael are modest.

3. Just as the *yonah* stretches its neck to be slaughtered, so, too, do the Bnai Yisrael, as it is stated, "For you [Hashem] we have been killed throughout the day."

4. Just as the *yonah* atones for sins [i.e., it is used as a sacrificial offering], so, too, the Bnai Yisrael atone for the nations. The seventy cows we bring on Sukkos as *korbanos* are offered so that the seventy nations of the world will not be eradicated.

5. Just as we find with the *yonah* that even if you take from it its young, it will never leave its nest, so, too, the Bnai Yisrael did not cease to make

their holiday pilgrimages to the Temple Mount even after the Beis Hamikdash was destroyed.

6. Finally, Rebbi said, "There's one type of *yonah* which, when fed, gives off a scent that attracts other pigeons to its nest. So, too, when the Elders of Bnai Yisrael expound on the Torah they attract many gentiles who hear them and become proselytes (Midrash Rabbah to Shir Hashirim, 1:15).

The prophet Yonah's destiny was almost entirely spelled out in his name!

Yonah, the bird represents the fervor with which the Jewish nation observes the festival pilgrimages. Yonah ben Amitai was outstanding in his observance of the festival pilgrimages (see #1, #5). His prophecy was given to him on Sukkos, when we offer seventy bulls as sacrifices to atone for the sins of the seventy gentile nations (Rashi, Bamidbar 29:35) and his mission was indeed to save a gentile nation from annihilation (#4). Modestly, he tried to hide his prophetic status from all, and escape from his mission (#2). When confronted by the storm, Yonah willingly offered his life, accepting it as divine retribution (#3). Finally, Yonah made such a deep impression on the gentile passengers of the ship that they all chose to convert to Judaism (#6). According to the Midrash (*Pirkei d'Rabbi Eliezer*, ch. 10) representatives of each of the 70 nations of the world were on board Yonah's ship, all of whom left their idols behind and turned to the ways of Hashem after their experience with Yonah (#4, again). Yonah eventually proceeded to Ninveh, where he succeeded in turning an entire city of gentile sinners to the ways of their creator (#4, #6).

May Hashem make us aware of the missions that He has prepared for each of us on this world, and give us the courage and determination to execute them!

PARSHAS HA'AZINU

Sukkos [The Feast of Tabernacles]: In The Shade Of The Almighty's Sukkah

Do the righteous need Divine protection in the World-to-Come? The evidence seems contradictory.

"You shall dwell in sukkos [shading shelters] for seven days..." (Vayikra 23:42). Rav Levi said: When someone keeps the mitzvah of Sukkah in this world, Hashem says of him, "He kept the mitzvah of Sukkah, so I will shade him from the scorching sun of the Day of Judgment."

Rav Yannai and Reish Lakish said: There will not be any Gehinnom in the World-to-Come (i.e., in the ultimate, eternal world that follows a person's initial reward or punishment after his or her death—Ran, Nedarim 8b). Rather, the sun at that time will scorch the wicked and burn them up, as it says (Malachi 3:19), "A sun will come which will burn like a furnace; all the wicked and all the evildoers will be like straw, and the sun will incinerate them...." At that time Hashem will make a sukkah [shading shelter] for the righteous to protect them from the sun, as it says (Tehillim 27:5), "He will conceal me in His sukkah on the day of evil; He will hide me in the seclusion of His tent" (Yalkut Shimoni, Emor #653).

Reish Lakish tells us in the Midrash, that as a reward for observing Sukkos a person is protected from the heat of the blazing sun that will scorch the wicked in the World-to-Come.

From this Midrash it would seem that the righteous will be protected from the scorching sun of the future by means of a special shelter provided by Hashem. This, however, seems to contradict Reish Lakish's own description of the events to take place in the future as it appears in the Gemara:

Reish Lakish said: There will be no Gehinnom in the World-to-Come. Rather, Hashem will take the sun out from its sheath and it will blaze intensely. The wicked will be punished through the sun, while the righteous will be healed through it, as it says (Malachi 3:19-20), "A sun will come which will burn like a furnace; all the wicked and all the evildoers will be like straw, and the sun will incinerate them.... But a sun of kindness will shine for those who fear Me, with healing in its rays." Moreover, the righteous will derive pleasure from the sun, as it says (ibid.), "...and you will become sated, as fattened calves entering their pen to feed" (Avoda Zara 3b).

According to this account, the righteous will not need to be sheltered from the burning sun on the Day of Judgment. The warmth of that day's sun will be beneficial to them rather than harmful.

How can we reconcile these two statements, both of them made by Reish Lakish? Why will the righteous both benefit from the sun, yet require shelter from it?

To address this question, we must first explain some of the basic themes expressed in these Midrashim, and attempt to understand their deeper meaning. Why is the *sun* chosen to be the agent through which Hashem will administer punishment for the wicked and reward for the righteous? What is meant by the sun's "sheath," and why is it normally encased in this sheath? What does the Sukkah that Hashem will construct for the righteous represent?

It should be noted that Aggadic statements [words of Chazal that consist of homiletics or narratives, rather than discussions of legal issues] are generally allegorical. They are intended to represent ideas that were not meant to be revealed to the unprepared lay person (stated by Maimonides, in his introduction to the Mishnah, s.v. *Achar Ken*). Aggadic statements are given to several different levels of understanding. By analyzing the terminology used in the above statements and comparing them to similar expressions used elsewhere by Chazal, we can perhaps scratch the surface of the deeper concepts alluded to in their words.

(Please realize that Aggadic themes are often difficult to convey in a few short sentences. Even if I were to understand them to their fullest, explaining them to a broad audience would not be easy, and I would still have to resort to metaphor or allegory occasionally. Please do not take everything that I say here literally, and give me the benefit of the doubt, realizing that nobody is perfect. May Hashem forgive me if I misrepresent His words, or cause them to be misconstrued.)

II

The Gemara (Sotah 10a) tells us that the word *Shemesh* [protector (Rashi)] can be used as an appellation for Hashem, as it says, "Hashem is a *Shemesh* and a shield" (Tehillim 84:12). The common biblical usage of the word *shemesh*, however, is as the Hebrew word for "sun." Why should the sun be referred to with the same word that denotes its Creator?

The sun represents Hashem's glory

"The heavens proclaim the glory of God...He made a tent in [the heavens] for the sun. The sun appears like a groom coming out of his bridal canopy; it rejoices like an athlete running his course. It emerges from one edge of the sky and it goes around to the other; no one can escape its heat" (Tehillim 19:2-7).

In what way do "the heavens proclaim the glory of God"? The psalm explains that it is through the sun's great strength that Hashem's power is demonstrated. This colossal nuclear furnace, radiating more energy every second than humans have consumed in the whole of our history, is the source of all life on earth. Holding in tow the entire solar system through its gravitational pull, the sun's light, heat, and "wind" of ionized particles affect planets and other bodies billions of miles away. The sun—our only directly observable star—is the greatest public demonstration of Hashem's awesome might and glory.

In fact, it was this very display of power that brought some ancient civilizations to worship the sun. We, however, who believe in Hashem, note that the sun itself can do nothing to change its predetermined, natural course. It persistently "emerges from one edge of the sky goes around to the other." Instead of worshipping it, we marvel at the great Power Who endows the sun with such tremendous power.

This is a key to understanding many of the words of Chazal involving the sun. Take, for example, the interpretation Rabbeinu Bachye (Spain, 1350) offers for a Gemara in Bava Basra:

Rebbi Shimon ben Yochai said: There was a precious stone that hung from Avraham Avinu's neck. Whoever was sick would come and gaze at the stone and be healed. When Avraham died, Hashem hung the stone on the sphere of the sun (Bava Basra 16b).

Avraham's ability to "enlighten people's eyes," in a spiritual sense, is being compared here to a brilliant gem. It was said to be hanging on Avraham's neck, because speech emanates from the throat, which is in the neck (and it was through his words that Avraham was able to enlighten people). "Whoever was sick..." means that whoever had spiritual shortcomings would—after being exposed to Avraham, become "healed" of his spiritual ailment. When Avraham died, he left behind no other human being who was capable of demonstrating Hashem's unity and greatness to others. This capability now rested only with the sun, as it says, "The heavens proclaim the glory of God...." (Rabbeinu Bachye, intro. to Parshas Yisro see also Kli Yakar, Bereishis 32:27.)

This, then, may explain why the word *Shemesh*, used in the Torah to describe Hashem, was borrowed as a name for the sun, His great emissary on this world. After all, an emissary is entitled to go by the name of his dispatcher.

III

This is the "sun" that both rewards and punishes, in the World-to-Come In this world, however, the "sun"—i.e., the demonstration of Hashem's glory to man that the sun represents—is "sheathed." After all is said and done, it is still possible to make the mistake of thinking that the sun operates of its own volition, as idolaters believe—or that the sun acts according to natural principles that developed spontaneously and randomly, as modern day atheists believe. The "brilliance" of the sun is thus cloaked, in this world.

This is the "sun" that both rewards and punishes, in the World-to-Come

In the World-to-Come, however, Hashem will take the sun out of its "sheath." As the Gemara (Berachos 17a) says, "In the World-to-Come there will be no eating or drinking; rather the righteous will sit and delight in the radiance of Hashem's presence."

Experiencing closeness to God will be in place of physical pleasure for the righteous. They will be able to perceive God in a way impossible in this world—the sun will be "taken out of its sheath." This is the reward for those who have sought throughout their lives to know Hashem and His ways better. (Knowing Hashem and His ways is our goal in life... "This is the only thing that a person may be praised for: knowing and understanding My ways...said Hashem"—Yirmiyah 9:23.)

Hashem will reveal His glory to each of the righteous in the World-to-Come in accordance with the amount of effort they invested in knowing and understanding Him during their lives in this world.

The wicked, on the other hand, will endure disgrace at that time. It will be made abundantly clear just how much they had distanced themselves from the source of eternal life during their lives on this world. On the Day of Final Reckoning, their disgrace will be revealed to all, and any existence that they merit will only be granted to them through the righteous whom they had so despised during their lives. The revelation of Hashem's presence in the World-to-Come will "burn" them, due the their distance from Him.

The reward of the righteous is granted based on an evaluation of how close they were to their Creator during their lives. It therefore stands to reason that even among the righteous, every person's experience in the World-to-Come will be different. Some will be closer to Hashem than others in certain aspects, while others will be closer than them in other ways. The righteous will therefore both "derive pleasure from the sun [the revelation of the Divine Presence]" for their accomplishments, and "be burned by the sun" for their failings.

Since they are righteous, however, and at least tried to "know Hashem," Hashem will make them a sukkah to protect them from being scorched for the latter. Thus, Reish Lakish's two statements can be seen to complement each other. The righteous will both be rewarded by the sun, and need protection from it.

IV

But exactly what is the "sukkah" through which Hashem grants protection to the righteous?

Torah is the "sukkah" that protects us on Sukkos and on the Day of Final Judgment

"No one can escape [the sun's] heat" (Tehillim 19:7)—but in the future there *will* be people who will be able to escape the sun's heat. Who are these people? Rav Acha explained: People who occupy themselves with Torah study—as the subsequent verse says, "The Torah of Hashem is perfect" (Yalkut Shimoni, Tehillim 19, #674).

The Torah that a person studies during their lifetime (in order to become closer to Hashem) forms the "sukkah" that shelters them from the damaging heat of the "sun" in the World-to-Come.

Why is a sukkah the metaphor chosen to represent the study of the Torah? First of all, like a shelter, Torah study protects a person and shields a person from the evil and destructive elements of this world (Gemara Sotah 21a).

A house also protects a person from the elements, of course, but the Sukkah is a better metaphor for the protection provided by the Torah. A sukkah, while providing shelter, still lets in the light of the sun (i.e., teaches one faith in his Creator) through its leafy roof. (In fact, one immersed in Torah study is said to be in the "tent" of Torah—"*oholo shel Torah*"—see Rashi Bereishis 25:27, and HaKesav Vehakabala ad loc.)

The sukkos we are commanded to live in during the Sukkos festival may also hint to us the importance, and the benefits, of Torah study. The Gemara (Sukkah 2a) tells us that the mitzvah of dwelling in sukkos involves "going out of our *permanent* dwellings and living in a *temporary* dwelling." The allegorical understanding of this statement may be that the "sukkah" of Torah brings us to realize that this world is not a permanent residence, but rather a temporary dwelling place only. It is only the World-to-Come, when eternal rewards and punishments are granted, that is truly important.

The Vilna Gaon, in his commentary to Yonah 4:5, develops this theme eloquently. The Gemara (Sukkah 11b) tells us that the roof of the sukkah should be made of "the refuse of the wheat and wine produce" (i.e., constructed from plant material, not of manufactured objects or food).

The Gaon explains that when the Torah tells us to use "the refuse of bread and wine" for our sukkah, it can also be seen as a metaphor. The

Torah (represented by the Sukkah) teaches us the lesson that we should turn our attention away from such physical pleasures as "bread and wine" (culinary pleasures and intoxicating beverages), and concentrate on spiritual pursuits. As the Mishnah in Avos (6:4) says, "This is the way of the Torah: eat bread and salt, drink but a small measure of water". (See also Chidah in *Nachal Kedumim*, Parshas Vayishlach, #11.)

As a friend of mine, haRav Avraham Ziskind of Jerusalem, pointed out, the Midrash that we started with may also be understood in this light. As the Midrash stated, keeping the mitzvah of sukkah earns one protection from the scorching sun of the World-to-Come. This may be understood to mean that if one truly appreciates the *message* of the mitzvah of sukkah—that it is important to shun physical pleasure and to instead pursue spiritual perfection through Torah study—then one will merit to sit in the protective "sukkah" of Hashem in the World-to-Come.

This may also be the association of the verses in the psalm starting "*L'David Hashem Ori*," (quoted at the conclusion of our original Midrash) as Rav Ziskind further pointed out:

"[My wish is] that I may sit in the house of Hashem (the house of Torah study) all my life, that I may see the sweetness of Hashem and visit in His palace (that is, that I may be able to enjoy the pleasure of perceiving his presence in the World-to-Come). For He will conceal me in His sukkah on the day of evil; He will hide me in the seclusion of His tent. (As a result of my studying the Torah, Hashem will conceal me in His sukkah, protecting me from being scorched by the sun of the World-to-Come.)" (Tehillim 27:4-5)

May Hashem grant us a portion in the World-to-Come with the righteous, and bathe us in the light of his healing and refreshing sun!

(The Vilna Gaon, in his commentary to the book of Yonah 4:5, elaborates on this theme.)

PARSHAS VEZOS HABERACHAH

Simchas Torah—How I Love Your Torah; It Is My Conversation All Day Long! (Tehillim 119:97)

Our Sages tell us that studying the Torah is a greater mitzvah than any other mitzvah of the Torah. "A person reaps the fruit of these mitzvos in this world, while the principal remains for him to enjoy in the World-to-Come...and Torah study is the equal of all the others [mitzvos] combined" (Mishnah, Pe'ah 1:1).

What makes learning Torah unique among the mitzvos of the Torah? The Rambam [Maimonides], based on Kiddushin 40b, offers the following explanation:

"There is no mitzvah which is the equal of Torah study...because study leads to performance" (Mishneh Torah, Hilchos Talmud Torah, 3:3).

Thus according to the Rambam, Torah study is more important than the other mitzvos of the Torah, because, in the final analysis, observance of all the mitzvos depends on Torah study. Even after one has learned the basic laws of a mitzvah, it is only through Torah study that one will gain a better understanding of the nuances of the mitzvah.

Learning Torah— the greatest of mitzvos

The Vilna Gaon, in his commentary to the above-quoted Mishnah, highlights another dimension of Torah study. Every single word of Torah that is learned is a new mitzvah. If a page with one-hundred words on it is studied, one has performed one-hundred mitzvos; if one spends the identical amount of time performing another mitzvah, one gains only a single mitzvah. This alone would make the study of Torah greater than the performance of any other mitzvah.

The basis for the Gaon's reasoning can be found in the Ran's teachings (Yoma 83b s.v. *vegarsinnan*), who explains that the repeated performance of a lesser transgression is more severe than the single performance of a much greater transgression. Inversely, we may conclude that the repeated performance of one mitzvah is more meritorious than the single performance of even the greatest mitzvah. This alone would make the study of Torah many times greater than any other mitzvah; when it is combined with the inherent importance of Torah study ("study leads to performance"), the mitzvah of Torah study is seen to be truly outstanding.

II

The mitzvah of Torah study differs from the other mitzvos in the manner in which it is executed as well.

Non-stop Torah "Rebbi Yehoshua was asked, 'May a man teach his son Greek wisdom (a wit-sharpening form of recreation invented by the Greeks)?' He responded, 'He may do so, but only during a time which is neither day nor night, for during the entire day and the entire night one is obligated to study the Torah and there is no free time in which to engage in the teaching or practice of Greek wisdom.' As the prophet says (Yehoshua 1:8): 'You shall ponder the Torah day and night!' " (Tosefta Avoda Zara 1:3; cf. Menachos 99b).

Any time of the day or night a person is not involved in the performance of another mitzvah, one is obligated to be involved in the study of Torah.

Similarly, the Gemara tells us (Yoma 19b) that the verse which states (Devarim 6:7), "You shall speak *those words* [of Torah]," is forbidding us to speak *anything* other than words of Torah. (As Rashi explains, the Gemara is forbidding idle pratter. Proper speech spoken to one's family or in the course of doing business is permitted, since earning a livelihood is a mitzvah in and of itself, as the Gaon points out in his commentary to Pe'ah 1:1.)

Tosafos (Berachos 11b, s.v. *shek'var*) uses the Tosefta's all-day-all-night ruling to resolve an apparent contradiction in the laws of blessings. Before eating in a sukkah, one recites a blessing. If one leaves the sukkah to perform daily business, the blessing must be recited once again before one next eats in the sukkah. In regards to the blessing recited before Torah study, however, the law is different. After reciting the blessing in the morning, one need not repeat the blessing throughout the entire day—even if business or other pursuits are done during the course of the day. Why is that?

Tosafos explains that the mitzvah to study the Torah applies during every spare moment of the day. Therefore, being involved in other tasks does not cause an interruption in one's Torah study. The mitzvah of Sukkah, on the other hand, only applies to us while eating. During times other than meals, one is distracted from the mitzvah of Sukkah. Because of this, one must recite a new blessing before performing the mitzvah a second time.

III

The Rosh resolves the contradiction between the two blessings in a slightly different manner, revealing to us yet another aspect of the obligation to study Torah. According to the Rosh (Berachos 1:13), only people who are fully immersed in the study of Torah are justified in not reciting a new blessing after a pause in their Torah study. Even when such people tend to their everyday affairs, they are eager to finish their chores and return to the study of Torah. Because their minds are never distracted from the study of Torah, their earlier blessing is still valid upon their return to the study of Torah.

Longing for the study of Torah

The Rosh discloses to us that a true student of the Torah finds all worldly pursuits to be no more than annoying distractions that temporarily interrupt Torah study. The Rosh's source is undoubtedly the Gemara's teaching that (Berachos 35b) "The earlier generations considered Torah study to be their *fixed pursuit* and earning a livelihood to be a *temporary diversion*, they therefore succeeded in both." (See also Yoma 19b, "Make the study of Torah a fixed pursuit, not a temporary diversion.")

Although the Rosh recognizes that one must take one's mind off Torah studies temporarily in order to tend to worldly needs, some later commentaries take a more extreme position. *Mishnas Avos* (a commentary on Avos written by Rav Yosef ben Yehudah Ibn Eknin, disciple of the Rambam, to Avos 4:10) asserts that even *while* one finds oneself involved in non-Torah matters one should be thinking Torah thoughts in the back of one's mind.

The Sefer Hafla'ah, in his introduction (par. 35; see also his introduction to *Sefer HaMikneh*, par. 32), elaborates further. How will one ever succeed in business, asks the Hafla'ah, if one's mind is always preoccupied with Torah? The answer: "Know Hashem while you go about your ways, and He will make your paths straight" (Mishlei 3:6). If you think thoughts of Torah while you work, Hashem will see to it that your business prospers. Similarly, "Happy is the person...who desires Hashem's Torah and ponders His Torah day and night...he will succeed in all that he does" (Tehillim 1:1-3). One need not be concerned that concentration on Torah thoughts will cause one to fail in worldly endeavors.

In a similar fashion, Rav Chaim of Volozhin (in his commentary to Avos 2:2) contends that the Mishnah's famous statement, "Torah is proper when accompanied with worldly activity," means that even while one is involved in worldly activity, it is good to think about Torah. (See also *Nefesh HaChaim*, 1:8.)

A contemporary Gadol, HaGaon Rav Shlomo Fisher of Jerusalem, pointed out to me that the spiritual height to which the Hafla'ah and Rav Chaim Volozhin are referring is discussed by the early commentators. When the

Torah tells us (Devarim 11:22) to "love Hashem, walk in His ways and *cleave to Him*," the Ramban explains that one who is on a truly high spiritual level should dwell on the love of Hashem even while occupied with business. While one is conversing with another person, one's heart should be thinking about Hashem and His ways. Similarly, the Ra'avad (end of Hilchos Teshuvah) refers to righteous individuals who perform all of their mundane activities in a distracted manner because their mind is absorbed by the love of Hashem.

However, most people will find this approach difficult, if not absolutely impossible, to follow. Rav Fisher noted that as the Ramban mentioned, cleaving to Hashem is a great accomplishment practiced by no more than a few elite individuals per generation. The everyday working person is certainly not expected to act in such a manner. What the average Jew can and should strive for is the diligence described by the Rosh. Any free moments during the day—such as those that pass while waiting for a customer to arrive or for some process to be completed—should be used for Torah study and not be wasted.

IV

Yehoshua and the angel

In an enigmatic incident in the book of Yehoshua (5:13-14), a heavenly angel threatens Yehoshua with a sword. According to the Gemara (Megillah 3a), the angel was admonishing Yehoshua for keeping his warring soldiers on active alert throughout the night. "Night is not a time during which nations battle," says the angel, "you should have used the nighttime for the study of Torah!"

Why indeed did Yehoshua stop his soldiers from studying Torah that evening? Hadn't Hashem warned Yehoshua to "ponder the Torah day and night?" Apparently, Yehoshua believed that one should direct one's full attention to the mitzvah at hand. Since the Jews were currently engaged in the conquest of Israel, Yehoshua felt that their full concentration should be devoted to the war effort. The angel informed Yehoshua that he was mistaken. As we quoted from the Rosh, no matter what kind of work one is engaged in, one should devote any spare moments towards the study of Torah and the love of Hashem. (See Rashi Berachos 32b, who compares the effort that a working person puts into working to the effort that a soldier puts into fighting a war.) Since night is not a time for active battle, Yehoshua's soldiers belonged in the *beis midrash*, studying Torah!

THE JEWISH HOLIDAYS

The Seven Liquids And The Seven Moadim

Preface

The seven Jewish holidays, or *Moadim*, provide the framework for the Jewish experience of time. During the time of the Beis Hamikdash every Jew was commanded to "appear before his Creator" in Jerusalem on Pesach, Shavuos and Sukkos. These three pilgrimage holidays commemorate momentous events that took place from the moment of our exodus from Egypt to our entry into Eretz Yisrael. On the High Holy days of Rosh Hashanah and Yom Kippur, Hashem judges the actions of every person and determines what each one will be granted in the coming year. The two rabbinic holidays of Chanukah and Purim remind us that Hashem continues to protect us even while we are under the rule of foreign nations.

Besides the explicit descriptions of the first five *Moadim* in the Torah, our Sages and later commentators have pointed out less obvious aspects of the *Moadim*. Rabbinic literature contains many discussions of the biblical and rabbinic *Moadim*. With Hashem's help, let us unveil one more hidden pattern to the Jewish holidays.

II

The Mishnah (Machshirin 6:4) tells us that a food product can become *tameh*, or unfit for sacred use, only after coming into contact with a liquid. Prior to contact with a liquid, however, food cannot become *tameh* even if it touches a source of *tumah* (ritual impurity).

There are seven liquids that render food capable of becoming *tameh*: dew, water, wine, oil, blood, milk and bee's honey. When any of these seven liquids are put into contact with a food, it becomes able to become *tameh*. It is as if the food is incomplete—i.e., not fully edible—until it is washed with one of these seven liquids. This exempts the food from the laws of *tumah*, since these laws do not apply to a non-edible and non-usable objects. (Rashbam, Vayikra 11:34).

Interestingly, each of the seven *Moadim* finds its parallel in one of the seven liquids.

III

1. Let us begin with Pesach. Pesach is related to blood, as Rashi explains, the Jews left Egypt at a time destined for the spilling of blood.

Pesach = blood [Pharaoh told Moshe,] "See that evil confronts you" (Shemos 10:10). It is stated in a Midrash that there is a star named "Evil." Pharaoh told Moshe and Aharon, "Using astrology I see that Evil's star is rising to greet you in the desert, this signifies blood and murder!"

Rashi adds that later—when the Jews sinned with the golden calf and Hashem wanted to destroy them—Moshe prayed, "Why should Egypt declare 'He took them out with Evil' (Shemos 32:12)?"

This verse refers to what Pharaoh had told them, "See that [the star] Evil confronts you!" Immediately after Moshe's prayer we see that "Hashem withheld the Evil" (Shemos 32:14). Hashem substituted the blood of circumcision for the blood which had been predicted as a sign of death. Upon entering the Land of Israel, Yehoshua circumcised the Israelites. That is what is meant by the verse describing Yehoshua's mass circumcision (Yehoshua 5:9): "Today I have removed the disgrace of Egypt from upon you." Until this blood of circumcision was spilled, the Egyptians said of the Israelites, "We see blood (decreed) upon you in the desert!" (Rashi to Shemos 10:10)

2. Pesach is also related to blood since the use of blood to serve Hashem was crucial to the Redemption from Egypt.

Rashi comments on Shemos 12:6: "And I passed upon you and I saw you and behold it was time for you to be loved" (Yechezkel 16:8).—Hashem meant by this, "The time has come to keep the promise I made to Avraham, to redeem his children!" But the Jews had no mitzvos through which they could merit His redemption, as it says (ibid. 16:7), "And you were naked and exposed." Hashem therefore gave the Jews two mitzvos: the blood of the Pesach offering and the blood of circumcision (the blood of the mass circumcision on the evening that they left Egypt) as the verse says, "You were soiled with your bloods" (ibid. 16:6)—i.e., with two bloods. Another verse says, "You, too, with the blood of your covenant, have I sent forth your prisoners" (Zecharyah 9:11).

Because the time of Redemption was fated for blood (as the first Midrash states), our complete Redemption had to come through the use of blood to serve our Creator (the second Midrash).

3. Aside from this, the entire stay of the Jews in Egypt was bloodstained. In fact, Rashi comments on Shemos 2:23 that the Midrash notes that Pharaoh used to bathe himself in the blood of Jewish babies to cure his leprosy.

The Pesach Seder is full of reminders of the Jewish blood spilled in Egypt. Tosafos comments on the *charoses* into which we dip our *marror*:

"The Yerushalmi tells us that some people [mix in wine] in order to remember the blood [of our fathers that was spilled in Egypt].... It is customary nowadays to initially prepare it very thick and then to thin it with wine and vinegar" (Tosafos to Pesachim 116a).

Halachic authorities (see *Mishneh Berurah* 472:38) also link the halachic preference to use red wine for the four cups at the seder to its similarity in color to the blood Pharaoh spilled slaughtering the Jews.

The bloody color of the wine and the *charoses* can also be seen as a reminder of the blood that the Jews themselves let flow when the Jewish men circumcised themselves and when they slaughtered their Paschal lambs prior to leaving Egypt.

IV

1. In many places it is customary to eat milk products on the first day of Shavuos (Rama, Orach Chaim 494:3).

Shavuos = milk

Many reasons have been suggested for the custom of eating milk products on Shavuos, the day we were given the Tablets of the Law (see *Taamei Haminhagim* par. 621-626). One reason is that when the Jews received the Torah on Shavuos, they could only eat dairy products. None of the previously slaughtered meat had been prepared according to the Torah's requirements of shechitah, salting and deveining, so only milk products were available immediately after the receipt of the Torah (*Taamei Haminhagim* par. 623; *Mishneh Berurah*, 494:12). Another reason is that the Torah is referred to as "sweet as milk" (Shir Hashirim 4:11), or as "butter" (Berachos 63b).

2. The eighth chapter of Shir Hashirim is understood by the Midrash to be a description of the giving of the Torah at Mount Sinai. The woman in the verse [representing the children of Israel] says, "I will lead you, I will bring you to my mother's house [where] you shall teach me" (Shir Hashirim 8:2). On this, the Midrash comments:

" 'My mother's house'—refers to Sinai. Rav Brachia said: 'Why is Sinai called "My mother's house?" Because that is where the children of Israel became like a newly born infant!' " (Midrash Rabbah to Shir Hashirim 8:2).

An infant only drinks milk (see Yevamos 114a, Kerissos 13b). The Jews were like newborn infants at Har Sinai, drawing their nourishment from the Torah as an infant sucks milk at its mother's breast. (Shir Hashirim 8:1 in fact alludes to the Jewish People as an infant nursing from its mother's breast.)

This is another reason to commemorate the giving of the Torah by eating dairy products.

3. The Kabbalists have an additional explanation, drawn from the Zohar, for the custom of eating milk products on Shavuos. The Zohar presents its theme in typically cryptic style, appropriate to the hidden nature of its message.

The seven weeks of counting the Omer between Pesach and Shavuos serve for the Jewish people as seven clean time periods, just as a woman waits seven clean days after seeing menstrual blood in order to become *tahor* (ritually clean).

According to the Gemara (Niddah 9a), the menstrual blood of a nursing mother is transformed into milk [which is why a nursing woman usually does not menstruate]. This metamorphosis represents a transformation from strict justice to mercy. (Similarly, on Shavuos, the "bloody" days of the Omer which follow the "menstrual period" of Pesach are transformed into a time of "milk" and mercy on Shavuos). (The Zohar, as quoted by the Be'er Hetev to Orach Chaim 494:8)

The physical and emotional stress caused by the loss of blood during menstruation stems from the punishment of Chavah, the first woman (Bereishis 3:16). Seven days are required to remove menstrual *tumah*, which represents strictness and punishment. Another way to "put an end to punishment" is demonstrated by lactation. A nursing mother has brought new life into the world, which partially compensates for the death that Chavah introduced to the world (Bereishis 3:19). As compensation, nursing temporarily halts the menstrual cycle with its accompanying discomfort and instead produces life-sustaining milk. Retribution, symbolized by blood, is replaced by the mercy of milk.

On Shavuos, the Zohar tells us, we also find the "blood" of Pesach, representing justice and punishment, converted into the merciful "milk" of Shavuos. Again seven time periods, in this case, weeks, are required in order to complete this process and bring an end to the omer count, with its connotations of harshness and punishment (See Yevamos 63b; Mishnah Eduyos 2:10). This period of retribution is followed by Shavuos—a time of mercy and compassion, a time of "milk." The Zohar clearly depicts Pesach as a holiday of blood and Shavuos as a holiday of milk.

V

Sukkos = water

Sukkos is associated with water. As the Mishnah (Rosh Hashanah 16a) tells us, "On four occasions judgment is passed on the world.... On Sukkos, the world is judged on its supply of water." Many of the mitzvos of the Sukkos holiday revolve around this theme:

Why did the Torah tell us to pour water [on the altar] on Sukkos? Because

Sukkos marks the start of the rainy season [in Israel]. The Holy One, blessed be He, said, "Pour before Me water on Sukkos, so that there will be blessing in the year's rains!" (Rosh Hashanah 16a from Tosefta 1:11).

We find in Taanis 2b the following: "When do we begin to mention rain [in our Shemoneh Esrei Prayer]? Rebbi Eliezer said: From the time one takes the lulav [i.e., on the first day of Sukkos]... The four species [mentioned in the Torah, in Vayikra 23:40] are taken on Sukkos in order to appeal to Hashem for water. Just as these four species cannot be brought without water [i.e., they need more water than other species in order to grow], so too the world cannot survive without water."

VI

1. Olive oil is central to the observance of Chanukah. We light our menorahs to commemorate the lighting of the menorah in the Holy Temple after the invading Greek armies were vanquished. Only one flask of undefiled olive oil for the menorah was found in the Temple sanctuary. It contained enough oil for one day; yet, miraculously, it burned for eight consecutive days without being consumed. Because the oil kindled in the menorah of the Temple was olive oil (Shabbos 21a), it is preferable to use olive oil, if we can, for the mitzvah of lighting the Chanukah Menorah (*Rama*, Orach Chaim 673:1; *Mishnah Berurah* #4 and *Sha'ar haTzion*).

Chanukah* = *oil

2. Olive oil represents the light of the oral Torah. ("Olive oil helps a person remember even the Torah he learned seventy years ago," notes the Gemara in Horayyos 13b.) It was the light of the oral Torah that the Greeks and the rebellious Jews (the Sadducees) failed to extinguish (see Bereishis Rabbah 2:4), and it is this light that shines from our Chanukah menorahs until today.

3. The Sefas Emes (Chanukah, 5661) reveals to us yet another aspect of the Chanukah oil. The war against the Greeks was a war against both assimilation and Hellenism, a manifestation of the Torah observant Jews' refusal to absorb Greek culture. Similarly, oil also does not combine with another liquid, and thus represents the Jewish people:

It is written in Devarim Rabbah 7:3: " 'And Hashem has singled you out today to be for Him a chosen nation as He had told you He would...and to place you above all the nations He has made, for praise, fame, and glory' (Devarim 26:18,19). Just as oil cannot be mixed with other liquids, likewise the Jewish nation cannot be mixed with idolaters, as it says, 'I have separated you from the nations to be mine' (Vayikra 20:26). In addition, just as when oil is mixed together with other liquids it rises above them all, so too are the Jews above all the other nations, as it says in Devarim 26:19, 'and to place you above....' "

The Chanukah oil represents our resistance to and eventual rise above all competing pagan cultures. The choice of the oil from the olive tree specifically highlights the traits of tenacity and loyalty of the Jewish people. When branches of most trees are grafted onto a tree of another type, hybrid fruits result. An olive branch, however, will produce only olives (Yerushalmi Kilayim 1:7; see also Rashi to Tehillim 128:3). The olive tree cannot be made to change its produce, and thus olive oil, even more than other oils, symbolizes the Jews' loyalty to their religion and their refusal to adopt alien products.

VII

1. One does not have to search far to find an association between wine and Purim. The Talmud accents the association of the two in a rather extreme statement:

Purim = wine

"Every man is obligated to become inebriated on Purim!" (Megillah 7b; see Orach Chaim 695:2 for various halachic interpretations of this Gemara).

According to Avudraham, the reason for this peculiar practice is that all the miracles of the story of Purim were centered around wine-drinking parties (*mishteh*): Queen Vashti was killed by her drunken husband, Achashverosh, during such a party (Esther 1:10); Esther's elevation to queen was celebrated with a drinking party (Esther 2:18); Esther later invited Achashverosh and Haman to two drinking parties, which led to Haman's demise and the neutralization of his cruel decrees (Esther 5:4,8). By drinking wine, we remind ourselves of the Purim miracles.

2. The Midrash (Esther Rabbah 7:12) describes Hashem's protection of the Jewish People from Haman's evil plotting in terms of intoxication:

"Haman told the king, 'There is (*yeshno*) one nation...' (Esther 3:8)—What Haman meant to say was, 'The "One" of Whom it is said, "Hashem is One," is sleeping (*yashen*) and not guarding his people!' "

"Hashem retorted, 'I have no sleeping moments, as the verse says, "Behold the guardian of Israel does not rest and does not sleep" (Tehillim 121:4), and you are saying that I am asleep! By your life, you shall see that I will "awake" my anger on "you," and remove you from the world!' [This is the meaning of the verse which says,] 'Hashem awoke as if from a slumber, as a mighty man awakening "from his wine," and He smote His enemies...' (Tehillim 78:65,66)."

Drinking wine reminds us that Hashem changed His relationship to the Jewish People during the times of Mordechai and Esther. From a state of passive supervision that is compared to a drunken stupor, Hashem aroused Himself to actively intervene and protect His people. Perhaps this is why some interpret the Talmudic directive to drink as a recommendation to "drink more than one is used to, and then to 'sleep...' " (*Rama*, Orach Chaim 695:2).

VIII

1. Dipping an apple in honey to request of Hashem "a pleasant and sweet year" (*Rama*, Orach Chaim 583:1), is a long-standing Rosh Hashanah custom. Honey demonstrates the transformation of the bee's sting into the sweetest of foods, symbolizing the transformation of justice into loving-kindness—something we pray for on the Day of Judgment. On Rosh Hashanah, Hashem relaxes His staff of justice and grants His beloved nation a reprieve (Tur Orach Chaim #581; Vayikra Rabbi 29:1)

Rosh Hashanah* = *honey

Maharil (Hilchos Rosh Hashanah) brings numerous sources from the Torah, Nevi'im and Kesuvim for eating honey on the Day of Judgment. (See also Rosh Hashanah essay, p. 259.)

2. Shmuel (I:14), describes how King Shaul had the entire Israelite army take an oath not to eat until after the impending battle with the invading Philistines (I Shmuel 14:24). But, we are told:

"Yonasan did not hear his father make the people take an oath. He stretched out the end of the staff that was in his hand, dipped it into the canes of honey [that were to be found all along the road] and brought it to his mouth" (I Shmuel 14:27).

Shaul realized that someone had eaten and betrayed the oath, and he swore that whoever had eaten, even if it was his own child, would be put to death. When Shaul discovered that Yonasan had eaten, Shaul kept his oath and ordered his son's execution. Only after the entire nation pleaded with Shaul, did he rescind his decree and allow Yonasan to live (I Shmuel 14:45).

The verses describing the repeal of Yonasan's sentence are recited as an omen of peace and well-being (Berachos 55b). By dipping an apple in honey, we appeal to Hashem to pardon us just as Yonasan was granted life even after the death sentence was pronounced upon him!

Interestingly, the Zohar (3:231a) notes that when the term "*vayehi hayom*" ["It was that day"] is used, it refers to Rosh Hashanah. This very term is the one used to describe the day that Yonasan was saved from execution (I Shmuel 14:1).

IX

1. Yom Kippur is the Day of Atonement, and as the following quotes demonstrate, dew is a symbol of Hashem's acceptance of our repentance:

Yom Kippur* = *dew

"The anger of the King is as a lion's roar and His goodwill is as dew upon grass" (Mishlei 19:12).

"Return, Oh Yisrael, to Hashem ('*shuvah Yisrael*')... I will accept their teshuvah; I will be as dew to Israel" (Hoshea 14:2,5,6).

This theme is made even more clear by the Midrash:

" 'The ways of your youth shall be like dew to you, [Avraham]' (Tehillim 110:3). Avraham worried, saying, 'I have sinned for so many years in my youth, during which I worshipped idols!' Hashem calmed him, saying, 'The ways of your youth shall be like dew to you, [Avraham]. Just as dew "flies off" (evaporates) and disappears, so, too, shall your sins fly off from you and disappear' " (Bereishis Rabbah "*Tal*" 39:8).

2. Dew is impossible to drink. It doesn't accumulate in pools, and a single dew drop is too small to drink. It is the least substantial of liquids.

Rashi tells us in his comment on Shemos 16:14: When the sun rose, the dew on the manna rose to "greet the sun" [i.e., it evaporated], as that is the nature of dew. Even if one filled a tube with dew and sealed it, the dew would evaporate when left in the sun.

Because it is so insubstantial, dew is the appropriate liquid to represent Yom Kippur, when all eating and drinking is prohibited.

The lack of physicality of dew is also connected to the spirituality attained by the Jews on Yom Kippur. On Yom Kippur, they rise, as it were, "to greet the sun," i.e., they enter a spiritual realm that is "closer" to their Creator. The Tur quotes from a Midrash: On Yom Kippur the accusing angel sees that there is no sin in Yisrael, and he says, "Master of the universe, You have a nation that is unique on the earth! They are like angels!" (*Tur*, Orach Chaim #606).

3. Dew is integral to the continued existence of the world:

"Dew and wind...never cease, because without them the world would not continue to exist" (Taanis 3a and Rashi ad loc.).

Similarly, the world could not continue to exist without repentance and atonement:

"If You took note of our sins, O G-d my Lord, who could survive? But You forgive our sins, that we may continue to fear You" (Tehillim 130:3,4).

The process of repentance and atonement reaches its height on Yom Kippur, which brings atonement for all the year's sins.

X

In conclusion

This completes our comparison of the seven liquids to the seven *Moadim*. How is this strange correlation to be interpreted? It would seem that just as the seven liquids complete a food and make it capable of becoming *tamei*, so too, the *Moadim* can "complete" a Jew. Then, as a Jew complete in mind and spirit, one is able to climb up the ladder of *kedushah* and *taharah*, or closeness to Hashem. Much more needs to be said to fully explicate this connection (such as how each of the *Moadim* complete a Jew in a certain aspect of the service of Hashem), but for now, let us simply rejoice in the depth and beauty of Hashem's Torah!

PARSHAS ZACHOR

Life Saving Shekalim

The ideas and sources mentioned in this week's Parsha Page are for the most part to be found in a fascinating article by Aryeh Naiman in the Summer 5751 edition of *Jewish Thought*. Aryeh Naiman, a lawyer by profession, currently resides in Har Nof, Jerusalem.

"It was known to Hashem that Haman would one day pay *shekalim* for [the annihilation of] the Bnai Yisrael, so He made sure that the yearly *shekalim* given by the Jews would precede those of Haman, as it says in the Mishnah (*Shekalim* 1:1), 'On the first of Adar, the announcement to give the yearly *shekalim* was issued. (Gemara Megillah 13b)' "

Our shekalim vs. Haman's shekalim

Every year the Jews were required to contribute one half of a shekel to the treasury of the Temple. This would be used to pay for the public sacrifices performed there. This yearly obligation is derived from Shemos 30:15. Another rule, derived from Bamidbar 28:14, states that each year's sacrifices should be bought with money donated for that particular year. Even if money was left over from the previous year it could not be used for the purchase of sacrifices; only "new" money was acceptable. The Jewish year begins (for most purposes) with the first day of Nissan. By this day, then, there must be sufficient "new" *shekalim* in the coffers of the Beis Hamikdash to cover necessary expenses. In order to allow ample time for the collection of funds for the new year's sacrifices, the collection of the half-shekel began one month before Nissan, on the first of Adar.

The Aggadah quoted above suggests that Hashem intentionally arranged that the date for the collection of these *shekalim* would be the beginning of Adar. These *shekalim* were the "antidote" to Haman's *shekalim*, which were paid to King Achashverosh in order to arrange the killing of the Jews on the thirteenth of Adar (Esther 3:9). The merit of the yearly collection of *shekalim* for the *korbanos*, which customarily began two weeks before the thirteenth of Adar, protected the Jews from Haman's evil decree. This is probably the source for the custom of donating a half dollar (or half of the equivalent amount in whatever currency is used in one's particular country) to charity, on the day before Purim as a remembrance for the half shekels donated to the Temple. It was the merit of those donations that brought about the miracle of Purim, so it is appropriate to remember them at the onset of Purim.

For some reason, the mitzvah of giving the half shekel is seen by Chazal as a way of neutralizing, or offsetting, the damage caused by Haman's *shekalim*. But what exactly is the connection between the two matters? And how can our *shekalim* act as an atonement for Haman's *shekalim*?

II

When Haman originally tried to persuade King Achashverosh to agree to annihilate the Jews, the first thing he told the king was that the intended victims were "one people, scattered and divided up throughout all the nations in all the states of your kingdom." At the end of that verse Haman added, "It is not worthwhile for 'the king' to let them be." In Esther Rabbah 3:10 we are told that any time the Megillah mentions the word "the king" without qualifying the word by specifying "the King Achashverosh," it may be interpreted to be a reference to the King of Kings, Hashem. The Sh'lah (c. 1600, in *Drush for Parshas Zachor*) and the Kli Yakar (in the end of Parshas Beshalach) suggest that according to this rule, we may understand Haman's words as follows:

A nation divided

"There is a people that is known to be one people—which is, a unified people (see II Shmuel 7:23: "Who is like Your people Israel, one nation on earth?")—which is now, however, scattered and divided up throughout all the nations. For this reason, it is not worthwhile for the King—Hashem—to let them be!"

Haman was trying to convince Achashverosh that there would be no Divine protection for the Jews. This was because there was no unity among the Jews and thus Hashem would not be interested any longer in preserving them. Thus, argued Haman, this would be the perfect opportunity to attempt to annihilate the Jews! According to this reading then, the sin that almost caused the greatest holocaust of Jewish history was the lack of harmony and love among Jews. When the Jews show a lack of unity, they lose their usual Divine protection. The first ones to take advantage of this weakness are always the Amalekites (from whom Haman descended).

In Devarim 25:18 we read that shortly after their exodus from Egypt, the

Amalekites "cut down all the stragglers in the [Bnai Yisrael's] rear." Rashi explains that this reference is to people who, because of their unworthiness, were expelled from the protective "tent" of the Clouds of Glory. The Jews who fell prey to Amalek were those who had lost their unity with the rest of the nation, those separated from the camp of the Bnai Yisrael.

Similarly, as Kli Yakar points out, immediately preceding the first account of Amalek's attack on the Bnai Yisrael (Shemos 17:7), we read: "They called that place Massa (which means, provoking) and Meriva (which means, quarrel), after the quarrel of the Bnai Yisrael and their provoking of Hashem." Once again we see that it is when the Jews display the trait of divisiveness and lack of unity they become prey to Amalek's aggressiveness.

III

Unity through the collection of shekalim

In the event of a national census, we are commanded that each Jew must donate half a shekel towards the *korbanos*. The Torah tells us (Shemos 30:12), "Every man shall give [one half shekel as] an atonement for his soul to Hashem...so that there will not be a plague among them when they are counted." Apparently, when we are counted we become prone to plagues. What is it about a census that makes the people suddenly prone to a plague? And how does the giving of half a shekel alleviate this danger?

The Malbim (c. 1900) explains that as long as the Bnai Yisrael are united in one cohesive group, their collective group merit is very great. But when the people are counted, and a stress is laid upon the *individual* identity of each person, this collective merit is no longer in effect. In order to offset the danger that this would pose, the half shekel was given as an atonement. Giving a *half* a shekel, the Malbim explains, will help to have each person realize that without the association of his fellow Jews he is not a "complete" person. One's power comes not from remaining an individual, but from being a part of the whole.

The half shekel donations of both the census and the yearly Temple dues, reflect this theme of unity in a number of ways. The Torah is quite insistent that the amount given by the people should be equal for all: "The rich man shall not give more, and the poor man shall not give less, than half a shekel" (ibid. v. 9). The giving of the half shekel was the great equalizer. This mitzvah, more than any other, stressed the unity and cohesiveness of the Bnai Yisrael.

This theme is seen further when we contemplate how the *shekalim* were used. The Midrash (*Pesikta Rabbasi* 10) comments, "The public sacrifices were bought with the *shekalim* of all of Israel, in order that all of Israel may be partners in these sacrifices." Again we see the concept of the shekel being a unifying factor.

Now we can understand how the mitzvah of the half shekel was interpreted by the Gemara as a neutralization of Haman's evil plans. Haman's entire "sales pitch" was based on the fact that the Jews were not entitled to Divine protection anymore as a result of their disunity. The *shekalim*, which were collected two weeks before Purim, showed that Israel *did* inherently possess the trait of unity, even if they occasionally slacked from it. Therefore, they were worthy of Hashem's protection from the diabolical scheming of Amalek!

IV

Purim: A time to reunite

We find that as soon as Haman's evil decree became known to the Jews, the first course of action—suggested by Esther herself—was, "Go *gather together* all the Jews who are in Shushan, and fast for me" (Esther 4:16). In order to stop Haman, the Jews must be "gathered together." Only through unity could they succeed in rescinding the evil decree.

Similarly, when Haman's plan was eventually foiled, Mordechai sent messages to all the Jews in the Persian Empire, telling them to "congregate [*lehikahel*] and protect themselves." They would conquer their enemies only through joining forces with each other, and showing their unity. And that is just what the Jews did (Esther 9:2,15)!

In conclusion, it is interesting to note that we commemorate the Purim salvation by "sending portions of food to one another, and gifts to the poor" (Esther 9:22). Through the tribulations of Purim, we learned the importance of unity. To this day we take advantage of the Purim holiday, using it for strengthening our *achdus* [oneness]!

PURIM

The Fight Over Jerusalem

The political turmoil in the Middle East of today is dizzying. The most skilled negotiators, heads of state and generals, all seem to be stumped. It is natural and wise, in difficult circumstances, to turn to historical precedents. Perhaps the most important (and exacting) parallel to our dilemma can be found in Megillas Esther. The story of Purim was nothing short of the main battle in the war over control of Jerusalem!

In order to understand this insight it is necessary to understand the historical and political setting in which it occurred.

Mordechai's wanderings The First Temple in Jerusalem was destroyed by Nevuchadnetzar, king of Babylon in 3338. The king of Judea, Yehoyachin, was sent into exile 11 years before. Mordechai was among those who traveled with him to Babylon (Esther 2:6). When Corash (Cyrus, a Persian-Median successor to the Babylonian empire) authorized the rebuilding of the Temple in Jerusalem in 3390, Mordechai returned with Zerubavel, the leader of the returning exiles to Israel (Ezra 2:1-2, see also Gemara Menachos 65a). According to Esther 2:6, Mordechai is found in Shushan, in the year 3398 (which was at least the sixth year of Achashverosh's rule [Esther 2:16]). The question is, why? What compelled Mordechai, who was already advanced in age, to return, perhaps even voluntarily, from the land of redemption to the wanderings of the Diaspora? The answer is, Jerusalem.

II

The book of Ezra recounts the bold efforts of Zerubavel, Mordechai and the original returnees to rebuild Jerusalem and the Temple. However, these returnees did not find the Land of Israel uninhabited. It is well known that the Assyrian conquest of the Northern Kingdom of Israel some 185 years earlier (3205) resulted in the expulsion of the Ten Tribes, who largely inhabited the area known as Shomron (Samaria). The Assyrians, true to their style of population displacement, settled a myriad of different groups of nations, from places largely unknown, in the then recently vacated Shomron. Although these new Shomronim had a tacit relationship with the Jews who remained in Yehudah (Judea), the Shomronim were not subject to the Babylonian exile resultant from the destruction of the First Temple. It was these people who Zerubavel and company encountered on their return home. They did not receive a warm welcome.

Haman's sabotage of the return to Zion

In the book of Ezra, the Shomronim are called the "*tzarei Yehudah U'binyamin*" the antagonists of Judah and Benjamin (Ezra 4:1). From the outset, the Shomronim were clearly not pleased at the sudden return of the Jewish natives. Perhaps they were growing accustomed to having the place for themselves. Perhaps they thought that the world had seen the last of the Jews. Whatever their motive, they set out to reverse the situation. Their strategy was simple: stop the building of Jerusalem, and checkmate the Jews indefinitely.

Stopping the construction forcibly was not considered, because the building effort was officially sanctioned and promoted by the superpower of the day. So they sent lobbyists, armed with petitions against the Jews to the king of the ruling Empire, King Corash (Cyrus). The building of Jerusalem was stopped. When the Jews tried to initiate the building again during the days of Achashverosh (a successor to Corash) the Shomronim again sent a petition to the king. Achashverosh accepted the petition and withdrew the building permit (Ezra 4:6,7 and Rashi).

The big surprise is the identity of the author of the petitions and the lobbyist dispatched by the Shomronim. The author was Haman's son(s), and the lobbyist was Haman himself! Rashi, quoting *Seder Olam Rabbah* (also brought in *Yalkut Shimoni* #1068), clearly identifies the ten sons of Haman with "the ones who authored the attack on Judah and Jerusalem mentioned in Ezra" (Rashi, Esther 9:10).

III

Textual proof of Haman's role

Although these Midrashic connections might seem ethereal, they are not. A close study of the texts themselves attests to the same conclusion. First, although the king had decreed that all were to bow down to Haman, it was the fact that Mordechai was a "*Yehudi*" which caused others to call Haman's attention to the insubordination of Mordechai (Esther 3:4). Here, "*Yehudi*" is clearly an appellation of his region or district of origin, Judea. Haman was apparently known for his antagonism towards the Judeans.

Secondly, the group which authored and dispatched the antagonistic petition was known as the "*tzarei* [antagonists of] *Yehudah U'binyamin*". However, wouldn't then a single member of this group be called "*tzorer Hayehudim* [antagonist of the Jews]", or "*Ish Tzar* [a man who is antagonistic] as Haman was so called (Esther 9:10, 7:6)? And who were the "*tzarim*" that the Jews prepared to avenge themselves upon on the thirteenth day of Adar? Could we not surmise that they were the ten sons of Haman, and the scheming Shomronim?

Our final, and perhaps most compelling proof, is the content of the petition of antagonism itself. The petition (Ezra 4:11-16) contains two basic arguments: The Jews will be rebellious, and they will not pay taxes when they build Jerusalem. These same two arguments feature prominently in Haman's argument against the Jews to the king: "...neither do they keep the laws of the king and it is not for the king's profit to suffer them" (Esther 3:8). Rashi (Megillah 13b) even adds that Haman contended that the Jews were not paying tribute, poll tax or land tax ("*misim, gilgaluyos, ve'arnonos*") in parallel with these same items of alleged non-payment in the petition in Ezra (4:13). In short, both argue that the Jews don't obey the king's laws and that they cause financial damage to the king. (For further scrutiny of this matter see M. Lehman's article "A reconstruction of the Purim Story" in *Tradition*, vol. 12, no. 3-4.)

IV

The final piece in this puzzle is, of course, Mordechai. Why did he return to Shushan? The Midrash fills in this missing piece for us.

Mordechai's role

"[You shall be punished] as a man who is running from a lion, and meets with a bear; later, when he finally arrives at the house and leans his hand on the wall, the snake bites him" (Amos 5:19).

"Running away from a lion"—i.e., from Babylon; "He meets with a bear"—i.e., with the Persian-Mede kingdom; "When he arrives at the house"—when the Bnai Yisrael started to build the walls of the Beis Hamikdash ("he leans his hand on the wall"), the wicked Haman and his son Shimshi tried to stop them ("the snake came and bit him"). That was why Mordechai the messenger went [to Shushan] to lobby to continue the building of the Beis Hamikdash. At the same time, Haman went to Shushan to try to permanently stop the building of the Beis Hamikdash (*Yalkut Shimoni*, Amos 545).

Mordechai arrived in Shushan at a time of great distress for the Jews. Their one hope of redemption, the rebuilding of Jerusalem and the Temple, was now shattered. And Mordechai arrived with a purpose—to counter-lobby against Haman. It was in this troubled political climate that our story of Purim is set.

Mordechai and Haman were veteran sparring partners from the old country. No wonder Haman was enraged that Mordechai did not bow to him (Esther 3:4). One can envision two political action committees feverishly lobbying at opposite purposes. Two opposing camps were lobbying the superpowers of their day for control of Jerusalem and the Temple Mount.

Conclusion

Our secret weapon

The lobbying efforts of Mordechai were to no avail. In the political arena of international diplomacy and power brokering, the Jew then had no power. The only strategy which had any effect, and which literally reversed the entire impending catastrophe, turning it into the downfall of our adversaries, was a humbling but courageous decision made by Esther. "Go gather all the Jews of Shushan and fast with me... for three days" (Esther 4:16). Esther instituted a fast of *teshuvah*. In this manner she was admitting that it is *not* our enemies that must be beaten and subdued. It is *we* who must change when faced with adversity. We must commit ourselves more strongly to our Father in heaven. "When Yaakov's [the Bnai Yisrael's] voice is low, the hands of Esav can overpower him. But when his voice is heard [in prayer], the hands of Esav have no power over him!" (Midrash Bereishis Rabbah 65:20). If Yaakov uses his voice properly, for prayer, learning and repentance, then the hands of Esav—and those of his descendants, such as Haman—will be subdued. Our voice will supersede.

Is the political situation not the same in our day? By now, it is well known that control over Jerusalem is the objective of the Palestinian agenda. The parallel between the Palestinians and the Shomronim runs even deeper when we note that the Palestinians, like the Shomronim of the past, are recent transplants to the region. (See the book *From Time Immemorial* by Joan Peters, JKAP Pubns, 1993).

What can the Purim precedent teach us? What skilled negotiating tactics can we learn from Mordechai? The simple answer is that we, too, must commit ourselves more strongly to our Father in heaven. With this in mind, let us humbly accept this responsibility in our present struggle. Let us courageously use our "voice of Yaakov," crying out to Hashem in *teshuvah*!

GLOSSARY

GLOSSARY

Acharonim—The later commentaries.

Aggadah, Aggadic, Aggados—Words of Chazal that consist of homiletics or narratives, rather than discussions of legal issues.

Aggunah—A woman who is prevented from remarrying because her husband has abandoned her, is missing, or refuses to give her a Jewish bill of divorce.

Akeida—Sacrifice to G-d.

Aleph-beis (א-ב)—The Hebrew alphabet: א-alef, ב-beis, ג-gimmel, ד-daled, ה-heh, ו-vav ז-zayin, ח-ches, ט-tes, י-yud, כ-chaf, ל-lamed, מ-mem, נ-nun, ע-ayin, פ-peh, צ-tzadi, ק-kuf, ר-reish, שׁ-shin, שׂ-sin, תּ-taf, ת-saf.

Al Hamichyah—The abridged version of Grace recited after eating any food prepared from the seven species for which Israel is praised.

Amah, Amos—Cubit measurements.

At-bash—A system in which each letter of the Hebrew alphabet is paired up with the letter on the "opposite side" of the alphabet. For example, the letter *alef*, at the beginning of the *alef-beis*, would be substituted with a letter *taf*, the last letter of the *alef-beis*.

Beis Hamikdash—The Holy Temple.

Beis midrash, batei midrashos—House(s) of Torah study.

Bikkurim—The dedication of the first of one's fruits to Hashem.

Birkas Hamazon—The Grace after eating bread.

Chalitzah—The removing of the shoe; a rite performed to release the widow of a childless man from the obligation of levirate marriage.

Challah—The mitzvah of separating a small piece from the dough which is to be baked into bread and given to the Kohen. Nowadays it is burned.

Chametz—Fermented or leavened bread forbidden on Pesach.

Charoses—Mixture made of apples, nuts, cinnamon, and wine used at the Pesach seder to symbolize the mortar that the Jews were forced to make in Egypt.

Chazakah—An act that accomplishes formal acquisition of real-estate through developing the real-estate in some manner.

Chazal—The Sages of the Mishnah and Talmud.

Chol HaMoed—The intermediate days of Pesach and Sukkos.

Dinar, Dinarim—A form of currency used in the times of the Gemara.

Drush—An exegetical derivation from a verse.

Emunah—Faith in G-d.

Gaavah—Pride.

Galus—Exile.

Gan Eden—Garden of Eden; paradise in the World-to-Come.

Gehinnom—Hell, purgatory.

Gemara—The Talmud, or a section of the Talmud.

Gematria, Gematrios—A talmudic numerical system in which letters of the Hebrew alphabet are given numerical values based on their order in the alphabet. The number thus derived from a word often reveals a deeper level of the word's meaning.

Halacha, Halachic, Halachos—Jewish laws.

Hashra'as HaShechinah—The dwelling of the Divine Presence in this world.

Kabbalah, Kabbalistic—Jewish mysticism, part of which was handed down orally and part of which was arranged in works of Kabbalah, such as the *Zohar* and later works.

Kares—Excision.

Kedushah, Kedushas—Holiness.

Kesiv—The way a word is spelled in the Tanach.

Kinyan—Act of acquisition.

Kohanim—Priestly tribe.

Korbanos—Sacrifices.

Kri—The way a word which is written in Tanach is to be masoretically pronounced.

Leviasan—A sea creature whose hide will be made into a sukkah for the righteous in the Messianic era.

Loshon Hara—"The evil tongue" or speaking ill of a fellow Jew in the presence of others.

Makkos—Plagues.

Mashal—An allegorical story.

Menorah—The seven branched candelabra in the Holy Temple.

Mesorah—The traditional rendering of the Scriptures.

Metzorah—Someone afflicted with *tzaraas*, a skin disease similar to leprosy, which imparts ritual impurity to the afflicted party.

Middah Kneged Middah—Measure for measure.

Middos—Character traits.

Mikveh—Ritual bath into which a person or an object is immersed to attain ritual purity.

Mishkan—The Tabernacle.

Mishnah—The concise written record of the oral law, composed in its present form shortly after the destruction of the Holy Temple.

Mitzvah, Mitzvos—Commandment(s) of Hashem.

Moed, Moadim—Holiday, holidays or set season(s).

Motzi-shem-ra—Slanderer.

Mussar—Personality development.

Nassi, Nesi'im—1. the leader(s) of the twelve tribes; 2. spiritual and temporal governor(s) over Israel during the period of Roman rule, beginning approximately c. 30 BCE.

Nazir—A man or woman who chooses to accept certain prescribed strictures in order to attain a higher level of sanctity and closeness to Hashem.

Ohel Moed—The Mishkan or Tabernacle.

Olam Habba—World-to-Come.

Orlah—The Biblical prohibition that disallows eating fruit grown during the first three years of a tree's life.

Parsha—The weekly Torah Reading.

Pasuk, Pesukim—Verse(s) or passage(s) in Tanach.

Regalim—Pilgrimage festivals i.e., Pesach, Shavuos, and Sukkos.

Rishonim—The earlier commentaries.

Rosh Chodesh, Roshei Chodoshim—The first day of a lunar month(s).

Shaatnez—A mix of wool and linen threads.

Shabbos—Sabbath.

Shechinah—Divine Presence.

Shechitah—Ritual slaughtering.

Shofar—A ram's horn, sounded to symbolically awaken the souls to repent.

Siddur—Prayer book.

Simchas Beis Hashoeva—The Celebration of the Water Drawing—an evening event, held daily from the second until the seventh days of the Sukkos holiday.

Selichos—"Forgiveness." Penitential prayers recited during the New Year season and on fast days, expressing remorse for our sins.

Shekalim—Coins referred to in the Torah.

Shemittah—Sabbatical year during which agricultural work was forbidden.

Sukkah, Sukkos—Shading shelter(s); scantily roofed structures that the Torah bids us to build for the holiday of Sukkos.

Taharah—Ritual purity.

Tanach—Acronym for Torah, Nevi'im and Kesuvim.

Tannaim—Sages of the Mishnah and Midrash.

Tefillin—"Phylacteries." Small black leather boxes which contain certain Biblical passages, worn upon the arm and head of Jewish males over the age of thirteen on a daily basis.

Teshuvah—"Return." The term used for repentance for past sins.

Tumah—Ritual impurity.

Tzaddik, Tzaddikim—G-d fearing person.

Tzaraas—A skin disease similar to leprosy that afflicts sinners.

Tzaros—Misfortune.

Tzedakah—Charity.

Tzitzis—Ritual strings that hang from the corners of four-cornered garments.

Tzom—A Fast.

Yeshiva—An institute of Torah learning.

Yetzer Hara—Evil inclination.

Yevamah, Yevamos—Widow(s) subject to *yibbum*.

Yibbum—Levirate marriage.

Yom Tov, Yomim Tovim—Major holidays when most work is prohibited.

Yovel—Jubilee, fiftieth, year.

Zt'l (zecher tzaddik l'vracha)—acronym for "may the tzaddik's memory be remembered for blessing."

Zerizus—Swiftness in the performance of a mitzvah.